D0371953

CHINA'S CENTURY

The Awakening of the
Next Economic Powerhouse

CHINA'S CENTURY

The Awakening of the
Next Economic Powerhouse

LAURENCE J. BRAHM

JOHN WILEY & SONS (ASIA) PTE LTD

Singapore • New York • Chichester • Brisbane • Toronto • Weinheim

This publication is designed to provide accurate and authoritative information in regard to the subject matter covered. It is sold with the understanding that the publisher is not engaged in rendering professional services. If professional advice or other expert assistance is required, the services of a competent professional person should be sought.

Other Wiley Editorial Offices

John Wiley & Sons, Inc., 605 Third Avenue, New York, NY 10158-0012, USA
John Wiley & Sons Ltd, Baffins Lane, Chichester, West Sussex PO19 1UD, England
John Wiley & Sons (Canada) Ltd, 22 Worcester Road, Rexdale, Ontario M9W 1L1, Canada
John Wiley & Sons Australia Ltd, 33 Park Road (PO Box 1226), Milton, Queensland 4064, Australia
Wiley-VCH, Pappelallee 3, 69469 Weinheim, Germany

Library of Congress Cataloging-in-Publication Data
China's century : the awakening of the next economic powerhouse / Laurence Brahm.
    p. cm.
  Includes index.
  ISBN 0-471-47907-2 (cloth)
    1. China--Forecasting.   2. Twenty-first century.   I. Title: Awakening of the next economic powerhouse.   II. Brahm, Laurence J.
  DS706.C51137 2001
  303.4951--dc21

                                                                  00-068630

Typeset in 10/12 points, Revival by Cepha Imaging Pvt Ltd, India
Printed in Singapore by Saik Wah Press Pte Ltd
10 9 8 7 6 5 4 3 2 1

CONTENTS

Contents

ACKNOWLEDGEMENTS

China's Century presents a cross section of viewpoints from leading specialists on issues covering a spectrum of concerns which decision makers worldwide, whether in business, professions, finance, media, diplomacy or politics, need to know in evaluating China's growth and potential in the future.

Each section begins with a chapter by the relevant Chinese government minister presenting the policies and targets to be achieved under his portfolio. Following chapters are prepared by either chairmen or CEOs of major multinational corporations who are pioneers in China business, leading lawyers, academics, or journalists, both foreign and Chinese, presenting views on their areas of expertise.

I would like to first express my deepest appreciation and thanks to State Council Premier Zhu Rongji for taking the time to prepare the foreword to *China's Century*. Premier Zhu's foreword best expresses both the vision of the Chinese government and the spirit of China's people, in setting forth the aspirations and goals China seeks to achieve in the new century.

I would also like to express great thanks to State Council News and Information Office Minister Zhao Qizheng for the enormous support which he has provided for this project, without which it would not have been possible.

Special thanks to both State Council News and Information Office Bureau Director Tian Jin for his support and keen interest, and Publishing Division Director Wu Wei for her tireless energy and effort in coordinating and working closely with me. Their efforts have made this project a reality.

I would also like to thank the publisher John Wiley & Sons, especially Nick Wallwork for working with me to conceptualize this idea, Janis Soo and Katherine Krummert for their detailed editorial assistance, Adeline Lim and Ira Tan in helping to make this project a success, and the many others involved. I would also like to thank Naga Group Director Stephen X.M. Lu for his work coordinating translation matters and economic research and Julia Zhang for her liaison and administrative assistance. Special thanks to my wife Eileen Chen Kaiyan for her support throughout this entire undertaking.

Laurence J. Brahm
Beijing, January 2001

FOREWORD

A BRIGHTER FUTURE

Zhu Rongji

State Council Premier, People's Republic of China

Together with the arrival of the new century, a rapidly advancing scientific revolution—represented by information technology is profoundly changing the means of production and lifestyles of people, becoming the emerging force propelling modern economic growth.

Accelerated adjustments and reorganization of the world's economic structure, the rapid development of new industries, and the obvious increase in the pace of economic globalization, will bring new opportunities for economic development and unavoidable serious challenges to all nations, especially developing countries.

Developing economic globalization calls for the further establishment of a new international political and economic order that is both fair and reasonable, demanding ever more effort on the part of all nations, especially developing countries, to deepen reform, adjust internal structures and strive to enhance economic competitiveness.

Since the founding of a new China 50 years ago, China has undergone enormous changes, especially over the past 20 years of reform and opening. China's economic achievements have become the focus of global attention.

In the 1970s, China was ranked the 11th largest economy in the world. It is now ranked seventh. Its export-import volume has risen from 32nd in the world in the 1970s to ninth today. China's foreign exchange reserves and volume of foreign inbound investment rank second in the world.

The standard of living of 1.2 billion Chinese people has realized historic strides, having gone from poverty, to securing proper nutrition and clothing for all, to now being on the threshold of affluence. Today's China is characterized by: political stability, economic prosperity, social progress, ethnic unity, and a high spirited people full of vigor, vitality and entrepreneurial spirit.

At this important moment of transition across centuries, China's economic development is at a critical period of deepening reform and structural adjustment. As we advance down this road, we have certain conditions in our favor. At the same time, we also face many difficulties and challenges, which we cannot neglect. From our present situation, we see a lack of sufficient demand and irrational economic structures, increasing unemployment pressure, and a decrease in farmers' incremental income growth, among other issues. Problems such as these arise in the course of development and can only be resolved gradually through further development. Already we have made some headway in this regard.

During the first quarter of 2000, China's economic indicators showed significant improvement. Compared with the same period of 1999, the gross domestic product (GDP) rose by 8.1% and industrial added value by 10.7%. Furthermore, greater efficiency and beneficial results were clearly evidenced by the 23.8% increase in financial revenue and the realization of a 200% profit increase for industrial enterprises.

The main factors underlying these achievements are:

First, over the past three years we have consistently implemented a proactive financial policy, which has played an important function in stimulating economic growth, especially in intensifying infrastructure construction, which has opened up the market for traditional industries.

Second, strengthening the social protection system construction has stimulated an increase in consumption. These strengthening measures have included: raising pension fund payments for retirees; increasing the support of basic living standards for laid-off workers as well as increasing the wages of government and institutional employees; and improving the psychological expectations of workers facing reforms.

Third, implementing a stable monetary policy has helped to stabilize the renminbi's (Rmb) value. In addition, adopting a tax rebate policy has encouraged exports on many fronts, causing export values to grow from zero and negative growth to positive growth. Export growth was 6.1% and 39.1% for the first quarter of 2000.

Fourth, increased input in education, science and technology has promoted the development of new high technology industries, further improving the industrial structure.

Fifth, through strengthening the state-owned enterprise reform, a portion of the enterprises have reorganized, implementing the shareholding system and listing on the stock exchange, while others have turned losses into profits through an intensification of sound management, technology upgrades, and debt-equity transfers.

A preliminary modern enterprise system has been established involving a transfer of enterprise operating mechanisms and the formation of standardized supervisory organs in large and medium state-owned pillar enterprises. Through these measures, most of the large- and medium-sized loss-making state-owned enterprises will step out of their plight.

China is accelerating the process of acceding to the World Trade Organization. I believe that accompanying this important turning point of WTO entry, will be China's opening to the outside, from which a new era will develop.

We will accelerate steps to promote the opening of the energy, transportation, telecommunications, and environmental protection fields to the outside. At the same time, we will further open the service sectors, such as finance, insurance, tourism, commerce and trade. Moreover, we will actively absorb foreign investment to participate, through various forms, in the reform and restructuring of state-owned enterprises.

We will follow the requirements stipulated by the World Trade Organization to adjust and amend existing foreign-related laws and regulations to rapidly establish an economic and trade system conforming with international practice, while reflecting China's domestic conditions.

China is the largest developing country in the world, possessing huge market potential. By raising living standards and upgrading the consumption structure of over one billion residents, a huge consumer demand will be created. Large scale infrastructure construction, industrial structure upgrades, and development of the western regions will certainly bring about the need for even greater investment.

Over the coming 10 years, China's GDP is expected to grow at an average of 7% per year, fixed asset investments to grow at an average of 10%, and total imports to exceed US$2,000 billion. The tremendous commercial opportunities that will be China's in the future belong not only to Chinese entrepreneurs, but to farsighted and daring entrepreneurs from all over the world.

Expanding China's market will be an important element in promoting world prosperity. We warmly welcome and anticipate entrepreneurs from all countries in the world and international investment institutions to come to China and establish businesses. Hand in hand, we shall march together toward a brighter future.

As a member of the Asian community, we pay very close attention to Asia's economic stability and development. China's economic development is inseparable from that of the rest of Asia. The prosperity of Asia in turn requires China.

Over the past decade, the Asian economies grew rapidly, causing our region to become one of the most vibrant in the world. We are pleased to note that the Asian countries which suffered the impact of the Asian financial crisis are undergoing an economic revival. The Asian financial crisis has left us with an important lesson that is, the need to prevent financial risk and prevent overspeculation, through establishing a sound, highly efficient and secure financial system.

Every nation should not only deepen its own financial reforms and strengthen financial supervision, put into play financial functions to support economic growth, and pay careful attention to preventing financial risks, but also actively participate in reforming the international financial system, and strengthening global and regional financial cooperation.

I believe that the Asian economies will certainly be able to adjust and perfect their own development models, becoming reinvigorated, and moreover, taking a more important position in the global economic structure of the new century. I can say with full confidence that the future of Asia's economy will be bright.

INTRODUCTION

THE CENTURY AHEAD

Beijing, October 1ˢᵗ, 1999: A heavy rain had poured from the sky the night before. By dawn the rain had stopped. Mist evaporated quickly against a sharp autumn wind. As I arrived in Tiananmen Square to attend celebrations for the 50ᵗʰ anniversary of the People's Republic of China, the sun had already pierced through clouds overhead. Red flags flew from the mammoth buildings—the Great Hall of the People, the Museum of Revolutionary History—lining the square. It promised to be a bright, sunny day.

Crowds of organized students had gathered, dressed in a pageant of colors. Red banners flapped in a pungent autumn wind. The first thing that caught my eye above the brightly dressed masses forming on the vast expanse of Tiananmen Square were two large, white-lettered, red signs flanking the portrait of Sun Yat-sen, the leader of the 1911 Revolution and in turn, founder of modern China. By tradition, the portrait of Sun Yat-sen faces Mao Zedong's own portrait over Tiananmen gate, eye-to-eye across the square every October 1ˢᵗ. The wording on the red signs, however, can change depending on the political wind.

I looked for changes. "Congratulating the People's Republic of China on the 50ᵗʰ Anniversary of Its Establishment," read one sign. "Carry High the Banner of Deng Xiaoping's Great Theory in Leading Us into the New Century," read the other, clearly and unequivocally stating to Chinese people that the next century for China would be driven by pragmatism.

Deng Xiaoping Theory arguably began to emerge with his "black cat, white cat" statement (color doesn't matter as long as the cat kills the mouse) in 1962. It was crystallized at the 13ᵗʰ Communist Party of China (CPC) Congress in 1987 when Deng explained that China is not a communist but rather a socialist country and, moreover, "only in the first stage of socialism," adding that "the first stage will take a relatively long period of time." Deng Xiaoping Theory fully came into its own during his "southern inspection" in 1992 when he demanded (to the chagrin of more conservative planners) faster growth and more open reforms, coining the phrase "socialist market economy with Chinese characteristics." For Chinese looking across the Square on the PRC's 50th anniversary—wondering what the next 50 years may hold—that simple sign about Deng Xiaoping Theory said a lot.

Like most Chinese events, National Day—the PRC's 50th anniversary—was laced with symbolism. The symbols on this occasion were clear, almost concise. As the celebratory events unfolded through the lens of China's official media, most Chinese observed the symbols and searched for messages that would affect their lives in the months, years and decades ahead.

While the military review and State Chairman Jiang Zemin's speech were the focus of Western media cameras, the parade itself seemed to say the most about where China will be heading in the next century. Yes, there were the expected Beijing lions dancing with their wooly manes, centrific dragon dancers, and of course, throngs of minority people in colorful costumes. However, beside the color, there were also a number of simple but potent messages, which most Chinese observed that day.

The parade was divided into three sections. The first section, titled "Founding of the Nation," began with a portrait of Mao Zedong announcing the new nation in 1949. It focused on several historical events that led to the creation of the People's Republic of China. Slogans were minimalist. Reference was made to "self-reliance" with a focus on "agricultural and industrial development." In fact, this was the shortest section of the three-part parade.

The second section, titled "Glorious Reform," was led by Deng Xiaoping's portrait. This section highlighted *chengbaozhi*, the self-responsibility system introduced in the early 1980s, which reversed the communalization process that had dominated China's economy since the late 1950s. Children marching with spring flowers was one of the most piercing symbols: the "spring story" is understood immediately by most Chinese as being Deng Xiaoping's 1992 *nanxun*, southern inspection, an event that permanently changed the direction and growth of China's economy. Quotations from Deng decorated the floats that followed: "Liberate thinking, seek truth from facts," "The basic task of socialism is to develop production forces," "Construct socialism with Chinese characteristics," "Science and technology are the first production force," "Education must face modernization," "Face the world and face the future." The messages were clear.

The third section, appropriately titled "Flying into the New Century," began with a portrait of Jiang Zemin making his report at the 15th CPC Congress, when Deng Xiaoping Theory was enshrined in the CPC constitution. Consisting of 34 floats, it was by far the largest flotilla of the parade. Achievements in priority sectors—transportation, energy, machinery, telecommunications, aviation, information industry, architecture, public health, environmental protection, and the development of special economic zones—were displayed in simple but powerful images on separate floats (even a huge DNA model was paraded before the crowd). High technology was without question the dominating image. The overwhelming message was that China will not be left behind in the next century.

As expected, there were floats representing the state-owned enterprises. Unexpectedly, there were floats representing China's burgeoning mixed economy: the "public economy," the township enterprises, and moreover, the private enterprises. The float representing private enterprise was topped with some famous local entrepreneurs happily waving. Emblazoned on its side were statistics of production and income earned by these enterprises and the contribution that the private sector is making toward re-employment and the economy as a whole. Even statistics on the government's fiscal revenues from the private sector were displayed on the float. Without question, open acceptance of the private economy and the role it will play in the new century, was being openly displayed with a lot of color.

The more human side of the parade by far outweighed ideology. A float decked with some of China's most stunning fashion models provided a new twist, followed by entire families parading as groups (American politicians also like to talk about "family values"). Newly married couples—registered that day—parading across the rostrum in Western tuxedos and long, flowing white wedding gowns were a far cry from the Red Guards who marched by just over 25 years ago.

After the event I was surprised at some of the Western media's reports. One of America's most influential newspapers commented that the event "looked a lot like the Cultural Revolution." This distortion on behalf of the American press disturbed me the most. Ironically, it did not send to American readers the same message being sent to Chinese here—in fact, it reported the opposite. Reading this statement, I asked myself why didn't they just report the messages being projected that day? Because for Chinese watching, a lot was said about the century ahead.

Today China is driving forward its policy of guided market economics, creating what is ironically fast becoming one of the most laissez-faire economies in the world today. The incredible materialistic drive of the Chinese people—a pent-up energy released through 20 years of dramatic reforms—is gaining an unprecedented momentum of its own. The unparalleled conspicuous consumption of China's "masses" is becoming a market force that will not only sustain China's growth rate in the new century, but may very well become a critical force in maintaining the prosperity of developed nations feeding into China's market.

China has come of age. This is now a fact of our times that can no longer be denied by negative journalism, buried in historic misunderstandings, or restrained by certain foreign policies of "containment." The century beginning in the year 2000 is China's.

Part I

ECONOMY AND REFORM

STARK CHALLENGES

A look at the past two decades of reforms in China gives a pretty clear indication of where China is going in the century ahead. When China launched its economic reforms and began opening to foreign investment nearly 20 years ago, the Central Government faced the stark challenge of turning around an economy of virtual scarcity in respect of everything—commodities, durable goods and foodstuffs—even basic staples. In those days, virtually all consumables were subject to a strict rationing system.

Today, as China drives into the new millenium, the Chinese Communist Party leadership faces a somewhat different challenge—how to stimulate consumption in a market of oversupply—in virtually every commodity, durable good, and foodstuff. This turnabout from scarcity to abundance speaks for the strength of the nation's economy, the policies of its leadership, and the direction being taken at the outset of this century.

Today China's leadership faces not the problem of raising production, but the more comforting problem of dealing with overcapacity. In the span of just 20 years, China has gone from being a nation of commodity scarcity to being one of oversupply of durable consumer goods. At the same time, this remarkable achievement has left national economic capacity unbalanced.

To a great extent, dramatic changes in China's urban coastal areas have left the lives of much of China's rural population unchanged. Basic facilities in the countryside remain backward. Without rudimentary hygienic facilities, water, and electricity in China's vast

1

rural hinterland, consumer demand for light industrial goods, necessary to sustain the momentum of China's growth, will not be able to mature to the next anticipated stage.

China has some 2,600 counties, each consisting of 10 to 20 townships, totaling 30,000 to 50,000 townships nationwide. The Central Government's vision is to develop these townships through infrastructure investments to be matched by local-level financing. This huge undertaking in the mass construction of modern towns and infrastructure throughout China's interior and rural regions will create job opportunities for local labor. This will then reduce the flow of rural itinerants to the coastal urban centers, relieving a problem that has had the effect of compounding social and economic pressures on China's industrial coast. Moreover, such massive projects will give China's rural households more income and, in turn, future spending power.

The quality of life for China's rural masses, who still constitute over 80% of the population, will rise sharply over the coming decades. As rural families move into modern townships with water, electricity, and modern conveniences, their lifestyles will change and a new wave of consumer demand will begin, stimulating production in China's now slack, but vast, consumer goods industrial sector.

INFRASTRUCTURE BLUEPRINT

The current program unveiled at the outset of this century involving the opening of central and western regions—China's vast hinterland—through a program of State infrastructure investments and measures to encourage both domestic and foreign investment, is the framework to advance this vision. China's leadership is also realistic, knowing that this entire program of investment and construction could take anywhere from 10 to 20 years to realize, with many critical social and economic pressures yet to be solved in the meantime.

Infrastructure spending by the State will lead this process. Some Rmb260 billion has been earmarked for roads to open up backwater provinces, and another Rmb270 billion to modernize the railroad system, which remains China's most essential and reliable transport network. The State will spend Rmb130 billion to expand agricultural irrigation in these areas, and another Rmb100 billion to develop public utilities to bring in theaters, cultural centers, and badly needed hospitals. This massive spending on infrastructure will in turn revive a number of China's pillar industries such as cement, iron, and steel. The surge in demand will provide new impetus for growth. An initial Rmb100 billion bond issue in 1999, followed by another Rmb160 billion worth of bonds issued during the first half of 2000, has spearheaded this effort.

After developing basic infrastructure in the first phase, the government plans in the second phase to attract the nation's more successful coastal enterprises to make commercial investments in the interior. This would be a logical response for the enterprises: facing already competitive markets in industrialized urban areas, they will be ready to tap the growing consumer expectations of China's hinterland. At this point, the State will be looking to the banking and financial sector—hopefully overhauled and recapitalized by that time—to support this new wave of commercial investments.

The blueprint for China's central and western provinces is not too different from that envisioned for the coastal regions 20 years ago. Shenzhen was merely rice paddies and a simple market town when I first passed through from Hong Kong at the outset of the 1980s. The infrastructure came from the State. Investment from Hong Kong and overseas followed. Now the State plans to implement that same game plan, albeit on a massive scale.

Ironically, Jiang Zemin, who was Shenzhen's first city planner in the early 1980s, now is Chairman of State and the central figure in China's corps of leaders undertaking this historic and unprecedented program of reform and massive development. The leadership sees China, with the size and diversity of continental Europe, as a microcosm of the dichotomy between developed and underdeveloped nations of the world. The industrialized coast will invest in the underdeveloped interior, which in turn will become the new consumer market for the industrialized coast.

MARKET OPPORTUNITIES

In the coming century, there will be no other industrialized or industrializing country so poised to grow and expand as China. Given its sustained high rate of growth and mammoth export potential, China's competitiveness as an international trading partner will be formidable. Projected levels of consumer spending, based on current savings, and a population which is one quarter of the world's total population, makes China's market ever more seductive. For multinationals everywhere, the equation is pretty clear: not to participate in China's economy is not to participate in the world's economy in the century ahead.

The opportunities to be created through China's long sought after entry into the World Trade Organization (WTO) will also open a Pandora's box of competition, which could threaten domestic pillar enterprises upon which the State depends for much of its revenues. The dilemma of restructuring China's state-owned enterprises and recapitalizing the banks stuck with enterprise bad debts, clearly remains the single biggest challenge for the leadership at the outset of this century.

This dilemma is underpinned by the need to stimulate domestic consumption. Without consumer demand, light and heavy industrial production will remain slack and worker redundancy and unemployment will rise, throwing into precarious balance many diverse interests and highlighting existing irrationalities in the country's economic structure. However, if consumer demand can be stimulated, then demand will spark production and in turn maintain employment at manageable levels. China will then be able to push forward its ambitious and broad-reaching program of state-owned enterprise reform.

STIMULATING DEMAND

In order to stimulate consumer demand, the government has attempted to draw into circulation some Rmb6,000 billion in personal savings, now locked in deposit accounts in the commercial banking system. A series of measures have been undertaken, to ranging from cutting interest rates seven times over the past two years, introducing personal loans on consumer goods purchases, to stimulating the domestic stock markets, to even taxing interest on bank deposits. Unfortunately, none of these moves has had the anticipated impact in stimulating consumer spending. Why?

In short, China's pattern of consumption has gone through a three-stage cycle since reforms were introduced in 1979. The first period was one of scarcity, meaning that whatever suppliers produced was eagerly absorbed by a market generally lacking in consumer goods. The second period was one of "irrational investments," when domestic and foreign enterprises assumed a limitless market, based on the existing mentality of scarcity, and therefore produced duplicate goods. The third period, the current one, is an era of oversupply, a condition created by the previous wave of irrational investments.

Intensifying the current problem of oversupply are the enterprise reforms themselves. In the past, people spent their expendable income because they assumed their basic needs would be provided for by the State. No one worried about buying or renting homes, or paying for insurance, medical care, their kid's education, or pensions. China's current enterprise reforms involving the commercialization of housing, insurance, medical insurance, and pensions are in fact pulling out the carpet from under consumers. With the shadow of imminent unemployment overhanging many workers, people are not spending but rather saving for those unexpected future costs which may no longer be underwritten by the State.

The "catch-22" is that unless those burdens of the state-owned enterprises—housing, insurance, medical care, education, and retirement—are commercialized, then the enterprises themselves will not be able to operate in a viable manner, to service their debts, and, in essence, to reform. This is the tremendous difficulty that China's leaders and economic think tanks now face. Currently, the intention is to revamp infrastructure within China's central and western provinces, with projects funded through State debt issues, in the hopes of luring coastal enterprises to invest in the interior, which in turn would create jobs, putting cash into pockets.

The long-term goal behind these measures is to stimulate consumer demand in the interior regions, which due to their underdevelopment, remain backwaters. To some extent, China's economic policies on the threshold of the 21st century are looking a bit like FDR's New Deal. In practice, implementation will be difficult. It will require a complicated balancing of wide-ranging and often disparate regional interests, a race against time, and the patience of people living in an economy that spans both past and present, juxtaposing sometimes very free and unregulated markets with policies of overguidance under the label of "macro-controls."

REFORM IDEOLOGY

Foreign analysts and journalists who repeatedly speculate over internal fighting between "reformers" and "hard-liners" in the Chinese government are just living in the past, seeing China through an outdated pair of lenses. In fact, there are no hard-liners in China anymore. China's entire leadership is one of reformers, albeit with different ideas on how to reform, which models to adopt, and how to apply certain monetary tools and social welfare systems to China's often unpredictable economic and social environment. It is fair to say at the outset of this century that China in fact has already undergone plenty of reforms—exactly 20 years of reforms for that matter—from the perspective of ideology, economics, finance, social security and the regulatory frameworks being applied to each.

Wave after wave of social change has also occurred, creating enormous disparities between generations with the kinds of gaps that emerged in America in the 1960s and Japan in the 1980s now apparent in China. Ideological parameters and values of the past which made sense to a generation growing up in an economy of scarcity do not apply or make sense to a new generation born in an economy of overcapacity driven by new conspicuous consumption. This new reality is further complicated by rapidly growing gaps between rural and urban residents that have yet to be closed by the trickle-down effects of expanding wealth or the telecommunications revolution, which is now occurring in China as fast as anywhere else in the world.

The problem is that diverse and often discordant parts of the economy have not caught up with the theory driving current policies of growth.

Political ideology has in turn been left behind. At this crossroads, the Communist Party of China is seeking to reinvent its ideological platform so as to speak to the realities of this century, while holding on to some ideals of the last.

ENTREPRENEURIAL SPIRIT RELEASED

Ironically, the year 2000 kicked off with great enthusiasm as announcements in the Chinese press heralded that individuals would be able to establish private companies with only one renminbi as registered capital! Many people believed this exaggeration and before long, the State Administration of Industry and Commerce (SAIC) was overwhelmed by a mad rush of enthusiastic entrepreneurs. What happened?

On January 1, 2000, the Private Individual Wholly Invested Enterprise Law officially went into effect. Intended to encourage domestic private enterprise, the new law covers a range of issues from establishment, investors, management dissolution, and legal liabilities. However, in all of its six chapters and 48 articles, the drafters neglected a very important issue—minimum registered capital. In doing so, they sorely underestimated the entrepreneurial spirit of China's new rising private business class, which they sought to encourage. Of course, entrepreneurial instinct immediately assumed that in the absence of a specified minimum capital, well, then just one renminbi should do it! In the spirit of "a hundred flowers blooming," China's one million private enterprises were about to erupt into the millions; that was until the SAIC announced that they were not about to register any "one renminbi" companies, at least for the time being, in the absence of implementing regulations.

In the wake of this mad enthusiasm for start-ups, a more realistic, yet quite encouraging view was expressed when State Development and Planning Commission Minister Zeng Peiyan spoke at a news conference organized by the State Council News and Information Office on January 4, 2000. During this conference Minister Zeng sent a clear signal of support for the growth of China's "non-state," or private, sector. Zeng revealed in his speech that, with the exception of sectors and regions, which for reasons of national interest or security need to remain restricted to state investments, basically all sectors would be open to private investment. Moreover, Zeng indicated that private enterprises would be afforded the same conditions and "opportunities" as state-owned entities in connection with listing on the domestic securities markets.

PRIVATE ECONOMY

For years, the very question of whether private enterprises should be allowed to list on China's securities markets has been a topic of

emotional debate between old and new generations of Chinese economists. The former expectedly argued that only state-owned enterprises—
which are intrinsically owned by the "public"—should be listed; as after
a "revolution," a "liberation," and a lot of political movements, it would
just be unthinkable to allow the private sector to take capital away from
the "public." The latter argued that unless private companies can be
listed, the stock markets can never become dynamic competitive markets, a point emphasized by *ziben liudong gaige*, "capital circulation
reform"—one of Premier Zhu Rongji's *wuxiang gaige*, "five items of
reform." Minister Zeng Peiyan's statements at the outset of the new
century clearly indicate which group of economists now has a louder
voice in the ears of central policymakers.

The revival of China's non-state economy actually began as a delicate
experiment following Deng Xiaoping's consolidation of power at the
Third Plenum of the 11th Party Congress in 1978. Throughout the 1980s,
when cautious experimentation was still the name of the game, China's
private sector witnessed an average 2% annual growth, which jumped to
an average of 5% during the bolder, more dynamic 1990s. Today, China's
private sector is growing at a rate of 20%, which represents the single
fastest growing aspect of China's domestic economy.

Two key events at the close of the 1990s represent major ideological and
substantive breakthroughs for China's private sector. The green light was
given at the 15th Party Congress, which recognized that "public ownership"
should not be limited to "state ownership," opening the door for a mixed
economy leading to acceptance of a broader definition for the term
"non-state," meaning private. In March 1999, the Ninth National People's
Congress adopted a constitutional amendment recognizing the private
economy as an "important constituent" of the "socialist market economy,"
which meant that for the first time in 50 years private assets were given
constitutional protection.

Today, China has approximately 3.85 million businesses, of which over 1.5
million are private enterprises. The registered capital of China's private
sector now exceeds Rmb590 billion and the sector employs over 78 million
people. In short, China's private sector now employs more than 10% of the
country's labor force. Clearly, encouraging private enterprise now presents
one of the few realistic solutions to China's growing layoffs of state-owned
enterprise workers and unemployment problems.

At the 15th Party Congress in September 1997, State Chairman Jiang
Zemin announced a policy of "grasp the large and release the small,"
which envisioned "grasping" large industrial pillar enterprises and
merging them into *chaebol*-syle conglomerates while "releasing" the
medium and smaller enterprises to the market. This policy, in its initial
stage of implementation, witnessed superficial restructuring of large
enterprises with the shifting of debt between them and a short-lived

sell-off of smaller state enterprise assets, usually to the families or friends of enterprise managers. Economist Wu Jinglian, a key advisor to State Chairman Jiang Zemin and member of the Chinese People's Political Consultative Conference, had been largely credited with brainstorming the "grasp the large and release the small" policy. Disappointed by its implementation, Professor Wu himself reconsidered the formula, proposing instead that the policy be reworked as "release the large and support the small."

The real question concerns what policies are needed in order to "support the small." While the possibility of stock market listings gives rise to new hopes, these opportunities will remain limited as the question of raising initial capital required to build critical mass remains a practical impediment. The current credit environment still favors state-owned banks lending to state-owned enterprises as the private sector's traditional skepticism remains. Just like the state-owned banks, foreign investment bankers and venture capital types have concentrated their efforts to date in searching the state sector for "mega deals" and "dot com ideas," ignoring opportunities created by these self-imposed systemic impediments.

Clearly the fastest growth point for China at the outset of this new century is concentrated among small private enterprises, many of which are engaged in solid manufacturing, distribution, trade, retail and services. They are drawing new management talent, which often knows how to use both capital and *guanxi* relations with more effective results than the lazy vision-lacking managers of China's state sector. Private enterprises are now legally protected and permitted to issue both A and B shares on the domestic bourses. State policy is quite clear: while large pillar enterprises will need to be retained and maintained, a green light has already been given to the private sector where growth will be encouraged in the years to come. Without question, this is the sector of China's economy with the greatest potential and where dynamism will be found in century ahead.

In the opening chapter of this section, Minister Zeng Peiyan of the State Development Planning Commission presents a sweeping overview of the economic reforms underway and the reform program that will guide China's economy over the first decade of this century. In the second chapter, Sidney Shapiro, a member of the Chinese People's Political Consultative Conference where he serves as a key advisor on economic reform issues, reviews the changes he has witnessed over his more than half a century of living in China. In the third chapter, Claude Smadja, managing director of the World Economic Forum, describes the challenge of globalization and the critical policy adjustments that China will need to tackle to meet this challenge of becoming a real world economic power. In the last chapter of this section, Huang Weiding, executive director of Red Flag Publishing House, and one of the China's most senior economists, candidly discusses the problem of corruption and the law, a side effect of economic reform that is threatening to undermine these very reforms.

ZENG PEIYAN

Minister Zeng Peiyan heads the State Development Planning Commission, which has authority to set economic development parameters and approve large-scale national infrastructure projects. Minister Zeng has served as both minister of the Electronics Machinery Ministry and previously as commercial counselor in China's U.S. embassy. He is a graduate of Qinghua University, having majored in electrical engineering.

In this chapter, Minister Zeng provides a comprehensive overview of the past 20 years of reforms, highlighting China's achievements in alleviating poverty and overcoming the structural impediments to economic reform. Minister Zeng discusses the challenge of maintaining high growth against the pressures which can easily emerge during the course of economic rationalization, drawing for us a roadmap of how the government plans to address these challenges in the years to come.

THE ROAD MAP

Zeng Peiyan
Minister, State Development Planning Commission

TWENTY YEARS OF REFORM

At this point in time as the human race enters the 21st century, China is increasingly becoming the focus of world attention. This is due primarily to the past 20 years of economic development and reform, the achievements of which are unprecedented. An ancient, civilized nation has obtained new life and vitality. Moreover, people can see with increasing clarity China's bright prospects in the new century and the Chinese people's revival as a historic trend.

Over the past 20 years of economic reform, China's national economic growth has increased rapidly; national gross domestic production has averaged 9.6% growth, achieving Rmb8,205.4 million, ranked seventh in the world. Agricultural and industrial products' production volume ranks foremost in the world. Corn, cotton, rapeseed, meat, coal, chemical fiber, yarn, cloth, cement, televisions, digital control panels, and steel also rank foremost in the world. Electric power capacity and fertilizer production volume rank second. China has left the stage of supply deficiency, or "economic shortages," achieving an historic transition from a seller's to buyer's market. The times when commodity supplies fell short of demand are now over.

The income levels and quality of life for urban and township residents have been raised. Having fulfilled our basic needs of food, shelter and clothing, we have realized the objective of comparative comfort. Staples (such as grain and rice), meat, eggs, and fish produce have already exceeded the world average per person. In 1999, the average income for urban and township residents was Rmb5,854, a 360% increase over 1978. The income of rural residents was Rmb2,210. This represents a 470% increase over 1978. Reflecting the quality of life of Chinese citizens according to the

11

Engles Index [a measure applied by economists in socialist countries to demonstrate reductions in poverty], in 1999, urban and township areas' per capita poverty levels were 41.9%, dropping 14.8 percentage points from 1980, while rural areas were at 52.6%, dropping 15.1 percentage points from 1978. Some 216 million rural people have been pulled out of poverty.

SOCIALIST MARKET ECONOMY

In this early stage of building a socialist market economy system, a basic market pricing mechanism is coming into play, which is functioning in the disposal of resources. The proportion to which the market is establishing prices for society's retail commodities exceeds 92%, and over 80% for sales of the means of production. Of these retail commodities, at least 80% of the "means of production" or materials and equipment used in production, are free from price controls.

With public ownership as the mainstay, a multi-faceted mixed economy is already developing. In terms of total national industrial production, the state-owned economy has already dropped from its former dominant position of 77.6% in 1978 to 28.5% in 1998, while the collective economy has risen from 22.2% to 38.5%, and the non-state (private) economy has risen from a mere 0.2% to 33%.

The state-owned enterprise management system and operating mechanisms are undergoing a deep transformation, establishing corporate systems that represent a major step forward in attaining the goal of enterprise modernization. A production and distribution system is now being implemented, one that still considers labor (how to use it most efficiently), yet considers capital and technology as key guiding elements. Already, the policy of permitting and even encouraging a certain segment of the population in certain urban regions to become prosperous through their own initiative and labor is yielding results.

Openness has formed the basis of the economy. In 1999, total foreign trade reached US$360.7 billion, representing 3% of total world export trade, ranking China number nine in terms of world trade. Over the past 20 years, our country has received an accumulated US$306 billion in direct foreign investment. For six consecutive years, China has been the largest recipient of foreign investment among developing countries. Of the 500 largest multinationals in the world, 400 have already invested and established factories in China. By the end of May 2000, foreign exchange reserves had already reached US$158 billion, the second largest in the world. In implementing an open policy, imported technology and management experience have promoted economic development.

At this time, China's economic development still faces many difficulties and problems. Mainly, the effective requirements are incomplete, economic structural irrationalities and conflicts are overt, employment pressures are increasing, and rural farmers' incomes are increasing at too slow a rate.

We are diligently adopting measures to solve these problems and especially over the past two years, have persistently expanded domestic consumption, adopted an active fiscal policy and encouraged an increase in both investment and consumption.

In the year 2000, the economy has already realized a major turn for the better, with growth increasing; economic efficiency clearly being raised; urban and township consumption stabilizing and tending to flourish with a major increase in fiscal income; and foreign trade undergoing a powerful increase. Foreign exchange reserves have continued to grow. These all indicate that in solving the lack of consumer demand, macro-control policy has played a major part in achieving results at the initial stage. The momentum of our national economic development is steady as we enter the 21st century.

DEVELOPMENT OBJECTIVES

Along with the new century, our nation will enter a new stage of develop-ment, constructing a comparatively comfortable society and moreover, basically realizing modernization. Our development objective is, by the year 2010, to realize a doubling of GNP over the year 2000, moving from a level of comparative comfort to affluence, forming a comparatively complete socialist market economy system. By the year 2020, our national economy will develop further, each system becoming more perfected. By the year 2050, modernization will be basically achieved, completing the construction of a prosperous, strong, democratic and civilized socialist nation.

Looking forward to the future, China's economic development has many positive favorable conditions and difficult challenges. Our nation's population is large, level of development low and moreover not balanced, possessing a huge blatant market demand along with the rising income levels of urban and township residents. An enormous market demand shall in the future serve as a powerful driving force behind sustained economic growth and productivity.

Over the past several decades, rapid economic growth has laid a foun-dation for a relatively abundant materials and technology base, with trans-portation, communications, natural resources, and water conservancy, among other basic infrastructure construction, advancing by leaps and bounds. These advances have helped break through the bottleneck restrictions that delay the effects of enhanced economic development.

Our nation's deposit rate is relatively high, having maintained a rate of about 41% throughout the 1990s. This has enabled a 32% rate of return on fixed investments, sufficient to support rapid economic growth. The market economy continues to evolve so that enterprises of all ownership forms may compete fairly. Future steps to promote and stimulate the cre-ative powers of hundreds of millions of people will provide new power for rapid economic growth. Promoting industrialization, urbanization, and infor-mation technology will provide powerful impetus for further economic growth and for new points of economic expansion.

Following our nation's entry into the World Trade Organization, we will continue to open to the outside, which will bring further opportunities for economic growth. The macro-control system continues to be perfected, with intervention ability continually being raised, giving us sufficient ability to avoid the fluctuations which can arise with economic growth. Perhaps of even greater importance is the experience we are gaining, which we can use to lay our road of "socialism with Chinese characteristics."

With comrade Jiang Zemin at the center of the collective third generation of leaders and the macro-economy under control, we can address any complicated situation, leading the entire nation to open up, advance forward, and take advantage of opportunities and favorable conditions in all aspects. We will adopt in the future even more powerful policy measures to guarantee the rapid and healthy development of the domestic economy, smoothly realizing these objectives of our struggle.

Strategic Adjustment Program

In accordance with our country's current status of economic growth, we must fully consider the world trends of rapid scientific and technological development, together with the accelerating changes in economic structures. We will soon concentrate our efforts on carrying out a strategic adjustment of our economic structure, including:

First, to promote the growth and expansion of new industrial structures more favorable to the economy. This involves efforts to further stabilize and strengthen agriculture and to continuously strengthen basic infrastructure and basic industries. This requires placing great effort on developing high technology industries and other new industries, using modern technology to restructure traditional industries and to actively promote creation of a national information economy.

Second, to continue to adjust and perfect the rationalization of economic structures and complimentary systems. In accordance with the principle of one step forward, one step backward, to adjust the role of the state-owned economy. With regard to key pillar industries and spheres that are the lifelines of the national economy, the State economy will have an allocated position. In terms of other spheres, the mixed economy will be encouraged to enter and operate, and moreover, through asset restructuring and adjustment of structures, raise the quality of state-owned assets in a comprehensive manner.

Third, to actively adjust urban and township structures. We will speed up urbanization, alleviate the expanding income gaps among urban and township residents, and work to lessen the obvious conflicts between urbanization and industrialization.

Fourth, to coordinate economic development between regions. While drawing upon the experiences and then putting into play the strengths of the eastern regions, we will simultaneously implement a strategy of opening the western regions for development, to accelerate the development of the western regions and open up empty areas to economic development.

SCIENCE AND TECHNOLOGY EQUATION

Scientific progress and creativity, as factors of productivity and forces of development, will in turn lead economic and social development. We must implement a progressive strategy for scientific education and highly skilled labor that will, in turn, make the nation prosperous. We must strengthen basic research and high technology research and expedite high technology industrialization. This involves strengthening the development and promotion of applied technology, promoting scientific achievements in the realization of production transformation, and concentrating on solving major technical issues of economic and social development.

We are adopting policies to deepen education reforms, support scientific research and encourage the merging of science, technology and education. In addition, we are working to build a corps of skilled and creative workers for the scientific and technology arenas. We wish to motivate creativity.

ACHIEVING AN ORDERLY MARKET SYSTEM

We continue to adhere to our basic national policies of birth control and environmental awareness to limit population growth and wisely use our natural resources. We continue to develop our natural resources but encourage sparing use. By strengthening control over environmental pollution, landscaping, and handling, we improve the ecological environment through soil and water conservation and prevent desert expansion and erosion.

Through deepening reform and perfecting the system of a socialist market economy, we can guarantee the realization of our main development objectives. It is necessary to accelerate state-owned enterprise reforms—and in accordance with the requirements of "clarification of property rights, defined responsibilities, separation of government from enterprise, scientific management"—to construct a modern economic system, so that enterprises can really become self-reliant in operation, as legal entities responsible for their own profits and losses.

Speeding up reform of the social welfare system; creating a national, unified, and standardized social welfare system; deepening economic and social reforms; adjusting economic structures; and protecting the labor force and ensuring reasonable mobility of labor—all will help ensure the long-term stability and security of the nation. Further progress in perfecting the market economy—emphasizing developing capital, technology, the labor force and real estate among others—while creating and enforcing market-related legislation, will help to form a unified, open, competitive, and orderly market system.

SIDNEY SHAPIRO

Sidney Shapiro serves as a member of the Chinese People's Political Consultative Conference in the capacity of an advisor to the
government on economic policy, frequently undertaking inspec-
tions of rural areas. Arriving in China in 1947, Mr. Shapiro stayed
behind after 1949 when others left, becoming a Chinese citizen
in 1963. His monumental translation of the *Outlaws of the Marsh*,
one of China's great literary masterpieces, has in itself become a
classic. He is also author of numerous books on China, including:
Jews in Old China, *The Law and Lore of Chinese Criminal Justice*,
and his most recent autobiography, *I Chose China*.

In the second chapter of this section, Sidney Shapiro provides
personal insight into the dilemmas, challenges and often conflicting interests that the government must balance at this crossroads
of China's economic transition.

UNPRECEDENTED EXPERIMENT

Sidney Shapiro

Member, Chinese People's Political Consultative Conference

PUBLIC ECONOMY RE-EXAMINED

How free the free market should be is a question faced by every country, regardless of political system, in accordance with its own practical circumstances. China has leaped over the capitalist stage and moved from feudalism directly into a form of socialism, in a world dominated by capitalist superpowers. China is cautiously feeling its way, in an unprecedented and unique experiment, and doing surprisingly well thus far. The end result will depend, in part, on how successfully China can juxtapose the structural and organizational mix it finds itself in.

In China, public enterprises are "owned by the people" as a whole and in turn operated either by the national government or local governments on behalf of the national government. The large public enterprises are directly controlled by the national government and run China's fundamental industries and build the infrastructure. The large enterprises are important, as 800 of them own 63% of China's total industrial assets, accounting for 70% of national industrial sales, and contributing 74% of China's industrial tax income. They produce half the gross domestic product, and contribute 90% of the output value of minerals, processed petroleum, electricity and water. To a large extent, these key enterprises have controlled domestic market supply, in turn influencing prices. As a social pillar, they employ hundreds of thousands of people and provide cheap commodities for lower-income families.

The problem is that more than one-third of the public enterprises operate in the red, burdened by huge debts, heavy taxes, and the obligation to support thousands of retired workers and employees. Most of these loss-making enterprises are small, operated by local governments under agreement with the central authorities. More than 90% of their working capital comes from bank loans. Their problems are compounded by bad management, an abundance of redundant employees and interference in their internal operations by government administrators.

A tentative program is shaping up whereby the local governments on the provincial level and below that operate public enterprises will have the power to reorganize, merge, lease, or sell these enterprises. In the past few years, local governments' powers have expanded and their financial income has increased. They now get over 70% of China's total revenue. The local governments claim their income is not excessive since they are burdened with all the costs of local development, economy, education, culture, and civil and judicial affairs. The central government has been able to limit their ballooning power somewhat by introducing a system of dividing taxes and exercising overall control of the economy.

The duel goes on. "You have your *zheng ce* (measures), we have our *dui ce* (counter-measures)," is a popular local saying. The local governments do everything they can to ignore or get around national orders, which they consider to be to their disadvantage. In some cases, local governments will even falsify reports to Beijing, to assure compliance when in fact there is none. This has become an extremely serious problem in achieving national legal standards, with no immediate solution in sight.

Township Enterprises

Ironically, their failings have proved a boon to township and private enterprises. Their more talented personnel resign and join the better-paying non-public companies. At the same time, these people retain their rights to the housing and social security provided by the public enterprises that formerly employed them. Some of the smaller public companies are now encouraged to merge or go into bankruptcy. This measure is adopted with caution. Putting too many unemployed people on the streets could cause unrest, and this remains a concern.

Today the policy is to encourage the development of efficient township enterprises, and at the same time enlarge existing small towns and cities, or create new ones, where modern planning and management can be implemented to absorb redundant labor from the farms. Healthy young men and women are leaving the farms in large numbers because government prices for agricultural products, particularly grain, are too low. Rural township enterprises seem an excellent practical way of employing much of the surplus rural labor. Some members of a farm family work in a newly established workshop or small factory of a township enterprise, while the rest remain on the land. Sometimes, they go to work in these enterprises only in slack agricultural seasons.

Unfortunately, all too often, greedy local officials will quickly ruin many of the more successful enterprises with fees and taxes as soon as they start to grow, or simply take them over through aggressive measures. The young people then gravitate to the already overcrowded cities, which exacerbates the increasing problems of crime, pollution, and housing supply.

The township enterprises in some places are themselves proving to be a problem. They tend to duplicate each other's products, turning out more than the market can bear, and quality is often poor. They heavily burden supply sources and transport facilities, and dump their waste into the nearest stream or field. Arable land is spoiled, water rendered undrinkable. Local officials are persuaded to turn a blind eye. While pollution is worse in heavily industrial regions, growing public pressure is beginning to force more restraint.

URBAN–RURAL GAP GROWS

Commentators within China have expressed repeated concern over the cultural effects of consumerism. They say urban youths especially identify more with consumer goods than with traditional values. The meaning of life is tied to money and luxury items. They fear this will widen the gap between rich and poor, and in turn cause social unrest.

About 80% of China's 1.2 billion people live in the countryside. One problem which China's rural farmers face is that officials have been underpaying the farmers for crops while the government has been decreasing its investment in agriculture on the whole. Meanwhile, the costs of farming have been on the rise, and taxes have increased as well. The prices farm families have to pay for consumer goods have also risen. With lower incomes farmers are buying less, thus adversely affecting China's domestic industry whose main market is in the rural areas. Improving the income of farmers—who account for the vast majority of Chinese people—has now become a fundamental and urgent problem to be addressed in the short term.

Beggars have appeared again on the streets of Beijing. I hadn't seen any in years. They are few in number. But what is disturbing is that many are professional beggars, not persons really in need. Often they are organized and operate in groups. This is an uncomfortable sign of the changing times.

The remote regions are rich in everything from oil, minerals, and cotton, to delicious perishable fruits. The problem remains a lack of efficient and reliable transportation. By bringing in railways and spreading the infrastructure, local income will increase and more foreign investment will be lured. This in turn will attract engineers and specialists, spread the population density, and create a boom comparable to the opening of the American West in the 19th century. Some of the investors presently concentrated along China's now industrialized east coast will start to seek a piece of action in the hinterlands as well.

Conspicuous Consumption

American economist Thorstein Veblen would surely have been startled had he lived to learn of "conspicuous consumption"—which he excoriated as an evil of capitalism—in a socialist society. We see it everywhere among the nouveau riche in China's business world. (It must be noted that the big spenders are conspicuous because they are a very small segment of a very large non-affluent society.) Not all of these are private entrepreneurs. Some are officials in government commercial organizations. One can't help wondering where they get their money.

A few of the larger public enterprises have found a convenient way to increase their earnings without increasing production. Because of their size and status they have easy access to bank loans. They often re-lend the money at higher rates to smaller firms that have difficulty obtaining credit. Sometimes they play the real estate market, or engage in other speculative activity. They spend more time playing the short-term money game than in developing new products for the market, despite the fact that the demand for good durable merchandise in China far exceeds supply. This is the real business climate in China today.

Getting rich is now highly respected in Chinese society. Unfortunately, certain firms and some individuals are not too fussy about how they get rich. Meanwhile, trying to bring prosperity to the average person is a lot more difficult. Yes, incomes have risen a bit, but so have inflationary costs and living expenses. The State is no longer underwriting the cost of living the way it did under the iron rice bowl system. The average Chinese is in fact not thinking about becoming wealthy, but trying to figure out how to maintain his own financially.

Open Door Question

Foreign enterprises know that in providing funding and technological and managerial skills they are creating potential Chinese competitors. But the Chinese market is so large and luscious they are willing to give away more than they would like in order to grab maximum big profits now, and let the future take care of itself. They also put up with outrageous rentals and other charges and the occasional need to pay bribes and kickbacks, which means that the advantages are not all on the foreign side.

Opinions vary among Chinese economists, not on the desirability of "opening the door," but on how wide and how quickly it should be opened, and how Chinese enterprises should respond to its opening. Some feel China should not rush into becoming a member of the World Trade Organization. They say it would expose tens of thousands of Chinese firms to competition from foreign goods, which are mainly of better quality and more attractively presented than domestic products. The main fear is that many workers could lose their jobs.

Others contend that foreign competition should be welcomed. They say it stimulates Chinese factories to improve the quality of similar merchandise. In practice, this is often not the case. The Chinese manufacturer is quickly driven from the relatively affluent and demanding urban market. But, instead of improving its products, more often the factory takes them to the rural areas, where the market is infinitely larger and people are willing to buy somewhat inferior goods if they are cheaper. The result is two markets—one for foreign imported goods, and one for domestic goods—with little improvement in the quality of domestic products.

Prevailing opinion is that the policy of opening and reform is theoretically sound. Foreign input and foreign competition are a stimulus, provided Chinese management, methodology, worker skills, equipment, incentives, and government assistance and guidance are intelligently employed. This policy is difficult to implement in practice. China has to offer sufficient returns to induce foreign entrepreneurs to invest, and yet not give so much away that she loses more than she gains. Excessive tax breaks and real estate bargains have been all too common, as have overly generous terms on income sharing and control.

The Chinese are often inexperienced and naive, and are easily deluded by foreign parties to a deal. Big foreign corporations are generally honest, though tough. But the smaller ones frequently engage in sharp practices and deliver shoddy products. Big or small, all the foreign enterprises play their cards close to their vests and reveal as little as possible of valuable technology and managerial expertise. The Chinese authorities are aware of this, but say privately they can accept being taken advantage of, until they have learned enough and are strong enough to act more independently. They call this "paying their tuition."

When the reforms and opening to the outside world began in the 1980s, morality was said to be as important as material gains. But then Deng Xiaoping was quoted as saying that it was not wrong for persons who had made special accomplishments to get rich before the general public. The tone of official newspaper articles and editorials began to change. Some insisted the economy had to be improved first. Once there was money around and more economic activity, that would be the time to start worrying about morality and ethics. In fact, material gains would themselves help raise moral standards. This was the thinking of the day.

Reality didn't work that way at all. Many interpreted Deng's dictum "to get rich is glorious" as meaning that any way you got rich was good, that you didn't have to be too fussy about how. Crime, graft and corruption grew. There was a flourishing of the old vices, and a few new ones invented as well.

Unfinished Work

To those holding on to antiquated, fussy concepts left over from feudal society, the "advanced civilizations" of the outside world were able to contribute twists made more interesting by their advanced technologies. It seemed as if overnight China was deluged with toothpaste, hamburgers, movies and TV programs stressing the torments of frustrated neurotics, lots of sex and violence, fashion shows with skinny vogue-ish models, and other blessings of the so-called "free world." When concern was voiced about this new foreign invasion, nonchalant freewheelers quoted Deng Xiaoping. Hadn't he said: "When you open the window it doesn't matter if a few flies get in." True enough, but Deng also added that you sometimes need to swat the flies that do get in.

In the blueprint for China's advance into the 21st century, the agenda calls for "cultural-ideological progress," which in my opinion is fundamental. None of the other goals can be attained without a moral rearmament. Immorality manifested in crime, vice, and corruption is obvious and serious. But its greatest danger to China's social stability lies in the immorality fostered and perpetuated by certain pernicious elements in China's feudal heritage, which have persisted to this day. Despite frequent lip service to the need to expunge them, the damage they continue to wreak has been underestimated. Little action is taken against them. It's rather like Mark Twain's remark about the weather: "Everybody talks about it, but nobody ever does anything about it."

During the Mao era China had a moral code. There were clearly defined standards—for the average citizen as well as for the Chinese Communist. People knew what was admirable, what was despicable, and most Chinese behaved accordingly. When the fanatic faults of the Mao era were discarded, the code was discarded with them. No new code has replaced it. Inevitably, greed and corruption rushed in to fill the vacuum. Today, using "connections," paying bribes, putting private loyalties above public good, and blind worship of authority—as widespread practices—are unfortunately considered almost required behavior for advancement and survival in Chinese society. In such an environment it is difficult to implement lasting reforms, regardless of how good the plans are, however honest and well-intended the leadership. China has won her political revolution, but the revolution against feudalism is still unfinished.

CLAUDE SMADJA

Claude Smadja has been the managing director of the World Economic Forum since 1996 and regularly travels to China where he interacts closely with China's top policymakers and leading economists. The World Economic Forum is an independent, impartial, non-profit foundation, the objectives of which are to further economic growth and social progress in the global public interest. The World Economic Forum represents a global partnership of business, political, intellectual and other leaders of society committed to improving the state of the world's economy.

In the third chapter, Mr. Smadja examines carefully the effects of globalization on China's economy, predicting enormous changes that China will go through following WTO entry, in rationalizing economic structures in order to integrate with the globalization trend.

Dealing with Globalization

Claude Smadja
Managing Director, World Economic Forum

Quantum Leap

In assessing the opportunities as well as the uncertainties, more than ever, China needs to be viewed through bifocal lenses. Accordingly, it is also essential to make sure that China's quantum leap into the globalization process, which WTO admission will represent, will be achieved successfully.

Preparing for the WTO and the added competitive pressure it will bring forces the government to accelerate the pace of rationalization of the industrial structure. There is, for instance, a 25–30% overcapacity in the household appliances sector for TV sets. The government is planning to close 2,000 out of 8,000 operating steel mills this year to rationalize production. Thousands of cement plants will be facing the same fate. In the same vein, there are today no less than 120 entities involved in car production in China and the government's plan is to bring that down to just four companies.

So the government priority in the coming period will be to sustain economic activity by whatever means necessary, so that the growth rate will remain at the level required to ensure social stability. This is why it is so crucial that this year proves to be the one during which the downtrend in the growth rate of the economy, which has been at play over the last seven years, would be reversed. This is also why the government is ready to pay the price—in terms of higher budget deficits and increased debt burden—for the continuation of expansionary policies over the next few years, which are going to look like "make or break" years for China.

Race Against Time

Of course, the question that comes to mind is the ability of the government to continue such policies long enough to sustain a very significant restructuring of the economy while ensuring a rate of growth compatible with social stability.

In this respect, China is considered to be in a reasonably good situation. When including the debts accumulated by the state banks, especially because of the heavy burden of bad loans to state-owned enterprises (SOEs), the overall (internal and external) debt of the country is estimated at between 50–60% of GDP—which remains still quite manageable. But this shows also that the expansionary fiscal policies of the last two years cannot be sustained at this level beyond the next two to three years. So there is an element of a race against time in the present effort to regenerate growth through the restructuring process already under way.

A reinvigorated growth rate will give the leadership the kind of "breather," or additional margin of maneuver, it absolutely needs as China enters a very critical period in its modernization process. This is a period which, in some respects, represents an inflexion point in modern history, as when Deng Xiaoping initiated the "four modernizations campaign," launching the process of opening up and modernizing the economy, or when he gave it a second start during his tour of the south in January 1992.

In many aspects, the first phase of China's economic take-off is now over, marking the end of an era where growth has been mostly generated by the injection of labor and capital. If it is to sustain the greater competition that its admission to the WTO will generate, China has now to enter the second phase of its economic development, in which it needs to achieve: a much higher level of efficiency in the allocation of resources; a much greater degree of integration into the global economy; and a significant improvement in its global competitiveness. It must also place a much greater emphasis on the quality of growth, complementing the present focus on purely quantitative factors.

This second phase is, in fact, a very delicate and sensitive one. It will challenge the ability of the leadership to navigate among quite a number of contradictory requirements and to find ways to reconcile them. It will also require an ability to fine-tune and to manage the conflicting pressures and the extremely sensitive balance in the triangular relationship among growth, reform and stability.

Over the next two or three years, there will be three key "prerequisites" to watch out for very carefully. These will be crucial "pointers" not only for the social stability and the economic progress of the country, but also in determining whether or not China can achieve its full integration in the global economy. These key prerequisites are reforms of the state sector, social security system, and banking and financial sector.

Pushing SOE Reform

Despite the fact that the reform of the state sector was identified during the 15th Congress of the Communist Party in September 1997 as the government's most pressing challenge, there was only incremental movement and progress for most of last year. But, according to most observers, there has been an increase of activity with respect to SOE reform since the signing of the agreement between Washington and Beijing in November 1999, with more bankrupt factories being closed down. In fact, there has been a very significant burst of activity in almost every sector of industry, prompted by the need to prepare for the shock of WTO admission. There seems to be a clear realization that despite the risks involved in the reform process, stopping it now would mean incurring even higher risks because it would mean a downward spiral for the economy. So there is no alternative to carrying on and accelerating the process in order to secure the necessary levels of growth in the coming year—to be able to meet the ever-increasing expectations of the population.

Beyond the tremendous waste and misallocation of resources that these enterprises represent today—snatching two-thirds of China's economic resources but producing only one-third of the country's GNP—the key issue is that it will be impossible for China to significantly improve its global competitiveness and to achieve the high level of sustainable growth that it needs without a much more significant shift—a dramatic shift—of resources and attention from the public to the private sector.

As with many other realities in China, the overall picture remains a very patchy one. In the coastal provinces in the Shanghai region, a lot of restructuring has been taking place in big enterprises and the process of re-employing laid-off workers in other activities is moving ahead. In other regions where SOEs still represent the only form of economic activity, progress is still extremely slow, and the injection of funds to keep operations going—even at a minimum level—continues, motivated by social stability concerns. In most regions, 70% of the small and medium-sized companies have now been de facto privatized, mostly through employee shareholding schemes. The word "privatization" is still something of a taboo. The remaining of these small or medium-sized enterprises are either in such a hopeless situation that they need to be closed down—which is happening in most cases—or their situation is so complicated that they are just left to die by themselves, waiting for the banks to pull the plug on their credit.

In some provinces, there is even now a very innovative process of redefining downward what a "big" SOE is, so that additional companies can be privatized through employee shareholding schemes, thus bypassing the central government policy of limiting the size and scope of the companies that can be moved out of the public sector. In trying to accelerate the pace, the government is also bound by the official deadline it set for itself, stating that the SOEs' restructuring process should be completed by spring 2001. It claims to have already achieved that objective with respect to the textiles industry. But realistically speaking, the overall process is still ongoing.

The risk will be that the leadership—having been too optimistic in its own rhetoric—would then be tempted to fudge the issue and claim success prematurely. Rather, there will have to be ways to readjust deadlines while keeping the pressure for restructuring at a maximum level. This problem of the government meeting the expectations it sets is linked to another issue that the leadership needs to confront: making sure that China avoids going the "Russian way." That is, the government must not develop a pattern through which a great part of public assets and resources are just snatched away by a small group of people under the guise of a privatization program. This is already happening in many instances, feeding a growing popular sense of anger and frustration.

But for SOE reform to proceed without triggering an unacceptable level of instability and social unrest requires an accelerated effort towards putting in place a social security system which, at the present moment, exists only in a few big cities such as Shanghai and Beijing. The government seems determined to move ahead in that domain. Social security reform is absolutely key because it will not only determine how far and how fast SOE reform can go, it also has a direct impact on financial reform; it determines the evolution of local finance reform since, with the growing number of plant closures, the pressure on local government to supply social welfare will increase in a dramatic way.

And of course, creating a social security net is absolutely essential in maintaining social stability in a phase of accelerated restructuring, a goal that the regime is more anxious than ever to achieve. And so far, the government has been quite successful at quieting down the demonstrations and the protest sit-ins in front of the town hall, by disgruntled laid-off workers or those still formally on the payrolls of SOEs, but getting only a fraction of their salary and without work. But, as transpired at the end of February 2000, the regime had to deal with what was presumably the worst case of industrial unrest happening in the northeast with the closure of a molybdenum mine. Angry miners offered only minimal severance compensation took violently to the streets, confronted the police and created chaos for several days before the army had to be brought in to restore order.

SOCIAL IMPACT

For the government this episode illustrated only too well where the danger lies ahead, as it tries to accelerate the restructuring of the public sector, in preparation for WTO admission and what impact this will have on China's economic structure. In fact, as the authorities know only too well, it is not the fact that the mine had to be closed that infuriated the miners. They took to the street after having discovered that what they were getting as a severance package was far less than originally planned because the top management of the company had allegedly diverted part of the funds. They were also furious to realize that part of the mining operation would continue after having been "privatized," at the profit of close relatives of the top managers of the mine.

This was one more illustration of the way the frustration created among the public by the widespread corruption problem, combined with the anxieties and despair created by the layoffs and destabilizing impact of the economic restructuring, can create at any moment a very explosive situation. This illustrates why at the last National People's Congress (NPC) session, Premier Zhu Rongji again devoted a good portion of his report to the issue of corruption. But despite a number of actions taken against corrupt officials—a former vice-governor was even executed during the session of the NPC—the problem is too widespread, and the political implications seem to be too complex, to expect any drastic change anytime soon.

The best that can be hoped for is that heightened concern about a growing and violent popular backlash against the increase of corruption, together with better supervision from the discipline enforcement authorities in the Party and the government—and very crucially—greater transparency brought by conformity to the WTO standards, will contribute to a gradual easing of this problem that today represents today a very serious destabilizing potential.

But even without the compounding problem that the growing popular frustration against corruption and graft represents, the issue of how to deal with unemployment, and how to accelerate the process of creating job alternatives, is in itself of critical importance for the success of the state sector reform. There is no alternative to addressing the SOE reform and the job creation process as two faces of the same coin.

In this respect, there is no underestimating the mind-boggling dimension of the challenge facing the government: According to the Labor Ministry, SOEs will have had to lay off 11 million workers between 1999 and the end of 2000, and if the process of industrial restructuring were to be fully conducted, it would mean altogether the redundancy of between 35 and 40 million people over the next few years. In addition, a huge number of township enterprises have also had to close operations because they are unable to adjust their production to the new expectations of the market and are going bankrupt. Add to that the fact that the ongoing crisis in the agricultural sector is forcing more and more people to leave the rural areas and try to find other alternatives in the urban centers. And then, there are of course the 15 million new people entering the job market every year.

And the situation gets even more complicated and pressing as the government intends to go this year into the second phase of the program, announced by Premier Zhu Rongji in 1998, of cutting by half the overall number of civil servants. After the first wave of implementation affecting the bureaucrats in the central government, this year the cuts are to affect the provincial and city governments and will then go down next year to the county and township levels. Presumably, the civil servants affected will have fewer possibilities than their counterparts in the central government to find alternative jobs in entities controlled at the provincial and city levels and this is expected to add to the pressure on the labor market.

Irrespective of what the official figures say, the unemployment rate in urban areas is estimated to be around 10 to 12%. Unemployment is not even officially accounted for in the rural areas where 900 million people live, but according to some rough estimates, unemployment and underemployment affect between 120 and 150 million people in the countryside.

There is no way on earth China is going to meet the daunting employment challenge it is facing without the private sector being fully recognized in its role as the key and unique engine for job creation, and being given the means to fulfill that role. There is now a clear recognition of that reality among the leadership. But so far, the fledgling private sector has been severely constrained in its development by the tremendous difficulties encountered in trying to get appropriate financing, especially in the absence of efficient financial markets. Things are just beginning to improve now, with recent government directives to the banks to be more forthcoming in provision of loans to the private sector.

ALLOCATING FINANCIAL RESOURCES

But, of course, the whole issue of efficient allocation of financial resources is closely linked to the requirement for a thorough cleaning up and reform of the financial and banking sector—which is itself linked to state sector reform. It is estimated that as much as 40% of the loans made by the banks to the SOEs are, in effect, non-performing ones. Altogether, the estimated amount of these bad loans is set at the equivalent of between US$200 to 300 billion, depending on the definition of a "bad loan."

There has been some progress made with the creation of asset management companies (AMCs) assigned the task of taking over the bad loans from the banks, to allow them to clean their balance sheet and to be able to recapitalize on a sounder basis. A few of these AMCs have now been formed, but a number of issues have not yet been solved regarding under what conditions they acquire bad loans from the banks, whether or not they can refuse to take nonperforming loans which have in fact no real value anymore. Thus, progress has been relatively slow so far and the priority now is to accelerate substantially the process. Although there has been a drastic reduction of loans to patently inefficient SOEs and in many cases the tap has been turned off, the practice of policy-directed loans has not disappeared, if only out of concern of not adding more unemployed people. So, the more the process of creating these AMCs drags on, the greater the danger of increasing the amount of irrecoverable debt and burdening the system even more.

Banking and financial sector reform is assuming even greater urgency as the forthcoming admission of China into the WTO means that Chinese banks and financial institutions face the prospect of competition from foreign banks in their own domestic market, in which they so far enjoy a monopoly. In this respect, the added pressure created by the WTO deadline would represent a very welcome development in spurring the evolution of the banking system towards a greater soundness in terms of management and decision-making processes, risk evaluation, but, also, in terms of its ability to finance economically relevant projects from private entrepreneurs.

The fact remains that despite the progress made recently with respect to access to financing for these entrepreneurs, in the growing competition for the allocation of resources between the public and the private sector, the bias is still tilted towards the former. China's private enterprises will not have the same possibilities to take full advantage of the opportunities created by the forthcoming WTO admission if they continue to have some-what restricted access to capital. Now, it is urgent that the bias tilt clearly towards favoring, in a very active way, the fast development of a vibrant private sector. This is especially true, betting on the dramatic changes that the Internet and the e-economy are beginning to bring not only to China's business structure, but to the mindset in the business community with the growing role of a new generation of e-entrepreneurs.

TOWARDS A COMPETITIVE MARKET

Of course, the development of efficient financial markets would go a long way in improving the situation by channeling at least part of the one trillion dollars of savings accumulated in China into the economy, and by helping to generate a much greater involvement from foreign investors. In this respect, an interesting development is the plan to open a second Board for listing new start-up companies, in Shanghai and Shenzhen. But there still exists, in the thinking of many government officials, an ambiguity: Capital markets cannot be expected, at the same time, to both help bail out SOEs and provide funding for private enter-prises. The markets will be able to play their role only when sound management practices, greater transparency and protection of minority shareholders rights are instituted.

This raises implicitly the whole issue of the status of private enterprise in China. A very important step was achieved in 1998 when the notion of private ownership was officially recognized and legitimized in the Constitution. But what is urgently needed now is to establish a legal framework to ensure the protection of private property, i.e., the protection of the results and benefits from private entrepreneurship. This is today a major requirement if the government wants to see the development of a new generation of private entrepreneurs able to make China a fully integrated part of the global e-economy.

Of course, this is a very sensitive political issue and the government may not yet be ready to address it because this would imply—or open the door to—the recognition that in the future the private sector, rather than the state sector, will be in the driver's seat. This is, in fact, the core of the issue. For all the effort towards the restructuring of the SOEs, reducing the public sector contribution to China's GDP to the SOEs in resource allocation, what needs to be revisited and substantially modified is the strategic role that will be assigned to the public sector over the next few years. Accession to the WTO will put tremendous pressures on the Chinese economic infrastructure to adjust in order to retain any chance at global competitiveness.

China has yet to change an economic outlook biased towards the public sector, or the notion of a production economy where, in many cases, the emphasis remains more on what is produced rather than what is sold or consumed. This helps explain why there is still a huge problem with the quality of goods and why inventories are estimated to represent as much as 15% of GDP, as factories keep producing a whole category of goods that the market does not want anymore. The shift towards a more "quality-oriented" approach to growth is certainly one of the challenges that the government needs to address in the new context that will be created by the admission to the WTO and the fiercer competition it will create for Chinese companies in the domestic market.

New Economy

The requirements for competitiveness in the global economy—transparency, unleashing innovative talent, flexibility, and the mindset which characterizes the Internet and the IT economy—are fundamentally at loggerheads with maintaining an ailing state sector into which the government keeps pouring billions of dollars each year. They are in contradiction with the "control" type of mindset and modus operandi that still prevails.

But the sensitivity of the issue and its implications for the political future of the country as a number of these problems are coming to a head, helps explain the nervousness of the regime. While moving ahead, the government wants to proceed by trial and error, keeping open for itself the option of freezing the process or backtracking if matters become too sensitive and difficult to control.

This is what is happening with the approach to Internet development. Of course, the leadership realizes the importance and the crucial necessity of making China a player in this domain and of favoring development of the sector. At the same time, it wants to retain elements of control with respect to content and foreign ownership or participation in Internet ventures. So, in parallel to very strict official limitations and prohibitions with respect to these issues, there is a much more complex picture where private entrepreneurs are, in some domains, going beyond what is officially authorized. The government turns a blind eye, but then from time to time sends appropriate signals when these private entrepreneurs are moving "faster than music."

We need to expect many cases of "one step forward, one step backward" on the Internet issue in China over the coming months. This is a strategic issue for the leadership and the immediate reaction of the bureaucracy is—and will continue to be—to use every single regulatory lever to assert control. But with the new generation of e-entrepreneurs, the start-ups can be expected to use all the possibilities that technological developments offer to bypass government regulations. The issue gets even more complicated as some of these regulations appear intent on providing state-owned Internet ventures with a market advantage over their private sector competitors.

This kind of "shadow boxing" is today an essential part of the day-to-day reality of business in China and is accelerating in many subtle ways the change in the corporate and business landscape. Of course, looking at the figures, one would be tempted to estimate that the Internet-based economy still represents today only a marginal or negligible fraction of the economy in terms of business volume and turnover. But this would be a major analytical mistake. There is no underestimating how far, how deep and how fast the new generation of e-entrepreneurs will change China's business and economic scene. They can take advantage of the government's disarray as so many new fields emerge and for which no existing regulations apply. The Internet-based economy is developing much faster than the government can control and regulate.

The best way to understand the full scope and complexity of the challenge might be to put it this way. Over the last 20 years, the regime has had to recognize that its legitimacy and continued power relied mostly on its ability to provide economic growth and sustained increases in the standard of living for a population exhausted by the tribulations of the Mao era.

This has proved to be so far a remarkably successful strategy. But now, if it wants to be able to ensure a continued increase in the standards of living of the population—and thus the continuation of its power—the regime has to embark into a number of new directions.

These new directions include a greater integration in the global economy, especially through accession to the WTO, and all the benefits and disciplines involved with it. This also means a much greater emphasis and reliance on the private sector as the key engine of economic dynamism and growth, and a drastic reduction of the public sector. This includes fully embracing the Internet, the telecom revolution and the e-economy, with all the free flow of information that goes with them. Such a course has tremendous psychological, social and, ultimately, political implications.

ECONOMIC REFORM AND MODERNIZATION

The process of economic reform and modernization will intersect more and more with this very sensitive issue of political reform. In other words, to sustain its legitimacy and continue its power, the regime must embark in directions that will put into question, more and more, the ways and modalities by which it exercises its power.

In fact, as always when confronted with crucial problems for which it does not have clear answers, the leadership is reverting to its longstanding practice of reacting by trying to assert its control even more forcefully. This helps explain why the tightening of the political grip is quite perceptible now. It is also in this context that the beginning of the preparation process for the 16th Congress of the Chinese Communist Party, due to be held by the fall of 2002, is adding to the complexity and—one might say—the opacity of the situation. Quite clearly, the jockeying for power and influence over the orientations of the Congress, and the new leadership line-up emerging from it, has already started.

But what is also clear is the fact that despite all the odds and uncertainties, there is no second-guessing that there is reform among the leadership. The only debate is on tactics and pace, not on whether to move ahead or not. In fact, the prospect of WTO admission is now forcefully used as a lightning rod in order to accelerate the reform process and help focus energies on it. And sensitivity to the social context and the urgency and complexity of the challenges ahead explain why it is so crucial for the government to use the margin of maneuver that any improvement of the economic outlook would provide, in order to accelerate the process of reform in view of the WTO admission deadline, on which it has staked so much of its efforts.

In this respect, much has been said about the sectors facing the most difficult adjustment process, be it the machinery and the pharmaceutical sectors or all types of capital-intensive activities. But there are two aspects which, maybe, have not yet attracted enough attention, especially in view of their implications not only for the future evolution of the country, but also with respect to China being fully able to fulfill its role and obligations in the context of the WTO.

FACING GLOBALIZATION CHALLENGES

The first aspect focuses on the agricultural sector, which still involves the majority of the Chinese population. The agricultural sector has been in crisis over the last few years and it will have to make a tremendous adjustment to be able to face the competition that will come when the WTO regime is implemented. If the agricultural sector is to survive in China, it must make a tremendous effort to restructure grain production and increase productivity to bring prices down to international levels; domestic prices are much higher now. This will also require shifting production toward activities in which China could have a comparative advantage on its own, as well as on the world markets: vegetables, fruits, and flowers for instance. This has, of course, significant implications for the concept of food security, to which the leadership has been very attentive, to reduce its vulnerability to the external world. But the restructuring process will have a very profound impact on transforming the physiognomy of the rural areas, accelerating the shift from agriculture to manufacturing and services.

One can be sure that in evolving towards compliance with the WTO regime, the government will be very careful not to create, in the rural areas, additional dislocations that it will not be able to manage. The pace and modalities of opening up and adjusting to foreign competition will be primarily dictated by what the internal context can absorb at a given moment. This might create the potential for friction between Beijing and its partners inside the WTO and one can expect that the dispute settlement system in the WTO will be put under substantial additional stress.

The second aspect has to do with the fact that over the last 15 years, China has undergone a very profound process of decentralization and de facto devolution of power from the central government to the provincial entities. In fact, it would not be too much of an exaggeration to say that China has today a relatively weak central state. There have already been many instances of provincial governments procrastinating on policies that Beijing was keen to enforce. We might well see a number of cases of that sort in the future as provincial or local authorities will try to delay—or shelter themselves from—the impact of measures decided by the central government in the drive to adjust to the requirements of the WTO regime.

The compliance issue will be a source of friction between the center and the provinces, as the tax issue has been for many years, and it took quite a protracted struggle from Beijing to increase its share of the tax revenues. In a similar way, the industry ministries—with all the sectors they control and the power that this situation provides them—are among those that can be expected to drag their feet on WTO compliance. Again it will be a matter of the leadership exerting enough pressure to get its way.

The result of this interplay—between the center and the provinces and between the leadership and the "obstruction capacity" of the ministries—will have an impact on the evolution of the power relationship inside China. China's standing in the WTO and its ability to fulfill its role as a "good" player inside the organization will also be affected.

But at the same time, there is no underestimating the tremendous impact of China's admission into the WTO for the country as well as for the world's trade structure. China has long suffered from seeing itself as having to cope with rules made by "others," that is, the Western world. It wants to be seen as it sees itself: as a rule-maker. There is an enormous amount of national pride in being able, through the WTO, to join the club of rule-setters. In many ways, this is considered to be a second and logical step in the process of international consecration after China regained its seat at the Security Council in 1973.

OPPORTUNITIES VS. COMPETITION

On the other hand, as much as the prospect of further opportunities created by the opening of the Chinese market is full of exciting promise for China's partners, they also face a significant challenge. There is no underestimating how much WTO admission will also allow China to become a more formidable competitor in a full range of products, from household appliances to textiles and even computers and electronic products. China's share of world trade is today around 3.2% and is expected to increase to about 7% five years after accession. This will have a tremendous impact on the international trade scene on China's relations not only with the U.S. and Europe, but also with its competitors and partners all over East Asia.

There can be no doubt that China's admission to the WTO is a development that the leadership in Beijing seems to have decided that for all it uncertainties, risks and difficulties, it must pursue. Any other option is—quite simply—even more dangerous to contemplate as it could mean a slower development pace, which would then create the risks of higher popular discontent, as expectations will become even more difficult to meet.

So, as China stands at this inflection point, as it gets to the point where the vibrancy and expectations and requirements and pressures of a new economy clash with the remnant elements of the command and control system and mindset, it is not surprising that the period ahead will likely be fraught with heightened tensions and uncertainties. From time to time, the regime will respond to increased problems by tightening its political grip. But in assessing the prospects ahead, and in keeping the present difficulties and uncertainties in perspective, two considerations need to be kept in mind.

First, over the last 20 years, the regime has demonstrated a tremendous capability for pragmatism, for ensuring that, overall, the direction remains set towards reform. In this respect, when it comes to the issue of economic reform and liberalization intersecting with political reform, one point is important. Whatever political evolution eventually takes place in China, it does not have to in any way copy the Western processes or formulae. Suffice it to say, the experiment of village elections launched a few years ago has been proceeding in fact very successfully, very quietly. It has changed significant elements in the daily reality of villagers. Now there are discussions about having some experiments with township elections, which will put the process at a much more—and complex—level. Nobody can predict how this will evolve, what lessons will be drawn from the first experiments or how, where and when they will take place.

One crucial and positive element, is the heightened realization among the leadership that whatever the differences on the pace or the modalities of the liberalization process, everybody is in the same boat. A major disruption could prove detrimental to everybody because it would then risk creating a chain reaction that nobody is sure to be able to control.

The second consideration lies in the fact that China is in the throes of a major generation change. This is quite apparent in the economic and business sector, of course, and much has been said about the new generation of entrepreneurs pushing the envelope every day with respect to what initiatives the system can live with. They are creating a wider breathing space for themselves, knowing how to slow down—in order to avoid any harsh adverse reaction—and how to put the general disarray and confusion to their advantage. Day-to-day business in China is definitely already much more complex and much more fluid that any reading of the present regulations or bureaucratic practices would let on.

But, the same process of generation change is happening at different echelons in the ministries, with the People's Bank of China and the Ministry of Finance being two very interesting examples. And this will also happen, at least to a certain extent, with the change that is supposed to take place at some echelons of the leadership as result of the next Party Congress in 2002. This will be a new generation for whom the parameters will not have been set by the previous dislocations and tragedies of contemporary Chinese history, be they the Liberation or the Cultural Revolution.

HUANG WEIDING

Huang Weiding is executive director of Red Flag Publishing House and a senior economist by profession. He is a member of the Publishing House Affairs Committee, which is the leading organization for Red Flag Publishing House and includes four committee members among which the chief editor is one. He simultaneously holds the position of secretary general of the Central Committee Ministry and Committee Publishing House United Publishing Organ.

The Red Flag Publishing House is a central government level publishing house, the main publication of which is *Seeking Truth* magazine (named after Deng Xiaoping's famous statement "Seek truth from facts") among other publications of the Central Committee of the Communist Party of China. These publications are directed at leading cadres and political theorists and also include social science books covering politics, economics, philosophy, history, and legal issues.

As author and economist, Huang Weiding has pioneered research of China's hidden, or shadow, economy. His representative works include *The Shadow Economy of China*, a best-seller that has been published in English, Japanese, South Korea, as well as in Chinese, continues to be republished. His numerous works include *The Puzzle of China's Current Consumption* and *Loss of Dignity — Memorandum of Penalizing Corruption*, among others. Huang Weiding's writing and research is viewed as critical in streamlining irrationalities in China's system of social distribution relationships and in highlighting problems of corruption which need to be corrected. Huang Weiding has personally participated in the investigation, cracking and handling of some of China's largest corruption cases. His work is highly respected by the Central Committee of the Communist Party of China and he is often invited to speak in China and overseas.

In this chapter, Mr. Huang explains how China's transition from a centrally-planned economy to one more market-driven has created opportunity for corruption, and what China is doing to remedy the problem.

Fighting Corruption Amidst Economic Reform

Huang Weiding

Executive Director, Senior Economist,
Red Flag Publishing House

Corruption with "Chinese Characteristics"

China's economic and social development achievements have attracted world attention. Entering the new century, China is full of both hope and challenges. Along with the deepening of economic reforms and implementation of macro-control policies, China's economy has already demonstrated a new trend of steady growth. Despite these strides, the spread and development of corruption is now seriously affecting China's economy and social development. This has become a focal point of attention of everyone, domestic and foreign, who wishes to see a prosperous and stable China.

First, the number of corruption cases involving large amounts of money is now overwhelming. In the early 1980s, bribes usually involved only a few thousand or at most tens of thousands of renminbi. In the 1990s, corrupt elements became greedier along with the course of economic development. As the tide of development rose so did the boat of corruption floating on the tide. Now there are frequently cases where a bribe will involve millions or tens of millions of renminbi. The largest corruption case to date has involved Rmb150 million.

Second, the number of high-level cadres involved in corruption cases has also been on the rise. In the 1980s, most cases of corruption occurred at the local or grass roots level. After the 1980s, the number of violations of both economic law and discipline by leading cadres increased dramatically. In 1999, 17 provincial-level and minister-ranking cadres (not including military cadres) received discipline from within the Party apparatus on corruption charges. It is also worth noting that during previous years, high-level

cadre corruption involved providing protection to criminal elements or taking passive bribes (that is, not aggressively asking for them), in amounts
that were not high. The former Vice Minister Li Xiaoshi of the State
Science and Technology Commission was a case in point, among others.

Recently, however, high-level cadres who have been penalized
actively sought bribes, taking the initiative to accumulate assets. The amounts
are also now extremely high. For example, the amount embezzled by
Jing Deqin, former vice chairman of the China International Trust and
Investment Corporation, among others, has involved tens of millions of
renminbi. Corrupt elements among high-ranking cadres are now being
uncovered routinely. This reflects the determination and achievement of
both the Party and Government to address the corruption issue. It also
reveals the difficulty in undertaking an open struggle against corruption.

Third, corruption cases involving extremely large organized groups have
now emerged. An especially massive smuggling and bribery ring in
Zhangjiagang Municipality involved over Rmb10 billion in corruption and
Rmb6 billion in tax evasion. This is what we call "collective corruption,"
a phenomena now causing national shock and furor. This case involved
over 200 government officials, with 12 cadres at the office or bureau-
level, and 45 cadres at the division level. The smuggling ring involved
a chain of command from the front line of customs, boundary police,
commercial inspectors, and harbor affairs, all the way up to the municipal city government and Party committee, including the highest ranking
leaders of the Zhangjiagang Communist Party Committee. At that time,
the media reported that the Zhangjiagang smuggling case was the largest-
ever smuggling case, involving the greatest amount of funds, and the greatest number of individuals at government and Party levels—as well as
judicial and enforcement department officials—since the founding of our
country. Recently, a case of smuggling in Xiamen involving even greater
amounts of funds and numbers of cadres and leaders, could make the
Zhangjiagang case pale in comparison.

Fourth, crimes committed by legal persons have also increased. While
state-owned enterprises are becoming more active, at the same time, many
are losing more money and laying off more workers. There are many reasons underlying the losses of state-owned enterprises, with corruption being
one of most critical causes. Among the cases of enterprises currently being
handled, at least half involve corruption and bribery among enterprise legal
persons or leading cadres. These worms use their power to serve their own
purposes and spend State assets luxuriously, shocking many people.

Fifth, corruption arising from economic sectors has now run rampant
through other areas. In Luo City of Guangxi Province, a deputy prison
director named Hu Yaoguang conspired with the director of the prison
hospital and key department heads, as well as the chief justice of the local
court criminal tribune, to collectively take bribes to bend the law for the

personal interest and benefit of friends and relatives by reducing the sentences and probations of over 60 criminals. Once this matter was publicly released, the entire nation was shocked. Some police even conspire with criminal groups to provide a protection umbrella while judicial personnel take bribes to bend the law. In addition, within the field of personnel matters, it has become vogue for officials to chase after promotions to higher office, which can then be bought and sold.

Sixth, corruption of power is expanding and spreading to become "professional" corruption. That is, the personnel of water, electricity and public facilities, city management and public transportation, among other government departments, can use their professional advantage to "eat, take, stop others, and make demands." The education department, once considered to be beyond the realm of money and corruption, is demanding fees and organizing classes of no value, simply to collect money. Another example is those stations or institutions that should serve agricultural production. Here, personnel can hold back quotas and increase prices of chemical fertilizer, pesticide, diesel oil, and other major agricultural products. "Eat the farmers, hold up their work, injure them" has become the pattern of government in rural areas. Leaders and cadres, as well as many management level officials, participate in these professional corruption activities. Those with great power use it against those with little power and limited use for it. Corruption of government administrative power has spread throughout society, a dangerous trend.

Rampant corruption causes great harm to the economy as state-owned enterprises are constantly being nibbled away at, with State assets being swallowed in their entirety. Corrupt elements are especially interested in targeting large-scale State investment and construction projects. Many "fried tofu"* construction projects result from embezzlement, not to mention duplicated construction projects and enormous waste. Corruption has destroyed China's investment environment, affecting inbound foreign investment. "Chaotic demanding of fees" as well as demanding contributions of all sorts, to a great extent have offset the advantages of investing in China in the minds of foreign investors. Commonplace bribery has created an environment of unfair competition, with these games of irregularity causing honorable businessmen who want to undertake proper business activities to just leave. When the government lends large amounts of money overseas, money laundering causes losses of tens of billions of dollars in capital to leak overseas.

These are the economic effects. Politically, corruption makes an extremely ugly impression upon the population. If corruption cannot be stopped in the long term, this will shake the confidence and trust of the people in both the Party and government, causing dissension and discord.

*Shoddy construction projects so poor in quality that they fall apart like fried tofu when picked up with chopsticks.

In terms of ideology and culture, corruption has confused the values and concepts of right and wrong in people's minds. The mindset now is to grab for oneself, a short-term action, lessening the cohesive force of the people and fighting spirit of the nation. Therefore, rampant corruption has become a prominent problem affecting and holding back the deepening of reforms, development of the economy and stability of society. This chronic problem has become a monumental obstacle for China in realizing its targets for development in the new century.

In facing this serious situation, many comments and views have been expressed by people both within China and overseas. Some people say that only a total westernization of China can solve the corruption issue. There are others who say that corruption has been caused by reforms and the creation of a market economy. They argue that at least during the political movements of the 1950s and 1960s, people were clean and honest.

What needs to be done is to recognize the phenomena underlying the corruption, which are inseparable from China's unique condition of being in the "first stage of socialism." Previously, China implemented a central-ized, planned economic system where production and living resources were distributed according to plans, creating a lack of consumer products, and which required a voucher system to purchase certain commodities. At that time, salaries served only as a supplement to this system of planned com-modity distribution. The distribution framework was built upon a low level of equality, which caused people to have limited tolerance toward expand-ing gaps in income distribution. In other words, in a situation in which the market mechanism had not yet developed, the conditions for corruption did not exist. At that time, society was honest and clean, but there was a price to be paid for this: the economic development was extremely slow and most people were poor. In addition, you could not rule out the existence of corruption, as corruption took the form of privilege through use or abuse of power. For instance, during the Cultural Revolution, Jiang Qing made a famous statement, "Money is meaningless to me." She could say this because she did not need money, as through her power she had everything.

After implementing reform and open policy, the target of econo-mic reform is to establish a socialist market economy. This new economic system was formed on the basis of the traditional, highly centralized planned version, upon which a market economy mechanism was gradually formed. Moreover, Deng Xiaoping's "crossing the river by stepping on the rocks" strategy of gradual transition from one track to another, in fact caused two systems to co-exist for a long time. Over the course of a 20-year economic transition period, neither the old nor new systems function completely. The planned system has already been broken up, while the new market economy has not been completely established. The result is that the factors that should normally halt corruption in both systems cannot function normally, therefore corruption has had a unique opportunity to become rife. The grey areas that have emerged in both systems have proved, in fact, to be factors inducing corruption. During the course of this special period of economic transition, a special mode of "transition period corruption" has emerged, the features or characteristics of which are as follows.

(1) Individual power interfering in the market is pervasive, creating conditions for transactions between money and power. Under a highly centralized planned economic system, the demands and potential for transactions between money and power are limited. Along with the market-oriented system reforms, many different independent bodies of economic interest are formed, allowing the market mechanism to play an increasing number of functions. However, reforms cannot be completed at once. The planned economic system still plays a function. Administrative power interference in micro-economic activities exists in a broad manner. In this situation, economic bodies will seek to optimize their interests in order to: obtain low-priced products and materials still under planning, to approve projects, to receive funds, or obtain favorable policy support such as loans, tax exemptions, or foreign exchange quotas. Unjustifiable measures involving bribes and kickbacks will be employed to attain these, corroding the administrative departments and officials who have the power to control finance, personnel, and property. Weak people are easily seduced by money to use their power as a chip to be exchanged. Individual power interfering with the market results in corruption in projects, engineering, and financing. Power interfering in the market is the greatest warming bed for nurturing corrupt opportunities.

As the breakthrough point in China's economic system reform, rural reforms, which achieved the greatest efficiency in reform, also had the same problems. First, the function of government at the grass roots level in rural areas has changed from directly organizing production activities, to supervising and encouraging farmers, to fulfilling sales tasks designated by the government. However, the working style and measures of government at this level have not changed accordingly. Second, farmers specializing in certain fields (such as animal husbandry) will sign contracts to use land, electricity, farming products and materials, in turn relying on township cadres in local village stations. Third, during the rapid development of the township enterprises, township cadres will use their management power to turn publicly-owned assets to private use. Therefore, in the meantime, the rural economy will quickly go the route of becoming a commercialized economy. The *san luan*, "three chaos," and use of power to serve private purposes, have begun to emerge, which does not follow the original concept of developing wealth through one's own labor. Some rural cadres who use their power become rich first.

(2) The market economy system is incomplete and remains imperfect, providing gaps within which corruption activities may occur. The lack of a

complete market economy becomes particularly obvious in that there is a market in the first stage but no market regulations. Market rules and systems may be required for economic development, but due to the gradual process of market economic reform, all kinds of systems, policies and measures cannot possibly be completed at one time. So these gaps can be fully utilized by those who wish to use their power for payment. For example, land which was once freely given out to be used now must be paid for. At first, this change marked progress toward a market economy; however, due to incomplete regulations, the approval of leasing prices does not go through the market or formal market sales. So the leaders will determine randomly how much can be sold and for what price and to whom, nursing corruption. Corrupt individuals may engage in power for money transactions through black box operations. Yu Fei, the former vice chairman of the Guangdong Province People's Congress Standing Committee, approved the sale and speculation of land obtaining huge price discounts, and allowed his children to obtain a Rmb166 million price difference. Another example occurs when the government encourages one section of society to become rich first, but does not offer the guidance and supervision needed to have them become rich through diligent work and legal means. These adjustments between poor and wealthy are neither useful nor efficient.

The break-up of the "iron rice bowl" has pushed workers to the market, but the necessary social welfare system has not yet been established. The problem of having too many people in government with too little to do has not been solved. In addition, when the state-owned enterprises relaxed their rights and profits, the management responsibility system invigorated the enterprises. Vague or unclear relationships between production and power within the enterprises, and a lack of efficient supervision and monitoring mechanisms over the directors and management, have given rise to peculiar situations. In short, the "temple is poor but the monks are rich." In other words, it is commonplace for the enterprise to lose money but for the directors to be personally rich.

(3) Irregular competition during this transition process has become the warm bed nurturing corruption. The essence of a market economy is competition. However, due to the immaturity of the market mechanism, a large portion of the competition in China is, in fact, irregular competition. In order to get hot products on the market or obtain resources still controlled by planning, many enterprises will directly offer gifts and kickbacks to government officials together with other commercial bribes.

In addition, flexibility in accounting among private or collective enterprises allows for bribes to be almost invisible. It is easy for officials to have a direct interest in the enterprise and to provide advantages to these enterprises over the state-owned ones, which are subject to a collective management and maintenance of accounts. Former Jiangxi Province Vice Governor Hu Changqing has already been executed for corruption. Within six years, he took over 87 bribes from over 18 persons. Most of these 18 persons were individual or private enterprise owners.

This irregular competition is also reflected in the foreign investment enterprises. Foreign enterprises in the coastal regions can, through the support of corrupt officials, engage in smuggling, black market arbitrage and sweatshop factories to lower costs. Foreign enterprises that follow the law will be in an uncompetitive position during this transition. In the mid-1980s, a duel commodity price system existed for raw materials. In the early 1990s, the development of real estate, funds and stocks created relatively typical examples of irregular competition. Some speculators used the duel system to become extremely rich overnight, completing their capital accumulation process. A number of officials gained huge benefits secretly.

(4) The policies and measures developed during this transition period have necessarily been short-term and expedient, which has given rise to corruption.

Due to lack of experience when adopting certain reform measures, the negative effect of these measures has been underestimated. For example, the State has, on a trial basis, tried forcing many administrative units to be responsible for their own losses and expenditures. The goal was to broaden sources of income and reduce expenditures; however, along with the differences between both, some units have tried to use their power and position to compete with other units of government in creating their own revenue streams. This has not only created chaos in the market order, but has also enhanced the lack of professionalism within various professions. Members of the Party, government, military, and political realm, as well as legal organs, have all opened enterprises, the original purpose of which was to provide employment for spouses and children so as to relieve social pressures. However, this has created a situation where power has interfered with the market, as power is used to do business and becomes a basis for transactions. After comparing the costs and benefits, it can be seen that these measures have in the end only raised the cost burden on society.

Therefore, the present phenomenon of frequent corruption is not much different from the corruption of privilege that existed under the planned economic system. It does differ from corruption existing in developed market economies. During this transition period, it is impossible for every link connecting both systems to be closely connected. Furthermore, the inability of both legal and system construction to keep pace provides many more opportunities for illegal and disciplinary conduct violations to occur, compared with a single system.

The transition from a planned to market economy system is a profound reform, during which many conflicts become unavoidable; however, we cannot shake our resolve to undertake reforms. The most important issue is to determine a breakthrough point at which we are able to grasp opportunity and test our strength and weaknesses. It is impractical to bring about change overnight. The former Soviet Union's collapse and subsequent internal disruptions offer us a profound lesson. Due to China's particular historic development and the realities of today, China's economic base is even more backward than that of the former Soviet Union. Development, therefore, could result in even greater instability. The enormous population and shortage of natural resources, combined with a low level of education, mean that if "shock therapy" were used, it would result in an economic disaster. Moreover, administrative power must continue to play an irreplaceable role in this period of market formation. Today's system of "macro-controls" cannot completely be separated from administrative measures. The problem involves how to gradually reduce the scope of interference using purely economic and legal measures to eventually replace administrative ones. China is seeking to realize a market economic system through gradual transition between one economic system and another. This involves seeking development through social stability. Reform must be carried out on the basis of economic development.

During this period of transition, developing an active economy and corruption are contradictions that may be expected to co-exist for a long period of time. How long will this last? During Deng Xiaoping's "southern inspection" he pointed out that, "I am afraid that another thirty years will be required for us to develop a more mature and solid system. Under this system, policies and guidance will have come into a fixed pattern." Deng said these words in the spring of 1992. On the basis of his own predictions, this period of transition could last until 2020.

It is of critical importance to understand this transitional aspects of China's corruption characteristics. Corruption is not the result of economic reforms; corruption is the result of the fact that economic reforms have not yet been fully completed. At present, corruption as a trend is still on the upswing, this is only temporary and one cannot assume that the corruption problem is unsolvable.

Of course, we must remain alert in seeking to eliminate the existing conditions which give rise to corruption. We cannot slow reforms for fear of corruption growing, but must increase the pace of reforms as this will eventually eliminate those very conditions which give rise to corruption. Although corruption cannot change the general trend of social development in China, it will destroy the reform process if allowed to run unchecked. It will even change the direction of reforms. The deepening of reforms and elimination of corruption must take place in parallel and be mutual, complimentary goals.

CORRUPTION AS AN INEVITABLE FACTOR OF TRANSITIONAL ECONOMICS

Based on the characteristics of the transition period of corruption, China's effort to build an anti-corruption mechanism is based closely around economics at its center and is coordinated with economic reforms to advance in steps.

First, high-level corruption must be severely penalized and cases of organized crime cracked. Only intense penalties can halt this trend and reflect the resolution of both Party and government to eliminate corruption. Only through such measures will the people regain confidence that corruption can be halted. On March 18, 2000, Hu Changqing, the former vice governor of Jiangxi Province, was executed for taking bribes exceeding Rmb6 million. This is the first case of a provincial or ministerial level cadre being executed on corruption charges since the founding of the People's Republic in 1949. Not long after, Chen Kejie, former National People's Congress Standing Committee Vice Chairman, ranked as a State leader, was first tried for the death penalty on charges of taking bribes involving Rmb41.09 million. In the meantime, organized smuggling cases in Zhanjiang and Xiamen are under investigation. The Chen case not only involves a shocking amount of money and number of individuals, but also has required an unprecedented number of officials to deal with a single case. One by one, high-level corrupt individuals are being penalized by the law. One after another, huge cases of organized crime have emerged, as complicated as twisted roots and branches. Of course, penalizing corruption involves conflicts of life and death among individuals, especially among certain corrupt elements that have long-term positions.

After many years, huge powerbroker networks have been built. For instance, Li Chenglong, the vice mayor of Guigang City in Guangxi Autonomous Region, was arrested for receiving bribes. During the course of the investigation, some Rmb14.16 million was discovered in his possession involving both goods and cash. At that time, however, individuals requested that the case be closed on the basis of only a single bribe involving Rmb45,000, stopping the investigation from including the rest. The procurator and disciplinary authorities were prepared to pursue the case to its logical conclusion. A power-ful figure stated, "If you pull up a carrot to get to its roots, it will pull up a lot of dirt with it as well. That dirt will need to be replaced, and this may not be so easy." That's why over the past few years, many investigations of major violations by high level cadres have involved investigators assigned by the Central Committee Disciplinary Commission, requiring very capable individuals able to put up with much hardship in pursuing cases to their conclusion.

Intensifying investigations of dereliction of duty has become a new measure in the battle against corruption. This crime does not necessarily involve putting money in one's own pocket, but rather results in neglecting duty, abusing power, and employing favoritism. In the past, people did not recognize such abuses as a crime, and many of these officials actually received promotions without anybody pursuing their legal liability. Now this is changing. There are two situations arising in connection with dereliction of duty as a crime. One involves lack of seriousness toward one's work, and dereliction of duty, often involving the trading of power for economic benefits even if evidence of such is difficult to detect. Over the past three years, organs nationwide have had cadres who have abused power or neglected their duties exposed. Cases of this nature have given rise to a strong social reaction against such abuses. In June 2000, Xu Yunhong, former Central Committee Alternate Member and Party Secretary of Ningbo Municipality, abused his power to take funds for private reasons in the interest of friends causing major losses to the State. This was the first known case involving abuse of power by a provincial level cadre since the founding of the People's Republic in 1949. One month earlier, the Central Committee Disciplinary Commission and Ministry of Supervision, announced the investigation and penalizing of a Vice Chairman of the Standing Committee of the People's Congress of Chongqing Municipality and a Vice Chairman of the Chongqing People's Political Consultative Congress, causing embarrassment and loss to the State. The local level procurate also seriously investigated and penalized a group involved in dereliction of duty and major loss of State assets. In the meantime, an investigation resulting in penalties of the judicial and law enforcement departments occurred, in order to promote the fair exercise of justice and law enforcement, and the fair use of administrative power in accordance with the law.

Third, intensified auditing and supervision has become one of the most important anti-corruption measures used over recent years. Violations of economic and financial discipline in the name of reform involving the embezzlement of State funds have created the worst damage for economic reforms. Under the leadership of the Central Committee and State Council, the State Auditing Department has discovered losses of Rmb214 billion in the grain supply fund carried over six years. The Department has assigned 50,000 auditors to jointly undertake with eight ministries and commissions to establish 16 State Council inspection groups to go to each region of the country to carry out investigations related to this case. This is the most extra-ordinary and massive coordinated auditing action since the establishment of the People's Republic. It involves a large amount of private embezzlement, as well as embezzlement by government departments, of funds designated for grains and staples, involving a plethora of legal and disciplinary violations and criminal activities. In addition, the State Auditing Department has discovered that the Ministry of Water Resources was involved in hiding and then transferring funds designated for projects that would transfer water supplies from the southern regions to the arid north. These funds were placed in a hidden account. The Ministry of Water Resources even embezzled over Rmb100,000,000 from the Special Project's Fund to invest in the purchase of residences, offices, and stock market speculation. The State Council has decided to confiscate the comprehensive office building complex illegally built by the Ministry of Water Resources and collect the embezzled water resources funds and reapply these to irrigation and water management projects. The liability rests on leaders and directly responsible individuals. A major auditing investigation of the central government's 1999 budget and other income revealed huge violations of rules and discipline, as well as of the law. Of particular interest, Rmb4.3 billion was embezzled from funds designated to relieve poverty amounting to one fifth of the funds under audit. The auditing department suggested that 60 individuals responsible for embezzling poverty relief funds be penalized by being kicked out of the Party and relieved from their official positions, with nineteen of them being sent to the justice department for prosecution.

The central government's resolution to attack corruption continues to intensify. Citizens signing their names to letters reporting corruption to government disciplinary organs is a growing trend. Based on statistics from the Nanjing Municipality, from January to May 2000, some 3,070 reports on corruption were received with 588 being personally signed by the individuals sending them. On average, for every five letters received, at least one is signed by the sender. Despite increased attacks and frequent acts of revenge against those reporting corruption, this continued reporting of corruption reflects the anger of the people over this phenomena as well as faith in the Party and government's resolve to penalize corruption. Over 80% of the cases now under investigation have arisen through reports submitted by citizens. Officials concerned with the grain fund audit being undertaken by the State Auditing Bureau have stated that, "auditing departments at the various local levels have received an enormous number of complaint letters. The State Audit Reporting Center has received over 1,300 such letters. The efficiency of such auditing activities has been increased as a result of such reporting.

Corrupt individuals in power hate those who report them and often their acts of revenge are extremely cruel and extreme. For example, in Pingdingshan City of Henan Province, the Party secretary in charge of political and legal affairs hired an assassin to murder the local deputy county chief when he reported the Party secretary's criminal activities. The assassin not only cut up the deputy county chief but killed his wife as well who was a model school teacher. In Lankao County of Henan Province, the Agricultural Machinery Bureau Director named Feng Xueliang, conspired with the deputy bureau director and five other people to "collectively research" to hire thugs to seal the door and ignite the home of an employee named Lian Haiqing for reporting their criminal activities. Lian's entire home, together with his four family members (including an eight-month-old baby girl) all burned to death in the fire. Almost unbelievable is that these thugs even went so far as to seek reimbursement for the receipts for the petrol and gas tanks purchased and used in setting Lian's house on fire. Feng Xueliang actually had the nerve to personally sign and approve the reimbursement slip.

The scale of threats and cruel revenge are not scaring the people, however, as many continue to demonstrate their strength and tenacity in struggling against such abuses. For instance, two workers from the Wuhan Children's Bicycle Factory were unfairly forced out of employment. In order to obtain evidence that the factory director received bribes, these two workers spent Rmb10,000 of their own money, travelling thousands of kilometers to north Hebei to obtain evidence of bribes he had received there. Finally, this factory director received the "deserved legal penalty." In addition, they had faced the risk of revenge when they received Rmb400 as a reward from the Procurator for reporting corruption. They explained their determination to expose corruption to the end.

Moreover, after years of efforts to struggle against corruption, which began with trying to curb corruption, full efforts are now underway to wipe it out by attacking corruption at its roots. The following summarizes various experiences and methods that are being used to achieve this end.

(1) The transition period of corruption is the product of power and money combined, and the methods of fighting corruption must approach the system itself and cut the channels for mixing power and money. On one hand, power must be regulated; on the other hand rules of the market must be standardized. A supervision system for preventing the convergence of power and money must be developed, and this mechanism must adopt the rules of a socialist market economy. This conclusion is one of the most important from the past few years of experience in fighting corruption. Through fixed exchanges between the economic administrative department and the law enforcement department and the dissolving of power and cross-functions, the links for the enforcement of power have been extended, thereby forming an internal system of controlling relationships. This is an efficient way to supervise the operation of power.

(2) Establishing an open system in order to handle these affairs. Only through transparency can people understand the truth and efficiently participate in supervision. Therefore, the Central Committee requires that "except for items which are State secrets, all matters and content dealing with procedures must be opened to society, so that it will be conducive for the understanding and supervision of the masses." A serious system for opening administrative affairs, village affairs and administrative affairs has already obtained positive results. Because the black box operation is being terminated, corruption will have no place to hide.

(3) The public now scorns the common phenomena of fees, penalties, and apportioning charges known as "chaotic collecting of fees." This is one

common form of creating income through the use of power. It destroys the market and gives rise to local department protectionism, causing serious losses to State financial capital. Many efforts to stop this have to date failed. In June 1998, the Party and Government enacted regulations regarding income expenditures under which all income must submit to the higher level government authority and all expenditure funds will in turn be appropriated through the budget. Only through the system itself can this fundamental corruption sickness which is inherent in the administrative and judicial systems be solved.

In the meantime, the military, People's Armed Police, and political-legal departments engaging in commercial activities easily gives rise to commercial phenomena. Some of these activities even involved the protection of smuggling and the sale of smuggled goods, destroying the socialist market economy order. In July 1998, the Central Committee decided that all of the military and armed forces as well as political and legal departments are not allowed to engage in commercial activities. At the end of December of the same year, all the provinces, cities and regions accomplished the complete separation of commercial operating enterprises from the military and government departments to which they were once attached, in accordance with the schedule for separation.

(4) Some government expenditures have mixed cheating and waste with deal-making involving power and money, due to the government's closed purchasing model. This now calls for purchase by tender. The government has introduced the new government purchasing system as urgent work to be dealt with. Over the last few years, Chongqing, Hebei, Shenzhen, Shenyang and other regions, have been test regions for purchasing through a bidding process, which has saved between 10–15% of the local budget. Some projects have even saved over 30% as a result. In addition, due to the purchasing activities conducted through open bidding, the black box operation in purchasing activities has been prevented, expanding the channels for intensified supervision and monitoring by the public.

A visible construction market has emerged pushing forward a system of assigning accountants and auditing systems to serve as a check on the economic liability of cadres, to regulate the operation of power and marketing mechanisms, and as important reform measures to realize the smooth economic system transfer.

ATTACKING CORRUPTION AT ITS ROOT

Corruption must be attacked to protect economic reform. In turn, reform must be expedited to eliminate the conditions for corruption arising during this transition to a market economy and while these two approaches are correct strategies, they are not enough. We will carry out the work against corruption to not just clean up corruption but to ensure the comprehensive progress of society. Only then can we fundamentally eliminate the condition that gives rise to corruption. There is a saying, "China's success is in commencing with economic reform. The Soviet Union's failure was in commencing with political reform." Some people even "turn pale at the mention of a tiger." They think only by freezing the political system and not undertaking reform for a long period can they ensure the correct direction of reform and development. Claiming that the success of China's economic reform is divorced from political system reform does not accord with the facts. We could not have the economic reform achievements of today without the Third Session of the 11th Party Congress—which ideologically, politically and organizationally set right the wrongs of the past—and without twenty years of open reform policy and democratic legal system construction. Therefore, since the reforms and open policy began, our country has ceaselessly carried out reforms of its political system. The success of our country's reform and the failure of the former Soviet Union's reform, is due to not the question of reform commencing from economics or politics, but rather a question of whether the reform track taken was correct or not. We should also be aware that in comparing economic system reforms, our political system reforms still lag behind. This is also an important explanation of why the anti-corruption campaign has had difficulty in digging corruption out at its roots.

The 15th Congress of the Communist Party of China provided a new direction in the way of thinking and approach to political system reform. Firstly, it expressly put forward both projects and tasks calling for law as the basis of rule in China, and the construction of a socialist country ruled by law. This fundamentally changes the situation of rule by man, and the past phenomena of Party and Government as well as Party and enterprises being inseparable. The trend and way of thinking of constructing a democratic legal system with Chinese characteristics will raise to a higher level the modern concept of rule by law. Constructing a modern society ruled by law is necessary in constructing a socialist market economy.

An important part of cleaning up our politics is for Party to be administered with severity and the concept of being a public servant intensified in the minds of leading cadres. Many of the older revolutionary generation are models in this regard. Marshall Chen Yi, one of the founding fathers of our country, once wrote a famous poem entitled "Don't Put Your Hand Out." In his poem, there was prophetic language to the effect of: "ordinary people have all kinds of weaknesses." A quote from Marshal Chen Yi's poem follows:

"Isn't it true, people do like power and position
Power and position tower over the mountain
Isn't it true, people like the beauties wearing heavy make-up
Drinking up the water of the love-river, but still feeling thirsty.
Isn't it true, people like to be loved and esteemed.
Hearing eulogistic songs and being happy like fairies."

His conclusion is absolutely clear: "Without people we cannot survive" and "We came from the people and cannot do them wrong." That's why his is the spirit of exemplary conduct and nobility of character which was not confused by "money, beautiful women, and the ten miles of foreign department stores"* or overwhelmed by the vices of power in his early years.

An older generation of cadres and leaders once said, "The older generation will not forget the masses. Anyone who forgets can still be reminded. However, as for the generation that will follow us, it is hard to say. They will forget the masses, and it is not easy for them to recall." Our Party has governed the country for more than half a century. The last twenty years has been the period of fastest economic growth in our history. A long period of peaceful construction and improvement in material conditions has created a new way of thinking among certain people which is not progressive but focused on seeking self-fulfillment, comfort and luxury, living in extravagance. These people have totally forgotten the hardship of the masses.

In 1999, the "three talks" education program was launched to cadres at the county level and above. In the year 2000, the "three representatives" education program began. From the Party to the people, this concentrated education is based on the basic principals of the Party and people's government. The central content is still raising the consciousness of cadres, cleanliness and self-discipline. In the meantime, the Party and government are constructing a government system by putting forward strict requirements for cadres based on the style of clean politics. Cadres are being called upon to make an example of themselves in terms of cleanliness and discipline. Afterwards, the Party and government will require leaders and cadres to go beyond cleanliness and discipline and to demonstrate responsibility to their spouses, children and working people around them. After that, they will be required to be responsible not just to their family, but to construct a clean government in the regions or departments for which they are responsible. This will include establishing a sound system of responsibility. It goes without saying that leaders must be responsible for the officials they promote. Based on reports from the Chinese press, in 1999 Wuhan City had 262 leading cadres who were held responsible for breaches in discipline among the cadres beneath them. Many were penalized through either Party of government-meted discipline. This is a vivid example of the ruling Party severely rectifying itself.

The core of political system reform is intensifying people's democracy and democracy within the Party. Democracy is a weapon that can kill corruption. For example, the phenomena of being able to sell or purchase a position of officialdom exists in situations where a single official can decide which officials to appoint under him without listening to the

---

* This is a literary description of old Shanghai which is used here as Marshal Chen Yi was Shanghai's first city mayor after 1949 following the liberation of the city by his own troops.

opinions of the public or others. The person who wants to purchase a position in government knows that he can do this not because of his own qualifications but because the leader has the power to give his nod. The buyer of an official position knows it is a good investment that will offer a return on principle and interest because from the position attained, many benefits will flow. If this situation does not exist, and a real democratic selection of officers is carried out with democratic supervision and dismissal, interference in administrative power will not be possible, as the market for officialdom will be effectively closed. Therefore, changing the system is more important than dishing out penalties, because ultimately the problem is with the system and solving the problem means changing the system.

Cadre system reform is gradually being adapted to the requirements of establishing a socialist market economy system and developing socialist democratic politics. Party and government used the expansion of democracy as a reform direction by insisting in and perfecting democratic recommendations, testing, and democratic systems of evaluation, a system of public notice may be intensified before officials are appointed. This will expand the right to knowledge, selection, participation and supervision. Of course, this is only the first step. Afterwards, a system of vigorously reform and perfection must occur to expand a system of selection candidates of choice. This will require perfecting a system of putting forward candidates by name, creating conditions to consistently expand conditions for direct election, impeachment and dismissal. Disqualified cadres may be replaced at any time, thereby forming a system of competition to remain in the political arena. Whoever is doing a good job will remain in power while those who are not will retire. In a nutshell, the transition from a system of high concentration of power and rule by man toward a democratic system must be realized. This is adapted to the transition from a highly concentrated planning system to a socialist market economy system.

Intensifying the supervision and monitoring of public opinion and media is another key point in attacking corruption and encouraging cleanliness. As the masses, the people are most qualified to evaluate the exercise of public power and reflect through the news media. Under the encouragement of the Party and government, public opinion supervision has been consistently increased. The central government and regional television, official newspapers, and web sites have all openly covered corruption. The supervision of the media has been greatly enhanced, providing immediate coverage of such tragedies as the collapse of the Jijiang Bridge, the Zhaozuo fire, and the shooting case in Bazhou. These reports came in time and grasped the trends covering the news, interviewing, investigating and disclosing corruption behind the scenes. Because of such coverage, those responsible cannot escape criminal liability in the end. Under this powerful supervision of public opinion, corruption activities are becoming increasingly risky.

While the struggle against corruption is still very serious, the economic reforms adopted by both the Party and government, and the guidance and mutual cooperation will move in step toward the same direction. This will accord with the basic conditions in China during this transition period. It is also an important guarantee for us to obtain this new period. We have full confidence and say in realizing the fundamental transformation to stop corruption.

Part II

INTERNATIONAL RELATIONS

FROM THE 19ᵀᴴ TO 21ˢᵀ CENTURY

In the early months of the 21ˢᵗ century, an odd event occurred, which in a way partially symbolized the closing chapter of a tragedy that unfolded in the 19ᵗʰ century and extended into the 20ᵗʰ. This tragic chapter closed when the Poly Group, a corporate entity under China's central government, spent Rmb30 million at a Christie's auction held in Hong Kong to purchase three bronze heads from a fountain in the Qing summer palace of Yuan Ming Yuan. These bronze heads were stolen when the ancient garden complex was looted by foreign invaders during the Opium Wars of the 19ᵗʰ century.

Yuan Ming Yuan, the architectural wonder built by the Kang Xi and Qian Long Emperors, once stood as the epitome of Qing imperial splendor and refinement. The complex was a vast sequence of interlocking palaces with gardens and fairy-like pavilions radiating outwards along crystal lakes covered with delicate bridges. The very existence of the Yuan Ming Yuan must have irritated Europe, which at that time, had not attained the advanced level of culture that China had enjoyed for tens of centuries.

Today, when you stroll through the public park that was once Yuan Ming Yuan, in the suburbs of modern Beijing, you see nothing of this splendor—virtually everything that was Yuan Ming Yuan has been obliterated. The delicate palaces that once housed imperial treasures dating from every period of China's history are gone; only the stone foundations, which could not burn, remain to mark the pillar supports of the once-classic vermilion palaces and pavilions. The treasures once held within are today on display in the museums of those European countries whose forces sacked Yuan Ming Yuan, or are in private collections. Today, when you walk through the shattered remains of Yuan Ming Yuan, you can only ask yourself what kind of hatred could fuel such destruction.

In 1860, foreign allied forces united in a single purpose: to cripple China politically and force it to open to the West—on Western terms—economically. The Emperor Xian Feng had already fled to Chengde in the north, the old hunting lodge palace complex of the Qings. His dynamic brother, Prince Gong, became diplomat of the day. He kept the foreign forces at bay and refused to open the gates of Beijing to them. Unable to attack the political nerve center of China, the allied forces attacked the cultural. Discovering the vast wealth outside Beijing's city walls, enshrined in the Yuan Ming Yuan and the Summer Palace, they broke into the palaces stealing every conceivable item of value and destroying what they could not take with them. Pearls, jade, rubies and gold of immeasurable quantity and value were removed. Century-old vases were shattered, paintings of priceless value were indiscriminately burned, the precious Peking dogs—specially bred by the imperial household—were hurled headfirst into wells, and gold-embroidered dragon robes were heaped and burned.

The entire complex of Yuan Ming Yuan and the Summer Palace was put to the torch. For weeks, the sky over Beijing was black with smoke. The statement was clear: precious items of immediate commercial value to China were to be had by foreign interests; precious items of cultural importance and value were to be destroyed completely.

In the weeks that followed, Prince Gong negotiated. The foreign powers wanted access to Beijing; they wanted the gates to be opened. Eventually, he was forced to acquiesce and the gates were opened. The foreigners entered; another treaty was signed. Trading ports, which included Tianjin, Beijing, Nanjing and Guangzhou, were opened, and foreign-occupied territories in China were put under foreign administration. Chinese law was not enforceable against foreign interests on Chinese soil in these foreign-administered enclaves.

The backdrop of these events cannot be forgotten or lost in understanding the dynamics of Chinese-Western relations today. It is not a question of old, unsettled grievances, but of the historical context upon which such relations have been established.

The key elements of Western policy towards China at this critical period in history were: to obtain unlimited access to China's market, that is, to sell Western-manufactured and finished goods to the vast Chinese population without restrictions or import duties; to have unlimited access to China's vast natural and crafted products at cheap labor costs; and to control trade. Foreign powers knew that a weak political system would have to tolerate their interests and commercial domination. In addition, the rights of foreigners in China could not be touched by Chinese law; foreign laws and administration were carried out within foreign enclaves and complete diplomatic immunity was accorded to all foreign interests. These elements of this diplomatic episode have remained part of the collective unconscious underlying both Western diplomatic and commercial initiatives today in opening the China market and the Chinese government's approach to dealing with them.

It is clear that the foreign powers did not have as their intention the toppling of the Qing imperial system. They chose not to attack the basis of the political nervous system of dynastic China. Rather, it was clearly their intention to have access and, moreover, control of China's resources. Leaving a weak political system in place was only to their advantage.

Likewise, in another context, a strong Communist China with a heightened sense of nationalism has predictably posed more obstacles to foreign exploitation of China's resources than Chiang Kai-shek's Kuomintang, which was, historically, always malleable as far as money was concerned. Is it any wonder that U.S. support and propaganda were for so many years (and even today) behind Taiwan and not China?

THE TAIWAN QUESTION

The United States' isolation of China coincided with its continued support for Chiang Kai-shek's regime, which the U.S. insisted upon believing held political ideals similar to its own. There is little debate over the historical facts surrounding Chiang Kai-shek's regime: corrupt to the core, intertwined with the Shanghai "Green Gang" mafia, suppressive and totalitarian. Nevertheless, the U.S. insisted on recognizing this regime as "Free China," even after it was popularly expelled from the mainland.

Washington determined that Chiang's regime be recognized and Mao's isolated. Reports from journalists in the field, such as Edgar Snow and Theodore White, were often not published, as editors felt compelled to reflect the views of the anti-Communist right wing which dominated Washington D.C. then, and to some extent today as well. Nobody in Washington really tried to understand what communism meant for "New China," or the ideals driving the new leadership and the problems confronting it as it sought to unify and reconstruct the nation. As a result, the Taiwan issue, with the collective unconscious of diplomatic baggage entangled within, remains as one of the major items topping the list of China–U.S. issues, which in turn weighs on China's relationship with the West, influencing strategic concerns of other Asian countries as well.

The ascent of Chen Shuibian's Democratic Progressive Party (DPP) in Taiwan's year 2000 local elections finally ended the Kuomintang Party's traditional 50-year grip on the island's power politics. On one hand, it represented an end to long-established channels of dialogue between the Communist and Kuomintang parties, which are rooted as far back as the Xian Incident in 1937 and the Chongqing negotiations between Mao Zedong and Chiang Kai-shek. On the other hand, this change in Taiwan's power structure may inadvertently present a new opportunity to move relations forward in a nonconfrontational manner never envisioned under the Kuomintang.

The historic clash between the Kuomintang and the Chinese Communist Party was brought to a new epoch last year with the introduction of Kuomintang leader Lee Teng-hui's "two-state theory." This theory soon became the single, key issue of confrontation between Beijing and Taipei, blocking unification progress on all fronts. Lee's "two-state theory" represented a major step backwards.

In order to clarify China's position on the Taiwan issue, in early 2000 the State Council issued a white paper on "The One-China Principle and the Taiwan Issue." The paper clearly enunciates China's position on the Taiwan issue. Most of the points are not new, but some offer wider scope for discussion, which may even be interpreted as concessions of an unprecedented form.

Most of the foreign media, however, ignored the content of the paper, and concentrated on reporting a single line in the document referring to China's right to reserve the use of force under specified conditions. In doing so, the foreign press largely ignored the fundamental meeting-ground points opened up under this unique document. It is useful to understand fully the cards that China now places on the table. The following key excerpts (which the foreign media all but refused to report at the time of their announcement) reveal how close negotiation positions are in fact:

One-China Principle: the white paper acknowledges that "both sides for a long time recognized that there is only one China" (Chiang Kai-shek also stated the same principle) arguing that only Lee Teng-hui (former Taiwan "President") has actually departed from this line by calling for "state-to-state" relations, adding that Lee Teng-hui "betrayed the one-China policy."

Military: The paper states, "Following reunification Taiwan will have a high degree of self-rule and the central government will not station military and administrative persons in Taiwan," adding that "this method in line with the one-China principle respects the hopes and wishes of Taiwan compatriots." This provides an even broader framework for a future Taiwan Special Administrative Region (SAR) than the Hong Kong SAR, where in negotiations with the British, Deng Xiaoping was adamant about stationing the People's Liberation Army in Hong Kong. This requirement has been dropped in relation to Taiwan.

Arms: "Nations having relations with China have no excuse to sell weapons to Taiwan," which could be interpreted as a specific protest against attempts by the U.S. Congress to pass the Taiwan Security Enhancement Act and to include Taiwan in a theater missile defense program. These moves can be seen as running counter to the three communiqués that form the basis of relations between China and the United States, and an interference in the cross-straits talks.

International Relations: "Taiwan has no right to participate in the United Nations as only sovereign states may participate in international organizations." However, "Taiwan can participate in certain international organizations under the name of Taipei, China," which Taiwan is in fact doing with respect to efforts such as the Asian Development Bank and the Asia Pacific Economic Cooperation (APEC) forum. Moreover it appears that this model would be acceptable to Beijing in connection with the World Trade Organization, representing an unprecedented concession on a very critical and practical issue to many in Taiwan. In short, aside from the question of participation as a sovereign state, which must be reserved for China under the one-China principle (in keeping with the three communiqués), Taiwan may have practical direct access to trading, economic, and other related international organizations. This position presents a practical solution for a long-outstanding issue.

Use of Force: "If Taiwan separates from China in any name or if there is an invasion by foreign forces or the Taiwan authority refuses to negotiate forever to solve the Taiwan issue, then China will have to adopt any possible measures including the use of force to protect Chinese sovereignty and territorial integrity." The last line of the white paper has been repeatedly the focus in both media coverage and in the U.S. Congress. This statement, however, should be understood in the entirety of the sentence in which it is stated. Force has been reserved to three specific conditions: (1) if "foreign forces" invade Taiwan, (2) if there is a clear act of separation, or (3) if the "Taiwan authority refuses to negotiate forever."

How do we define "forever?" Foreigners doing business in China long enough should know how to read between the lines. Through a face-saving maneuver, it seems as if an opening has been presented. Chinese, who are very practical, should know how to negotiate with each other. This can be evidenced by statements made during the 2000 National People's Congress sessions by both Jiang Zemin and Zhu Rongji to the effect that within the one-China policy, "anything can be discussed." Practicality is also evident in recent statements by the recently-elected Chen Shuibian to the effect that his party, the DPP, can drop its independence platform and the recent announcement that Quemoy and Matsu islands (under local administration of Taiwan) will begin direct trade with Fujian Province.

So why did the U.S. Congress and State Department become so upset about the white paper? The contents are in fact consistent with the three communiqués that ground China–U.S. relations, which are summarized as follows:

The Shanghai Communiqué (1972) established the one-China principle adding an American commitment to gradually withdraw military installations and troops from Taiwan.

The Communiqué for Establishing Relations between China and America (1978) formally established diplomatic relations on the mutual acceptance

of principals relating to Taiwan's return to the mainland and the termination
of the previous America–Taiwan defense pact.

The Communiqué of August 17 (1982) emphasized that Taiwan's return
to the mainland is entirely an internal issue of China's and agreed to a
reduction of U.S. arms sales to Taiwan.

Dialogue across the Taiwan Straits has been unavoidably linked
to dialogue between Washington and Beijing. This has been the case
since 1949. Such dialogue is now overshadowed by the Taiwan Security
Enhancement Act, the proposed theater missile defense system
for Taiwan, and Washington D.C.'s continued arms sales to Taiwan.
What's happening?

When speaking in relation to the Taiwan issue in early 2000 at Johns
Hopkins University, President Bill Clinton suggested, "There must be a
shift from threats to dialogue across the Taiwan Straits."

When speaking shortly thereafter to journalists at the close of
the Third Session of the Ninth Plenum National People's Congress, Premier
Zhu Rongji suggested that in order to make President Clinton's statement
more precise, two words should be changed. Zhu suggested, "There must
be a shift from threats to dialogue across the Pacific Ocean."

CHINA–U.S. RELATIONS

Washington's policy towards China, in broad terms, has not changed
all that much over the past 40 years. Following a strong reception given to
Kuomintang leader Lee Teng-hui by a number of U.S. senators
and congressmen during his visit to New York in 1995, it was clear
that the predominant thinking of America's right-dominated Congress
remains locked in the mind-set of the 1950s and 1960s, at least in terms
of China.

Foreign businessmen on the ground in China are often frustrated trying
to explain to corporate headquarters the dynamics of change in this now
very market-oriented market. This frustration is compounded by the difficulty of trying to break through the rather fixed negative images in the
minds of both corporate and political decision makers often painted by the
foreign press. Opportunities are lost as a result of slow and indecisive
decision making back home.

Duanzhi She, the former public relations manager of the American Chamber of Commerce in China (AmCham), described his impressions during a
visit to Washington D.C. of the knowledge possessed by U.S. Congress
members concerning China issues:

> Congress members need to raise their level of understanding about
> China. Most of them have never been to China. Thus, their knowl-
> edge of China comes second-hand from the mass media, which

tends to emphasize negative stories—human rights violations, weapons proliferation, child labor, belligerence, religious persecution—and other buzzwords. Little wonder the U.S. legislators told us all kinds of weird things about China.

One Congress member, for example, accused China of taking over the Panama Canal. In his mind, the People's Liberation Army bought the support of a Hong Kong tycoon, who in turn bought control of the Panama Canal, threatening U.S. strategic interests. Another legislator said he did not support PNTR because Communist China is preparing for war against the United States. He asked his AmCham visitors if they knew how many missiles China has targeting the United States. "Eighteen," he pronounced. Fortunately, an AmCham delegate with knowledge of such issues was able to reply that the United States has 2,000 missiles targeting China. Moreover, we informed him that China and the United States have signed a de-targeting treaty.

While Congress often frustrates American companies wishing to invest or sell technology to China, to conduct joint satellite launches and joint research, China's market continues to evolve. Opportunities pass by. One must ask couldn't more be gained in these areas from the perspective of both business and closing gaps in understanding and perspectives through cooperation rather than "containing" or "engaging" China?

On the eve of President Clinton's visit to China in 1998, Henry Kissinger noted succinctly:

> Republicans see China as a threat; Democrats view it as a laboratory for the spread of American values. Both view China through the prism of their party's experiences over the last 30 years.
>
> Unfortunately, too many Republicans have substituted China for the collapsed Soviet Union and seek to deal with it by the methods that accelerated the collapse of the Soviet empire: diplomatic confrontation, economic ostracism and ideological warfare. Too many Democrats act as if the principal goal of American policy should be to replicate our institutions and principles in China, even at the cost of our many other interests at stake in Asia and without regard for the complexities of Chinese history.

China continues to change certainly with more speed than Congress can comprehend or Washington's best think tanks can keep up with. When Clinton entered the White House, America's China policy was called "containment." We all know what that means—certainly the Chinese are clear. Clinton progressed his policy to one of "comprehensive engagement" which may be seen as a positive step, although many Chinese question whether there is any difference in substance from "containment." Maybe it is time for America to consider changing its strategy toward China again. On Clinton's trip to China, Jiang Zemin himself suggested an avenue worth consideration. Jiang called it a "strategic partnership."

Today, without question, many if not most Chinese greatly admire America's inroads in technology, science, computers, finance, and management—areas where they would welcome a "strategic partnership." These are the things about which Chinese wish to learn and apply to their own system, not political ideals. When American magazines publish photos of Chinese children stuffing their mouths with McDonalds hamburgers and write that American values have come to China, they are only touching on superficial images. The investments of foreign corporations, the skills that are taught to Chinese employees, new horizons in management training and ways of systematically approaching market share, gain far more in promoting similar values than political grandstanding. This is the reality of China and America's relationship, which needs to be redefined, if "strategic partnership" is to become a reality.

ON SUNSHINE AND STORMS

China's State Chairman and Party General Secretary Jiang Zemin was interviewed by Mike Wallace of the CBS program "60 Minutes" on August 15, 2000. Jiang used this occasion to express his own views on China–U.S. relations as follows:

> We are now in the new century and China–U.S. relations should strive to advance to constructing a strategic partnership. Whoever is the next president, regardless, from the perspective of world strategy should try to straighten out the China–U.S. relationship... . Sometimes China–U.S. relations are good and sometimes in a storm. There are certain people in America who do not want to see China and the U.S. having good relations. They always make some problems.

In his interview, Jiang went on the explain differences in China's political system:

> China's system of a National People's Congress involves a system of consultation under the leadership of the Communist Party together with other parties cooperating. Eight parties are participating. Some [U.S.] congressmen ask, who is the opposition party? Why do we need an opposition party? America wants to apply its concept of values to the whole world. They think that every region of the world will use the American political system. This is simply unintelligent. Every country's election system must be based on their

own situation, historical traditions, culture, economic and development level, and education level.

China's political system has developed from China's history and 5,000 years of unbroken cultural development. During this period, the geographic land that is China, even when ruled by a people from beyond the Great Wall (Mongolians during the Yuan Dynasty and the Manchurians during the Qing), has consistently been developed under the cultural dominance of the Han (Chinese) people, with other minorities partly involved. Under the weight of 5,000 years of history, cultural values and social behaviors, modern China cannot be quickly changed, although since commencing its economic reforms, Western culture has come to China in large doses. However, Chinese culture has consistently remained the overriding force and continues to influence the Chinese people's thinking—a basic and essential factor to consider when developing a body politic.

China has always been large in scale, at least from the Tang Dynasty through to the Qing Dynasty, during which time its borders remained more or less constant. Today, China is one of the largest countries in the world—it is certainly the most populated. This is what makes China different. The proportion of natural resources to people is in fact, relatively small. China's landscape is dominated by mountains and deserts, and naturally irrigated and arable areas are few. At the same time, China is aiming to become one of the world's most developed countries, which will demand both industrial expansion and agricultural efficiency. In order to achieve this objective, China still has a long road ahead of it; it will require constant and careful planning to maximize, without destroying, the few (proportionate to population) natural resources China has.

The topic of China–U.S. relations is always a sensitive one. Why should it be more so than U.S. relations with any other country? A quick review of China–U.S. relations throughout the Clinton administration is revealing and places much into perspective. The Clinton administration initially adopted a policy of "containment" during the first term, which changed to "engagement" in the second. We witnessed the first visit of an American president to China since 1989, followed by Clinton blocking Premier Zhu Rongji's WTO bid during his sensitive Washington visit, followed by the bombing of the Chinese embassy in Belgrade.

From this abyss in relations, an 11th hour "win-win" deal on China's WTO entry was struck, largely due to Zhu personally intervening in the negotiation as it began to break down. This year witnessed Clinton appealing to the U.S. Congress to grant China PNTR. Topping off events was Jiang Zemin's recent visit to the United Nations to attend a millenium summit for international heads of state. Using Jiang's own appropriate words, "Sometimes China–U.S. relations are good and sometimes in a storm."

NEVER BORING

Over half a century ago, in 1949, China's relationship with the Soviet Union was an uneasy continuation of relations rather than an alliance. Mao Zedong himself wished to see China align with the United States and establish relations with this less immediate threat, a wish torpedoed by America's embargo which followed the establishment of new China. China's long years of economic and political isolation between 1949–79 represented a political imposition—none of the economic embargoes (those placed against Cuba, Vietnam and Cambodia) lasted as long (with North Korea as exception), or had such an effect in real terms, as the embargo placed against China by the United States.

It is clear that straightening out China–U.S. relations is an item paramount on Jiang Zemin's list of business for the new century. Shortly after his arrival in New York to attend the millenium heads of state summit at the United Nations, Jiang spoke to a small group on the nature of the current international configuration of power, and relations between nations. Jiang's discussion sheds some light on China's own concerns about the future of China–U.S. relations, which has been pockmarked by a host of sensitive and complicated issues.

On the relationship of human rights to sovereignty, Jiang Zemin explained that, "Respecting human rights and sovereignty are basic equal principles. These principles have been in existence for many years, but must now be reviewed and considered. Every country has the responsibility to respect international human rights documents, linked with the character of each country's situation for the promotion and protection of each country's human rights and basic freedoms."

"However," he added, "on the other side, mutual respect of sovereignty and non-interference in internal affairs are still standards of international relations. The people of each country have the right to select their own social system and route of development according to each country's situation, to create their own life. China respects human rights, we also respect the rights of sovereign nations."

On the function of the United Nations, Jiang explained, "The purpose and principle of the United Nations must continue to be developed. After more than 50 years, practice indicates that the purpose and principle of the United Nations remains valid. We should calmly and jointly protect the authority of the Security Council. We cannot work outside the Security Council. We must jointly strive to intensify the functions of the United Nations in the areas of development. Most nations are developing nations and priority should be placed on solving their problems. We should jointly strive to have a democratization of the decision-making of the United Nations. All members should be equal regardless of whether they are big and small, strong or weak, rich or poor. The reform of the United Nations should reflect the common will of a broad number of countries especially the rational demands and basic interest of the broad developing countries."

China's own diplomatic outlook on the world has been—as in the case with virtually every other nation—shaped by its borders. Nations bordering China include: North Korea, Russia, Mongolia, Khazakstan, Kyrgyzstan, Tajikistan, Afghanistan, Pakistan, India, the Jammu and Kashmir regions, Nepal, Bhutan, Myanmar, Laos, and Vietnam. Compare China's border situation with that of the United States, which neighbors only two countries: Mexico and Canada. As a simple fact, this explains a lot concerning basic outlook.

Compare the tone of Jiang's words at the United Nations to the tone of President Bill Clinton's when Clinton explained his reasons for supporting PNTR made on May 21, 2000: "Yes, China is still a one-party state...but by forcing China to slash subsidies and tariffs that protect inefficient industries which the Communist Party has long used to exercise day-to-day control, by letting our high-tech companies in to bring the Internet and the information revolution to China, we will be unleashing forces that no totalitarian operation... can control."

Jiang's own explanation given to Mike Wallace of "60 Minutes" on the system which China is now trying to evolve sets a completely different tone from Clinton's: "We are trying to construct socialism with Chinese characteristics, the idea of which is to first allow a certain portion of the population to become affluent," Jiang explained. "Becoming rich is glorious. It is not necessarily capitalist. We need to study Western culture and particularly technology, but this must be adapted to Chinese customs."

"The West wants us to become Westernized," Jiang added, "but if everywhere in the world was like the West, wouldn't it be pretty boring?"

In the opening chapter of this section, Minister Tang Jiaxuan, who heads China's Ministry of Foreign Affairs, paints a broad-brush picture of China's current policy of international relations and diplomatic initiatives covering most regions of the globe. In the second chapter, Canadian Ambassador to China Howard Balloch discusses the changes he has witnessed in China's own approach to diplomacy, paralleling economic development from the perspective of relations with Canada and his own personal insight. Danish Ambassador to China Christopher Bo Bramsen discusses the emerging strategic commonalities between China and Europe evolving through the ASEM forum in the third chapter of this section. Both the Canadian and Danish ambassadors contributing to *China's Century* are unique among the foreign diplomatic corps in Beijing as the grandfathers of both were China traders active in China's early foreign commerce over a century ago. In the fourth chapter of this section, Mark Daniell, author of *World at Risk* and managing director of Bain & Company SE Asia, examines global hot spots and China's pivotal role in preserving world peace and stability in the century ahead.

TANG JIAXUAN

Tang Jiaxuan is minister of the Ministry of Foreign Affairs, China's high-powered diplomatic corps. A graduate of the Oriental Languages Program of Beijing University specializing in Japanese, he has served a number of terms in the Chinese Embassy in Japan. Formerly vice minister of the Ministry of Foreign Affairs, he was appointed to the top post in 1998.

In the following piece, Minister Tang provides an overview of China's recent diplomatic initiatives and a framework for understanding China's current agenda for furthering international relations.

CHINA'S FOREIGN AFFAIRS IN THE NEW CENTURY

Tang Jiaxuan
Ministry of Foreign Affairs, The People's Republic of China

POLICY OF FRIENDSHIP

Turning the century, the international situation appears to have undergone significant changes since the cold war. While the general trend of the international situation is one of ease, hegemonism and power politics arise at times, attacking the United Nations Charter and other publicly recognized principals of international relations. The world is still not at peace.

Facing the shifting international situation, China maintains a peaceful, independent and self-reliant foreign affairs policy, determined to uphold state sovereignty, territorial integrity and national dignity, striving for a more influential international position to effectively promote international peace and development, and create a positive environment for domestic modernization.

The friendly, cooperative relationship between the Chinese people and people from all over the world has been continuously enhanced. In 1999 only, Chinese President Jiang Zemin, National People's Congress Chairman Li Peng, and State Council Premier Zhu Rongji, visited 40 countries in five continents. In turn, 40 foreign state presidents and government leaders visited China. Entering the year 2000, high-level visits continued to be very frequent. They enhance mutual understanding and deepen trust, laying a positive foundation for the further development of bilateral cooperation, which will bring mutual benefits in the new century.

Over the past year, positive relations between China and neighboring countries have been consolidated and strengthened. China's and North Korea's state leaders jointly agreed to increase bilateral cooperation to a new level. The relationship between China and South Korea has been strengthened as well. The traditional friendship between China and Cuba has deepened. The constructive partnership between China and India continues to develop. The cooperation between China and other Asian countries has showed positive signs, witnessing the signing of joint announcements regarding future bilateral cooperation with Vietnam, Thailand, Malaysia, Indonesia, Singapore, Philippines, and Myanmar. The fifth meeting of the "five countries'" presidents, of China, Russia, Kazakhstan, Kirgizistan and Tadzjikistan, as well as the holding of the first meeting of these "five countries'" foreign affairs ministers and state defense ministers, has further enriched the mechanisms of friendship and cooperation.

There have been new developments of friendship and cooperation in political and economic arenas between China and other large developing countries. Chinese state leaders have visited many Asian, African and Latin American countries over the past year. China established a "New Model of Cooperative Partner Relationships" with Turkey, established "Partnership Relations" with South Africa, and reached mutual understanding for the establishment of a "Facing the 21st Century Strategic Cooperation" relationship with Egypt. All of these mark the deepening of relationships between China and developing countries.

RELATIONS WITH MAJOR POWERS

The relationship between China and the world's large countries has been continuously developing. China and U.S. relations have gradually recovered after having experienced a winding road in 1999. On May 25, 2000, the U.S. House of Representatives passed the proposal to grant China Permanent Normal Trade Relations (PNTR). Resolving China's status as PNTR is a positive move toward developing economic and trade relations based on equality and mutual benefit between China and America. However, China decisively rejected and will not accept the past proposals, which contained terms interfering in China's internal affairs and hurting China's interests. China and Russia's relationship has been steadily and continuously developing. In March 2000, Vladimir Putin was elected the new President of Russia and President Jiang Zemin expressed congratulations to him over the telephone. The two countries' state leaders jointly expressed that their strategic cooperative partner relationship will be further developed in a positive and well-rounded form in the new century. China reached a bilateral agreement with the European Union to join the WTO, the development of their bilateral economic and trade relationship is steady, and discussion and cooperation for international affairs has been enhanced.

The relationship between China and Japan has maintained a healthy momentum. After the death of Japanese Prime Minster Keizo Obuchi, his successor Prime Minister Yoshiro Mori expressed his effort to further develop relations with China, meanwhile sending executive special diplomatic mission leaders to represent him in visiting China. In May 2000, some 5,000 representatives from all walks of life and cultural fields from Japan formed a Sino-Japanese Cultural Tour Exchange delegation to visit China, a historical breakthrough commercially as well as in terms of the number of people involved in this Sino-Japanese friendship exchange. President Jiang Zemin attended the Sino-Japanese cultural tour exchange meeting and delivered an important speech. This exchange further enhanced the Chinese and Japanese people's friendship and mutual understanding, which is significant in opening up a new phase of Sino-Japanese friendship for the 21st century.

China has played an exclusive and aggressive role in the United Nations and multilateral international organizations. In March 1999, during President Jiang Zemin's visit to Switzerland, he put forward the five principals of establishing an international, political, economic new order and new security proposal, by forming mutual trust, mutual benefit, equality, and cooperation as core centers, which received enthusiastic responses. China, in attending the 54th United Nations General Assembly meeting, stressed the principals of: feasibly strengthening national sovereignty; respect and mutual noninterference in internal affairs; settling international disputes by way of peaceful negotiations; enhancing the role of the United Nations; and protecting the Security Council's authority, among other points, which received positive responses from many countries.

NATIONAL REUNIFICATION

China will continuously push forward the unification of one country, and decisively maintain national sovereignty and respect. In December 1999, the Chinese government resumed the exercise of sovereign rights over Macao, "a hundred years' travelling son returned back to its mother's embrace."

The task of realizing a complete, unified, single country is still outstanding, after smoothly completing the return of Hong Kong and Macao. We made a firm struggle over the "two states" statements and the actions of Lee Teng Hui, who attempted to disrupt the country, effectively attacking the "Taiwan Independence" force. The proposals of "Taiwan rejoining the United Nations" and "Initiating Taiwan as an Observer to attend the World Hygiene Meeting" put forward by a small number of countries were again frustrated.

The 21st century is walking toward us. This is a time full of challenges, full of wishes, a time to open up, to keep forging ahead and to go all out to make the country strong. It is a time of moving forward from the past and opening a way for the future and realizing a revival. China's prospects are bright in the new century. China's foreign affairs' prospects in the new century are ever more expansive.

In the course of the new century, China will continuously and carefully implement Deng Xiaoping's foreign affairs ideas, maintain peace and independence and keep the initiative in its own hands on matters of foreign affairs policy. On the basis of the five principles of peaceful coexistence and other publicly recognized international relations norms, we will call for developing friendship and cooperative relations with every country in the world, and further create a peaceful international environment and a sound environment for domestic socialist modernization construction. In dealing with international affairs, we will continuously uphold justice, and determine our policy according to what is right and wrong, true and false. China will continuously endeavor to promote the development of world peace for the sake of establishing justice and a reasonable international political and economic new order.

Chinese people will decisively push forward the unified industry of the country and carry out battles without compromise for all forms of disrupting behavior. In March 2000, the Taiwan region elected a new generation of leaders, which will not change the fact that Taiwan is a part of China. Our attitude towards Taiwan's leaders is to listen to what they say and observe what they do; we wait and see in which direction they want to lead the relationship between mainland China and Taiwan. To realize the goals of "One Country Two Systems" and "Peaceful Reunification" according with the mutual benefits of both mainland Chinese and Taiwanese people, is both the desire of the Chinese people and the general trend of our times. The One-China principal is the basis and premise of peacefully solving the Taiwan issue. We are firmly against any form of "Taiwan Independence."

RELATIONS WITH DEVELOPING NATIONS

In the new century, to strengthen broad cooperation and unity with developing countries will still be the basic premise of China's foreign affairs. In the 20th century battle of fighting for national independence and prosperity among strong countries, China formed a profound friendship with a wide range of developing countries. On the road to the 21st century, in dealing with global challenges, establishing justice and a reasonable international new order, China will continue to cooperate with developing countries through support of each other, closely coordinating, jointly opening up friendship, mutual benefits and new cooperative achievements. China will forever stand on the side of developing countries.

In October 1999, President Jiang Zemin officially proposed to the African countries' leaders and the Organization of African Unity Secretary General to hold the "Sino-African Cooperation Forum—Beijing 2000" ministerial level meeting and received an enthusiastic response. During autumn 2000, this historic meeting was held in Beijing. On the occasion, issues such as how to further strengthen Sino-African relations in the new era and how to protect the mutual benefits of developing countries in the process of globalization, among others, were deeply probed. This important event aimed at promoting friendly Sino-African cooperation at the turn of the century. We believe, through joint efforts of all various parties, this important meeting achieved success. The unity and cooperation between China and African countries will open a new chapter in the new century.

CHINA'S ROLE IN THE CENTURY

China has already established various forms of partnerships with every large county in the world. These partnerships will be further developed in the 21st century. China, as the largest developing country in the world, is aggressively developing relations with every large country, strengthening links and exchanges which serve well in promoting world peace and stability and are positive in developing multi-polarization.*

In the new century, China will continuously play its role as a large developing country with Chinese characteristics in the United Nations and other multilateral organizations, and contribute responsibly toward world peace and development. In September 2000, the United Nations held the "Millennium Presidential Summit" to explore the prospects of world peace and development and to discuss the United Nations' future reform and development. President Jiang Zemin attended this meeting and delivered an important speech. China has always protected the United Nations' position of authority in dealing with international affairs, on the basis of maintaining the aim and principal of the United Nations Charter, fully representing the wide range of member countries' mutual benefits, approving the carrying out of relative reforms to the United Nations and its Security Council in order to make it better able to fulfill the United Nations' responsibility in protecting international peace and security.

The 21st century bell will be sounded. Farewell to a hundred years of humiliating history. Hundreds of millions of children of the Yellow Emperor will stride vigorously and proudly ahead into the threshold of the new century. China's foreign affairs in the new century will make a great contribution toward creating a long-lasting, peaceful and generally prosperous new world.

*Referring to balanced multiple relationships between developed and developing countries as opposed to a purely lineal or polar relationship such as between east and west, communist and non-communist and so on.

Howard R. Balloch

Howard R. Balloch is Canada's Ambassador to China. Having spent his childhood in eastern Canada, he attended the University of Laval in 1969 and received his bachelor's degree (Political Science and Economics) in 1971 from McGill University; his master's degree from McGill University (International Relations) in 1972; and his doctorate (between 1973 and 1976) at the University of Toronto and the Fondation Nationale de Sciences Politiques in Paris.

Ambassador Balloch joined the Department of External Affairs in 1976 and served in a number of positions at home and abroad including: the Southeast Asia Relations Division; Canadian Embassy in Jakarta, Indonesia; Head of Transportation Policy and Assistant to the Chief Air Negotiator; Personnel Division; Canadian Embassy in Prague, Czechoslovakia; and as Director of Resource Management at Headquarters. From the mid-to late-1980s, he was the director of the North Asia Relations Division, and during the early 1990s, was assistant deputy minister for Asia Pacific. Mr. Balloch is married and has four children.

Ambassador Balloch has a unique family connection to China, as his grandfather was a tea trader in the coastal regions of Fujian and Hong Kong over a century ago.

In the following chapter, Ambassador Balloch draws upon his particular background and experience in providing insight into the changes occurring in China, from Canada's perspective, and where they may lead in the century ahead.

THE CANADA-CHINA RELATIONSHIP: A PERSONAL PERSPECTIVE

Howard R. Balloch

Ambassador of Canada to China

SKETCHES OF VANISHING CHINA

My grandfather spent 30 years of his life in China. A hundred years ago he was still in Fuzhou, where he had been a tea trader for many years. He was soon to move down to Hong Kong for another decade or so before retiring and heading home. When I was a child, the few oddments left from his effects were the source of great mystery and magic. Photographs of over-dressed Europeans at leisure at the racetrack on the island in Fuzhou, of scenes of the tea plantations further west in Fujian and of the Hong Kong waterfront, and a book of watercolors entitled *Sketches of a Vanishing China*, told of a world that could not have been much further away, figuratively and literally, than the eastern Canada I knew as home. There were a few other treasures, like a silver 1899 horseracing trophy, that he took away from China, but not many, for little had survived his death shortly after settling back in the Highlands. My father, orphaned as a boy, took what there was when he emigrated to Newfoundland in the 1930s.

Not many Caucasian Canadians can trace a family history back into imperial China. I can do so only because my grandfather was a Scot and my father, driven by family misfortune, sought a brighter future across the Atlantic. My father could count to ten in Chinese, had happy memories of an *ayi* brought home to Scotland, and told us that our grandfather had been a simple and kind man, fair to the Chinese with whom he dealt and who served him. I suspect that my father really had little idea of his father's life in China, and whether in fact he had been as disdainful of those around him as so many of his Western counterparts. I wonder what the signs said at the

Fuzhou racetrack, where my grandfather won his trophy, and whether dogs or Chinese other than servants were permitted entry.

It was just barely more than one hundred years ago, on August 14, 1900, that the foreign troops broke through to Beijing and lifted the Boxer-led siege of the Legation Quarter. While many European countries and the United States and Japan had legations there, Canada did not. And it may be in that differentiation, and in the fact that my country does not have to share whatever historical burden I might personally carry as the grandson of a Westerner benefiting from the forced opening and exploitation of China, that we might start our look at Canada–China relations.

A LESS BURDENED RELATIONSHIP

Of all the G-8 countries, Canada has had the shortest and least historically burdened relationship with China. We cannot claim Marco Polo or the rich knowledge the Jesuits built, nor the trading routes charted by the Anglo-American clipper community. While Canada established a small trade office in Shanghai just after the turn from the 19th to the 20th century, we had no concessions and sent no troops or warships to break blockades. In fact, the first real engagement we had inter-governmentally with China did not come until the Second World War, when we established our first resident embassy in the wartime capital of Chongqing. And until that time we largely had let China come to us. Unfortunately, while this left us without some of the historical demons that others have had to expunge, or in some cases seem still haunted by, it did not lead to any greater tolerance or foresight in our early dealings with China.

Unlike our European counterparts, the early Canadians in China were not for the most part big traders. From our small Shanghai office, we sold Canadian furs to the affluent and wood and ores for the newly emerging industry of the lower Yangtze. Only two or three Canadian firms were active in the trans-Pacific trade of silk and tea, although there were a few colorful figures who crop up in the footnotes of history, like Two-Gun Cohen, a tough Albertan who carried two Derringers and who served in his mature years as the bodyguard to Sun Yat-sen. The largest dimension of our early relationship was moving what our industrialists considered a commodity, Chinese labor, easterly to the mines and railroads of the Canadian West.

Shortly after Confederation in 1867, the opening up of Canada's West became a major priority for our young country. New provinces from Manitoba to British Columbia were brought into the federation, and the task of building a truly continent-wide country began. No endeavor in fulfilling this nation-building dream was more important than the construction of a coast-to-coast railway. In building eastward from Vancouver, the Canadian Pacific (CP) Railway needed vast numbers of laborers, far more than the still sparse Canadian population could provide. And so the Chinese were recruited in the thousands from a series of townships in Guangdong province, and thus began the first significant flow of ethnic Chinese to Canada.

While it would be nice to describe a welcome environment for the tens of thousands of Guangdong workers who arrived to work for the CP Railway in the late 1870s and 1880s, the truth was harsh. Denied the right to bring wives or children, the workers we paid very modestly, housed together in crowded dormitories and given a minimum of freedom or time off. But they were not forced to return to China at the end of their contracts, and as the railway work began to diminish, gradually established themselves in the lower mainland of British Columbia and in many of the towns and villages along the line from Vancouver to Calgary. Soon they were to fan out further east, finding gainful employment as cooks and laundrymen and in a few other trades for which they were accepted according to invisible but clearly understood ethnic barriers, in spite of a determined work ethic and growing prosperity. For the most part, and except for the limited interchange imposed by their commercial endeavors, these Chinese communities lived apart from their Caucasian neighbours.

Yet shortly after the turn of the 20th century, certain changes began to emerge. First, the growing tumult in China brought Chinese issues to Canada. Sun Yat-sen's famous trip through Canada brought real political attention to Chinese issues, not just within the Chinese communities to which he turned for financing, but also among the more established political order. Shortly afterwards, Chinese communities edged towards the Canadian mainstream by volunteering to serve in the First World War. Across the country, but particularly in British Columbia and Alberta, ethnic Chinese students started to be accepted into universities and colleges, emerging frequently as professionals whose practices were limited to the communities whence they had come. There was still a special fee for Chinese immigrants, including wives and family members sponsored by men already in Canada, called the Head Tax, part of a discriminatory immigration policy that was not made race-blind until after the Second World War.

EARLY ENGAGEMENT

Canadians themselves were becoming more engaged in China at the turn of the century. Missionaries established themselves in many parts of the country, and by the 1930s, the Canadian missionary presence in places like Chengdu (where they founded Southwest Medical College) was notable. For the most part, Canadian missionaries were not concentrated in and around the treaty ports like their European and American counterparts, undoubtedly because there were no Canadian communities or Canadian concessions established there. An interesting footnote to later diplomatic relations between the two countries is that one of Canada's wartime diplomats in China (Chester Ronning, later to be an outspoken proponent of

early recognition), and the first three Ambassadors of Canada to the People's
Republic (Ralph Collins, John Small and Arthur Menzies) were all
Mandarin-speaking children of missionaries. But at home in Canada, just as
the Chinese communities remained largely apart from, and largely ignored
by, other Canadians, so too did the government of Canada take only marginal interest in developments in China during the inter-war period.
Although the government had moved relatively soon, after the final constitutional authority for foreign affairs was transferred to Ottawa from Britain
as the colonial power, to establish a full embassy in Japan, the government
deferred establishment in a China still rocked by internal conflict and chaos.

   While the government in Ottawa was taking little interest in the turmoil
in China, a number of Canadians were getting personally engaged very
deeply. Among a number of young idealistic doctors, nurses and volunteers
who were to join the fight against the Japanese, and sometimes against the
Nationals as well, none would become more famous than Dr. Norman
Bethune. Bethune became the chief doctor for the 8th Route Army, bringing
simple but advanced techniques to battlefield medicine, and introducing
simple medical systems into the rural areas through which the army moved.
He became a friend to a number of the revolutionary leaders, and earned
their respect because of his fierce determination and selflessness. He was
to die of septicaemia and exhaustion in Tanxian, Hebei, at the end of 1939.
Norman Bethune was later eulogized by Mao Zedong, who exhorted all
young Chinese to learn from his selflessness, and every schoolchild from
the early 1950s to the 1970s grew up associating Canada with Bethune. I
am reminded of this every time in even the remotest corners of China;
whenever I tell someone that I am Canadian, I see their eyes light up as
they say the name "Norman Bethune!"

   The Second World War, however, galvanized Canadian attention to China.
Two regiments of Canadian troops participated in the hopeless defense of
Hong Kong. Ottawa opened its first full embassy in the wartime capital of
Chongqing, and advanced substantial war loans to the coalition government
to help finance Canadian-built weapons and supplies. Canadians participated in the airlifting of those supplies across the Himalayas. After the war,
the embassy moved, along with the Nationalist government, to Nanjing, and
it was assumed that a continuous relationship with China would follow.

   When the Nationalists were defeated and the People's Republic
established in 1949, the Canadian Government kept its mission in China
open, and began discussions on a formal diplomatic relationship with the new
country. The negotiations were difficult, however, stymied by two principle
roadblocks: acceptance by the new Chinese government of their obligations
to repay—as the successor state to the Nationalist-led wartime coalition—the
loans advanced during the war for military equipment; and the disposition of
a number of ships being held in Vancouver, which had been the property of a
private Shanghai shipping firm and which the new PRC authorities claimed as

being state property. There was no significant ideological impediment to recognition and Canada took no step, as some others did, to follow the Nationalists to Taipei. Unfortunately, before the remaining roadblocks could be overcome in the negotiations, the Korean War broke out, and Canada quickly committed troops to the UN Command. This effectively terminated the recognition negotiations, and the remaining Canadian diplomats were withdrawn from the People's Republic.

From the end of the Korean War until late in the 1950s, no effort was made to revive the suspended bilateral talks. The Cold War had broken out and successive Canadian cabinets had no taste for dealing with a country with which we had been effectively at war. The formal relationship with China remained with the Nationalists. While no mission was ever established in Taipei, there was an embassy representing the Nationalist government in Ottawa. It is interesting to note from Cabinet papers released in recent years, that the government periodically looked at the China question, generally recognizing that talks with the PRC would have to be some day re-engaged, but as there was no domestic pressure for haste, and some substantial pressure from Washington not to break ranks with those who shunned the Communist regime, the issue was repeatedly deferred.

In late 1959 and early 1960, however, the very difficult food supply situation in China became evident to the outside world. It was the Conservative government of John Diefenbaker which took the decision to engage quietly with the Chinese on a major wheat supply deal, which eventually saw very large quantities of Canadian prairie wheat shipped to a China gripped by famine. The shipment of the wheat was opposed by the Eisenhower administration in Washington, which saw it as violating of its "trading with the enemy" principle, and any use of U.S. ports was initially denied. But Ottawa remained committed and proceeded with the shipment, beginning a friendly and problem-free relationship of wheat sales that celebrated its tenth anniversary at the time of formal diplomatic recognition and 40th anniversary this year.

DIPLOMATIC RELATIONS

It was also in 1960 that two young Canadian journalists went to China and interviewed Mao Zedong and a number of other leaders. They subsequently travelled by bus and train to other parts of the country, and after leaving published a book entitled *Deux Innocents en Chine Rouge*. The book painted a picture of a far more benign China than many Canadians had pictured, and the journalists themselves began to argue for recognition and the formal establishment of diplomatic relations.

On several occasions during the 1960s, the Canadian Cabinet looked again at the "China Question," as it was known. Most Cabinet ministers, and certainly Prime Minister Lester B. Pearson, favored normalizing our relationship and argued the inconsistency of sustaining relations with the Soviet Union and other Communist countries while continuing to shun China. However, a consensus could never be reached in those years, and cabinet documents suggest that the strongest opposition was voiced usually from the Defense Department, which tended their minister a rather predictable—maybe even made-in-Washington—line about the dangers of kowtowing to the reds and the risk of a rift with our friends to the south.

However, one of the journalists on the 1960 trip was Pierre Elliot Trudeau, who entered Parliament in 1966 and was named minister of justice in the 1967 Pearson government. A year later, when Pearson stepped aside for reasons of ill-health, Trudeau replaced him as prime minister, surfing a great wave of popularity—"Trudeaumania"—and began a long and creative tenure frequently marked by foreign policy initiatives very independent of either American policy or core NATO doctrine. Not surprisingly, one of the principal elements of Trudeau's foreign policy platform was recognition of the People's Republic of China, and shortly after winning his first election, he initiated the beginning of serious negotiations.

The bilateral negotiations of 1969 and 1970 were not easy for many small and two big reasons. China was in the midst of the Cultural Revolution, infusing the talks with complicating ideological debate and limiting flexibility by Chinese negotiators. Canada was also among the first countries to negotiate recognition since the issue of Taiwan had crystallized. The latter issue was finally bridged in mid-1970, using a formula on Chinese territorial integrity and the Taiwan issue that was to become the boilerplate formula for more than 40 countries that would subsequently recognize the PRC. As a result, in spite of opposition occasionally reiterated by our neighbors to the south, on October 13th, 1970, the two countries formally established diplomatic relations and moved quickly to establish missions in each other's capitals.

Since the establishment of formal diplomatic relations in the middle of the Cultural Revolution and nine years before the United States was to follow suit, the evolution of our relationship since then has been accompanied by a process of change, and I hope growing maturity, on both sides.

The first few years after 1970 saw a rapid expansion in political, cultural and educational relations. Leaders paid reciprocal visits. Revolutionary opera troupes and collections of archaeological treasures visited Canada, while collections of the Group of Seven landscape artists and the Canadian Brass quintet toured China (the latter actually performing in factories to recognize the importance of the workers in modern China). Student and scholar exchange programs were begun as early as 1972.

On the economic side, substantial wheat shipments continued, and an effort was made to encourage other trade as well. While a gradual growth in other commodity trade was evident, a more robust expansion of the commercial relationship would have to await economic reform. There were some early and notable exceptions, including the first Nortel (then North-ern Electric) sale in 1972, which was to provide the telecommunications and telephone equipment for the historic visit of U.S. President Nixon; U.S. companies, of course, were banned from trading with China!

During the process of reform and opening up of the Chinese economy since 1978, trade between Canada and China has risen dramatically, increasing tenfold by 1992, and more than trebling again during the period between 1992–1999. China is now our fourth largest trading partner, with total trade for 1999 over a record $10 billion. And when trade figures with Hong Kong are included, China moves into third position.

IMPACT OF REFORM

The period since Deng Xiaoping's historic 1992 visit to the South, which gave a great boost to economic reform, has seen the nature of Canadian exports to China change dramatically. Whereas in 1992, up to 50% of Canadian exports were grain, this ratio has now fallen to less than 10%. Now Canada increasingly offers China technology and services, including the CANDU technology sold to China to build two nuclear reactors for $4.5 billion on the seaside in Zhejiang province, which will provide electric-ity for Shanghai. Nortel, passing its 25th anniversary in China in 1997, has now become a major player in China's telecommunications, operating research and development centers and manufacturing plants, transferring and developing state-of-the art technologies for the Chinese market.

Smaller Canadian high-tech companies have sunk substantial roots in China as well, in wireless technologies, paging, satellite ground stations, aircraft simu-lators and so on. Internet firms, software companies, distance education pro-viders and film animators have all more recently joined the growing list of Canadian enterprises established in China. Canadian companies are bringing their expertise in financial and insurance services to China as well, for example, Manulife, which in 1996 became the second foreign life insurance company to obtain a license. At the same time, the flow of wheat has continued, although the bumper harvests of the past five years have seen a substantial reduction in volume, made up for by sustained levels of potash sales and growing demand for canola, live beef cattle and animal genetics.

According to statistics gathered by the Ministry of Foreign Trade and Economic Cooperation, there are now some 4,800 Canadian joint venture projects registered in China. I cannot possibly account for all of these, for they range from the big joint ventures, with which we are of course famil-iar, to tiny firms established with a small investment by a Canadian, per-haps even in his or her town or county of origin, to grow mushrooms, make underwear or run a restaurant (these are real examples I have inadvertently stumbled across as I have travelled throughout China). For many of these ventures, it has not been easy-going over the last decade or so, for China has remained an unpredictable place to do business, with little recourse to law and frequent intervention by local authorities to skew the playing field or change the rules after a business has been established.

Regrettably, corruption too has eroded the quality of the business environment. At the embassy, and in our consulates in Shanghai, Guangzhou and Chongqing, we have spent an unconscionable amount of time and effort intervening with central and regional authorities trying to solve commercial problems that never should have arisen. This, of course, is very much part of why for us and for others, getting China into the World Trade Organization (WTO) has been such an enormous priority. We want a fair and level playing field for our businesses, which of course will also result in a more predictable, transparent and productive domestic market, which will be a great spur to economic change throughout the country. It is also why we are closely watching the current campaign against corruption launched by the Chinese leadership.

PUBLIC POLICY SUPPORT

While we have, of course, negotiated our bilateral market access deal with China as part of the WTO accession process, Canada has also worked with China to support China's readiness for accession. Canada has provided assistance to China in developing a rules-based environment for commerce through two special programs, the Public Policy Options Program and the Public Sector Reform Program, which we fund through the Canadian International Development Agency. Included to date within these broader reform programs are projects related specifically to China's need to implement expected WTO obligations in the automotive, fisheries and high-tech sectors.

The Public Policy Options and Public Sector Reform programs are in fact good indicators of the general approach the Canadian government has tried to take in its broader relationship with China. What we have tried to do is to recognize and respect the dynamics of change underway in China, and to see if there are not means by which we in Canada can engage where positive contributions can be made. Take, for example, three of the big change vectors currently being pursued through determined policy intent: marketizing the economy; changing the structure of the state and various levels of government; and shifting the basic relationship between the individual and the collective.

As China has moved towards a market economy, it has faced obstacles of all sorts in addition to the enormous attitudinal change that such a shift has required. The lack of supportive legal structures, the paucity of professional and management personnel, and the lack of efficient intermediaries in the capital markets are among many very substantial challenges that have not been easy to rectify overnight. We in the

Canadian government have tried to recognize that these are areas where more than criticism is merited, and so have engaged with the Chinese authorities in diverse but, we hope, well-focused efforts to assist those agents of change to actually achieve what they are trying to. For example, rather than simply lobby for better access for Canadian mining firms, we have chosen to work with the Chinese Ministry of Land and Resources, sharing Canadian and other international practices so that China can benefit from the experience of others in putting into place a stable and transparent legal and regulatory environment for the exploration and development of its mineral resources.

In another area, we have directly supported the teaching of basic accounting by major Chinese business schools, adapting the curriculum used by the Canadian Chartered General Accountants Association, leading to such well-known universities such as Qinghua, UIBE and Fudan now all granting CGA degrees. Similarly, we have sponsored projects and activities aimed at sharing western, and particularly Canadian, experiences in the securities sector, believing that an efficient mutual fund industry will be critical in mobilizing large amounts of underutilized private savings and allocating them to companies—both private and para-state firms—that have the best chance of becoming the modern dynamic business sector the Chinese government has made such an effort to encourage. These efforts to assist the process of change in China also have the potential benefit of improving the long-term prospects for Canadian firms in the Chinese market, but that should not be viewed as somehow deleterious to their positive impact on the reform process in China and on broadening the participation of those who benefit from it.

We are also conscious of the high social costs of economic reform and of the somewhat complex circle of challenges it creates. Without effective social programs to mitigate the impact of higher levels of unemployment and the reduction in medical, housing and other subsidies, both state enterprise reform and a further withdrawal of the state from the marketplace becomes socially too damaging. Yet without effective fiscal and financial sector reform, those social programs are simply far beyond the capacity of the state to pay for. Without further state-owned enterprise (SOE) reform, the burden to both the state directly (and indirectly through continued questionable lending by the state banks) will remain so great that revenue growth derived from fiscal and financial reform will be retarded and the dangers increased in allowing too fast a growth in competitive private capital markets. Now we know that Canada cannot solve these problems, but what we can do (and have done) is to share with China our own experiences in center-provincial fiscal management and in universal medical insurance and universal social assistance programs.

Dynamic Economic Relationship

Our development cooperation relationship with China is not, of course, limited to assistance in economic and social policy reform. Begun in 1982, our development assistance vocation here had an early concentration on agricultural productivity, energy and higher education linkages. Today, while we continue work in agriculture (drylands agriculture, balanced fertilizing) and transportation (such as intermodal transport and capacity-building in specialized fields), we have also branched into environmental projects, both at the policy and remedial technologies levels, and our support for university linkages is now really limited to cooperative activities in applied research. And at the far end of the spectrum of large-to-small projects, we also continue to finance more than 100 small projects that respond to local development initiatives in some of the poorest western provinces of China (this we call the Canada Fund, active in Tibet, Xinjiang, Qinghai, Ningxia, Gansu and Guizhou) and a similar slightly smaller program aimed at supporting non-governmental organizations and the emergence of a truly civil society here in China.

Among the most important and remarkable characteristic of the dynamic economic relationship between Canada and China is that it has a history that continues to this day, of being relatively problem-free from a political standpoint. There have been no debates in parliament about the annual renewal of Most Favored Nation (MFN) treatment to trade from China (indeed, Canada has granted permanent MFN, or Permanent Normal Trade Relations (PNTR) status, as it is now referred to in U.S. circles, to all trading partners), and there have been few calls for making access to the Canadian market conditional on changes to Chinese domestic or foreign behavior.

There are certainly those in Canada who have argued that the substantial development assistance program Canada has with China, or the establishment of a sequential series of concessional lines of credit should be canceled or used as leverage to pressure for improvements in China's treatment of political dissidents or religious freedoms. Yet for the most part, there has been a very wide national consensus that a broadly-based and constructive engagement with China is more likely to pay long range dividends than an on-again off-again relationship in which conditionality or sanctions prevent the sustained development of linkages and networks of relationships with many sectors and groups in China. This has allowed the Canadian private sector to pursue its trading and investment interests without fear of being buffeted by sudden political squalls. Consequently, the business community, particularly through such organizations as the Canada–China Business Council, has been able to use its partnership with government positively, and to seek help when needed in obtaining a fairer or more level playing field, and to build strong and longstanding relationships with business partners, both inside and outside the state sector.

The current Canada–China relationship goes far beyond the economic and commercial areas, however. There are growing numbers of people in China who are studying and teaching about Canada. There are now more than 20 active Canadian Study Centres in China, and some 300 "Canadianists." I noted earlier the growing numbers of Chinese people who have immigrated to Canada. This may not be matched by reverse flows, but there are increasing numbers of Canadian students, tourists, artists, business people, and experts in various fields who have chosen to make China a part of their lives. With this growth in people-to-people ties has flourished a rich dialogue of culture and values. Many Chinese immigrants to Canada, or their children, have also returned to China to work or invest, either independently or for Canadian companies.

Today's exchanges range from artists like Canada's renowned baroque ensemble, Taflemusik, to the more modern Bryan Adams and Alanis Morissette. Celine Dion and Diana Krall have great followings in China. Beyond the cultural world, there is an increasing involvement of non-governmental organizations such as Trees for Life, who plant trees and provide environmental education in places like Yunnan. Canadian and Chinese officials as well as non-governmental academics and experts now meet on a regular basis to undertake dialogue on human rights. Canadian development assistance supports poverty alleviation projects in poorer parts of China, including villages in Gansu province, which Canadian Prime Minister Chratien visited while in China in 1998. Canadian and Chinese experts engage on fiscal management, criminal law systems, public service reform, the establishment of legal aid systems, and the global problems of environmental degradation, particularly climate change. The Canadian and Chinese military have gradually increased their inter-service contacts, notably with reciprocal visits in 1998 and 2000 of ships of the Canadian Navy to Shanghai and Qingdao and ships of the Chinese Navy to the Canadian West coast. We have also been deeply engaged in trying to find solutions to international problems, sitting as we have over the last two years side-by-side on the UN Security Council.

EXTRAORDINARY BROAD WEB OF HUMAN RELATIONSHIP

Underpinning this historically open-minded interest by Canadians in China, and the increasingly comprehensive nature of the Canada–China relationship, has been a significant change in the orientation of Canada, as it has grown aware of the growing importance of Asia generally and China specifically. One of the motors behind this shift has been the changing makeup of Canada, with a substantially growing population of people of Chinese origin.

While Canada has always been a country of immigration, what has changed radically over the last half century, and particularly over the last 20 years, is the makeup of our immigrant population, and in particular the new importance of immigrants from Asia. In 1950, our population was primarily of European origin, Britain and France, but also virtually every other European country. Over 90% of all immigrants who arrived before 1961 were born in Europe. Only 3% of pre-1960 immigrants were Asian-born. Their proportion has been growing steadily every since. Asians accounted for 12% of those who arrived in the 1960s, and 33% of immigrants who came in the 1970s. The most remarkable growth of our Asian population, however, has been in the current decade. Of the roughly two million persons who arrived in Canada during the 1990s, almost 70% were born in Asia.

This means that Canada now has a very large number of citizens who have strong ties—of language, family, property, business interests—to China and to other Asia Pacific countries. I am thinking particularly of the approximately one and one-half million Canadians of Chinese origin, many of whom have come to Canada in the past 20 years. These people have not only enriched the multicultural fabric of Canadian society and made great contributions in all fields, but have also formed a pool of people with close and enduring ties to China. These links have been invaluable in cementing our economic and cultural ties.

It is the engagement of ever larger numbers of Canadians, regardless of origin, in business, economic, academic, cultural, and people-to-people exchanges and dealings that have given the Canada–China relationship the breadth and strength that it has today. The governments of the two countries also continue to play a role, however, both in ensuring that the inevitable frictions that arise in such a complex relationship do not get out of hand, and in encouraging even wider engagement.

Since 1970, Canadian and Chinese leaders have paid frequent visits to each other's country. Since 1993, it has become an annual tradition to have either a head of state or head of government visit every year. By the end of 2000, Prime Minister Chratien will have visited China four times in six years, with visits to Canada interspersed between those by Premier Li Peng in 1995, by President Jiang Zemin in 1997 and by Premier Zhu Rongji in 1999. Every year for the past five, an average of eight Canadian ministers from the federal government and three provincial premiers have visited China, and a roughly equivalent number of senior central government and provincial leaders have travelled from China to Canada.

Given the theme of this book, it seems only logical to ask about the future. While predictions, particularly about the future, are always risky, I personally am a great optimist about the future of the Canada–China relationship. The reason is simple. I am an optimist about the future of China.

These are indeed extraordinary and exciting times in China. The magnitude and breadth of transformations underway are unparalleled in the modern world. I believe that the commitment to deep systemic reform, and to a substantially different but still Chinese future, is also widely shared by the country's leadership of both today and tomorrow, the latter group representing as competent, intelligent and globally-aware a class as one can find anywhere on the face of the globe.

That in the end is the source of my greatest hope and confidence. While it is beyond anyone's ability to give an accurate prognosis of what the huge transformations now underway will mean for China a generation from now, I can tell you that it is the integrity and ability of those I see ready to take tomorrow's helm that gives an observer confidence about the prosperous, responsible and law-abiding great power that China is destined to become. As it does so, Canada will be there as a partner and as a friend, but will itself be changed and enriched as a result.

As I look at the extraordinarily broad web of human relationships, both familial and formal, that underpin the Canada–China relationship today, at the complex of intergovernmental and academic and private linkages that are the very warp and woof of that relationship, and at the mutual respect which runs like a current through them, I cannot help but think back to the early pioneers. I would like to show what we have built, and continue to build, to the railway workers and indeed to my grandfather. I like to believe that they would be proud of those who have followed them.

CHRISTOPHER BO BRAMSEN

Ambassador Christopher Bo Bramsen was born in Copenhagen in 1943. With a law degree from the University of Copenhagen he entered the Danish Foreign Service in 1970. He has held various posts at home and abroad, including in Washington, D.C. and Brussels. During his term as permanent secretary of the Ministry of Industry (1990–1994), Ambassador Bramsen visited China for the first time in 1991. As consul general, he opened the Royal Danish Consulate General in Shanghai in 1994, and was appointed as Denmark's Ambassador to China in 1995. He is also accredited as ambassador to the governments in Mongolia and the People's Democratic Republic of Korea.

Ambassador Bramsen has written several books relating to international affairs. His books on China include a book about his grandfather's life in China during the first part of the 20th century. The book was published in Danish in 1993, in Chinese in 1996, and in English at the end of 2000 under the title *Open Doors— Vilhelm Meyer and the Establishment of General Electric in China.* Furthermore, as a tribute to the 50th anniversary of the diplomatic relations between the People's Republic of China and Denmark in May 2000, another of Ambassador Bramsen's books was published, *Peace and Friendship—Denmark's Official Relations with China, 1674–2000.*

Ambassador Bramsen draws upon his extensive experience in China and his deep family roots going back to his grandfather in providing insightful perspective into new foundations for furthering relations between Europe and China.

ASEM — A New Dimension in Asian-European Relations

Christopher Bo Bramsen
Ambassador of Denmark to China

The Ancient Silk Road

In 139 B.C., more than 2,000 years ago, China's Emperor Han Wudi sent his envoy Zhang Qian on a journey from China towards the West. The expedition went as far west as the present Uzbekistan and has later been described in the classic Chinese novel from the 16th century, called *Journey to the West*. The route followed by Zhang Qian and later by many merchants with caravans of camels loaded with silk and other goods from the Far East developed into an important commercial link to Europe. The route ended on the East coast of the Mediterranean Sea, thereby linking together the two largest and most influential capitals in the world, Chang'an and Rome. The most famous European to have traveled this route, later called the Silk Road, was the Italian merchant, Marco Polo, who at the end of the 13th century traveled from Italy to China, where he stayed for a number of years before returning to Venice.

The Silk Road was not just a network of trading routes. Contacts between countries and peoples far apart led to a cross-fertilization of technical skill and ideas. Merchants were accompanied by craftsmen and monks. Religions found their way to foreign countries. Most noteworthy was the spread of Buddhism from India to China and other countries in the Far East.

When ships from Europe began to reach the shores of the Far East 500–600 years ago, the old network of silk roads was taken over by new trading routes along the coasts of Africa, India and South East Asia.

Today, at the beginning of the new millennium, the world is no longer run by a small number of colonial powers and empires. Today there are 188 members of the United Nations, and a global framework of cooperation in all fields has developed and made the UN a true world organization.

The large number of states in the world has also led to a high degree of regional cooperation, where a group of neighboring countries within a region establishes a special framework in order to strengthen their relations within certain areas of common concern. The European Union (EU) is a remarkable example, but other organizations can also be mentioned, such as North American Free Trade Association (NAFTA), the North Atlantic Treaty Organization (NATO), the Association of South East Asian Nations (ASEAN), and the Asia Pacific Economic Cooperation (APEC), to mention a few.

The newest development in international relations has been the establishment of region-to-region cooperation. In this respect the ASEM framework, the Asia–Europe Meeting, is among the latest examples of two regions looking into questions of common interest, and setting up a number of projects and programs with a view to strengthen their mutual cooperation.

As we enter the 21st century, ASEM might well become a major factor in the development of the Asian–European relations. Countries from both sides are given the role of coordinators for a specific period, and in this regard, both China and Denmark will be playing leading roles within ASEM during the next few years. The old Silk Road between Asia and Europe has now been replaced by a modern framework, the ASEM, facilitating not only trade between the two old continents, but also cooperation in a number of other fields.

ASIA–EUROPE MEETINGS

While relations between America and Europe and between America and Asia have developed extensively during the last 20–30 years, the relations between Europe and Asia, with more than two-thirds of the world population, have not experienced the same growth. In July 1994, the European Commission issued a report, "Towards a New Asia Strategy." Later that year, at a meeting in Karlsruhe in Germany between members states from the EU and ASEAN, Prime Minister Goh from Singapore proposed to enlarge this European–Asian framework by inviting China, Japan and the Republic of Korea (South Korea) to join. Thereby, the Asian participants in the Asian–European cooperation would be the same as in APEC.

With this background, heads of state and government from Europe and Asia met at a summit in Bangkok, Thailand, (ASEM I) in March 1996. Here they agreed to establish a framework for the development of a comprehensive Asian–European partnership.

Since their first summit in Bangkok, the ASEM participants have included 25 countries. On the European side, all 15 Member States of the European Union, as well as the European Commission, take part in the ASEM, while from Asia, the original seven ASEAN countries, as well as China, Japan and the Republic of Korea participate.

ASEM Participants

Asian Participants	European Participants
Original Members of ASEAN:	Members of the European Union:
Brunei	Austria
Indonesia	Belgium
Malaysia	Denmark
Indonesia	Finland
Philippines	France
Thailand	Germany
Vietnam	Greece
	Ireland
Others:	Italy
China	Luxembourg
Japan	Netherlands
Republic of Korea	Portugal
	Spain
	Sweden
	United Kingdom, and
	the EU Commission

The ASEM Summits are held every other year, alternating between cities in Asia and Europe. ASEM I was held in Bangkok in March 1996, followed by ASEM II in April 1998 in London. Under the heading "Partnership for Prosperity and Stability in the New Millennium," ASEM III was held on October 20–21, 2000, in the Korean capital of Seoul. ASEM IV will be held in September 2002 in Copenhagen, Denmark.

ASEM meetings are also held at the level of foreign ministers, who met in 1997 in Singapore and in 1999 in Berlin. In May 2001, China will host the next ASEM meeting of foreign ministers.

Furthermore, both the ASEM finance ministers and the economic ministers meet regularly. In 1999 the ASEM Ministers of Science and Technology met for the first time.

Outside of these summits and ministerial meetings, regular "Senior Officials Meetings" (ASEM SOM) and are held twice a year in order to prepare the talks at the summits and the ministerial meetings. Officials also meet to prepare the meetings of the ASEM finance ministers and economic ministers. The ASEM framework can be described as follows:

ASEM Decision-Making Structure

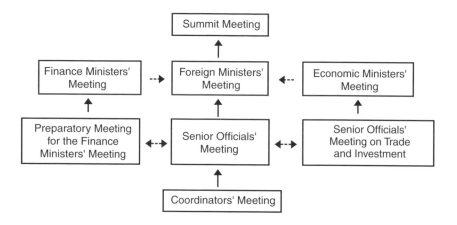

At the ASEM Summit in London in 1998 the participants agreed on a text, a cooperation framework, spelling out how the process of cooperation should proceed. This document was expanded at the ASEM Summit in Seoul and is now referred to as "Asia-Europe Cooperation Framework (AECF) 2000." The AECF 2000 sets out "the vision, principles, objectives, priorities and mechanisms for the ASEM process for the first decade of the new millennium."

To prepare for the ASEM meetings, the participants appoint two coordinators on both sides. Until ASEM III in Seoul, the Asian coordinators had been South Korea and Thailand. They are now China and Vietnam. On the European side, the coordinators are the country with the EU Presidency, as well as the EU Commission. The EU presidencies, lasting six months each, are as follows: in 2000, Portugal and France; in 2001, Sweden and Belgium; and in 2002, Spain and Denmark.

The results of the talks at each of the ASEM summits are contained in a Chairman's Statement. This text is issued at the end of each Summit. It is the head of state or government of the host country who issues the statement, but the text reflects the general agreement of all the participants.

At the first ASEM Summit in 1996 it was agreed that the work within the ASEM cooperation should concentrate on three areas: political affairs, economic affairs and affairs relating to education and culture. In 1998 in London, the ASEM leaders confirmed that the ASEM process should "carry forward the three key dimensions with the same impetus: fostering political dialogue, reinforcing economic cooperation, and promoting cooperation in other areas."

At ASEM II in London in 1998, the heads of state and government established the Asia–Europe Vision Group. This group, consisting of a special representative from each of the 26 ASEM participants, including the EU Commission, was asked to write a report with recommendations on how to strengthen Asian–European relations. The Vision Group published their report in March 1999, "For a Better Tomorrow: Asia–Europe Partnership in the 21st Century."

In the introduction to the report, the group wrote, "The Asia–Europe Vision Group is convinced that Asia and Europe can and must make concrete and concerted efforts to create a prosperous living space in the 21st century. Basically the vision of the 26 co-writers is "gradually to integrate Asia and Europe into an area of peace and shared development, a prosperous common living sphere in the 21st century." The report, presented to the ASEM foreign ministers in Berlin in March 1999, contained a number of recommendations, some of which have now been discussed and decided upon during the recent ASEM Summit in Seoul.

In the AECF 2000, adopted in Seoul, the visions and the broad scope of the ASEM cooperation is listed as follows: "ASEM leaders envisage Asia and Europe as an area of peace and shared development with common interests and aspiration such as upholding the purposes and principles of the UN Charter, respect for democracy, the rule of law, justice and human rights, concern for the environment and other global issues, eradication of poverty, protection of common cultural heritage and the promotion of intellectual endeavors, economic and social development, knowledge and educational resources, science and technology, commerce, investment and enterprise."

The ASEM process is intended to promote mutual understanding and develop consensus through dialogue on a wide range of issues and lead to cooperation in the common interests of the two regions. European and Asian participants usually hold respective caucus meetings to coordinate their positions before ASEM meetings. It should be noted, however, that the ASEM process is not a "bloc-to-bloc" dialogue. It is, rather, a unique type of "region-to-region" dialogue, where each member country participates on an equal footing.

Whereas political coordination has been practiced by the EU Member States for many years, it is only recently that the Asian participants in ASEM have organized summits and other meetings in order to take a look at international issues, as seen from an Asian perspective. These East Asia Summits, referred to as ASEAN+3, were held in Malaysia in 1997 and in Vietnam in 1998. When they met in Manila in November 1999, the heads of states and governments affirmed the importance of meeting on a regular basis and adopted a Joint Statement on East Asia Cooperation. Singapore hosted the fourth East Asia Summit in November 2000.

POLITICAL DIALOGUE

ASEM has proved to be a useful forum for the exchange of views on questions relating to the international political situation. This dialogue serves an important purpose in clarifying positions and building confidence, both within and between the two regions. As described in the AECF 2000, "ASEM efforts should focus on issues of common interest, proceeding step-by-step in a process of consensus-building, with a view to enhancing mutual awareness and understanding between partners, drawing strength from our diversity, while not excluding any issue beforehand, but exercising wisdom and judiciousness in selecting topics for discussion."

Although the post-cold war era has led to a significantly reduced military tension in the world, it is widely held that we face a number of new, more diffuse threats to peace and stability. They cover a broad spectrum of challenges to the political, social, economic and environmental fabric of our societies. As a result, the concept of security has become wider, and the security of one country or one region has become more and more intertwined with that of other regions. Today, diplomacy, trade and good governance have become important elements in the concept of security, thereby adding more weight to crisis management, preventive diplomacy and conflict resolutions.

This development in modern international relations is also reflected in the ASEM political dialogue.

In Seoul, the main political topics included the Korean Peninsula, East Timor, Southeastern Europe and the Middle East. The ASEM leaders also discussed the UN system, human rights, prevention of conflicts and arms control. A number of other global issues of common concern were on the agenda in Seoul: migratory flows, transnational crime, international terrorism, the fight against illegal drugs and the fight against HIV/AIDS. The problems related to energy and the environment were also given a high priority at ASEM III.

The ASEM political dialogue has also been extended into the area of socio-economic issues. In this respect, the ASEM Conference on "States and Markets," held in Copenhagen in March 1999 and hosted by Denmark and the Republic of Korea, proved to be an important milestone in the ASEM process. The conference focused on the question of the roles of public authorities and private actors in the promotion of economic and social progress.

ECONOMIC COOPERATION

Together the ASEM countries of Asia and Europe account for 44.2% (about 2.27 billion people) of the world's population and 54.4% (about US$15.3 trillion) of the world's GNP, as shown in the next page.

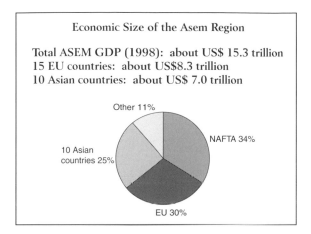

The ASEM countries together count for 35.4% (about US$6.3 trillion) of world trade.

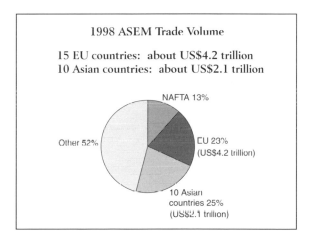

Together the 25 ASEM member states can enlarge their role in the world economy by actively engaging in ASEM cooperation. Their aim is to strengthen dialogue and cooperation between the two regions with a view to facilitating sustainable economic growth, contributing together to the global economic dialogue and addressing the impact of globalization.

The finance ministers as well as the Economic ministers now meet once a year. They have agreed on a number of ASEM initiatives involving government and business sectors, covering areas such as trade, investment, and environment. These initiatives now include:

- The Asia–Europe Business Forum (AEBF)
- The Trans-Asian Railway Network

- The ASEM Trust Fund (ATF)
- The Trade Facilitation Action Plan (TFAP)
- The Investment Promotion Action Plan (IPAP)
- The Asia–Europe Small and Medium Enterprise Conference
- The Trans-Eurasia Information Network

At ASEM III in Seoul, it was decided to intensify efforts to increase trade and investment flows between the two regions. E-commerce has been added as a new priority area, and the leaders agreed to "accelerate efforts to address the digital divide to promote the joint prosperity of the two regions." They emphasized the importance of the WTO system, and the ASEM activities "aimed at strengthening cooperation in the financial area, particularly in preventing the recurrence of a crisis."

CULTURE AND EDUCATION

In the third dimension of ASEM cooperation, covering the social, cultural and educational fields, the aim is to promote enhanced contact and strengthened mutual awareness between the people of the two regions. This cooperation not only involves government and business, but also direct people-to-people exchanges. Among the many initiatives in this field are the following:

- The Asia–Europe Foundation (ASEF)
- The Asia–Europe Young Leaders Symposium (AEYLS)
- The Asia–Europe Environmental Technology Center (AEETC)
- Protection and Promotion of Cultural Heritage
- Community Health Care (Asia–Europe cooperation in combining traditional and modern medicine and treatment for community health care)
- ASEM Education Hubs (AEH)
- Cooperation on Environmental Disaster Preparedness
- Seminar on Labor Relations
- Promotion of the Welfare of Children
- Asia–Europe University (AEU)

The third dimension of ASEM cooperation has been extended to include the social sector. The initiatives set in motion in 1995 at the UN World Summit for Social Development in Copenhagen, and at the follow-up conference in June 2000 in Geneva—Copenhagen+5—are now also reflected in the ASEM process, where the participants have agreed to strengthen their dialogue on socio–economic issues and on social development. In Seoul, the ASEM leaders shared the view that social and human resource development, including lifelong learning, were instrumental in alleviating social and economic disparities within and among ASEM countries.

In Seoul, the people-to-people exchanges were boosted by the decision to launch a special DUO Fellowship Program, aiming at increasing exchanges of students and teachers between the two regions.

The Future of ASEM

The ASEM process does not include all countries in Asia and Europe. The present 25 ASEM partners have agreed that the ASEM process should be open, evolutionary and conducted in progressive stages. They have also agreed that the two sides decide for themselves which new candidates they will propose from their own region, and that a decision on new participants is made at the ASEM summits by a consensus of all member states. This procedure is referred to as the "two-key approach." Among possible candidates on the Asian side are the new ASEAN member states, Laos, Cambodia and Myanmar. On the European side, the 13 European countries that have applied for EU membership are potential future members. Russia, belonging to both the European and the Asian side, has also announced an interest in joining ASEM.

Whereas ASEM II in London in 1998 was marked by the financial crisis in Asia, the mood at the Seoul Summit was much more positive and forward looking. A large number of initiatives, proposed by the ASEM partners, were endorsed.

As a new partner in regional as well as inter-regional cooperation, it is interesting to note that China is now seriously engaged in the ASEM-process. Amongst the 16 new projects adopted by ASEM III, China is co-proposing the following four:

- Anti-Corruption Initiative   China/UK
- Cooperation in combating Transnational Crimes   China/Italy
- ASEM Environment Ministers' Meeting   China/Germany
- Forestry Conservation and Sustainable   China/Finland
  Development

China will host the ASEM Foreign Ministers Meeting in May 2001 and is now one of the Asian coordinators for the next two years. As we are entering the 21st century, China faces the opportunity and the challenge of becoming an active and committed political actor in Asia and within ASEM. If the ASEM cooperation becomes the Silk Road of the new millennium, China will again have an important role to play in building new links between Asia and Europe.

MARK DANIELL

Mark Daniell is managing director of Bain & Company SE Asia, Singapore. He joined Bain & Company in 1980 in Boston and became a member of the London office in 1982. He joined the Singapore office in 1997 on a full-time basis, having worked actively in Asia from 1983 on specific projects. Mr. Daniell founded the global mergers, acquisitions and integration practice of the firm in London in 1987. Bain & Company is one of the world's leading global business consulting firms, and has established "bainlab," an active incubator and accelerator of Internet companies. Bain's client work in China has covered a wide range of industries, with a focus on financial services, consumer goods, technology and telecommunications, focusing on growth strategy and change for large multinationals and local companies.

Mr. Daniell's industry experience includes financial services, telecommunications, consumer products, banking, manufacturing and distribution. He is the author of the internationally acclaimed book, *World of Risk: Next Generation Strategy for a Volatile Era*. In the following chapter, Mr. Daniell analyzes China's enhanced global role in bringing stability and peace in a world of increased financial risk and political volatility.

CHINA IN A WORLD OF RISK

Mark Daniell
Managing Director, Bain & Company SE Asia

NOT JUST THE ECONOMY

In his book, *The Clash of Civilizations and the Remaking of World Order*, Samuel Huntington described the next great risk threatening world order as the clash between Muslim and Christian civilizations. He describes a great conflict arising from the "fault line" separating groups with fundamentally different and irreconcilable world views. In many ways, Huntington's conclusions are well-founded. The risks of the simmering Middle East and crisis in Kosovo bear out their validity. However, based on an analysis of trends in the new economy, the environment, crime, poverty, human rights and cultural development, China will also play a key role in determining the shape of the new global order—and possibly creating another great fault line between and across competing civilizations. As China evolves and continues to emerge from its economic isolation, the risk of a new global bipolarity also grows. At this critical juncture, we can set out on one of two paths—one leading to greater global integration and lesser risk, the other to a future fraught with a constant risk of escalating conflict—economic, cultural and even military. It is obvious that a thoughtful approach on both sides, one that can lead to a more positive, and more sustainable, state of affairs is the preferred choice.

A policy of deep and continuous engagement that encourages this great nation to participate as a constructive member of the global community can support the emergence of a more positive policy structure within China and can lead to a more positive future for Western nations as well. China is the beneficiary of a 4,000-year-old civilization that differs in almost every aspect from its Western counterparts. As one of the world's great societies, China cannot be fully understood or engaged in constructive dialogue without a full understanding of a full, complex Chinese perspective—past, present, and future. Failure by the West to engage thoughtfully with the complex Chinese system now will unnecessarily increase risk and contribute to a certain failure to capture opportunities to build bridges over these looming fault lines between East and West.

In the economy, China's sheer scale and growth patterns, emerging trade and investment balances, currency management policy, capital markets influence, control of market access, evolving governance practices, and protection of foreign investment rights are all issues that will require substantial engagement for appropriate resolution on a mutually beneficial basis. An internal need for capital, job creation, technology, and open trade relations will ensure China retains a seat at the table on a global economic matters for years to come.

However, China's contribution to major global events—positive and negative—will not be confined to the economy. In the area of crime, China will play a pivotal role in the global response to piracy, software piracy, corruption, drug trading, women's rights, and triad expansion.

In the environment, China's rising use of chlorofluorocarbons, potentially catastrophic use of lignite, deforestation, sulfur dioxide emissions, contribution to acid rain, coastal degradation and other environmentally unsound practices are of concern to Chinese citizens and neighbors alike. In the military sphere, Taiwan, the Spratlys, and other flashpoints will need to be carefully managed to avoid regional, or even global, military conflagration.

On the cultural front, China is one of the few civilizations to have a comprehensive set of cultural attributes that have survived the tests of time and the travails of transportation into new lands. The Chinese language, literature, medicine, philosophy, arts, architecture, cuisine, religion and belief system, family structures, performing arts, martial arts, clothing, and other pillars of the Chinese civilization have remained intact and influenced the West for centuries. The need to retain the essence of this civilization while moving forward in inevitable social evolution is one of the major cultural challenges of the coming centuries.

MUTUAL SUSPICION

There is a dangerous trend developing in the West to position China as the next Evil Empire. Such an adverse positioning strategy serves the narrow interests of selected groups in the U.S. and Europe and is based on a shallow understanding of Chinese intention, capability and history. Allowing these narrow interests to prevail in the East–West debate would indeed be a tragedy on both sides.

From a Chinese perspective, the United States is also positioned by many influential policymakers as bent upon "hegemonic" domination of the world. This view is "proven" by the embassy bombing, support for Taiwan, protest at the treatment of Tibet, the North Atlantic Treaty Organization (NATO) bombing of Yugoslavia, the broadening of alliances with countries bordering China, conflicting claims on oil and gas fields surrounding the Spratlys, hedge fund attacks on Asian shares, currencies and economies, and even the arrest of General Augusto Pinochet. These events are all seen as heavy-handed attacks on national sovereignty in general and China's future integrity in particular.

Although apparently unrelated from a Western world view, these events take on a different meaning from the perspective of a country that has been force-fed opium by the English, brutally colonized by the Japanese, and cast into economic exile by the capitalist countries for nearly half a century.

Attempts to reconstruct a Russian–Chinese alliance and promulgation of the view that the United States is attempting to control the world—and hence China—through a vast pincer movement involving alliances with NATO on the west and Japan on the east reflect deep-rooted feelings of isolation and powerlessness.

U.S. military exercises with armies in Tajikistan, Kazakhstan, and Kyrgyzstan and visits to the United States by Mongolian officers have further fanned the flames of concern. All of these countries share a border with China. Past fears of being encircled or invaded led, in part, to China's involvement fighting U.S. forces in Korea in 1950. A better understanding of interests and resolve on both sides early on could avoid unnecessary conflict at a later date.

In many ways, it is simplistic to talk as if China were one single entity capable of speaking and acting as one indivisible unit. Economic, cultural and political differences vary enormously from rich coastal regions to an underdeveloped interior. Within the political and policy infrastructure of China itself there are also many complex factions. China's New Security Concept, a proposal of a more aggressive approach to foreign policy, is the brainchild of some of the more hard line factions within the military and government hierarchy. This concept reflects but one of the contending forces that make leadership and reform in China one of the world's toughest balancing acts. In Jiang's own words captured in a *Time* magazine interview in October 1997, "In the past few years, the Chinese people have scored very exciting achievements. But there are brain breaking questions and problems for us. It's hard for me to tell what's the biggest challenge."

The history, culture, and nature of the two systems—Chinese and Western—are so fundamentally different that the perspectives held by each often share little in common. The point of departure for China is a highly complex, centrally administered country of one billion citizens inhabiting diverse regions and enjoying vastly different levels of economic benefits and prospects. The entire system is struggling between conflicting tensions of an old, centrally-controlled economic and political system, and a new reformist drive toward modernization, economic liberality, and greater human rights. The imperatives for economic growth to underpin the reform movement are essential for an understanding of Chinese politics and economic policy. The system is characterized by a constant battle between advocates and forces of reform against conservative elements motivated by a desire to preserve the power and security of the old order.

Underlying these modern tensions is a four thousand-year history of the Han civilization. Attitudes toward money, religion, fate, diet, medicine, family, language, central authority, the state, and even life and death are colored by a rich and deep vein of history and collective experience stretching back over millennia. The concept of the Middle Kingdom, a vision of a China suspended between heaven and earth, is also an enduring part of the Chinese view for the future. Yet, also, memories of past losses and humiliations remain close to the surface. This mix of confidence and insecurity will require deeper understanding and more thoughtful engagement by the West to move forward together on a balanced path of peaceful progress.

Difficulties in establishing a clear bilateral policy are shared with the U.S. and multilateral accords merely compound the complexity. Each American government, for example, has navigated in the treacherous waters between a One China policy and a Taiwan Act that requires protection of Taiwan from mainland military adventures.

It is also important that China understands fully the Western perspective. Failure to engage the West from an equally thoughtful perspective will increase the risk of the emergence of another destabilizing global duality. The last Cold War cost trillions of dollars, redirected a high proportion of scarce global intellectual capital into unused weapons research, and contributed to a climate of fear that spanned an entire generation. Comprehensive engagement on both sides will be necessary if an East–West repeat of the Cold War is to be avoided.

In every system, the complexity of reaching an effective decision increases geometrically with the number of parties involved. In China, hard-line, centrist, and reform factions all crowd the space for input on China–U.S. relations. On the American side of the issue, the House, the Senate, the Administration, the media, and the electorate all wade in on delicate issues of bilateral relations. Even when the leadership of the two nations approach agreement, the complexity of reaching closure conspires to keep the parties apart. During Premier Zhu Rongji's 1997 trip to the United States, this problem of complexity arose as a major obstacle in the closing stages of obtaining a World Trade Organization clearance for China, which has taken years to overcome.

"In my view, the gap between the two sides is really already not very significant," a frustrated Zhu said at a joint White House press conference with Clinton. "If you want to hear some honest words, the problem does not lie with some big gap, but with the political atmosphere."

Of course, Zhu knew that before he arrived in the United States, but could do little to redirect the forces aimed at stalling the approvals. Clinton also struggled awkwardly to temper the media's feeding frenzy. "We cannot allow a healthy argument to lead us toward a campaign-driven cold war with China," he warned shortly before Zhu's arrival. "No one could possibly gain from that except for the most rigid, backward-looking elements in China itself."

New Levels of Risk

As the Chinese economy steams ahead, building vast reserves of dollars and piling up an enormous trade surplus with the developed world, Chinese military capabilities are rising at nearly the same pace from a similarly low base. Only recently, China successfully tested a new ground-to-ground missile, the Dong Feng-31, which is reportedly capable of delivering a single nuclear warhead 8,000 kilometers—or nearly the distance required to reach the mainland of the United States. China already has a real, but still limited, nuclear and neutron bomb capability.

Although nuclear arsenals and delivery capabilities still lag the U.S. dramatically, and China historically has not shown great interest in international military adventuring, the combination of major trade and economic influence, coupled with a growing military capability and apparent willingness to use that capability thousands of miles from the U.S. or Western Europe, make China an awkward force to be reckoned with.

The new nature and risk of a disengaged or threatened China is easy to see. *Unrestricted War*, by Colonels Wang Xiangsui and Qiao Liang spells out concerns over potential escalations of future conflict in a multi-dimensional arena. According to the authors, future war will be fought out along new dimensions, which include: terrorism, drug trafficking, environmental degradation, and computer-virus propagation. They conclude, "Unrestricted war is a war that surpasses all boundaries and restrictions. It takes non-military forms and military forms, and creates a war on many fronts. It is the war of the future."

It is also the full realization of some of the worst risks facing us as a united humanity. A better approach that diminishes this risk, through the application of the best available strategy and investment to build broad and constructive links, is a need of the highest priority. It is both urgent and important.

Benefit

One recent editorial in the *New York Times* described the current state of relations as two parties "in a diplomatic fog attempting to negotiate a path toward a common goal with few common reference points and no understanding where the other party was." Occasionally bumping into each other, the leadership of China and the United States often find themselves placed on a collision course by political or media forces on both sides of the Pacific. The media or contrary political forces can be seen to be operating to a very different agenda from the positive engagement favored by Zhu Rongji and the Clinton administration.

It is thus even more important for leaders on both sides to double their efforts to create bridges and buffers to link these different civilizations as comprehensively as possible. Public and private sector investments and initiatives need to be launched and sustained to overcome the constant presence and erosive impact of divisive forces on both sides.

To date, President Jiang Zemin and Premier Zhu Rongji have master-minded a highly charged and risky rush to the future in a peaceful man-ner—balancing reformist and hard-line political factions, and responding to a nationalistic sentiment while steering China more firmly into the currents of a global economy. At times, the balancing act has wobbled dangerously, notably after the embassy bombing when the Foreign Ministry announced it would cease cooperation with the United States "in the fields of prolif-eration prevention, arms control, and international security." Highly vocal allegations of a deliberate attack on the Chinese embassy in the *People's Daily* and other mass publications highlight the need to keep open channels of communication and to build a broad platform of issues of mutual inter-est. An agenda that encourages the East and West to find common interests as well as antagonisms is essential. A series of task forces to combine public and private sector interests to address non-geopolitical issues such as the economy, the environment, crime, the poverty gap and other issues affect-ing the common welfare of both countries would be a major step forward in bridging the current gap and reducing future risk and volatility.

Systemic Nature of Chinese Development

In order to prepare an effective program of constructive engagement, it is instructive to review the nature of China's current development trends from the full set of paradigm principles of dynamic macro-economic sys-tems. For each recurring principle, there is a fit with important aspects of China's current point of departure. The increasing globalization of China's trade patterns, investment sources, and political influence is perhaps the most salient characteristic of the systemic development of the world's most populous country. The increasing complexity of China is equally evident—its evolving languages, political structures, religions, beliefs, collective memory, and fundamental worldview are but a few of the elements making up the essence of the Chinese civilization.

The apparent contradictions are not, by Chinese standards, inconsistent. A unique blend of feelings of strength and powerlessness can only be understood on Chinese terms. The dynamic and accelerating pace of change is reflected in a century of dramatic swings in political and economic structures from a feudal base 100 years ago through agrarian communism and the tribulations of the Maoist era, to a modern reforming Communistic structure operating on the threshold of a new millennium.

Through waves of war, colonial oppression, rebellion, occupation, starvation, uprising, and growth, the Chinese system has demonstrated a pattern of obsolescence and reinvention, constantly reinventing itself and recasting the structures of modern society on a foundation of millennia of old values and beliefs. Over time, the Chinese system is converging toward a more international set of economic principles, discarding inefficient doctrines of state intervention in the economy, and using the resulting growth to consolidate the country's disparate regions and industries to the fullest extent possible.

Vaclav Suvil, a professor at the University of Manitoba, has summed up well the resulting systemic volatility in an essay entitled "China's Unstable Past and Future," published in the *International Herald Tribune*. Noting abrupt and dramatic changes in policy, he identifies an underlying instability in many fundamental policies and draws the appropriate systemic conclusion: "...There is very little likelihood that the country's future will be a linear extension of the recent past, a matter of continuity, and stability. The lessons of the past tell us to anticipate more great reversals."

New businesses like China.com and a highly educated and technologically literate population will accelerate this convergence through participation in the international culture of the cyberworld. The operative model has moved from the static to the dynamic and accelerating reforms are making up for lost time. Eventually new leadership will emerge in China, replacing the old guard of the 1949 Communist era. A more independent, worldlier, and flexible approach is expected to emerge. Li Qiang, sociology professor at the People's University in Beijing, described the emerging new generation as better traveled and more tolerant of other cultures as a result. Most strikingly, "they automatically accept reform; they know it must happen." The transition of leadership from old guard to new generation is yet another element in the changing face of modern China.

Internal and external turbulence also characterize modern China—internal turbulence arises as a result of change, as new systems clash with old. External turbulence arises as a historically self-contained Middle Kingdom steps out carefully into a global economy, a global communications net, and an increasingly global value system.

Ultimately, the Chinese system is essentially rational, seeking to find the most effective relation of means to its own shifting ends, but only pursuing those ends on a basis of a uniquely Chinese rationality. These means, ends, and the logical and historical structures linking them together cannot be fully comprehended from a Western perspective—any more than a Chinese perspective can fully apprehend a Western system. There is a shared need to reconsider policy and actions to bring the two nations together, on a foundation of clearer understanding.

Kipling's famous phrase, "The East is East, the West is West, and n'er the twain shall meet," is a dangerous prescription when so much of the world's future lies in a successful joining of the twain in a mutual effort to build a sustainable new global balance.

RULES OF ENGAGEMENT

The risk of not building bridges over the fault line between the world's largest and the world's most powerful countries is enormous. At a simple level, it is obvious that the world's most populous and the world's most powerful countries should be engaged in broad and deep dialogue on a full range of issues. The current three pillars underpinning the U.S. approach will need to be extended and deepened by a full range of bridging initiatives: a One China policy; active dialogue; and peaceful resolution of issues.

The period following the 1949 Revolution, which cut many of the ties that could have bound the countries together, caused the two civilizations to diverge rather than to develop common areas of interest. This repelling historical force will need to be counterbalanced by far more action and a wider range of compensating initiatives consistent with a vision of a more fully engaged pair of nations in the future. The same principles of science and nature, and the same recurring patterns of dynamic systems apply here as elsewhere—and the regained focus, scale of effort and sustained application will need to be increased dramatically to overcome the systemic energy of separation which has characterized these two countries for half a century. Trade should be maintained. Investments should be accelerated and protected. Joint task forces should be set up to investigate new opportunities to improve environmental, criminal, cultural and economic ties. The public and private sector should come together to strap these two differing civilizations together wherever possible.

Now, with the legacy of that historic division leaving many gaps that should have been filled, a new opportunity is also created to build bridges unencumbered by the past. It is possible to design a new policy of engagement that takes into account the systemic nature of the two countries and the full set of opportunities to build constructive bridges between the two cultural and economic foundations. The ties that bind the countries together are still too few and too weak, and both sides are too ready to sever even these flimsy points of contact. New strategies to create bridges across these fault lines of civilization will need to be seen as critical steps towards realization of a vision of a less volatile world.

PARALLEL PATHWAYS

This list of challenges should not be taken to single out China for special criticism. The same criticisms and risk assessments would apply to the major nations of the West. Rapid deforestation in China, which contributed to recent flooding that adversely affected 300 million people, has a historical precedent in America deforestation one hundred years ago—at a similar stage of industrialization and development. Substantial engagement will require a deep and honest understanding of both pasts in order to move forward toward a sustainable common future.

The momentum, power, and directions of the Chinese and Western systems can follow one of two paths. One path leads to separation, constant conflict, or even catastrophic collision of the two. A new global duality between China and the United States is already emerging that could lead down this path and replicate the costs and risks of past bipolar follies. A second path leads to a deep and constructive engagement that can provide counterbalance in advance to the strains and stresses of change and can reduce volatility and prepare as best we can to respond to the inevitable nonlinear or systemic catastrophic discontinuity in the future.

The list of risks and challenges which extend beyond the economic into every major area of societal challenge and risk provides, in fact, a significant opportunity for enlightened leaders to address major future risk today, and to build effectively toward a better and more united world for tomorrow.

Part III

INVESTMENT AND TRADE

ADOPTING LOCAL CUSTOMS

"Knock-knock." It was 6:00 am. We had just traveled through the night for six hours by car, cutting across the dusty Hebei landscape, the factory chairman's driver swerving like a maniac between oncoming lorries on the long dark country road. Physically and emotionally exhausted, we finally "crashed" in the hotel after midnight. And now—"knock-knock."

"Who is it?"

"Little Liu. Remember me? I am factory Chairman Wang's driver. I just dropped you off here at the hotel six hours ago."

"Then why are you back so quickly?" I reached for my glasses in the dark.

"Chairman Wang wants to invite all of you to a breakfast meeting," Little Liu shouted through the door.

"Breakfast meeting?"

"Chairman Wang says after long drive last night, need to have welcome very warmly. So we start with welcome breakfast meeting. Chairman Wang says all Americans like breakfast meeting, so he wishes to warmly welcome you too. Chairman Wang always thoughtful for honored guests!"

"Oh. When does he want the breakfast meeting?" I opened the hotel room door.

"Now!" the driver burst into the room excitedly waving his arms as if he were going to fly. "Chairman Wang wants you all to come NOW!"

I ran up and down the corridor knocking on doors of other colleagues in the negotiating team. "Sorry," I explained. The negotiations will be starting at breakfast, which will start NOW!"

109

Little Liu the driver drove our team into the state-owned enterprise, and led us into a room. Chairman Wang stood up and shook everyone's hand. He then waved for us to sit at a round banquet table covered with piles of Oreo and chocolate chip cookies. I have never seen so many cookies in my life.

The room was dominated by a huge television screen that blasted out the latest Chinese karaoke love song hits. Four factory girls in Victorian-style ball gowns with dangling plastic diamond earrings served cookies. Mr. Wang picked up the microphone and began to sing. Then it was my turn, then the turn of our general manager, accountant, and so on. Everybody sang. Then Mr. Wang ordered the Maotai liquor to be opened. Maotai, a sorghum-based schnapps, is stored in stone bottles because it can burn through glass. Then the *gan-bei* (bottoms-up) toasts began. It was only 8:00 am.

The drinking and singing went on through lunch. In fact, we never left the room. Finally, the translator who had been forced out of politeness to drink every round with Chairman Wang couldn't take it any more. He ran to the toilet to vomit. After a while he did not return. Chairman Wang sent someone to see what was wrong. Wang's deputy returned to report that the translator was afraid to come out of the toilet for fear of having to drink more rounds with Wang. Feeling an instant "loss of face," Chairman Wang ordered that platters of *jiaozi* (the local dumplings) be brought into the toilet. Wang's strategy was to flush out the translator, which he succeeded in doing. Pale and exhausted, the translator downed another two thimble-size glasses of Maotai. Chairman Wang beamed, laughing to his own amusement. He had regained "face."

The merriment ended around 3:30 that afternoon when Chairman Wang led our negotiation team into a formal conference room on the third floor of the factory. In fact, nothing of any serious nature was actually discussed over breakfast-cum-lunch. Finally, as *molihuacha*—the Jasmine tea so common in north China—was being poured, we were sitting down to serious discussions.

Wang opened the meeting, "Welcome to our factory. We can have friendly negotiations in the spirit of mutual benefit, cooperation and equality—that is, until 5:00 pm. Then we must stop all discussions. You see, at 5:00 pm the mayor of our city will be coming here to welcome you to invest in our city. And of course, to show our respect and thanks, we must throw a banquet for him as well."

Doing business in China may come as a series of culture shocks. To succeed, one must be prepared to throw away some of one's own cultural baggage and as the Chinese say, *ruxiang suisu*—"when entering the county adopt the local customs."

LEGAL FRAMEWORK

Over 20 years ago at the Third Plenum of the 11th Party Congress, Deng Xiaoping pushed forward his program of reform which would be known as the "open policy" ever since. Within a year, on July 1, 1979, the Fifth National People's Congress passed "The Law of the People's Republic of China on Chinese-Foreign Equity Joint Ventures" (the Joint Venture Law). This law established the basis for investing in China through the form of a joint venture, a structure modeled along the lines of a company, with a board of directors, a separate legal personality, and liability limited up to the contributions made by the parties to the joint venture. The concept may sound elementary, but at the time it represented a tremendous, unprecedented breakthrough for an economy which had been pretty much closed for 30 years.

On September 20, 1983, the State Council adopted "Regulations for the Implementation of the Joint Venture Law." These regulations provided procedural details for establishing joint ventures, contributing capital, transferring technology, and the operations of the board of directors. This would become the pattern of legal development for foreign investment over the next 20 years, into the new century: that is, a law will first be promulgated with subsequent implementing regulations filling in the gaps. The latter may be altered as necessary to meet the changing needs of China's investment environment.

China's willingness to improve continuously on its legislation is demonstrated by the fact that on April 4, 1990, the Seventh National People's Congress revised the Joint Venture Law. The revised Law allows the foreign party to a joint venture to appoint the chairman of the board of directors (disallowed under the 1979 Joint Venture Law), and permits multiple parties to be participants in a joint venture (formerly restricted to one foreign and one Chinese party). The Joint Venture Implementing Regulations were shortly thereafter amended to allow joint ventures to be extended for periods of up to 50 years (formerly restricted to 20) and further amendments are being made. A new set of implementing regulations applying to cooperative joint ventures was adopted in 1996.

In the years following the adoption of the Joint Venture Law, many contractual joint ventures were established along the structure of a partnership. In the absence of any specific law, these enterprises followed loosely the concepts laid out in the Joint Venture Law. To address the question of this gap in the legislation, on April 13, 1998, the Seventh National People's Congress passed the law on "Chinese-Foreign Cooperative Joint Ventures."

The National People's Congress adopted the law on "Wholly Foreign-Owned Investment Enterprises" in 1986. This law permitted wholly foreign-owned enterprises to be established within the People's Republic of

China, and made the Chinese legal system in this regard far more liberal than many other jurisdictions in Asia. While local participation is required in many other Asian countries such as Malaysia and Thailand, China permits complete foreign ownership of a legal entity, provided that such entity is engaged in activities which involve either technology transfer or export production. Subsequent legislation has permitted the establishment of wholly foreign-owned holding companies to hold equity in and controlling management in multiple China investments.

To further clarify the procedures involved in establishing a foreign investment enterprise in China, the Chinese government has implemented a number of regulations addressing such issues as the management of labor, the registration of joint ventures and the contribution of capital. Liberalization and relaxation of the current maze of restrictions is on the cards with WTO entry requiring extensive changes in existing legislation. This process is complicated by the multiple government departments involved, the regulatory authority of which is itself being redefined by WTO and the market forces now in full play within China's economy. MOFTEC Minister Shi Guangsheng announced a key breakthrough that is about to revolutionize the foreign investment landscape—the recent policy shift allowing and even encouraging foreign investment enterprises "which meet the conditions" to list on the A and B share markets in China. This development will present a breakthrough for foreign investors as it allows for the first real exit strategy for China investment plays.

GUAN XI

Given the recent proliferation of Chinese legislation, it is easy to assume that the written law in itself is the law. Unaware of the informal systems functioning beyond the statute, a foreigner may find himself working with only part of the system.

China's traditional political system was fundamentally a pattern of personal relationships. Today, personal relationships, known as *guan xi*, form an invisible network that often provides the most expedient way of getting anything done (from buying a train ticket to seeking official approval in establishing an enterprise). Therefore, the extent of one's own personal *guan xi* may determine the legality of what one does when it comes to investing and trading in China. Using one's *guan xi* to understand the informal systems beneath the law may also help one second-guess policy which is always subject to change.

Despite China's enormous strides in introducing new legislation, China's legal system continues to develop within the context of Chinese culture and an economy under transition. Internal politics, policy considerations and traditional influences are often dominant factors operating behind the law. In many respects, the practical application of law in China actually begins not with the written law but with a complex network of informal systems operating beneath the formal legal one. These informal systems, although social in nature, play an implicit, pervasive role in the way law functions in China.

While *guanxi* and connections still play a very important part in doing business in China, the once widespread and broad decisionmaking powers of officials have to a great extent been curtailed and reformed into procedural decisionmaking within the scope of the legal system. We are also seeing the rise of the National People's Congress—in the past often criticized by Western observers as being a rubber stamp of Party policy—now maturing and exerting its powers as the nation's highest legislative authority. The various ministries and departments, while often still subject to the whim of personal discretion of certain officials within, are operating increasingly within the framework and structure of China's rapidly growing legal system. In short, China's bureaucracy is evolving into a civil service.

ENTERING THE DRAGON

"Enter the Dragon"—how to do it? This is the first question foreign investors face when coming to China. From taking the first step to establish a liaison presence, to eventually establishing a holding company to manage a conglomerate of joint venture production facilities, choosing and structuring the right vehicle is always a question of paramount concern.

Foreign companies usually start off by establishing a presence in the form of a representative office. This is a good approach as it allows the company to get a foot in the door, put manpower on the ground, begin to establish relations and learn the lay of the land. While a representative office in itself cannot conduct business in its own name, it can serve as a convenient way to establish business relations and as a contact point for the company's foreign headquarters.

When investing in China, one may choose between establishing an equity joint venture, a cooperative joint venture, or a wholly foreign-owned enterprise. Choosing the right vehicle depends on the industry in question, the potential partner (maybe necessary for development in a particular sector), and the foreign company's own management philosophy and long- or short-term strategy.

Many multinationals find that once they have established several joint ventures or wholly foreign-owned enterprises, it behooves them to establish a "wholly foreign-owned investment enterprise," in this case known more commonly as a holding company. Foreign equity in the various joint ventures or wholly foreign-owned enterprises will then be transferred from the foreign corporation's offshore vehicle to the holding company onshore. This allows for consolidated management and a concentration of resources.

When coming to China, whether to trade or invest, foreign business people will find that one of the most prevalent of China's "Chinese characteristics" is the need to obtain approval for virtually every activity one wishes to engage in. This system of obtaining approvals particularly affects investors seeking to establish a formal presence in China and can be prove to be a frustrating experience. Inevitably building one's own *guan xi* network over time helps one surmount barriers more easily.

Whether it be a representative office, equity or cooperative joint venture, wholly foreign-owned enterprise, or holding company, approvals are essential before operations can begin. Approvals often require several stages: project approval, feasibility study approval, and contract and legal documentation approval, before proceeding to the stage of registration and obtaining a business license. At any stage, discrepancies in documentation can cause delays. Good relations with the government approval organizations at each level should be maintained, at all times. Due largely to traditional factors, personal relationships are still more important than written law. This situation is unlikely to change much over time, despite WTO entry.

FURTHER ENCOURAGEMENT

As China enters the new century, further investment and trade liberalization will help bring China's complicated investment environment closer in line with WTO requirements. In order to encourage foreign investment into China's central and western regions, MOFTEC has announced imminent relaxation of foreign investment restrictions. Key highlights of specific preferential measures follow:

- Restrictions on foreign equity control, currently applied nationally, will be lifted for investments in the central and western regions.
- Extensions on income tax exemptions and reductions will be extended to foreign investors with existing investments on China's coastal regions which invest in the interior.
- Coastal enterprises may *chengbao*, or contract-manage, local enterprises located in the central and western regions.
- In order to increase services and trade, foreign investment will be "promoted" in sectors relating to insurance, finance, foreign trade, commerce, securities, telecommunications, and tourism.
- Foreign investment in retail and commercial shopping malls (previously limited to certain coastal cities) will be opened to cover all provincial cities, autonomous regions and economic zones.
- Foreign investment approval procedures will be simplified.
- The former approval ceiling (US$30 million) on local provincial level approvals will be removed in regards to general investments and applied only in sectors deemed sensitive and requiring national approval.

- Foreign multinationals will be permitted to increase their scope of operations for holding companies and their business scope.

On a first read, many foreign investors may ask themselves whether any substantive changes are underway, or are these broad policy announcements just bait to lure investment. While past experiences may be a reason for caution, some real breakthroughs could be emerging from China's program to revitalize it's western regions. At a recent "Large Enterprise Group and Western Economic Structure Adjustment Seminar" held in Chengdu, Sichuan Province, MOFTEC Vice Minister Long Yongtu provided rare insight into the policies underlying China's program to dramatically open the central and western areas to foreign investment. Long pointed out that, "The opening of the western economy is not just to support those at the poverty level and it is not just a blood transfusion project, moreover it is a program to develop a market economy."

Toward a Market Economy

Underpinning China's central-western region development program is the recent announcement of a project to develop an inland region gas transport pipeline covering 4,200 kilometers stretching from the Talimakan Desert in Xinjiang to Shanghai, to transport 12 billion cubic meters of gas across the country every year. Total investment in the pipeline project will be Rmb440 billion with a projected 8–10 year investment return and a 12% internal rate of return.

The key point is that this project is open, and moreover, targeted to foreign investment, representing an unprecedented relaxation over the once tightly State-controlled transport and energy bastions. In addition, foreign investors will be allowed to hold majority equity in the pipeline projects transporting gas from western to eastern regions. Furthermore, pipeline network construction projects may be contracted to foreign parties. It has also been mentioned that "several companies may establish an investment bank" for purposes of cooperation on this project. In addition, the following principles have been offered and put on the table for foreign investor cooperation:

- All aspects of the project will be opened to foreign investment.
- The project will not be state-owned and foreign investors can control majority shares without any limitation on equity at all.
- Means of cooperation are unrestricted and can include equity, cooperative joint ventures or "other forms of cooperation."
- Exploration and exploitation rights for minerals will be offered on a reduced basis and all imported equipment will be exempt from taxation.
- Special preferences for transferring land-use rights will be offered.

It should be noted that according to past "Foreign Investment Guidelines," (issued annually by MOFTEC and the State Economy and Trade Commission together with the State Development Planning Commission) "any project related to gas or strategic construction project must be controlled by the State." These same guidelines also required that city gas supply pipeline projects be closed to foreign investment. In short, both areas have historically been "prohibited" to foreign investment. Consequently, this mega-pipeline project represents a major breakthrough in allowing direct foreign investment, and moreover, equity control in what was once considered an extremely sensitive protected sector of the State.

Vice minister of the State Development Planning Commission and Group Leader of the Western Gas Construction Working Group, Zhang Guobao has described this policy of special treatment as a "major breakthrough." In a rare disclosure of the thinking underlying these new policies, Zhang pointed out that the project is seeking foreign investment to "underwrite costs" and in particular, "foreign management to assure timely completion."

This is an experimental project on a massive scale, expected to pull up many other sectors alongside the development of accompanying service industries and infrastructure stimulated through this project. In summary, there are several reasons why this mega-pipline represents the cutting edge of China's western region pioneering:

- It symbolizes an enormous gesture to signal that China will be opening to foreign investment in an unprecedented manner following its entry to WTO.
- China's earlier announcements concerning opening the western regions have not been backed by concrete content, and this presents an enormous investment opportunity with specific preferential terms outlined in detail for the first time.
- In the process of opening the western regions, China has taken the view that advanced western management experience and technology are critical and this project will allow Chinese technicians to study carefully how to manage a massive energy infrastructure project on a commercial basis without government interference.

MOFTEC Vice Minister Long Yongtu, when addressing key officials from the central and western provinces during recent talks in Chengdu, provided some of his own insight behind this project and other breakthrough decisions which may be expected to follow. Long stated, "Your Party secretaries and governors are all very busy. Many foreign investors come and want to make appointments with you to understand the economic situation in your provinces and cities. One day when the foreigners stop making

appointments to ask questions and don't want to see you, then you will
know that you have really done your job in creating a market economy."

In the first chapter of this section, Minister Shi Guangsheng of
the Ministry of Foreign Trade and Economic Cooperation reviews
the policy changes underway in order to bring China into the World Trade
Organization (WTO) and to improve the atmosphere for foreign investment as China enters the new century. In the second chapter, George
Fisher, the chairman of the board of Eastman Kodak, draws upon his
extensive experience in leading pioneering investments in China on a massive scale for two major multinationals, providing unusual and rare insight
into the secrets of success in penetrating the China market. In the third
chapter, Michael Furst, managing director of the American Chamber of
Commerce in China, looks back at his years of experience in providing
support to the American business community and lobbying in Washington
to provide clarity in respect of the significance of China's WTO entry and
its impact on business. In the fourth chapter, André Desmarais, president
and co-chief executive officer of the Power Corporation of Canada, highlights the experiences of his group in undertaking diversified investments in
China and examines how China's WTO entry will impact future investments in this complicated market. In the fifth chapter, Robert Theelan,
chairman of the board of Chinavest, the earliest venture capital firm pursuing risk investments in China, will discuss his company's approach to
venture capital in this emerging and dynamic market.

SHI GUANGSHENG

Shi Guangsheng is minister of the Ministry of Foreign Trade and Economic Cooperation (MOFTEC), the government organ responsible for overseeing all foreign trade matters, and approving and regulating foreign investments in China. In addition to setting foreign trade and investment policy, MOFTEC also spearheaded China's decades' long negotiations leading to WTO entry.

In this regard, Minister Shi has a remarkable career background in foreign trade matters. Prior to assuming the position of MOFTEC Minister in 1998, Shi served as MOFTEC Vice Minister holding the portfolio for foreign trade. Prior to this, Shi served as assistant to Li Lanqing (now first Vice Premier) when Li was MOFTEC Minister. Indeed, Minister Shi's entire career has been linked with foreign trade, having served as director of MOFTEC's Import-Export Department and before that as deputy general manager of China National Metals and Minerals Import–Export Corporation. Shi speaks fluent French.

In the following section Minister Shi presents an overview of the foreign economic and trade policies being adopted by MOFTEC in facilitating overseas trade and encouraging foreign investment in the century ahead.

CHINA'S FOREIGN ECONOMIC TRADE IN THE 21ST CENTURY

Shi Guangsheng
Minister, Ministry of Foreign Trade and Economic Cooperation

RAPID DEVELOPMENT OF CHINA'S FOREIGN-RELATED ECONOMY AND TRADE

As mankind enters the 21st century, the continuing scientific and technical revolution will propel forward the developing trend of accelerating economic globalization, and China will continue adhering to our basic national policy of opening to the outside. China will vigorously develop foreign economic trade, constantly strengthen economic and trade relationships with other countries of the world, actively participate in economic globalization and make new contributions to promote the common development of China's economy and the world economy.

Since the founding of new China, China has consistently devoted itself to developing trade on the principals of equality and mutual benefit through economic and technology cooperation with other countries and regions of the world. Particularly over the more than 20 years of reform and opening, foreign economy and trade have consistently expanded both in depth and range, as an important substance of our basic national policy of opening to the outside. The quality and level of foreign investment has been consistently enhanced over this period, playing a significant function in promoting economic and social development in China. It has made economic and trade relationships between China and other countries of the world closer, promoting mutual friendship between Chinese people and people of other countries of the world.

Since reform and open policy, China's foreign trade has developed rapidly. In 1999, China's total import and export trade value reached

119

US$360.7 billion, ranking ninth in the world. The value of exports was US$194.9 billion and imports US$165.8 billion. While the scale of foreign trade is constantly expanding, the structure of commodity exports from China has clearly been optimized. Chinese commodities, with their low prices and high quality, are generally welcomed by people of all countries in the world. China's trade partners are spread all over the world, reaching the present 227 countries and regions from just a few dozen in 1978.

Absorbing foreign capital was the initial move in opening China to the outside. It is also one of the practices of building a socialist economy with Chinese characteristics. Through the end of 1999, China cumulatively approved more than 340,000 foreign investment projects and actually used US$307.851 billion in foreign capital.

China, which is undergoing constant development, has provided a huge market and commercial opportunity for capital and technology coming from all countries of the world. At present, investments in China have originated from more than 180 countries and regions. Among the world's top 500 large multinational corporations, approximately 400 have invested in China. Other large multinational corporations are also preparing to come to China to make investments. Accumulated foreign investments in other forms, including loans provided by foreign governments and international financial institutions, have also reached more than US$14 billion. Since 1993, China, for seven consecutive years, was the developing country that drew the most foreign investment.

Foreign contract engineering projects and labor cooperation are also progressing steadily. China's investments in foreign countries continue a steady trend of growth. Through the end of 1999, China had signed foreign economic cooperative contracts valued at US$96.5 billion. Its businesses have spread to more than 180 countries and regions covering all five continents of the world. In 1998, among the top 225 international contractors that were selected by the U.S. *Engineering News Magazine,* 30 of the contractors were Chinese enterprises. MOFTEC has approved and filed about 6,000 overseas investment enterprises with US$6.95 billion of contracted Chinese investment. Markets involving Chinese overseas investment cover over 160 countries and regions. Those investments have made active contributions to developing the local economy and increasing local employment. Along with the development of the economy, China will further encourage able enterprises to actively develop their overseas investments based on the principle of equality and mutual benefit and further deepening economic and trade cooperation with countries all over the world.

Currently, China's rapidly developing foreign economy and trade has become an important part of the national economy. The rapid development of foreign economy and trade increases the comprehensive strength of China. It speeds up the formation of a unique Chinese open economy and promotes the adjustment and optimization of our national economic structure. It also enhances the international competitive power of the Chinese economy, raises the operational efficiency of the national economy and plays an increasingly important role in steadily boosting China's rapid economic growth. In the meantime, the development of China's foreign economy and trade also drive China toward undertaking certain responsibilities, making contributions that are bound to promote the prosperity and development of the world economy.

ENTERING WTO: OPPORTUNITY FOR CHINA'S FOREIGN ECONOMY AND TRADE

Since the second half of 1999, the negotiation process for China to enter WTO has sped up. At present, all the bilateral negotiations for China to enter WTO will soon be completed. The multilateral process is also entering its final stage. At the time of this writing, China's entry into WTO is not far away. China's entry into WTO is the objective requirement of China's constant development, reform and openness. It is conducive to the development of world economic trade and will make the WTO as an organization complete.

WTO membership creates more favorable conditions under which China can further implement and expand its openness to the outside. It will enable China to carry out international trade and economic cooperation under the multilateral, steady and unconditional most favorable treatment principle provided by member countries of WTO and create an international environment favoring development of China's national economy and foreign economic trade relationships. Entering WTO will further promote the openness of China in all fields and raise the attractiveness of China to industrial and commercial circles of countries all over the world. Entering WTO will also speed up the adjustment of China's industrial structure, promote development and the growth of prevailing industries, and, on an ongoing basis, raise the international competitiveness of China's economy.

After entering the WTO, China will take a more active stance to further expand its openness to the outside. China will further open its markets in the areas of commodities trading and trade services. China will gradually open further to the outside in the areas of commerce, foreign trade, finance, insurance, securities, telecom, tourism and agency services. The Chinese market has huge potential and broad prospects. Along with the constant deepening of China's open policy and increasing economic strength of China, the relationship between China's economy and the world economy will be increasingly closer. The huge market potential of China will be gradually transferred to actual purchasing power, thereby providing more commercial opportunities for industrial and commercial organizations in countries the world over.

After entering WTO, as a responsible large country, China will strictly observe the rules of WTO in accordance with the principle of balancing rights and responsibilities. China will also undertake the commitments made by it and speed up economic system reform itself. At present, in complying with the rules of WTO and the requirements of establishing a socialist market economic system, China is carrying out the overall clearing up of existing foreign economic laws and regulations, processing amendments and supplements in accordance with legal procedures, and speeding up the establishment and perfection of a foreign economic management system in connection with international common practices. In the meantime, China will energetically spread the knowledge and rules of WTO and accelerate the training of personal. China will also constantly raise the macro-adjustment and control capacity of the government and its international competitive power and be ready to welcome more intense international competition.

In order to adapt to the trend of economic globalization and to meet the requirements of entering the WTO, China is actively implementing a strategy of "walking out." Over the past 20 years, China mainly adopted the open policy of "leading in" and promoting the continual development of the economy through energetically importing capital, technology and management. Along with the increase of Chinese economic power and the enhancement of opening to the outside, we will push forward Chinese enterprises' "walking out" or going outside China to do business. We will better utilize both of these approaches and markets, both domestically and internationally. By doing so, we will enable these "walking out" and "leading in" approaches to realize reciprocal unification and integration. The implementation of the strategy of opening known as "walking out" is conducive to China seeking a new scope of global economic development and more participation in the international division of work and cooperation by taking the initiative; it is also conducive to China in its intensifying economic relationships with other countries all over the world and its promoting economic development of the countries and regions concerned.

Of course, while on one hand WTO entry brings opportunities to China, on the other hand, development in China is relatively low and the reform of state-owned enterprises has not yet been complete, thus, the international competitiveness of certain professions is not strong. In addition, the legal and regulatory systems needed to adapt to a modern market economy have not yet been completed.

After entering WTO, the economic administrative system of China may not be able to adapt and will need to be further perfected. Certain industries and enterprises may, to some degree, suffer some negative effects from the assault. However, after 20 years of reform and openness, the comprehensive national power of China has been constantly strengthened. China has accumulated experiences that will enable it to cope with the complicated and varied international economic situation. China's international competitiveness and capacity to withstand risk have greatly increased. As deeper reforms and openness are implemented, the stronger our capacity to withstand the risk. Therefore, we are confident and determined to channel this pressure into motivational power through deepening reform and expanding openness, welcoming the challenges brought by entering WTO and promoting the national economy to constantly achieve new horizons of development.

The events surrounding China's WTO entry will not only promote the development of China's economy, but also vigorously promote the development of the world economy and pour new vigor into the development of the world economy. After entering WTO, China will actively participate in a new round of negotiations of WTO as a member and play a constructive role with regard to making and perfecting multilateral trade rules. We are willing to join the other member countries of WTO to actively push forward to establish a fair and rational international economic new order, thereby allowing more countries, including other developing countries, to share in the opportunities and interests brought by multilateral trade and to realize the balance of interests and common development.

We deeply trust that China's entry into WTO will certainly push forward the development of Chinese foreign economic trade into a new era and push forward economic trade cooperation between China and the world to a new epoch. This will create new opportunities for the world economy, and for stability and prosperity in the new century.

CHINA'S NEW DEVELOPING OPPORTUNITIES PRESENTED BY WORLD ECONOMIC TRADE COOPERATION

Facing the 21ˢᵗ century, China will adopt more effective measures and take a more proactive attitude toward further opening to the outside. China will consistently perfect its pattern of opening each level and broad areas. Under this new situation, the economic trade cooperation between China and other countries of the world, including the United States, faces new and unprecedented opportunities.

China's economy will continue to maintain the positive momentum of rapid growth, thereby creating more trade and investment opportunities for foreign merchants. After experiencing 20 years of consecutive rapid growth, China's economy has established the necessary critical base and technical conditions. At present, Chinese politics and society are stable. The market economy system and legal system are being increasingly perfected. The mechanism of fair economic competition, in terms of various ownership forms, is also being constantly perfected, creating a favorable system and environment for consecutive economic growth.

At the beginning of the new century, China will provide ongoing guidance with respect to expanding domestic consumption. China will combine expanding domestic consumption with adjustments in its economic structure, pushing forward scientific and technical progress and promoting openness to outsiders by making efforts to maintain rapid consecutive economic growth. Forecasts for 2010 show that China's GDP will double based on the current situation. This requires more foreign capital imports, advanced technology and managerial experience, and continued vigorous development of foreign economic trade to provide broad room to developing Chinese–foreign economic trade and cooperation.

China is now implementing its strategy for developing the western regions. This provides an unprecedented opportunity for foreign investors to participate in the cooperation and development of central and western regions of the country. Implementing the development of western regions is a significant decision made by China in facing the new century. Utilizing openness to promote development and lead the western regions in developing their economies is a major aspect of implementing the strategy for developing our western regions.

At present, China is speeding up infrastructure construction including transportation, telecommunications, and energy resources, among others, in the western regions. In the meantime, China is also intensifying environmental protection efforts and treatment, giving priority in developing science and education and making efforts to cultivate talented personnel in the western regions. Policies have also been adopted to provide the necessary support. All these measures have laid the basis to invigorate the western regions and create a good environment for foreign investment. As long as foreign investors fully use the existing industrial basis and technical strength available in the western regions of China, and combine their advantages with the advantages of the western regions—which possess rich natural resources and labor resources—certainly they will turn these advantageous resources into economic advantages, marketing advantages and achieve great success.

China is now vigorously carrying out a strategic readjustment of its economic structure, which provides broad marketing prospects for foreign investors to develop economic trade with China and to come to China to invest in the new high technology industry. The important tasks for China for developing its economy involve adopting the domestic and international demands as guidance, relying on scientific and technical progress and creation, vigorously promoting efforts to upgrade, industrialize, adjust and optimize the economic structure.

China is now accelerating the elimination of backward equipment and techniques and striving to renew its productive capacities. It is also focusing on developing a technical equipment manufacturing industry and transportation machinery manufacturing system aimed at enhancing the development and manufacturing capacities for large completed equipment. In developing the new high technology industry, China is also actively pushing forward the "informationalization" of both the economy and society. China has huge market demands for advanced technical equipment. We hope that developed countries, including the United States, will release their restrictions on exporting their technologies to China, promoting and realizing even greater development for bilateral technical trade.

In the meantime, China very much welcomes foreign investment enterprises to set up research and development centers in China, or to invest in new, high technology industrial technical research and development projects. China also welcomes foreign investors to participate in the industrialization of high technology and the technical reform of traditional industry. While transferring advanced and applicable technologies to China, foreign investors will be granted favorable treatment. China needs new high technology. Meanwhile, China has tremendous technical strength and talented personnel. Cooperation between China and foreigners in high technology areas will be promising and profitable.

China encourages foreign investors to participate in China's ongoing and deepening reorganization and reformation of state-owned enterprises through a variety of means. One of the most important aspects of this is absorbing foreign investment to participate in the reorganization and reformation of China's state-owned enterprises. Currently, the Chinese government is actively undertaking research on administrative measures regarding the transfer of property rights of state-owned assets to foreign investors. Under the premise of satisfying the interests of both sides, China is willing to discuss all kinds of methods, including share holding, lease, sale and cooperative operations with foreign investors aimed at intensifying cooperation in various areas and promoting the reorganization and reformation of state-owned enterprises in China.

China will further deepen its foreign economic trade administrative system reform and perfect foreign-related legal system construction in order to provide a good trade investment environment to foreign merchants. China will speed up its pace to establish a unified, standardized and open foreign economic trade system in accordance with the requirements of a socialist market economic system, adopting international common practices. China will strengthen the construction of its foreign economic legal system and gradually establish a more perfect foreign economic legal system. China will strictly implement administrative power in compliance with the law and strengthen protection of intellectual property rights.

In addition, China will gradually establish and perfect an import and export commodity administrative system. The following will be done in this regard: the system shall be opened and standardized; the policies will be unified and transparent; all kinds of non-customs duties will be reduced.

China will vigorously improve the operating environment for foreign investment enterprises and financial services for foreign investment enterprises, and support the technical development and creation of foreign investment enterprises. China will encourage foreign investors to invest in the central and western regions and will simplify the approval procedures for the establishment of foreign investment projects and speed up the process of examination and approval. China will resolutely stop collecting fees and inspecting randomly, ceasing all kinds of apportioned charges imposed on foreign investment enterprises and further improve the management and services provided to foreign investment enterprises.

China in the 21st century will be more open. Based on the principle of equality and mutual benefit, China will consistently create a new phase of economic and trade cooperation with all countries of the world, including the United States, and go forward hand in hand and jointly create prosperity.

GEORGE M.C. FISHER

George M.C. Fisher is chairman of the board and former president and CEO of Eastman Kodak Company. Before joining Kodak, George Fisher was chairman and chief executive officer of Motorola, Inc. He is chairman of the National Academy of Engineering and is a member of the boards of the University of Illinois Foundation and the U.S.–China Business Council, having served as chairman of both of these organizations from 1997–1999. He is a member of the Council on Competitiveness, having served as chairman from 1991 to 1993. Fisher is a member of the boards of AT&T, Eli Lilly and Company, Delta Air Lines, Inc. and General Motors Corporation.

He has been active in U.S. international trade issues through such advisory groups as the U.S. Trade Representative and the U.S. Secretary of Commerce. Currently he is an appointed member of the President's Advisory Council for Trade Policy and Negotiations (ACTPN). Formerly, he was chairman of the Industry Policy Advisory Committee (IPAC).

Kodak's experiences in China can be outlined by a series of milestones, beginning in 1909, when George Eastman asked Alfred Parker, his export manager, to travel to China to set up Kodak's first business there. Through the century, Kodak expanded its operations throughout the region, and in 1994, Kodak dedicated itself to its "Grand Plan"—and a significant expansion of operations—which Fisher discusses in detail in his chapter below. George Fisher led both Kodak and Motorola to pioneer expansion in China, and is credited with making these investments unusually successful.

Drawing upon his extensive leadership experience in pioneering these major China investments, he reveals in the following chapter proven formulas for success in China.

KODAK AND CHINA
SEVEN YEARS OF KODAK MOMENTS

George M.C. Fisher
Chairman of the Board, Eastman Kodak Company, with Michael More

On September 19, 2000, as I was preparing to send this to the editor, the U.S. Senate, in an overwhelming bipartisan vote, voted for permanent normal trade relations with China, thereby essentially bringing China into the world trading system. This landmark agreement represents a "win-win" for the U.S. and for China. It will benefit both countries for generations. For Kodak, there could be no more gratifying evidence that our efforts there have promoted economic freedom in China and, thereby, a more stable, peaceful world.

I joined Kodak as its chairman and CEO in late 1993. By January 1994, I had made three decisions intended to guide Kodak into the 21st century.

First and fast, we would divest large businesses—chemicals, pharmaceuticals, household products—then quickly sell off some smaller ones. We would define and establish Kodak as the "World Leader in Imaging." We would offer everything required for capturing memories through beautiful color photographs and for capturing pictures useful for their information and entertainment value. The divestitures were successful. We paid off large debts and began to focus on pictures.

Second, we would embrace an apparent threat to our dominant technology, not flee from it. Within months, we would consolidate a platform that would leave us stronger, smarter, and more nimble in digital imaging than any competitor. People now take some 3,000 pictures a second worldwide, most on conventional film. But no one knows whether or when digital will displace film as the dominant technology in photography. Our digital patent position, product line, and marketing record are supreme. Kodak is ready for anything.

Third, over the next few years, Kodak would negotiate with China's leaders. We would become China's leading imaging company. We would grow that giant market rapidly, and thereby contribute to China's economic reforms. As I prepare to leave Kodak, my extended contract concluded, I am most pleased about China. In 1998 we announced an unprecedented cooperation with the Chinese government to overhaul China's imaging industry. In the process, we would acquire most of the state-owned enterprises (SOEs) that made up the Chinese photographic industry. We now are well ahead of plan. Kodak is poised to do well in China for a very long time.

The story of Kodak in China could fill this book. It's not only about planning, negotiating, and implementing. It's also about two cultures, with different habits and expectations. But most of all, it's a story about great people from two great nations living out great expectations and a story of cooperation and trust with a government for the benefit of an entire industry—something perhaps possible only in China.

WHY DID WE DO IT?

Because we could not afford not to.

As Jack Welch, chairman and CEO of General Electric, noted, "If you want to be the world leader in your industry you must be the leader in China."

There was (and is) no base so large, no market so promising, for picture taking. China's population was then just over one billion people (today it's 1.27 billion). There were enough potential photo-active consumers to equal or exceed their U.S. equivalents, since the U.S. population is nearly one-fifth theirs. China was poised to become the largest photo market in the world.

China's economy had begun (and now continues) to bloom. Consider three indicators:

(1) Shorter workweeks, the one-child policy (that child receives lavish attention), high savings rates, and high literacy rates were spurring economic growth and creating more leisure time.
(2) If all of China used film at the rate of consumers in Taiwan, global sales would jump 50%.
(3) In 1986, fewer than 20% of urban households there owned a color TV. Today it's 100.5%.

I'D BEEN THERE BEFORE

I had come to Kodak from Motorola, where we moved aggressively into China. Motorola's wireless telecommunications products become wildly popular overnight. And Motorola's US$2 billion investment in Tianjin proved U.S. companies could not only sell products in China, but make them there, too, with considerable economic benefits to the country itself.

Thus in October 1994, when now-Premier Zhu Rongji and I discussed the possibility of Kodak's revitalizing the SOEs that made up the Chinese Film Industry, we were eager to try.

First Steps

In early 1994 we established within Kodak the Greater China Region (GCR), comprising China, Taiwan, and Hong Kong. GCR was on the organization chart alongside the U.S. and Europe. People inside and outside Kodak realized we were serious. In 1999, with GCR running smoothly, we incorporated it into our new Greater Asian Region.

We knew the China project would take all-stars. Under Bill Prezzano, executive vice president of Kodak, we staffed GCR with the very best people from around the world. In a country changing as fast as China, and so alien to Western habits and tastes, our people needed to be very smart, flexible, and adaptable to surprise, stress, and culture shock. The screening process was nearly as rigorous as NASA might apply to selecting astronauts.

Equally important, we hired excellent people from China, and worked with dozens of skilled Chinese professionals in China to make the project a reality.

The Grand Plan would take a lot of money. China support became the one untouchable budget line, immune from across-the-board cuts.

But there was more to it than the team and the timing. We felt welcomed by the Chinese. We were confident we could open up a new frontier in photography in a way that would benefit not only Kodak but also the Chinese people. A snapshot may have the most immeasurable consumer value in the world. If we could cause exposures to grow, delight our customers, and help the Chinese economy, we could take pride as well as satisfaction from our work.

Negotiating

But first we had to "do the deal."

Negotiating business agreements in China is made interesting by three forbidding factors.

First, I knew from Motorola, we had to have a win-win. If conspicuous benefits to China were not evident from our first proposals, we could spin our wheels for years.

Second, the Chinese are superb negotiators. They are smart, no-nonsense, experienced managers who understand exactly what they need, what they want above that, and the value of extracting even more above that.

Third, there is no such thing as one-stop negotiating in the Chinese bureaucracy. Nearly one person in 30 there is employed by the government. In all, we had to deal with:

- Seven state-owned companies
- Six provincial governments
- Ten city governments
- Five ministries and commissions

- Several banks and trust companies
- Local tax authorities everywhere

When they realized how difficult this was going to be, senior government officials stepped in. They formed a Central Coordinating Committee that served as a single point of contact for all our negotiations. This saved months, probably years. (Our gratitude was boundless.)

THE LISTS OF "MUSTS"

We knew there could be no deal unless the Chinese could walk away with three essential "wins."

First, they had to have help with the overcapacity and underemployment in the SOEs. The plants were old and decrepit. There were too many employees. Product quality was second-rate and inconsistent.

Second, the industry had acquired enormous debt; the government could no longer afford to continue propping these businesses up.

Third, they needed new technology to make world class products.

Kodak naturally had its "musts" too. We needed a return on our huge investment. We could not keep supporting nonproductive assets. We had to be compensated for our new technology. We needed to keep complete management control, yet work hand in hand with local partners. We also needed a transition period to start up the business, during which our huge commitment would not be threatened by other foreign investment. This stipulation, consistent with the rules of the World Trade Organization, was especially important if we were to have time to prepare to compete.

The discussions took nearly four eventful years. There were dramas and complications all along the way. The negotiations were particularly difficult because we were making history. No other company had done what we were doing, and there was no regulatory road map to guide us. In fact, China's investment laws and regulations had to be rewritten because of our project. But finally we had a deal (albeit a complex one) that left both sides with their essential requirements. Its main points were:

(1) Kodak would commit $1.2 billion to overhauling much of China's imaging industry and revitalize key factories.
(2) Two obsolete plants would be closed.
(3) There would be a four-year moratorium on additional foreign investment.
(4) Two companies would be formed under Chinese law with Kodak keeping flexible management controls.

The Vision was Becoming a Reality

We built a world-class plant in China in no time, informed by eleven decades of manufacturing experience. We modernized others. We hired and trained great workers. We redoubled our effort to build a network of retail stores across China. We began to make more products in China. We honored the environment. We put safety first. We focussed on employees' health and working conditions. We worked tirelessly to understand what Chinese customers wanted from their pictures.

Sales climbed. Then they soared.

The stories of these demanding, exhilarating years could provoke a semester-long graduate school case study. (In fact, a three-part case study is already being used in business schools around the world.)

But we learned our lessons, too. You can't assume anything. Nothing is over until it is really over. There is a Chinese saying: "If it's not in your stomach than it's not really yours." In China, multiple approvals from varying levels of government bodies are required from what may seem the smallest to the most complex issues. And each level of approval will result in additional complications, particularly for complex deals. Any company thinking they can force through a $1billion dollar investment is greatly mistaken. We knew we had to plan diligently, review often, and question everything. But China taught us to anticipate the unexpected.

Take one example: It is easy to invest in China, but getting money out is another thing entirely. After the 1949 revolution, the People's Bank of China instituted the national currency, the *Renminbi* (Rmb: "the people's money"). Its unit of currency is the *yuan* It is difficult to borrow Rmb, or exchange it for U.S. funds, since the yuan is not a fully convertible currency. And when you are talking about large sums that must be transferred often, you must get your processes in place. There are many ways to do this: payments for goods and services purchased offshore; royalties paid for use of technology; interest on inter-company loans; dividends from future profits; and so forth. But you have to square this away early and be prepared to spend a lot of time on the details.

Another watch-out. In your negotiations, you can't assume you will automatically be able to secure domestic sale rights for products and services. Many Western companies have not. We kept this in mind as a key requirement, but you can see why the Chinese might resist. The best win for them might be an agreement whereby their factories continue to supply the domestic market, while the benefits of hosting a productive export company (employment, duties, etc.) return to them.

A third financial note. The July–August 2000 issue of the *Harvard Business Review* contains an article by Wilfried R. Vanhonacker, "A Better Way to Crack China," describing how Kodak was the only multinational company to register as a "joint-stock company," on the Shanghai and Shenzhen stock exchanges, thereby keeping a "high degree of operational control."

It concludes: "Many companies will be following Kodak's lead." I'd urge any CFO heading for China to read this article carefully.

One of the keys to our success was that both sides knew we were embarking on something special. We all sensed that this was a pioneering venture suffused with risks for both sides. If only one side won, both would eventually lose. Everyone in the room had to tolerate a lot of ambiguity and surprise. Without genuine good faith, collateral goodwill, and a keen desire to succeed, talks could have, more than once, broken down.

And it was equally important to connect with the Chinese on a human level. Despite cultures, backgrounds and perspectives, everyone has the same basic wants and needs. We understood this. We listened intensely to our Chinese hosts as they expressed their difficulties, and in turn they listened to ours. Together we worked hard—there were many sleepless nights—to resolve the outstanding issues.

And part of that good faith is making sure that no one loses face. This is very important in China, perhaps more so than in any other culture. In one or two instances, we actually made a small concession to prevent any possible embarrassment across the table.

There is not space here to detail the meetings, the discussions, the visits, the plane trips, the dinners, the late nights, the weekends devoted to this task. Anyone who signs up to do business in China must understand that full commitment means *full* commitment. But from that can come astonishing achievement.

RESULTS IN 2000

As I write this, in the summer of 2000, we are well ahead of plan. To summarize:

- In 1996, China was the 17th largest roll film market in the world. It is now number two.
- Kodak in China now has the number one market share in all categories: film, paper, and chemicals. (In 1996, we were no higher than third in any.)
- The Chinese central government approved and published an investigative report on the Kodak project in China's official voice, *The People's Daily*, on August 10, 1999. The report crowned Kodak as a model corporate citizen and the Kodak project as a successful model for foreign investment and state-owned enterprise reform.
- The number of Kodak employees has gone from 30 in 1993 to more than 5,000 today.
- There were fewer than 100 Kodak Express Stores in 1993; there are more than 5,000 today.
- Our quality meets Kodak's rigorous world standards. In fact, we are exporting China-made film to Japan.

- Kodak's first six-sigma (the highest standard for quality) camera production has been verified in our Shanghai factory.
- We have achieved ISO 9000 standard (another world-class quality benchmark) in film and equipment made in China.
- We are especially proud of our unprecedented safety record. We have 21 million safe work hours on the construction in Xiamen, to cite one example among many.
- In Xiamen, we paid more taxes in the first six months in 1998 than the previous SOE company, Fuda, did in the past 14 years.
- From such conspicuous success, we derived the credibility that makes expansion possible. We're leveraging investment into more manufacturing. We are producing digital cameras in Shanghai, and One-Time Use Cameras in Xiamen.
- Our workforce in China now stands at 5,000 employees, whose average age is 27. We established a training and development center in Shanghai that has transformed their lives and assured their future.
- We also operate a software development center in Shanghai that develops Kodak's latest digital products.
- Finally, when we committed to invest $1.2 billion in March 1998, we expected to be profitable in five to seven years. We will achieve full profitability in China this year, well ahead of our own schedule.

NOTES ON INTANGIBLES

Every major project has stories within the official stories. These notes reflect what I might tell others considering a large investment in China.

First, make a sign for the office wall: PATIENCE, PATIENCE, PATIENCE. China's long history has left its people with a different sense of time. They value the need for considered reflection over American business managers' chronic sense of urgency. And, too, each person you're negotiating with is reporting back to others, who in turn confront their own surprises and may have other agendas. Things will change. Stuff happens. Always keep your goals in mind. Always keep your cool.

Never underestimate the Chinese. Despite economic disparities, history tells they will hold their own and then some. The Yale historian Jonathan Spence wrote a fascinating book, *To Change China*. It shows how, from the 1640s onward, Western institutions and interests entered China with a view to bestowing something valuable in exchange for influence or power. Spence chronicles:

> "Every technique that Western advisors had brought had eventually been assimilated: heliocentric theories and calendaric science, sophisticated medical surgery, economic planning, engineering, interdisciplinary universities, long-distance communications, mechanized warfare,

nuclear physics. The Westerners had presented their expertise as the wrappings around an ideological package, however, and had tried to force the Chinese to accept both together. It was this that the Chinese had refused to tolerate..."

Spence demonstrates that no one has ever been able to inculcate change into China, or trick the Chinese into doing something they did not want. The Chinese change themselves only when they see a real need, consistent with their view of their immediate condition and their long-term future. Don't go in with a camouflaged agenda.

Americans tend to be pleased with themselves. American business leaders can be extremely pleased with themselves. Why not? By most methods of keeping score, they are winners. But more than once I have witnessed Western arrogance cost some companies greatly in China.

Indeed, I'd say that working well in China requires a measure of cultural humility. China is a great civilization, worthy of immense respect. Again, remember historical scale. When the pilgrims arrived in America in 1620, China had been China for more than 5,000 years. Such a heritage has ingrained both identity and a sense of community deep within the culture. Whatever problems they face today—and these are many and urgent—the Chinese people know who they are. They are incapable of cultural envy. They might reasonably wonder why more Westerners don't envy them.

Then there's the human scale. The Chinese population stands at 1.27 billion people, or 4.6 USAs. That's more than the combined populations of North and South America, Western and Eastern Europe, Russia, Australia and Indonesia. Regional differences ramify endlessly across 33 provinces and autonomous regions teeming with languages, dialects, customs, traditions, and legacies. China is more a continent than a country. Be wary of simplified conclusions, of too terse an analysis of market trends. Do not assume that what's right for one region will work in another, especially since household incomes in some are less than $100 a month, while other regions exceed $1,000 a month.

Many Chinese people live below the world standard for poverty ($2.00/person/day). The exciting progress in the urban centers will be the engine that drives the economy forward. But the economic tasks facing Chinese leaders seem immensely intimidating. It can be easy to judge the country on headlines or on 40-second news reports from CNN. And no leadership will ever guide with perfect judgments. That said, the desire to improve their people's general welfare is the propelling motive for the leaders of modern China. And nothing will bring that about so quickly as economic reform.

Many Chinese customs, practices, arts (think of Chinese music) seem wholly alien to Western tastes. We cannot fully grasp them, but what may appear quaint, primitive or eccentric to us may have profound significance. While viewing a Kodak-sponsored exhibit of Chinese Archeology at the National Gallery in Washington in 1999, I was reminded once again of a proud and accomplished people with a rich culture and illustrious tradition, some of which still remains with us today. I felt treated to a silent symphony full of force and teasing secrets. The bronze masks, the lacquered deer, the terra cotta soldiers—all seemed at once inscrutable and sophisticated, products of cultures one would give much to better understand.

And in the foreground: daily dramas of intense, ceaseless change. To visit China is to witness a nation so fixed on a better future that a certain dedicated tirelessness seems instilled. In Beijing I saw workers running across a construction site for a new subway system, each balancing a wheelbarrow piled high with soil. Above the shafts that led down into the tunnels were wooden tripods lashed together from rough-hewn wooden poles, each bearing the weight of the pulley and a bucket carrying tools and materials to the workers below. A black and white photo of that scene might resemble work being done in San Francisco a century ago—except that it was nearly midnight and the intensity in the workers' faces was unlike anything I'd ever seen.

One gathers the sense of a civilization intent on catching up to the best practices of the world around it, yet in a manner and toward a larger design that the Chinese alone can intuit. One senses, too, their internal steeliness, their readiness to undertake "the long march" to a better country, a fuller life.

The next night I found myself in a restaurant high above Hong Kong. Looking out at the glowing skyscrapers and down at superhighways streaked with speeding cars, I couldn't help thinking: yes, *this* is the future. *This* makes New York City look old.

When thinking about China I keep these two contrasting scenes in mind. The country seems poised between a timeless past and an utterly contemporary future, made possible by a rare single-minded intensity, the swift adoption of new technology, and the benefits of a more disciplined economy.

We've seen a lot during the last seven years. What will happen over the course of the next generations is anyone's guess. But we're seeing wonders already. And I'd bet that the energy on the bustling streets of Chinese cities, coupled with a new generation of committed, educated young people, will produce progress that may some day seem miraculous. I'd urge any CEO looking at investment in China to consider a "Grand Plan" the potential opportunity of a lifetime.

Michael J. Furst

Michael J. Furst, the executive director of the American Chamber of Commerce in China, was appointed to this position in November of 1997. He previously served as the Mitsui Professor of Business at MOFTEC's University of International Business and Economics in Beijing from August 1996 until January 1998, and is currently a visiting professor at UIBE. He is the former managing director of Omega Management Limited, a Hong Kong-based consultancy firm.

Dr. Furst has over 20 years' experience as a banker and consultant specializing in the areas of financial structure and strategy as well as managing organizational change, total quality management, and team building. Until 1994, he also served as an adjunct professor of management at Cardinal Stritch College in the midwestern U.S. In the 1970s, he studied with Peter Drucker, the world renowned management expert. He has been active in China/U.S. trade and exchange issues since 1988. Dr. Furst has a Ph.D. from the University of Santa Barbara, an MBA in Management from the Drucker Management Center at Claremont Graduate School and a B.A. from the University of Vermont.

Dr. Furst has led numerous AmCham delegations to Washington D.C. to lobby on behalf of the American business community in China. Such lobbying efforts have focussed on trade issues in particular and extensive meetings with Congressional members, contributing to adoption of PNTR status for China, paving the way for WTO entry. Dr. Furst draws on his extensive experience in discussing the significance of China's WTO entry and the realistic impact that it will have on foreign business.

CHINA'S WTO ACCESSION—THE BIG PICTURE

Michael J. Furst

Managing Director, The American Chamber of Commerce of China

LONG MARCH TO WTO

At this moment, China's "long march" towards WTO accession, begun in July 1986, is nearing its destination. Then China was just opening its door—closed to the outside world since 1949—and the importance of integrating into the global trading community, and the ramifications therefrom, was not fully realized. In fact, by some accounts, the West was more eager than China to have China in GATT. The bar was low, and Deng Xiaoping's China was a gloriously promising frontier. Deng himself was selected as the Man of the Year three times by TIME magazine.

The process came to a halt in 1989, when the tragic Tiananmen Incident took place. Within China, the conservatives took hold of power, and fear of "peaceful evolution"—a euphemism for capitalism—was prevalent. The West was believed to have instigated the anti-government movement. Internationally, China relegated overnight from the Wonder Story of the late 20th century to a pariah, resulting in less interest in the West in having China become "one of us." Economically, as the Uruguay Round of talks progressed, the bar for entry was also raised significantly, prompting China to claim that it did not want to join GATT/WTO if it meant the country had to sacrifice its national interests.

In 1992, Deng Xiaoping made his historic trip to southern China, resuscitating the faltering "reform and opening" program. During that trip, Deng, for the first time in the history of Communist China, said that a market economy was possible in a socialist system, and that the ultimate goal of reform in China is to build a "socialist market economy." These bold statements triggered progressive waves of economic boom, rekindling the outside world's interest in China and also China's interest in the outside world. The WTO accession process picked up momentum. In 1995, when the WTO was formed, China officially applied to join the organization. Since then, China has reached bilateral agreements with most members of the WTO.

A major breakthrough came in November 1999, when the United States penned a historic deal with China on market access. Then the Europeans reached an agreement with China in May 2000. Barring any contingency between now and the end of the year, China is expected to join the WTO near the end of 2000.

WTO Significance

China's WTO accession is by no means a mere trade arrangement. It is first and foremost a political statement and a commitment on the part of the Chinese leadership that the current policy of reform and opening up will continue and intensify. In fact, the current regime, headed by President Jiang Zemin, sees WTO accession as a monument to its leadership. Jiang hopes history will remember him by this move. In addition, reformers within the Chinese government want to use WTO accession as a lever to both pry open the resistance to positive change and to break the stalemate in the reform process. Currently, China's reform program stands at a crossroads: the huge but inefficient state sector seems virtually incurable; domestic demand is sluggish; unemployment is soaring; corruption is proliferating like a skin rash or worse; political reform has almost become a forbidden zone; and many foreign investors are on a side track, waiting to see how things will be going. To the reformers in the Chinese system, there is no single remedy that will address all those issues except, perhaps, for the rules-based WTO, which will prompt a much greater reliance on rule of law, accountability, transparency of government process, national treatment of foreign businesses, international compliance, and more foreign investment. In short, the WTO provides China with a path to market economics, which will help break local and departmental monopolies that have proven so hard to crack from inside. Reformers can now point to the expectations and requirements of the WTO system as a justification for necessary reforms.

Taiwan also has played a part in this drama. The island negotiated bilateral agreements with all its partners ahead of the mainland. Beijing, however, insisted that it had to be admitted into the WTO first. Beijing also realized that once both the mainland and Taiwan are admitted into the WTO, links between them will be closer than ever, thereby aiding the unification cause, another great objective that President Jiang wants to achieve.

The face factor is also at work. To China, WTO membership affords it long overdue face and dignity. The WTO, sometimes known as the "economic United Nations," is the only major international organization that China is not a member of. Given its growing international standing in recent decades, the Chinese leadership is uncomfortable not being part of the global trading community. As Vice Minister Long Yongtu of MOFTEC explained once to an audience of state-owned enterprise managers, China is a member of the United Nations, the World Bank, the International Monetary Fund, the international Olympic movement and countless others, so why can't it join the WTO?

On the diplomatic front, WTO membership will solve China's Normal Trading Relations problem with the U.S. permanently, thus removing a long-standing obstacle to improved relations between the two countries. This annual ritual, with its outcome always predictable, wastes a tremendous amount of resources from both sides and both the U.S. government, and the Chinese leadership earnestly wishes to put it behind them. The American business community could hardly agree more. Businesses dislikes almost nothing more than uncertainty.

Being able to participate in global trade rule making was another motive for the Chinese to join WTO. While claiming that the current international order is not fair enough, China hopes to be able to rewrite some of the rules of the game in the international arena; staying outside WTO does little to advance that goal. China's leaders, watching growing globalization gallop along, anxiously want to be a part of the race towards prosperity.

To the world at large, a WTO without China, the largest country in terms of population, the seventh largest economy and the tenth largest trading power in the world, is an unfinished organization. Add in the factor of China's rapid economic growth and one can only ask, "How can the WTO be 'world' without China?"

Culturally, China's WTO accession, if sustained by future events, represents a milestone event in Chinese history—this is China's "coming out party." The Middle Kingdom has, for the most of its history, been a country that has been more comfortable behind the Great Wall than it has as a participant in the great trading markets of the world. China has always perceived itself to be the center of the world and of civilization. In addition, throughout its history, China has been a country accustomed to rule by man, not rule of law. Never in its history have we seen a China as keen as it is today to join the international community.

Economically, the benefits for both China and the rest of the world are indisputable. To the West, China's 1.2 plus billion population, long considered the largest potential market to be developed, is meaningless unless China opens itself to the outside world. After insisting for years on a "commercially viable/meaningful/sound" deal with China, the United States unexpectedly got significant concessions from China in April 1999 during a trip to the country by Premier Zhu Rongji. When details of the agreement were made available publicly, senior executives of American companies in China described the deal as "astounding." During the congressional debate on China's PNTR in 2000, few questioned the economic benefits Americans will get from China's accession.

To China, most agree that accession will present both "opportunities and challenges," with the opportunities over-weighing the challenges. The immediate and most important benefit for China, perhaps, will be a drastic increase in the inflow of foreign direct investment (FDI). A study recently done by the Development Research Center (DRC) of the State Council, a top Chinese economic think tank, indicates that with improved predictability, a more transparent regulatory environment and the extension of the WTO's required "national treatment," China will attract more than US$100 billion of FDI in the first five years after accession.

WTO NEGATIVES

The decision to accede to the West-dominated WTO, however, is not an easy one for China. As one leading official with the State Development Planning Commission (SDPC), perhaps the most powerful Chinese ministry, put it during a small-group meeting with U.S. business representatives, the top Chinese leadership took a great chance in making that decision. Already, on the domestic front, the leadership is often being labeled as weak and excessively pro-Western.

Resistance also comes from bureaucrats at all levels who fear the prospect of losing their privileges and powers. Reform cannot proceed if limited to the realm of economics. Among the SDPC, the State Economy and Trade Commission (SETC), the Ministry of Foreign Trade and Economic Cooperation (MOFTEC), the Ministry of Information Industry (MII), the People's Bank of China, and all the industry-specific regulatory bureaus—none of them are volunteering to give up power. In fact, as one official from the SETC bluntly put it, the reform of SOEs is not an economic issue but a political one; if the Communist Party gives up control over the economy, what is the legitimacy for its existence, let alone its leadership of the country?

In addition, foreign competition will cause massive dislocations as faltering SOEs disintegrate and unemployment rises. Studies show that after accession, only the textile and clothing industry will probably benefit greatly; automotive and agricultural sectors will be hardest hit. Chinese researchers estimate that between 1999–2010, nearly ten million farm laborers will have to be retrained and moved to other sectors of the economy, while many poorly-managed SOEs will be edged out of their markets. Rising unemployment, coupled with institutional resentment, will constitute a great challenge to the power base of the Communist Party.

Furthermore, many fear that with an influx of Western goods and services will come "decadent" Western influences: lifestyles, values, pop culture and money worship. All this will eat away at the already fragile national pride and cohesion that the leadership desperately needs at a time of great social upheaval. An identity crisis, it is said, will creep up, particularly among the country's youth. This may explain the recent campaigns of *sanjiang* (stress on politics, justice and learning) and *sange daibiao* (representation by the Communist Party of the most advanced productive forces, culture and the interests of the vast majority of Chinese people), in an attempt to win back the popularity and legitimacy of Communist rule.

FUTURE IMPLICATIONS

To foreign investors, it is important to remember that change will occur incrementally, not dramatically. After so many years of waiting, they place great expectations on China's WTO accession. The truth is, however, that WTO is not a panacea; it will not solve all the problems of foreign businesses in China. The regulatory approval system will remain; the big ministries will fight to retain their power; enforcement is less than certain; the rule of law is yet to take hold; and there may even be more confusion in the initial stage.

Having said that, though, it will be equally wrong to underestimate the impact of WTO accession. After all, China made international commitments that are legally binding. Failure to comply with them will not only result in the diminution of China's international credibility but will also stall the domestic reform process, discourage foreign investment from coming into China, and put the legitimacy and power of the current leadership at risk. Change is taking place and will pick up momentum but, as always, one needs to be patient to let the drama play itself out.

ANDRÉ DESMARAIS

André Desmarais has served as president and co-chief executive officer of Power Corporation of Canada and deputy chairman of Power Financial Corporation since 1996. He is also a director of Great-West Lifeco Inc., Investors Group Inc., London Insurance Group Inc., Pargesa Holding S.A., Groupe Bruxelles-Lambert S.A., and RTL Group. Mr. Desmarais is also a Director of CITIC Pacific Ltd., The Seagram Company Ltd. and Bombardier Inc.

Mr. Desmarais is chairman of the Canada China Business Council; member of the Chief Executive's Council of International Advisors for the Hong Kong Special Administrative Region; member of the International Advisory Council of CITIC; member of the Beijing Mayor's Business Leaders Advisory; member of the Chairman's Advisory Council of the Americas Society; member of the Business Council on National Issues of Canada; and a member of diverse foundations and trusts within the Canadian community.

Power Corporation of Canada (PCC), established in 1925, is an international investment holding and management company with headquarters in Montreal, Quebec, Canada and its holdings include assets in North America, Europe and Asia. In North America, PCC's subsidiaries are operating businesses mainly in the financial services—covering mutual funds, life insurance, financial planning services, and other financial products. In the United States, Great-West Life & Annuity Insurance Company is now the eighth largest publicly-owned managed care company.

In Europe, through Pargesa, PCC's holdings include investments in a limited number of large operations and strategic industries including communications, specialty minerals, utilities and energy. In Asia, PCC has a growing portfolio, especially in the People's Republic of China through investments in mainland China and Hong Kong. PCC's holdings include an important investment in CITIC Pacific, a diversified conglomerate listed in Hong Kong, and a portfolio of direct investments in China. PCC's European affiliated companies hold interests in China through operating joint ventures and wholly owned companies.

Mr. Desmarais draws upon the experience of PCC's extensive and diversified interests in China in commenting on the challenges and opportunities which foreign investors will face following China's entry into WTO.

CHINA, UNLIKE ITS FAMOUS CITY, IS FORBIDDEN NO MORE

André Desmarais
President and Co-Chief Executive Officer, Power Corporation of Canada

PREPARING TO EMBRACE THE WORLD AND FUTURE

The world's new economy, while still driven by capital flows, is more clearly linked to the value created through the knowledge economy. The Chinese leadership has made it clear that its objective is to modernize China through investment in education and advances in technology. Indeed, these are fundamental themes in China's plans for economic development.

President Jiang Zemin, in a guest editorial entitled "Science in China" published in *Science* magazine (Vol. 288, 30 June 2000), emphasized this goal: "A high-calibre scientific community supported by an increasingly astute workforce is China's engine for change, ensuring our continuing modernization and preparing the nation to embrace the world and the future. Thus, scientific research and education are both national priorities and are incorporated in all of China's development strategies." This statement encourages foreign investors of high-value activities and points to expanded opportunities for strategic partnerships as China moves to become a high-tech economy. As foreign investors, our interest is to seek opportunities that help China and its people achieve their economic goals for a high-value economy in ways that are commercially aligned with our capabilities and investment objectives.

Power Corporation has had 22 years' of experience in China, dating back to 1978 when Prime Minister Pierre Elliott Trudeau, supported by the government of China, invited my father to participate in the opening of the Chinese economy to the outside world. Shortly thereafter, we began our relationship with Rong Yiren, founder of China International Trust and Investment Corporation (CITIC), a state enterprise, which had been mandated by Deng Xiaoping to act in a commercial manner, on behalf of the Chinese government, with foreign investors. This marked the beginning of a long and fruitful relationship that has grown stronger over time. And after 22 years of regular visits to China, I still continue to enjoy the added learning that each visit brings.

Experience has taught us the vital importance of a solid Chinese partner and the value of spending time to foster relationships. This is not unique to doing business in China; our growing activity in Europe has been based on the same belief in the importance of building a strong relationship with the right partner. But these years of relationship building in China have been especially useful because the cultural differences were so wide and we had so much to learn about each other. Over time, China will continue to rely on relationships that work—these will be the winners. So it is important to find and develop those relationships. And for us, our interest, like that of other leading Canadian companies, is in long-term projects that build value, not short-term or one-shot deals. This focus on long-term value-creating relationships is just as important for China.

IMPORTANT PRINCIPLES UNDERLYING BUSINESS RELATIONS

Our earliest joint venture business was founded on a few important principles: The first joint investment would be made in Canada; we would be equal partners with CITIC for any and all decisions; we would have our interests completely aligned; and we would make a symmetrical investment in China which would allow access to each other's assets in case of dispute. Guided by these principles, together we managed a pulp mill in Canada, which became one of China's largest foreign investments at the time. Working side by side, both parties gained the opportunity to learn from and about each other. While the mill has since been sold, the experience from this initiative proved most valuable for both partners.

More recently, our experience in creating a joint venture with Bombardier Inc., (the leading Canadian company in rail, recreational products and aerospace technologies) and China National Railway Locomotive and Rolling Stock Industry Corp. (LORIC), and its subsidiary Sifang, provides another example of how to create a strategically important new enterprise of long-term value. This joint venture will have the potential not only to meet China's growing needs for rail-passenger coaches, but to develop a manufacturing platform for a wide range of rail technologies, from subway cars to high-speed trains, that will serve global as well as Chinese markets. LORIC is linked to China's Ministry of Railways and is an established manufacturer of rolling stock and locomotives.

The original memorandum of understanding was signed by the three companies in April, 1994, and was followed by an agreement of the three partners to invest C$100 million in a new manufacturing facility at one of Sifang's existing sites. Under the agreement, Power Corporation and Bombardier owned 50% of the joint venture and Sifang the other 50%, with Bombardier's technology and production expertise to be employed in manufacturing, initially, inter-city passenger rail cars.

In November, 1997, Power Corporation, Bombardier Inc., LORIC and its subsidiary Sifang signed a further memorandum of understanding with China's Ministry of Railways, establishing the basis and the framework under which the joint venture would be formed, with the support of the Ministry of Railways. It specified Bombardier's commitment to provide personnel training and technology transfer. The agreement confirmed the site of Sifang's Jihongtan factory in Qingdao, as the location for the manufacturing investment. The plant will help meet the demand for higher quality railway service in China with the implementation of its first contract for 300 units of high-grade inter-city passenger rail cars which began in early 2000.

In pursuing this joint venture with our Chinese partner, it was important for us to address our Chinese partner's key goal, which was access to technology and manufacturing know-how. So we needed a true relationship, real technology transfer, and a business in which the interests of all the partners were commercially aligned. We felt we could develop a project that was both economically interesting to us and attractive to our Chinese partners. Now that the parameters have been set, we face the critical challenge of executing the plan; a key challenge is to reconcile the deeply different approaches to corporate governance.

IMPORTANCE OF BUILDING LONG–TERM RELATIONSHIPS

These positive experiences taught us of the importance of building a long-term relationship with a Chinese partner, and this will be just as important in post-WTO China as it has been in pre-WTO China. In China, before you negotiate a contract you first must establish a relationship based on mutual trust. This can be a lengthy process. It almost certainly means many visits to China and it also means understanding the values and vocabulary of the Chinese partner.

Getting expectations right is also critical. It is too easy for a foreign investor to approach China with high expectations for easy and quick success based simply on the sheer size of the Chinese market. This can make the idea of simply trying to buy a share of the market very appealing. But such an approach is almost guaranteed to fail. Expectations must be based on a realistic understanding of what is required for a successful project and recognition that entry into China takes time. And of course, any business plan to enter China must have a solid commercial basis. But realistic expectations are important for potential Chinese partners as well. Chinese enterprises have just as great a stake in ensuring they have the right foreign partner and those projects are based on reasonable expectations of what the foreign partner can contribute. Any commercial initiative must make good business sense. Otherwise, the partners may find themselves involved in a relationship that cannot succeed.

In our experience, business councils can also play an important role in building a strong relationship with both government and enterprise in China. This is why we established the Canada China Business Council in 1978, following the suggestion of the Chinese government to create such a body. Over the past 22 years, the Canada China Business Council has become the principal vehicle through which Canadian and Chinese commercial interests interact. I have been honored to serve as the Council's chairman since 1993, and today the Council has 20 full-time employees, with offices in Toronto, Vancouver, Beijing and Shanghai. Business interest has also grown. In 1993 we had 83 companies in our membership; today we have almost 300. The Canada China Business Council has become the key voice of Canadian business in helping to reach policy decisions or solve problems in dealing with the Canadian and Chinese governments.

The Council is fully funded by its business membership, and focuses not only on helping major corporations develop long-term relationships with China, but also on expanding the opportunities for small and mid-size businesses. The Council carries out its mission by fostering contacts in China and Canada from its member companies and in holding policy and information sessions for its members. It raises the profile of Canadian companies through its annual meetings, which include high-level political participation. Prime Minister Jean Chretien attended all the Council's annual meetings from 1994 to 1998 and participated in a special meeting of the Council in 1999, also attended by Premier Zhu Rongji. In addition to Premier Zhu Rongji, Premier Li Peng and President Jiang Zemin have all attended and addressed annual meetings of the Council, which alternate between Canada and China. The Council also acts as the host organization in Canada for visiting Chinese political and business leaders.

This special political-business relationship found in the Council has resulted in a number of important joint ventures and other enterprise initiatives. In 1995, for example, agreements were signed for Nortel Networks and SNC-Lavalin. The following year, additional agreements were signed, for example, granting Manulife Financial the first joint license for a foreign insurance company to operate in China, a contract for the construction of two CANDU nuclear power stations near Shanghai by Atomic Energy of Canada Ltd., and a contract by Westcoast Energy to build a power plant in Shanghai fuelled by waste blast furnace gases. The Council played an active role in facilitating these and many other projects.

The Challenge of Overcoming Differences

Cultural differences clearly add to the complexity of doing business anywhere in the world, including in China, with compromises necessary on each side. This means that a Western partner must adjust to the Chinese culture and the Chinese way of doing business, just as we expect a Chinese partner to understand international standards of business. For example, as we found, Western business people tend to have a legalistic approach to business arrangements, setting out in great detail all the possible contingencies in writing a business contract. For their part, the Chinese pay much less attention to the details of a contract and focus instead on the principles underlying the business arrangement. So it is the principles which must be negotiated first. Chinese contracts are typically very general and focus primarily on the underlying principles of the business agreement, leaving the partners to work out problems as they arise. Chinese partners operate on the assumption that over time things will work out.

At the same time, different notions of time, decision-making processes, corporate governance and expectations represent important cultural differences that can add to the difficulty for a foreign investor in doing business in China. These cultural differences should become less important over time as a result of WTO accession and as reforms already underway in China bring its domestic economy closer to international business practices.

Economic issues will not be the only challenges facing China as its economy progresses and the living standards of its people improve. The challenge of building an economy based on sustainable development is also a priority. China does not want the health problems that arise from widespread pollution, nor the long-term risk to the quality of its water, soil or air that come from environmental degradation and the loss of natural capital. Foreign investors can be important partners in pursuing methods of production consistent with this need for sustainable development and Chinese laws and regulations on the environment could be another element of compliance that foreign investors would be expected to meet.

While Canada and China are at different stages of development, they both share the need to incorporate concern for the environment into their business practices. Foreign investment is one way to incorporate sound environmental practices into China's future economy. Leading international corporations tend to be environmentally responsible; to utilize advanced technology and pollution control facilities and to practice advanced environmental management systems in their operations. China can expect and indeed encourage clean technology from foreign investors by strengthening its environmental laws and their enforcement, and by strengthening its intellectual property protection.

These are all challenges that can be overcome. So as we look to the future, and China's momentous decision to enter the WTO and adjust to the obligations of WTO membership, it is important to focus on the broader business implications.

THE SIGNIFICANCE OF CHINA'S WTO ENTRY TO FOREIGN INVESTORS

China's decision to join the World Trade Organization marks its bold next step in its "long march" toward becoming one of the world's leading economies. Even though this will mean major, and at times, painful domestic changes, it shows in the strongest possible way that China is prepared to be part of the process of globalization and is basing its future on growing ties and integration with the rest of the world.

While levels of foreign trade and investment are already significant, WTO membership means both trade and investment should grow even further in the years ahead. Acceptance by China of its WTO obligations will provide greater access and transparency under the rule of law in a world where there is growing global competition for value-added investment. This will give greater comfort and opportunity to foreign investors. This decision to join the WTO underscores China's expectation that high-quality foreign investment will continue to play an important role in supporting both the reform process and modernization of the Chinese economy. Foreign investment will bring technology, enhanced management skills and marketing know-how, thereby improving the vital connections to the global economy. These are good reasons to be optimistic about China's future.

China's WTO membership is particularly reassuring to foreign investors because it demonstrates a further commitment by the Chinese leadership to continue far-reaching domestic reforms. These reforms are an integral part of the process of building a technologically advanced and highly productive economy based on sustainable development. The signs here are promising. Even before joining the WTO, China's programme of modernization has shown courage and vision, as well as a readiness to take the painful steps toward domestic reform. No major country in modern history has tried to do so much in such a short period of time. These changes would have been a challenge for any country. But for a nation of China's size, with 1.2 billion people, the challenges have been even greater.

The level of reform and restructuring that has already occurred in China's economy, in its industry, in its legal and institutional arrangements, and in its openness to world trade and investment is remarkable. It adds credibility to China's commitment to meeting its new WTO obligations. And China is clearly on the right track for continued modernization and reform, streamlining the role of government ministries and agencies, developing effective capital markets, recognizing the importance of ownership rights, and accepting the WTO principle of national treatment.

In turn, WTO membership reinforces an earlier and also positive signal from China on the importance of equal rights for diverse forms of ownership. The 1998 amendment to the Chinese constitution gave "equal standing" to different forms of ownership. This demonstrated an improved understanding of the importance of ownership and property rights and the ultimate decision-making power of potential Chinese partners, suppliers and customers. The combination of China's acceptance of WTO obligations along with the constitutional recognition of diverse forms of ownership are confidence-building steps for foreign investors. These initiatives are in keeping with the central government's commitments to continue to develop a more complete and market-oriented legal and regulatory framework.

For China, WTO entry will mean a broadening of its gradualist approach to economic reform. China will need to adhere to agreed timetables on further reform and market opening, as set out in its WTO obligations. While China's gradualist approach has served it well so far, allowing the Chinese leadership to test various approaches and ideas for economic modernization, WTO membership is a signal that this step-by-step and "contained experiment" approach will be replaced by a more comprehensive approach to reform, based on the rule of law, transparency and national treatment, and a closer adherence to international business practices. This is important if China is to remain a most attractive and competitive destination for high-quality investment. And it is as significant for China's goal to develop its own high-tech Silicon Valleys as it will be for high-value foreign investment in more traditional industries.

FOREIGN INVESTORS' REQUIREMENTS

Foreign investors need predictability in the business environment; confidence in their ability to successfully implement a business plan; and sound assurances that the key factors affecting the success of the enterprise can reasonably be controlled by them if the eventual business achievement or failure is to be determined by the enterprise's ability to compete in a market-driven economy.

China's attention to strengthening the rule of law and the judicial system, and its acceptance of the WTO principle of national treatment, shows that it understands the importance of creating a business environment that will encourage long-term trade and investment. A transparent and reasonable legal and regulatory environment, an autonomous judicial system, protection of intellectual property, well-functioning capital markets and the availability of skilled people, along with stable macroeconomic policy, will go a long way to encouraging foreign investors.

At the same time, China could encourage high-value foreign investment by providing for greater flexibility and timeliness in decision making. The time-value of money is an important consideration for foreign investors. Under this concept, investors seek to maximize the return from capital by constantly keeping it at work. But if capital is tied up due to lengthy delays in decision making, then it is likely to flow elsewhere where it can be invested more profitably. Likewise, once an investment is made, the investors in an enterprise need to be able to make decisions in a timely manner to respond to new competitive conditions and take advantage of new opportunities.

CHINA: AN ATTRACTIVE INVESTMENT DESTINATION

With Chinese entry into the WTO, other steps would be helpful to facilitate and encourage foreign investors. One useful step would be to continue to clarify the role of government ministries and agencies. Premier Zhu Rongji initiated a major restructuring of central government ministries and other agencies in 1998, when he assumed his present position of leadership. This has resulted in a significant reduction in the number of ministries and a refocusing of their activities. This reform was based on the recognition that ministries should act as regulators, distinct from direct commercial interests of their own.

By separating commercial linkages between ministries and state-owned enterprises (SOEs), SOEs are becoming more commercially oriented. At the same time, the confidence of foreign investors has been boosted since this reform is reducing the potential for conflicts of interest. The threat of conflicts of interest existed because ministries, as well as pursuing regulatory responsibilities affecting enterprises, also had their own commercial interests. The steps taken so far have been helpful, and this initiative deserves to be continued.

This is why foreign investors in China would be greatly encouraged by a system that forgoes the need for a multitude of approvals from government ministries and agencies and instead relies on compliance with clearly established Chinese laws and regulations. Under a system of compliance, China would set out the rules in advance, so that lengthy negotiations for government approvals would not be necessary. Instead, the obligation of investors would be to demonstrate they are in compliance with China's laws and regulations. This would create a more dynamic business environment in what will be, in the 21st century, an increasingly competitive world. The results would be reduced transaction costs and greater investor confidence, thereby adding to the flow of foreign investments.

There would be another benefit. Experience in many different parts of the world shows that where there are several layers of approval, and a consensual system of decision making, this can lead to unfortunate and improper practices that are costly both to the host country and the foreign investor. A system with multiple layers of approval, along with consensual decision making, slows the process of economic advance and can foster costly misunderstandings. Similarly, decision makers responsible for approvals may avoid flexibility or new approaches out of fear of punishment or loss of face.

By reducing the need for government approvals and shifting to a compliance system, enterprise managers and investors will feel they have more leeway to experiment and take risks. China would benefit from this flexibility since, in addition to providing room for more risk taking, it should lead to timely business decisions, and therefore improved competitiveness for the enterprise.

A further helpful step that the Chinese government could take to facilitate foreign investment would be to establish clear implementation regulations, reflecting agreed commitments to the WTO, and timetables for the introduction of changes in its economic system. It would also be helpful if China could signify that it is determined to adhere to them. With the accession of China to the WTO, a large effort is underway in China to draft and implement the necessary laws and regulations to fulfil China's WTO obligations. The task is daunting but clearly proper management of this transition phase is vital to assure a credible government-led reform process. To reduce the uncertainties of the transition process, it would also be helpful to develop regulations spelling out how implementation will occur in different economic sectors, along with timetables, and to publicize these regulations.

Likewise, reforms that improve the potential viability of enterprises, including customs clearance, supplier chains, skilled workers, infrastructure and a level playing field that provides for open competition will provide considerable comfort to foreign investors.

Technology transfer is clearly a critical goal for China in modernizing its economy and in entering the industries of the future. But for real technology transfer to occur, adequate protection of intellectual property will be essential. The intellectual property issue is crucial today. It will become even more so in the future as the Chinese economy advances to even higher levels. China itself will have its own stake in intellectual property protection. With the high quality of graduates from China's leading universities and China's growing investment in scientific research and development, China will become a growing source of intellectual property. It, too, will wish to protect these valuable assets worldwide.

LOOKING AHEAD

While China's entry into the WTO does impose significant obligations, membership also offers it enormous opportunities in the global economy. And this will strengthen China's position as an important destination for foreign investors, not only to serve the Chinese market but also to make China a production and research base for world markets.

The obligations of WTO membership will lead to many changes in business practices. But in many respects, the underlying ingredients for success in China will not change. In particular, the need to find the right business partner will continue to be fundamental to success, just as it is in operating in many other parts of the world. So, investing time and money to build a relationship, and to understand Chinese culture and values, will continue to be critical.

There is much that China can do to improve the predictability and transparency of the business environment so that foreign investors can more easily enter into strategic partnerships with their Chinese counterparts and be in a better position to make timely and flexible decisions. In particular, moving from a complex governmental approval process to a system that allows enterprises to operate by complying with established laws and regulations would be a very helpful step. For a successful enterprise, the ability to make timely decisions is essential, and will be even more so in the 21st century as global competition becomes even more intense.

My experience in China suggests that for those willing to make the effort, there are significant opportunities. This is why we intend to be in China, as a partner, for a long time to come. China's membership in the WTO makes that future potential even more attractive and provides additional confidence in China's prospects to become one of the world's leading economies.

China, unlike its famous City, is forbidden no more.

ROBERT A. THELEEN

Robert A. Theleen, chairman and chief executive officer of ChinaVest, Inc., is one of the founding members and chief investment strategist of the company.

Founded in 1983, ChinaVest is the oldest independent venture capital firm in Greater China. Established with the singular mission of investing in companies operating in the "Greater China" economies of China, Taiwan and Hong Kong, ChinaVest has raised and managed over US$300 million from institutions including the Ford Foundation, IBM, Bell Atlantic, John Hancock and the University of California Regents. ChinaVest has raised a total of five funds that have spanned and tracked the economic development of Greater China from its roots in export-oriented light manufacturing to the recent emergence of telecommunications and information technology. A pioneer in bridging American management with Chinese entrepreneurship, ChinaVest prides itself on having introduced and inculcated the concepts of financial transparency, corporate governance and shareholder value to the companies it has invested in. ChinaVest has offices located in Beijing, Hong Kong, San Francisco, Shanghai and Taipei.

In the following chapter, Mr. Theleen discusses the emerging role of venture capital in China and how private equity financing is impacting the present and developing investment climate in China.

Private Equity in China

Robert A. Theleen
Chairman, ChinaVest

Defining Venture Capital in China

When ChinaVest established its first private equity fund in 1983, there was no term in the Chinese language to describe "venture capital." The idea of applying equity capital from independent or institutional investors to fund business growth was a concept foreign to Chinese businessmen. For a majority of these businessmen, business growth was mainly financed by operating profits or bank loans.

When we finally were able to convey the sense of what it is that venture capitalists do, a pragmatic Chinese official developed a character set which, translated into English, read "total loss investment." It seems we stressed the risk more than the reward in those days...

In fact, the choice of characters was an interesting illustration of China's economy during the 1980s. The fact was, state-owned enterprises (and those were the only enterprises that existed) were typically horribly managed and the generation of profits was not the goal of business activity. During this time, business was driven by politics and social factors, not by economic fundamentals.

So why would my partners and I decide to create the first U.S. venture capital company focused on China in that period? Because China was in transition—its command and control economy was loosening and entrepreneurial activity was bubbling from the bottom up. We wagered that there would be strong, profitable businesses to be built once the shackles were removed. And we also believed that it would be difficult for young companies to get the financing they needed from banks—which created an opening for U.S.-style venture capital, in our view.

This entrepreneurial activity centered first in the special economic zones (established in 1979) and later in the "open" cities (established in 1984). In these areas, the local governments were permitted to take measures to encourage economic development without the need for approval from the central government, while business enterprises were allowed to make their own investment, production and marketing decisions. Moreover, private ownership and foreign investment were legalized in these areas. These special economic zones and open cities effectively become laboratories for venture capital investment.

BACKING THE OVERSEAS CHINESE

In 1984, I was watching an American play in Hong Kong called "Greater Tuna," a comedy about a small town in Texas with big ambitions. I was struck that China might also expand its horizons by aligning itself with the larger overseas Chinese community. In a speech the next day I coined the phrase "Greater China" to refer to the enlarged Chinese community, and this became ChinaVest's investment mantra as well.

That is because the first real entrepreneurs in China were not mainland Chinese, but rather the overseas Chinese. Unlike some early American companies that moved into China with a view to selling into the Chinese market, these overseas Chinese businessmen wanted to make use of China's cheap land and labor for export. We believed that the overseas Chinese understood China's market development better than most of the foreign investors.

During the 1980s, therefore, Hong Kong entrepreneurs invested millions of dollars into southern China to move their manufacturing operations to the mainland. A majority of these manufacturers financed their expansion from retained earnings and debt, but some of these companies turned to venture firms like ChinaVest to fund their growth. Let me give an example.

Luks Industrial Company, a designer and manufacturer of television sets, approached ChinaVest in 1987 with a plan to build an assembly factory in Shenzhen. ChinaVest agreed to provide the capital to fund the plant expansion into China, but our activity with the company went beyond that: sitting on the board of directors, ChinaVest also helped the company develop stronger internal financial controls and helped develop a strategy for domestic sales as well. As with all good entrepreneurs, CT Luks saw what few other companies did, that Luks could sell expensive televisions in China not by trying to sell to individuals, but instead by focusing sales efforts on collectives and workgroups. This program was so successful that the company's domestic sales ultimately reached 70% of its revenue, eclipsing its exports. ChinaVest would later help Luks Industrial become one of the first companies with a mainland manufacturing capability to be listed on the Hong Kong Stock Exchange.

This was a very successful investment for ChinaVest financially. But, just as important, our investment helped turn a good small company into a very good big company, it helped deliver products and services to Chinese consumers that they might not otherwise have had, and we helped bring credibility to the company's IPO in Hong Kong. In the end, the best venture capital investment supports innovation and best-of-breed management, whether in technology, or business models, or services.

MOVING UP THE VALUE CHAIN

While private enterprise manufacturing boomed in southern China in the mid- to late-1980s, the private sector service industry in China was non-existent. Again, ChinaVest made several calculated investments at the early stages of China's service sector opening.

We liked the sector because, as a whole, the service sector was new and therefore there was not the weight of mismanaged state-owned enterprises to compete against, as there was in the manufacturing industry. On the other hand, there was a higher degree of regulation in the service industry and, in many cases, the regulator was also the competitor, for example, in telecommunications or aviation or distribution.

It is generally agreed today that government regulators should not also be competitors with industry, but that is often a difficult point to make to regulators! And China is not alone in this regard: some of the most bruising international trade battles have been in financial services and telecommunications, where governments around the world try their best to ensure an uneven playing field in favor of the dominant incumbent company. Still, the evidence in China is clear on this point. For example, China's airline industry flourished after the China National Aviation Corporation's regulatory powers were split from its management of regional commercial airlines. We believe the same is also proving to be the case in telecommunications.

One of the areas in which ChinaVest invested in the mid-1980s was the distribution and transportation sector. In 1986, Sante Fe Transport, a startup transportation company based out of Hong Kong, approached ChinaVest with a plan to provide distribution services for the multinational oil industry that was establishing drilling operations in China and offshore. However, obtaining a license to engage in distribution services on the mainland was not an easy task. Nonetheless, Sante Fe would become the first foreign transportation company to form a joint-venture permitted to operate in the PRC.

Sante Fe obtained its business license through what we call the "oblique approach to the Chinese bureaucracy." Business licenses in China are typically controlled by the relevant industrial ministry and, as a result, most foreign companies try to partner with companies that are affiliated with that ministry. However, this creates a clear conflict-of-interest, since many times the Chinese ministry or company does not really want the foreign partner to succeed.

In Sante Fe's case, the company would have needed to receive authorization from the Ministry of Communication. The industrial partner associated with MOC was Sinotrans. Neither Sinotrans nor the ministry had any interest in facilitating Santa Fe's entry to the market.

Instead, ChinaVest took Sante Fe into the Ministry of Petroleum. The Ministry of Petroleum did not have any vested interest in Sinotrans, but it did have an interest in expanding China's production of oil and gas. As a result, it was pleased to provide a specific business license to the company for its work with the Chinese petroleum industry. When this case was ultimately referred to the powerful State Planning Committee, the officials had little trouble seeing the cost/benefit equation for China, and it supported the granting of the license to Santa Fe.

In this case, ChinaVest helped Santa Fe significantly expand its revenue and services base. We provided financial advice and strategic planning. And, once the company was successful, we helped engineer the sale of it to a much larger European logistics company. This was a win-win outcome, since it gave Santa Fe additional marketing and financial muscle, it gave the European company a foothold in China, and it gave ChinaVest and management the chance to realize a reward from their years of hard work and risk.

THE MATURING OF VENTURE CAPITAL

From the 1980s to early 1990s, increasing amounts of venture capital were being invested in China's manufacturing and service sectors. It was used to finance the construction of factories, to open offices and hire staff. But it was also increasingly used to support the application of unique and innovative business practices that helped companies succeed in this period of China's economic transition. Venture capital firms like ChinaVest were increasingly appreciated by government officials as something like a measuring stick—since we are independent, and we can leave China if we perceive there to be greater investment value elsewhere, officials began to monitor the degree of capital flows controlled by venture capital. If the investment was moving up, then that was probably a good indicator that China's economic reforms were moving in the right direction; if the flows abated, or if certain sectors were not receiving investment, then perhaps there was something wrong.

By the mid-1990s, a new Chinese term was being used to describe venture capital. When translated in English, the new term read "entrepreneurial investment." That's more like it! Venture capital had indeed gained much respect during the 15 years since the initiation of Deng Xiaoping's economic reforms, but China was still far from being the ideal environment for venture capital to flourish. The continuing transformation of the Chinese economy would present new challenges for venture capital investment.

THE ROAD AHEAD — MANY SILICON VALLEYS

With these lessons and experiences in mind, what does ChinaVest see in the years ahead in venture capital? Frankly, the time has never been better to be investing private equity into China, in our view. At the same time, venture capital, which is by its very nature a risky business anywhere, faces some additional risks in China that, one hopes, may be diminished with policy reforms in the years ahead.

Living in Hong Kong and now in San Francisco, I can attest that there is no spot on earth more people want to emulate than Silicon Valley. Its imitators are everywhere, from Melbourne to Oslo, from Brazilia to Seoul. And why not? Famous Valley venture capitalists like to boast about being responsible for the largest creation of wealth in the last 100 years. Not bad for a place that you cannot find on a map and did not even exist as a concept in Californian's minds 20 years ago.

But I think that is actually part of the problem: international visitors come to "Silicon Valley" and expect to leave with a check list of items which, if they are faithfully reproduced, will create prosperity in their new location. Whereas in truth, Silicon Valley is a success in large part for factors totally beyond the Valley's control, factors to do with the depth and efficiency of U.S. capital markets, the strength of the U.S. consumer market, and the freedom with which commercial ideas travel and yet are protected in the United States. To my mind, there is no single economy in the world that can reproduce all these assets, with the single exception of China.

From my perspective, the following are the key ingredients for a vibrant and successful venture capital industry in China going forward:

- Capable entrepreneurs willing to lead, to take risk, yet willing to listen to outside advice and to put shareholder interest above all else
- Strong research-based universities, with an emphasis on basic research without regard to business applications or profit
- A ready supply of skilled and unskilled labor
- Middle management talent, in areas such as finance, marketing, sales, and business development or strategic planning
- Liquid and efficient capital markets
- A strong and growing domestic consumer market
- A diverse economic base, and
- Rule of law.

Looking down this list, the reader can make his or her own judgment about where China would stand in the rankings.

HIGH MARKS FOR EDUCATION AND SKILLS

Without question, China has strong universities and is quickly producing a highly skilled workforce. How many people are aware, for example, that there are more engineering undergraduates in China than in all of Western Europe? The caliber of such learning institutions such as Qinghua University and Beijing University is as high in the sciences as anywhere in the world. This is especially remarkable given how the Cultural Revolution decimated China's institutes of learning.

As for the labor force, China is well known for its unskilled labor pool. But, as ChinaVest's investments in Chinese software companies and high-end manufacturing prove to me, China is going to be increasingly appreciated for the depth and breadth of its skilled workforce as well.

China also has a ready supply of risk-taking entrepreneurs. And, what is rather interesting, mainland entrepreneurs have some stark differences from their overseas Chinese counterparts that may make them even more amenable to venture capital.

MAINLAND CHINESE ENTREPRENEURSHIP AND TRADITIONAL CHINESE CAPITALISM

Dr. Gordon Redding, at Hong Kong University, has conducted extensive studies of Chinese capitalism, which he argues is a form of capitalism different from either Anglo–Saxon or Japanese capitalism. More specifically, he argues that Chinese capitalism is highly trust-based and highly oriented around the family. To paraphrase Dr. Redding, Chinese capitalism had to become trust-based because, at the outset, the rule of law in China was not well developed. In an environment in which courts could not reliably settle contractual disputes, it became very important to know and trust your business partners. This tendency also reinforced what is a natural Confucian principal, namely, that one was supposed to respect and follow the father (and CEO) without question.

All of us in Asia can readily rattle off a dozen major families and the business empires they control. In many cases, they have managed these enterprises incredibly successfully. However, while there are many benefits to this style of capitalism, it is not especially conducive to venture capital. For one, venture capitalists and entrepreneurs do not have time to build up years of knowledge and trust. More importantly, since venture capital investment is almost always in a minority position in the company, it can often be very difficult for a venture capitalist to have any real influence in a family-run Chinese business. We have watched family-run companies fail—making us lose our investment—when the founder/CEO was not willing to listen to outside advice or relinquish control.

However, we see an important contrast in this respect in mainland China today. Because free enterprise was banned by Mao Zedong and business families were broken up or exiled from China, there is today not such a strong culture of "Father (or the CEO) Knows Best." The mainland entrepreneurs in whom we have invested welcome an active board of directors and do not believe they have all the answers. This is much more similar to the U.S.-style entrepreneur: one who wants above all else for the company to succeed, whether or not he is running it. I think this is an important intangible asset for China's growing venture capital industry.

THE IMPORTANCE OF A STRONG DOMESTIC MARKET

I will not dwell on this factor except to say, every team does best on its own home field. American companies have a natural advantage in the United States over foreign companies: they have broader contacts, understand the market, and live and breath with the competition every day. And since the U.S. is a $7 trillion economy, the potential prize is huge—if they win, they will win big.

I recall a conversation with a U.S. telecommunications executive in Hong Kong several years ago. He was planning to invest over $12 billion in Asia, including a sizable portion in China. It sounded like a lot of money to us, until he told us what the headquarters was planning to invest in the United States. "China is a nice market for us—but if we lose the U.S. market to competition, we lose everything," he said.

Needless to say, this gives an enormous advantage to start up companies in the United States. The consumer market here can reward good companies with rapid sales and profits. And, if they can compete successfully in the U.S.—one of the most competitive in the world—then they can probably compete in all global markets. There are very few markets in the world where the domestic market can nurture global competitors, but I think China's will soon be one such. The rise of Chinese brands like Haier, Kelon and Legend are examples of this.

CHINA'S INFORMATION TECHNOLOGY EVOLUTION

Note that the title is not "revolution," as it would commonly be in the West. Instead, ChinaVest sees China's development of information and life sciences technology as the natural evolution of China's economy from low-end to high-end. This is also one of our most important investment areas for the next decade.

A case in point is AsiaInfo, China's leading systems integrator that has built over 50% of the Internet backbone in China and is a leading supplier of software for the telecommunications industry as well. AsiaInfo is a case study for many of the points made above, and for one important point with which I will conclude.

When AsiaInfo's founders came to ChinaVest and other venture capitalists in 1997, there were many features that helped them stand out from the
hundreds of other business plans we review. First, they were obviously a
terrific bunch of hardworking and smart engineers and entrepreneurs. Born
on the mainland, they were educated in the United States and trained by
multinationals, so their background suited their business. Their business
model—to use their engineering talents to help Chinese telecommunications companies construct the information networks that they were sure
China would need—was clearly in demand, yet competitors would be hard
pressed to keep up. (We have one abiding principal when investing in
China: pick companies that have an "unfair competitive advantage," because
as soon as you succeed, there will be a host of imitators who try to take
your market away.) And, in addition to having high integrity, we were
confident that this was a group that would value and listen to the input of
their investors and advisors.

We invested in that first round of finance, when AsiaInfo was a small
company and highly risky. But, our gamble in this case paid off: AsiaInfo is
today a publicly-traded company on NASDAQ, and their company is worth
10–20 times more than when we invested. In other words, one of our
dollars invested in 1997 is today worth at least $20, and conceivably much
more. AsiaInfo also happens to be one of the best managed, most innovative companies in China today.

CAPITAL MARKETS AND CAPITAL GAINS

Ultimately, the goal of venture capital is capital appreciation and the realization of that value. We will enjoy some astounding successes—as with
AsiaInfo—and hopefully they will outweigh the investments we make in
other young companies that do not work out.

While we are delighted that AsiaInfo was able to list on the U.S. stock
market, it is not an easy thing to do. There are many good Chinese companies that will never be big enough or well known enough to tap into
foreign stock markets for growth capital.

A logical alternative would be listing on the domestic stock market.
However, today this is not feasible for us as foreign venture capitalists—
companies capitalized with foreign investment cannot pursue public offerings on either the Shenzhen or Shanghai A Share stock exchanges. This
situation has restricted foreign venture firms to invest only in companies
domiciled in foreign countries, which typically position them for public
offerings in foreign capital markets such as the Stock Exchange of
Hong Kong and NASDAQ. And it has held us back from making certain
investments when we judged that foreign stock markets would not support
such companies.

As a Greater China venture firm, ChinaVest's mission has always been to build and grow value in China. For the Chinese economy, it is unfortunate that home-grown businesses funded with foreign investment are required to list on overseas stock markets to raise additional capital. It hurts the local economy and to a certain extent the company. It affects companies because, by and large, public investors in the U.S. and Europe are not familiar with Chinese companies and therefore, interest in the stock can easily fall. It is also a challenge for Chinese companies to communicate effectively with foreign investors. The optimal solution would be for these Chinese companies to make public offerings on domestic stock markets whose investors possess a deeper understanding of local companies and their businesses.

Another avenue for realizing value in young companies is through a sale of interest to strategic investors, as we did with Santa Fe. Again, this is much more easily accomplished if the headquarters of the company is not located on the mainland, but rather in Hong Kong or offshore. Over time, I believe this hurts China, since the corporate and legal headquarters for a company does matter. But today, the process of transferring share ownership in China is complicated, and so most venture capitalists try to avoid the problem.

NURTURING POTENTIAL

Until China's regulatory environment becomes more conducive for financial investors to sell their investment interests to others, venture funding for Chinese companies will not reach its full potential. However, I am confident that today's leaders in China understand this point, and will do what needs to be done to ensure a vibrant and successful venture capital industry in the years ahead.

China is poised to create extraordinary businesses and wealth in the decades ahead. Its markets, its universities and its entrepreneurs convince me that this is true. And some small portion of that success will, I believe, be attributable to venture capital, and the risk that we as a group are willing to take to back young companies and unproven business ideas and technologies. Certainly, in our own small way, ChinaVest hopes to nurture and grow China's best companies for many years to come.

Part IV

INDUSTRY & COMMERCE

HISTORICAL BURDENS

Hsssss ... the pig iron smoldered as it rolled off of the rack. We were walking along the production line. Gas belched in all directions. Workers turned their heads and looked at us for a minute. It was a rare respite from the endless monotony of years on the same production line.

The factory general manager continued to explain what they were doing. "You see, all our equipment dates back to the 1960s and 1970s," he said. "Therefore we cannot make products that can compete with imports—unless we can buy the necessary technology. For that we need a huge capital injection. But how to get the funds? No investor would want to take on the burdens that our enterprise carries."

After leaving the production facility, we drove through the living areas—schools, kindergartens, cafeterias, medical clinics, recreation centers. A worker could be born, live and die within the confines of the enterprise without ever having to set foot outside. The corporation had enough people living on its premises to be a small city unto itself.

"We have 50,000 people here, including retirees and families of workers, whom we must support," the general manager explained. "As for workers themselves, we have about 20,000. To achieve maximum efficiency, however, we need at most only 2,000, using the current equipment and production facilities. And if we obtained modern equipment—which we need to improve product quality and compete with South Korean exports—we would require even fewer workers."

We stepped into a school run by the factory. The head teacher greeted us. Children were running around everywhere. Classrooms, cafeteria, play area—everything was neat and orderly. As kids scrambled around us, the

165

general manager continued to recite the litany of challenges he faced. "In fact, our enterprise must support all these facilities—housing, medical care, hospitalization, retirement, education, nursery," he said. "So how can we be competitive as a business?" A state-owned enterprise, the manager continued, had a responsibility to provide for its workers. "Actually, the government should help us sort out these problems," he said. "If we are to be competitive as an enterprise, the government should support our social burdens. But you must understand that these are historical burdens. It is not so easy to wipe out history and start afresh!"

RE-ENGINEERING CHINA

China's ambitious effort to reform its state-owned enterprises involves a tangled web of issues. Enterprises employ too many workers and are inefficient as a result. When the state corporations were established in the 1950s and 1960s, their purpose was to feed, house and care for people— not necessarily to be competitive. Today, however, both China and the world have changed.

Achieving competitiveness requires technology upgrades, which must be funded. But no private investor, foreign or local, will touch an enterprise that employs four times as many workers as it actually needs. Indeed, the expense of laying off these people—forcing them to *xiagang* ("stand down" from their jobs)—makes the investment opportunity a prohibitive risk. After adding the enterprise's debts to the entry costs, most potential investors will merely nod politely that "the tour of the factory was most interesting," laugh and walk away.

So if China is to undertake a program of industrial restructuring on its own, the government must inject huge amounts of capital. In fact, unprecedented bond issues over the past year have underwritten such a cash injection. At the same time, a thorough overhaul of the country's social-welfare system is essential.

If enterprises are to leave behind the burden for medical care, retirement benefits and insurance, these costs must be picked up by either the state or the financial sector. A mature insurance system is needed, as well as a pension structure. Neither exist to the extent that workers can be assured of the safety net their enterprises once provided after they leave their jobs. As a result, the burgeoning *xiagang* problem is a potential time bomb.

If enterprises will no longer be responsible for housing, workers have to buy their own homes and banks must be prepared to provide loans. China's banking system, however, remains inefficient. The ability to obtain enforceable security over property as a mortgage pledge lacks a basis in law. People do not trust real-estate developers. And they do not want to sink their cash into assets, particularly at a time when their company is no longer picking up the bills for medical care, education and retirement.

The restructuring of a state-owned enterprise—or turning it into what the Chinese now call a "modern enterprise system"—unleashes a host of issues. They are intertwined with the reform of the country's financial system, evolving social problems and the volatility of new expectations. Can China re-engineer itself?

The nation's ongoing reforms are entering uncharted territory. They have exposed "contradictions" within Chinese society that lay dormant under a system in operation for the past half century. To some extent, the current set-up had come into being in the course of addressing social dilemmas that had evolved over centuries.

Today, unforeseen changes may, in turn, spark a social and psychological crisis. And that could throw into question the course of reform that the country has been traveling. Re-engineering China, above all, will mean social re-engineering. Can Chinese society cope?

COPING

In October 1997, the 15ᵗʰ National Congress of the Communist Party opened with a keynote address by Jiang Zemin. It proved to be a watershed in China's efforts to reform its state enterprises. While acknowledging the importance of Marxism–Leninism and Mao Zedong Thought, the party general secretary confined it to a historical context.

What would move China into the next century? Jiang told the congress, Deng Xiaoping's theory of constructing "socialism with Chinese character-istics." By reaffirming Deng's platform, the conclave provided an ideological basis to develop a market economy according to China's realities, without departing from the historical ideals of the party.

Jiang sought to outline a broad policy framework that would give politically correct sanction to the growth of the country's non-state sector. Blanket approval would be given to the private acquisition of state-owned enterprises either through leasing arrangements, mergers, acquisitions or even auctions.

The Congress adopted a proposal to grant shares in state enterprises directly to their workers through a ticket system. The concept of a coop-erative joint-stock company was introduced. In his address, Jiang repeatedly stressed that China was only at the "primary stage of socialism," which meant that market and welfare mechanisms could be simultaneously applied in the management of the economy.

The 15ᵗʰ Congress approved ideological initiatives as well as policies to push reform forward. The theoretical advances included:

- A recognition that "public ownership" should not be limited to state ownership and that there were important roles for "multi-forms of own-ership" (meaning state-private, state-collective, collective and private) to play in what was now essentially a "mixed economy;"

- Acceptance of the need to develop the broadening "non-state sector"— in effect, the private sector. Such concepts were to be implemented within a framework under these policy guidelines:
  - to "grasp the large," or consolidating big, currently uncompetitive, industrial enterprises, in order to achieve an adequate critical mass and rationalization of production systems;
  - to "release the small," or allowing virtually all enterprises not included in the consolidation process to be transferred to the non-state sector, permitting the private ownership of state enterprises through the purchase of shares, auction sales, takeovers, (employee share options) or listings;
  - to absorb capital from the domestic market, where substantial liquidity had led to unproductive management of privately held funds, through more relaxed policies for the domestic listing of enterprises, and through managed trust funds;
  - to allow the conversion of outstanding enterprise debt into creditor equity under a policy of "loans converted into investment;"
  - to use state-held funds to clear the debts of selected enterprises;
  - to promote "cooperative shareholding enterprises" (yet to be legally defined) and to push the large-scale transformation of state enterprises into "shareholding companies."

Thus emerged the policy of "grasping the large and releasing the small." The state would hold on to big enterprises, injecting capital into them and supporting their growth. In practical terms, some 1,000 state corporations would continue to be held by the government, while the remainder would be released to the private sector.

On the back of this policy, an experiment began with the selection of 100 state-owned enterprises to serve as pilots for the creation of large conglomerates. Another 400 corporations were chosen from the country's various regions. The idea was to merge big state enterprises in key industrial sectors, along the lines of Korea's *chaebols* or Japan's *zaibatsu*. The aim was to create an economy of scale in the selected industries, while small enterprises were to be largely released to the private sector.

Another initiative of the 15th Party Congress called on the State to support the development of other key sectors, namely banking, finance, insurance and pension funds. The moves were necessary to remove certain social burdens from the enterprises and shift them to the financial sector. Such obligations included housing, insurance, medical care, and retirement benefits and pensions for employees of state-owned enterprises.

The financial sector was not only to take over these functions, but also to commercialize them. That would require the development of a mortgage lending system for residential housing and the promotion of adequate insurance and medical care programs. Comprehensive pension schemes would also have to be created.

The 15th Party Congress laid out a framework within which state-enterprise reform would be implemented. The placement of Deng Xiaoping Theory on the same plane as Mao Zedong Thought opened the way for pragmatism to lead the way without rejecting ideology. The decision Jiang announced, to define the "public sector" as encompassing more than the state sector, gave formal sanction to developing the private sector, as well as the concept of private ownership. Open acceptance of the "non-state sector" and the "mixed economy" in effect blessed the private economy while avoiding the ideologically sensitive word "privatization."

FIVE ITEMS OF REFORM

In March 1998, Zhu Rongji assumed the position of State Council Premier, from which he would oversee government affairs and a package of complicated reforms spanning the millennium. Topping Zhu's agenda was the issue of state-owned enterprise reform and invariably, the question of debt restructuring.

When asked by journalists about the depth of this dilemma, Zhu explained, "The foreign media have exaggerated this problem ... there are more than 79,000 state-owned enterprises in China, some of which employ less than a dozen people. Many of these are losing money, so if you look at the total number of enterprises in China, it appears that many are losing money. But you must remember that China has some 500 large-scale enterprises, of which only 10% lose money. Taxation revenues and profits from these account for 85% of the revenues and profits of the whole nation. Of these large enterprises, only 50 are losing money. I am quite confident that we can get rid of the loss-making enterprises in three years."

In order to untangle the conundrum of asset, debt, and social welfare problems entangling China's state-owned enterprises, Zhu announced an incredibly ambitious program described by the 1-3-5 acronym of *Yige Quebao*, *Sange Daowei*, *Wuxiang Gaige*, or "One Guarantee, Three Achievements, Five Items of Reform."

The "One Guarantee" referred to China's need to protect itself from the devastating effects of the Asian financial crisis, then raging at its peak. The One Guarantee actually consisted of three: maintaining high economic growth, low inflation, and a stable currency with no devaluation of the renminbi.

The "Three Achievements" set forth objectives to be pursued by Zhu's administration during its first three years. The first of these targeted achievements was to pull most large and medium-sized state corporations out of the red, and to establish a modern enterprise system. The second goal was to overhaul China's financial system by strengthening the central bank on one hand while allowing the commercial banks to operate independently on

the other. The last aim was to streamline the bloated government bureaucracy by reducing the number of officials by half.

Zhu's "Five items for Reform" included reforming the grain distribution
system, opening new channels for capital circulation, commercializing
housing, introducing a medicare program, and massively overhauling China's
financial and taxation system. These five items of reform basically turned
China's former social welfare system inside out, effectively shattering the
iron rice bowl. Where people once looked to their enterprise or government
unit for housing, medicare, pension and a host of basic "guarantees," including assurances of life-time employment, Zhu's message was clearly that this
system would have to change in order to really modernize China. Individuals would now have to rely on their own savings, and look to the financial
sector for the appropriate financing tools with which to obtain loans for
homes, education, insurance and pensions.

AUCTIONING STATE ASSETS

In 1998, in adopting the policy of "grasping the large and releasing the
small," the municipal government of Shenyang, Liaoning's capital, reportedly sold 192 small state-owned enterprises. The moves attracted much
attention, especially when 21 companies were publicly sold at one go.
Liaoning was gearing up for a major fire sale, putting 600 medium-sized and
small enterprises on the open market.

However, authorities encountered problems. Of the 192 enterprises put
on the market, only a third were actually sold. And some sales procedures
seemed not "entirely proper." Many government departments handled the
sales "according to the old way of thinking," with "irregularities" occurring
everywhere.

One example was the sale of the Shenyang Combustion Equipment
Factory. When the enterprise was put on the auction block, there were bids
of Rmb4 million, Rmb3.1 million and Rmb1 million. Instead of the deal
going to the highest bidder, it went to the party bidding Rmb1 million. The
successful bidder happened to be the factory's deputy director, who made
the offer in his own private capacity.

In July 1998, the State Economy and Trade Commission issued a notice
requiring every local state enterprise undergoing restructuring to "carefully
carry out procedures in accordance with local conditions." Many local
officials reportedly "did not understand" the concept of "grasping the
large and releasing the small." The result: "chaotic situations" that could
"undermine social stability."

The bureaucrats, often interpreting the policy to mean that anything not
obviously large could be sold off took outrageously creative approaches.
Some even adopted the old method of fixing targets for the number of
enterprises to be sold off. Officials would use state authority to force down

the prices of companies to be sold in order to fulfill their own self-imposed quotas. Through "back-door" arrangements, these assets were more often than not sold to friends or relatives, who in turn gave the bureaucrats a cut. Such problems further complicated the process of re-employing laid-off workers, a critical condition that could ignite social unrest.

"MODERN SYSTEM OF ENTERPRISE MANAGEMENT"

The central authorities selected a corps of inspectors to make sure the ambitious program of enterprise consolidation was on track. The trained personnel were sent to more than 500 major industrial corporations to monitor their operations. If the inspection system proved successful, Beijing intended to expand it to some 1,000 enterprises. The inspectors' chief task was to check corruption at regional levels as officials sold off state assets. To protect the system from abuse, no two inspectors were to be sent together and there would be no repeat assignments. The program, a bid by the central government to directly supervise local experimentation in enterprise reform, was said to be the brainchild of Premier Zhu Rongji.

During the National People's Congress in March 1998, Zhu indicated that 100 inspectors would be required. Candidates would be cadres with the rank of vice minister or above. The premier's plan was to have a hundred working groups monitoring large state-owned enterprises as they underwent restructuring. Each team was given specific tasks: to represent the central government, to inspect the assets of state-owned enterprises, to boost the asset base of the corporations, and to discipline cadres managing the enterprises as necessary.

Promotions and dismissals of state-enterprise managers would be based on reports by these working groups. In fact, many of the inspectors were either former vice ministers or ministers laid off during Zhu Rongji's ongoing campaign to streamline the central government. They retained their rank, but instead of heading entire government departments, they led inspection teams of about four persons.

The special inspectors were empowered to monitor the management of the enterprises assigned to them, primarily to ensure that company finances were not tinkered with. But the inspectors themselves were not allowed to become involved in management. Each was in charge of restructuring five enterprises. The mandate was limited to three years, after which another five enterprises would be assigned. Such an arrangement sought to minimize the chances of graft occurring should inspectors grow close to enterprise managers under their supervision.

At a special training seminar in Beijing, Zhu Rongji told the inspectors: "Within three years, the state-owned enterprises that are losing money must be turned around. We must create a modern system of enterprise management." The premier underscored his determination by adding: "This time, the methods of the state enterprises must change, and the way we manage the managers of these enterprises must undergo fundamental changes. That would bring us into line with international practice."

SHEDDING DEBT

Despite Premier Zhu's tall order, the bad debt from state-owned enterprises has remained the single most acute problem for China's banking system. The legal crystallization of enterprise bankruptcy, in fact, opened a Pandora's box of clever avoidance schemes. Creative enterprise bosses, especially those wrapped in protective networks of *guanxi*, local personal relationship in provinces, have adopted strategies such as the following.

Tuoke jingying ("shedding-the-shell operations"), which amounts to the legal separation of an enterprise from its overseeing government department. The government department in turn creates a new enterprise by transferring over its good assets and leaving the creditor bank with an empty shell when it tries to collect from the old enterprise.

Wuchang huabo ("transferring assets without compensation"), which involves a local government-owned enterprise declaring bankruptcy while its assets are appropriated and transferred to another enterprise being set up by the local authorities, leaving the creditor bank with nothing.

Sizi qingzhang ("privately clearing the debts"), which involves the enterprise management secretly distributing all enterprise assets to private interests (friends and relatives) before declaring the enterprise bankrupt and leaving the creditor bank in the lurch.

The question of solving the debt conundrum between state-owned enterprises and state-owned banks continues to top the agenda of issues to be addressed as China enters the new century.

On a positive note, State Economic and Trade Commission Minister Sheng Huaren announced during a recent news conference that "state enterprise shedding of debts should be realized within the three-year schedule." In fact, in 1997 there were 6,600 loss-making large industrial enterprises. Now there are only 3,100. This could be interpreted as major progress in solving the problem. In fact, the past three years have witnessed a national program of enterprise mergers involving loss-making enterprises either being conglomerated or being taken over and carried by those profitable ones.

True, at the outset of the new century, a majority of state-owned enterprises in 12 industrial sectors reported profits or at least a cessation of losses. In the first four months of 2000, state-owned enterprise profits surged by 3.5 times, reaching Rmb44 billion. Conversions have taken place; but a host of problems have yet to be solved.

In the first chapter of this section, Minister Sheng Huaren of the State Economy and Trade Commission, discusses China's overall industrial and commercial reforms within the context of the comprehensive state-owned enterprise reforms that are currently underway, and which have become a pillar of the China's total package of reform measures. In the second chapter, Dr. Heinrich v Pierer, chairman of the managing board, president and CEO of Siemens AG, examines the challenges and applications which China will be adopting in the critical sectors of electronics, communications, transportation and energy in the century ahead. Don H. Davis, chairman and chief executive officer of Rockwell International Corporation, discusses the importance of automation as a critical component in China's industrial growth and economic development in the third chapter. In the fourth chapter, Dr. Charles W. Pryor, Jr., president and chief executive officer of Westinghouse Electric Company, examines the role that nuclear power will play in providing a green source of energy in fueling China's growth into the new century. In the final chapter, Dr. Manfred Schneider, chairman of the managing board of Bayer AG, examines the key sectors of fine chemicals, agri-chemicals, health care and polymers in discussing the importance of the chemical industry in China's overall industrial development.

SHENG HUAREN

Sheng Huaren is minister of the State Economy and Trade Commission, China's key macro-economy and industrial policy-coordinating organ. Prior to assuming this key position in 1998, Sheng served as CEO of SINOPEC, China's enormous state petrochemical firm. As this sector is targeted as a spearhead for reforms, it is appropriate for Sheng to assume the reigns of this key government organ.

Under the auspices of the State Economy and Trade Commission fall the key industrial sectors of coal, machinery, metallurgy, ferrous and non-ferrous metals, domestic trade, light industry, textiles, petrochemicals, chemicals, tobacco, construction materials, and power generation. The body is also empowered to supervise trade policy and technological reformation of key industries. Paramount on the agenda of the State Economy and Trade Commission is the reform of China's state-owned enterprises.

In the following chapter, Minister Sheng outlines in detail the steps undertaken and the complicated challenges faced in China's ambitious industrial reform program for turning around loss-making state-owned enterprises.

STRIVING TO REALIZE THE THREE-YEAR TARGET OF STATE-OWNED ENTERPRISE REFORM AND SEPARATION OF LOSSES

Sheng Huaren
Minister, State Economy and Trade Commission

PROGRESS IN SOE REFORM AND SEPARATION OF LOSSES

The First Plenary Session of the 15th Congress of the Communist Party of China proposed that China will take around three years to pull most of its loss-making, large and medium-scale state-owned enterprises (SOEs) out of plight. The objective of this struggle is to strive towards establishing an initial modern enterprise system for most of the key large and medium-scale, state-owned enterprises by the end of this century. The proposition being put forward to revive the SOEs reflects the resolute determination and extraordinary courage and resourcefulness of the Central Committee of the Party. It also plays an extremely important function in mobilizing the Party and the country to push forward state-owned enterprise reform and development.

The Fourth Session of the 15th Congress of the Communist Party of China made decisions on certain major issues regarding reform and development of state-owned enterprises. It emphasized that China will try its best to realize this target and carry out overall arrangements for reform and development of state-owned enterprises spanning the millenium. China adopted a series of powerful policies and measures in this regard.

Under the leadership of the Central Committee of the Party and the State Council, the different levels of government, various departments and large-scale enterprises will rise with force and spirit. They will take the lead in facing many of the difficulties, striving to develop and work solidly in order to greatly improve the operations of the state-owned enterprises

175

and play a key function in the emergence of a turn for the better in the national economy.

At the earlier stage of proposing a three-year target for state-owned enterprise reform and separation of losses, China experienced a series of tough tests, being hit by both the Asian financial crisis and catastrophic domestic floods. The efficient demands of society were inadequate, and the economic efficiency and profits of the enterprises were slashed by large margins that imposed various difficulties for the realization of the three-year target.

In 1998, the profits for the state-owned and state-controlled industries reached Rmb52.5 billion, decreasing 34.9% in comparison with that of 1997. The Party Central Committee and State Council abruptly adopted a series of tough measures to address this. After making diligent efforts to push through these difficulties, 1999 became the turning point in connection with state-owned enterprise reform and separation of losses. The profits of the state-owned and state-controlled industries reached Rmb96.7 billion, increasing 84.2% in comparison with that of 1998. It marked the best achievement yet for the past five years. In the first half of the year, the state-owned enterprise reforms and efforts to turn around losses continued to maintain positive momentum and development. The state-owned and state-controlled industries realized profits of Rmb90.3 billion, increasing about 2.06 times compared with the same period for the previous year. The increased margin of economic efficiency and profitability exceeded any of the last few years.

As was obvious, increased economic efficiency and profitability for most regions were becoming apparent. In comparison with the same period last year, state-owned and state-controlled industrial enterprises throughout the 31 provinces, autonomous regions and the cities directly under the administration of the central government, demonstrated profits. Thirteen regions had an increase in profitability. Ten regions transferred their losses to profits. Among the six regions that suffered overall losses, five regions have reduced their net losses. As major regions are shedding their losses within the targeted three years, all three northeast provinces have increased profits by a large margin. Our forecasts have shown that by the end of this year, except for autonomous regions, most of the regions are expected to continue to increase profitability or turn losses into profits.

The economic efficiency and profitability of key industries are continuing to take a turn for the better. In comparison with the same period of last year, among the fourteen key industries, the profits for the industries of metallurgy, petrochemicals, machinery, electronics, light industry, textiles, pharmaceuticals, tobacco, and gold have increased. The electric power industry continues to maintain a relatively high profitability level. Ninety-three major large and medium-size enterprises in the metallurgy industry have realized profits of Rmb5.43 billion, increasing 3.5 times. The petrochemical industry has realized profits of 39.43 billion yuan, increasing 2.7 times. A turning point in the three-year reform and shedding of losses has occurred for the textile industry, which realized profits of Rmb2.41 billion based on the elimination of losses one year in advance. The amount of reduced losses and increased profits reached Rmb3.66 billion compared with the same period of last year. The nonferrous metals and construction industries have also turned losses into profits. The coal and military industries have reduced their losses.

The large and medium-sized enterprises have achieved new progress in eliminating their losses. When the Central Committee of the Communist Party proposed this three-year target in 1997, the loss-making large and medium-sized state-owned and state-controlled enterprises reached 6,599. By the end of June 2000, the loss-making enterprises had been reduced to 3,626, reducing by 54.9% the number of loss-making enterprises. Gratefully, the operating situation of state-owned small sized enterprises, which had consecutively suffered from overall losses, has improved. In the first half of 2000, the amount of losses has been reduced to Rmb2.18 billion, decreasing their losses of Rmb4.11 billion compared with the same period of last year. If work proceeds well, the losses may be eliminated and turned into profits within this year.

There are several reasons why such incredible achievements have been made in terms of state-owned enterprise reforms and development. First, the policies and measures adopted by the central government are proper and forceful. The Fourth Session of the 15th Congress of the Communist Party of China clarified that in order to expand domestic demand and boost economic growth, the Central Committee of the Communist Party and State Council will implement an active financial policy for three consecutive years. This has created a positive macro-economic environment for state-owned enterprise reform and the shedding of losses.

The policies and measures issued by the central government are aimed at improving state-owned enterprises—especially those policies for enhancing mergers, for bankruptcy, for transferring debt to equity share rights, and for deducting interest for loans granted to technical reformation. Such policies will directly promote the elimination of losses, pulling the enterprises out of their plight and improving their economic efficiency and profitability.

Second, all the regions and departments have diligently and efficiently performed the necessary work in accomplishing this goal. The provinces, autonomous regions and cities directly under the administration of the central government all put the target of realizing these tasks within three years on the top of their agenda. The main leaders all personally bear the responsibility to adopt various measures to carry out comprehensive treatment. Meanwhile, the clear-cut responsibility system has also been established, that is, the tasks and responsibilities of government departments

have now been more clearly defined and specified. The different departments concerned have supported each other in completing many tasks.

In addition, as a main part of undertaking the task of reform and shedding of losses within three years, enterprises have generally intensified their
reforms and administration. Facing tough market competition, enterprises
have generally focused on transferring their methods of operating and deepening internal reform. The enterprises have made diligent efforts to separate their losses as quickly as possible, and to enhance their competitiveness
through laying off and dispersing workers, and increasing the efficiency
of administration.

The economic efficiency and interests of state-owned enterprises have
been greatly enhanced, which further reinforces our confidence of realizing
the target of completing the reform and separation of losses within three
years. The practice proves that the objective of completing reforms and
shedding of losses within three years proposed in the First Session of the
15th Party Congress has greatly encouraged the fighting will of all of the
Party, the nation and people. It has mobilized the energy of the people in
various respects. Consistent with this target, the people throughout the
country have unified their will and are striving jointly to surmount numerous difficulties. All of this has resulted in today's positive situation in
connection with the state-owned enterprise reform and development.

REALIZING REFORM AND SHEDDING LOSSES WITHIN THREE YEARS

The objective of realizing reform and shedding of losses within three years
has bright prospects and is full of hope. The achievements of the past two
years have laid the foundation for realizing the three-year target. The international economic situation is improving. The domestic economy is developing further in the direction of the fine circle, which provides a positive
outside environment for further improvement of the operating situation for
the enterprises.

In the last few years, the State has issued certain major policies and
measures to activate state-owned enterprises. Those policies and measures,
especially the ones in connection with mergers, bankruptcy, transferring the
debts into equity share rights, subsidies in the form of technical reformation
policy loans and the construction of a social protection system among
others, will further demonstrate their efficiency and results.

We should also be aware that we are still facing many difficulties in
reaching our objectives of realizing state-owned enterprise reform and shedding losses within three years. To turn around enterprise efficiency and
profits to a great extent relies on the assistance of the state policies in
addition to the efforts made by the enterprises themselves. It is also inseparable from the revitalization of the international economic environment.

At present, the operating mechanism of the enterprises has not been completely transferred. The capacities of self-development are generally in a state of relative weakness. The basis for those enterprises to shed their losses is still not strong. Most of the enterprises that have gotten out of their plight maintain a low level of profitability. The internal management of those enterprises is still not strong and they have little ability to cope with emergency situations. During the past two years, those enterprises that can most easily shed their losses have already done so. Most of the enterprises that have not shed their losses have abundant labor and heavy debt burdens. The technology and equipment of those enterprises are out-dated and aging. They have to make more arduous efforts to get out of this plight. Due to inadequacies of the as yet evolving market system and the imperfection of the social welfare protection system, a set of enterprises that should exit the market cannot exit the market in time. All the above increases their hardship in realizing the objective of completing reform and shedding of losses within three years.

We must also be aware that state-owned enterprises completing their reform and sheding losses is only one stage of achievement. There are also many contradictions and problems in terms of establishing a truly modern enterprise system for operating well the state-owned enterprises in their entirety. The problems can be found deep in the layers of the organizations, for example, inflexible mechanisms, overstaffing, and overburdening debt, all of which have existed for a long time but have not been fundamentally resolved. These enterprises' creative ability, competitive capacity and the ability to withstand risks are relatively weak. They lack mechanisms of protection and technical assistance in ascending the way of a fine circle. Worldwide economic structural adjustment and scientific and technical progress are speeding up. Especially upon entering WTO, the enterprises of our country will face much tougher international competition.

All these matters require that we be modest and prudent and maintain clear minds in facing the achievements we have made. We shall absolutely not be blindly optimistic and treat it lightly. We must not slack off, rather we must fully recognize the long-term nature, arduousness and complications of reactivating the state-owned enterprises. We shall certainly continue to work hard and pay close attention to the specific tasks and ensure the realization of the objective of completing this reform and shedding of losses within three years.

COMPLETING REFORM AND SHEDDING LOSSES WITHIN THREE YEARS

The Central Committee of the Party has clarified its guidance and policy regarding state-owned enterprise reform and shedding of losses. The major policies and measures have been issued. At present the key challenge is to assure that the policies which have been set by the Party Central Committee are implemented and appropriate arrangements made at each level of government. We must insist on unification between speed and efficiency, between scale and structure and between quantity and quality. We must give priority to improving quality and enhancing efficiency. We must follow market guidance and actively push forward adjustments and control total volume. We shall resolutely eliminate, through selection, the productive capacities, overcapacity, and prevent against duplicated construction.

We should combine the current program, realizing the long-term objectives of state-owned enterprise reform and development, with an emphasis on enterprise mechanisms, while improving technology applications. The achievement of completion of the reform and shedding of losses shall be better embodied in the enhancement of efficiency, transfer of mechanisms and incremental competitiveness. We will maintain the momentum which has been gained through these reforms, while further advancing reforms which have now been put into play in the interest of developing these enterprises undergoing reform.

At present, we must focus on the following tasks:

1. Intensifying Mergers and Bankruptcies, and Perfecting the Exiting Mechanism of the State-Owned Enterprises

Based on the premise of guaranteeing social stability, we shall further intensify closures and bankruptcies. Viewing structural adjustment from a strategic vantage, we should concentrate our forces and focus on this crucial point. Currently, we shall pay close attention to solving the problems of closing down and bankrupting enterprises that need to exit the market in major industries, including in the coal, nonferrous metals, metallurgy, sugar manufacture, wool spinning, silk and military industries.

Through the means of closing down and bankrupting a set of enterprises with no hope of getting out of their loss-making plight, such as in the case of mining enterprises, the resources of which are exhausted, we shall strive to eliminate more loss-makers. Taking the whole situation of reform, development and stability into account, we should undertake the tasks of allocating and re-employing the workers of bankrupted enterprises and speeding up the establishment of a social protection system that is independent from the enterprises. We should also actively seek to set up an efficient road map with which some of the state-owned enterprises can exit the market. By doing so, we can reach a situation in which the enterprises have room to develop and have a door to exit the market. The resources thereby can be concentrated in the industries and enterprises with advantages. The competitive mechanism of survival of the fittest has been formed.

2. Speeding Up Implementation of Transferring Debt to Equity Rights and Implementing Various Reform Measures

Most of the enterprises that were advised to undertake the transfer from debt to equity last year have signed agreements for transferring their debt to equity shares held by financial asset management corporations. We must stress the organization and implementation of those plans of transferring enterprise debt to equity shares and intensify supervision. In this manner, we can really reach the objective of both helping the enterprises to get out of their plight and avoid and solve financial risks, both of which are of mutual benefit to the banks and enterprises. We should combine our efforts of transferring debt to equity shares, deepening enterprise reform, intensifying management and structural adjustment, with the aim of promoting the enterprises to expedite setting up a modern enterprise system, and realizing and optimizing the structure to upgrade industry.

3. Speeding Up Enterprise Technical Reformation and Enhancing Technical Creation

As for technical reformation projects, we should implement reform plans and quicken the pace of examination and approval, as well as ensure that the capital funds of enterprises, bank loans and discounted financial charges on capital are appropriated on time. In addition, we must intensify supervision and management to reach the symbolic objective of timely technical reform.

Technical reform must focus on assortment, quality, efficiency, profitability and expansion of exports. Adopting new high technology and advanced and applicable technology, we should reform a set of key enterprises, form superior products and specifically prevent duplicate construction. We shall also quicken the pace of constructing new technical creative systems with the enterprises as the main bodies, give full play to technical development as central to enhancing the self-creative capacities of established enterprises. In addition, we shall also further push forward various combinations of production, learning and research to speed up the transfer from scientific and technical achievements to actual productive forces. In the meantime, we shall promote the industrialization of new high technology and strive to realize a leap in China's development of industrial technology.

4. Continually Implement the Policy of "Grasping the Big and Releasing the Small," and Actively Push Forward the Strategic Reorganization of Enterprises

We shall meet the requirements of economic globalization in entering WTO. We shall further optimize and reorganize large-scale enterprises and enterprise groups, which were organized in the last few years, raise their core competitiveness and make them real pillars of our national economy with enhanced strength to participate in international competition.

We shall also implement the opening strategy of "walking out" and encourage the industries that possess superior competitiveness domestically and relatively large production power to move to developing countries and set up trade and resource development bases overseas. In addition, we shall continue to adopt various forms to further release and activate the state-owned small-sized enterprises. In the meantime, we shall stress the construction of a socialized welfare service system for the medium and small-size enterprises. Measures will be adopted to solve the difficulties of medium and small-size enterprises raising funds. We shall push forward the enterprises to unite and reorganize them in accordance with the specialized division of tasks and cooperative principles and form an organic association and cooperative development pattern among the large, medium and small-size enterprises.

5. Managing Enterprises by Intensifying and Improving Overall Enterprise Management

We shall implement the spirit of instruction of the Central Committee of the Party and the State Council regarding the intensification of management. Directing against the weak links in the management of the enterprise, we shall stress the management of costs, capital, quality and security production. We shall learn from the Han Steel Factory and Ya Xin examples, and push enterprises further toward facing the market. The enterprises shall intensify and improve overall management operations, reduce expenditures and enhance competitive capacity. The enterprises shall also improve safety during production and resolutely eliminate the occurrence of especially large accidents. Based on collective experience, we shall establish sound large-scale enterprises and enterprise groups with management systems that adapt to the market economy and are in line with the characteristics of China.

6. Actively Pushing Forward the Construction of a Modern Enterprise System and Specifically Transferring Enterprise Operating Mechanisms

In accordance with the basic requirement that large and medium-size, key, state-owned enterprises shall initially establish a modern enterprise system, we shall severely further regulate and perfect the enterprises that have completed the reform to a corporate system. These enterprises shall establish a sound, legal person management structure, and deepen the internal three-system reform covering labor, personnel and distribution within the enterprises. They shall also transfer the operating mechanism of the enterprise and separate the functions of the enterprise to deal with social affairs. We shall widen the channel of fund-raising of the enterprises and realize the multiplication of investment bodies. We shall also actively pay close attention to the task of listing the enterprises, especially the listing of large-scale enterprises and enterprise groups in the areas of petroleum, petroleum-chemistry, telecom, metallurgy and aluminum industry among others.

We will continue to place stress on coordination and control of the total volume in accordance with market demands. We will comprehensively utilize all kinds of measures with the three industries including coal, steel and iron and sugar manufacturing as the major focus, and give full play to the function of the market mechanism. We will resolutely eliminate backward productive capacities, condense production of long-term products and optimize the structure of these products. We will also continue to develop and regulate the market, deepen circulation system reform, quicken the construction of the market system and provide a market environment of fair competition to the enterprises.

The year 2001 will be decisive in our battle to realize our objective of enterprise reform. Under the leadership of the Central Committee of the Party, with comrade Jiang Zemin at the core, we must seriously implement the important ideology of "Three Representations" and further implement the spirit of the First and Fourth Sessions of the 15th Party Congress. We will strive for decisive victory in completing reform within three years, thereby laying the solid foundation for cross-century reforms and the development of state-owned enterprises.

DR. HEINRICH VON PIERER

Dr. Heinrich von Pierer, chairman of the managing board, president and CEO of Siemens AG, was born on January 26, 1941 in Erlangen, Germany. He graduated with a master's degree in economics and a doctor's degree in law. In 1969, Dr. von Pierer joined Siemens' legal department of corporate finance. Between 1977 and 1987, Dr. von Pierer held a number of positions in the sales and marketing departments of Siemens' Power Generation Group and in several corporate departments. In 1988, he was appointed commercial head of the Siemens Power Generation Group. One year later, he was appointed member of the Siemens AG managing board and group president. Dr. von Pierer has been the chairman of the managing board, president and CEO of Siemens AG since 1992.

Over the last decade, China has developed into a major pillar for Siemens business in the Asia–Pacific region. By the end of September 1999, Siemens' total investment (Siemens AG; Siemens Ltd., China; subsidiaries and BOT projects) reached DM1.1 billion. Siemens has 52 operating companies (42 joint ventures, 8 wholly-owned subsidiaries and 2 BOT projects) and 28 regional offices in the country, which provide employment for over 21,000 local people. The key targets of Siemens' business in China include expanding technology transfer, increasing local R&D activities and financing. Siemens will continue to establish and develop local partnerships, cooperation and local competencies to ensure sustainable long-term growth in China.

In the following piece, Dr. von Pierer draws upon the collective sector experience of Siemens in discussing the challenges that China faces in the areas of electrical supply, information, communications and transportation in the new century.

Progress from Tradition — China Moves into the 21ST Century

Dr. Heinrich von Pierer
President and Chief Executive Officer, Siemens AG

China's Transformed Image

The great Roman philosopher Seneca once said, "The greater part of progress is the *desire* to progress." The will and the power to change made China great in the past and also distinguish the country at the threshold of the 21st century. A leaner government bureaucracy, the fight against corruption, the accelerated opening to the West, and the encouragement of the growing private economy are only a few examples of the new directions being taken by the country. Economic and social changes have fundamentally transformed China's image.

In view of its size, enormous population and economic power, China plays a special role in the world economy. It already enjoys a solid ranking among the world's leading industrial countries and will continue to build up its position in the coming years. China's upcoming membership in the WTO will substantially accelerate this process.

A number of facts spotlight China's enormous potential. From 1996 to 1999, the country's economy grew an average of eight percent a year, an impressive figure in international comparison. Over half of all direct foreign investments made in Asia in 1998 flowed into the People's Republic of China. And measured on its economic performance, China is now one of the world's leaders. It is only a question of time before China becomes the world's largest economy. Whether that will occur in 2015 or in 2025 is irrelevant. What matters is the trend.

China impressively demonstrated its economic stability during the recent Asian crisis. While many other countries in the region were thrown into major difficulties by the turbulence, China was far less affected. Previous structural changes in the country's economy were in large part responsible for the country's robust health throughout this difficult period. China's responsible fiscal and currency policies also helped ensure that the domestic economic boom was stabilized and sustained. Interest rates were reduced seven times since 1996. This has been a positive incentive for foreign investors and a clear signal in favor of private consumption.

Obviously, important steps have already been taken. The future of China and its people now depends to a great degree on the further development of its infrastructure. One should differentiate two different aspects of this theme:

- First, the question is how quickly the country will succeed in building a solid nationwide infrastructure that extends beyond the urban and industrial centers. This will be the key factor determining the growth rate of the country's overall economy.
- Second, the question is how the country will meet the challenges of providing adequate infrastructure for its rapidly growing cities. The key task here is to offer people work, living space, and good living standards.

China's nationwide infrastructure is the key that will determine the speed of the country's economic development. Ultimately, the well-being of all its people depends on the quality and functionality of the infrastructure. Three infrastructure segments are particularly important:

- Energy supply
- Good transportation systems and intelligent traffic concepts to ensure the mobility of people and goods
- A modern information and communications infrastructure for voice and data transmissions.

SECURING ADEQUATE ENERGY SUPPLY

Securing an adequate energy supply for its growing population and rapidly expanding industry is one of China's biggest tasks. In doing so, it isn't enough merely to build new power plants and transport power to end-users. In view of growing environmental awareness, the country needs an efficient and environmentally compatible supply of electricity and heat. One solution is to boost the efficiency of existing power plants with the help of innovative technology and to utilize the energy-saving potential offered by coupling the generation of electricity and heat.

State-of-the-art technology, for example, allows the efficiency of coal-fired power plants to be increased to 45% from today's average 32% level. By using gas-fired combined-cycle power plant, generating efficiency can be raised to nearly 60% while significantly reducing emissions. Advanced power plant technology, then, not only sharply cuts generation costs, but also helps protect the environment. Future-oriented power generation also means increasing the use of energy sources that do not produce carbon dioxide. These sources include renewable energy, such as hydropower and solar energy, and naturally, nuclear energy as well.

Efficient energy supplies also require the optimization of transmission and distribution networks. The great distances that have to be covered in China need low-loss transmission technology and intelligent power grid management. Energy-saving, high-voltage direct current (HVDC) lines and superconducting cables help minimize energy losses. Two examples of this modern technology are the Siemens-built HVDC line that has transported electricity from China's largest hydro-electric plant in Gezhouba one thousand kilometers to Shanghai since 1990, and the Tian–Guang line that links two hydropower plants with the Guangzhou region and began operation this year.

COMMUNICATIONS

Economic growth and a high standard of living will require overcoming often enormous distances, regardless of whether it involves people or goods. Whether by plane, train or by car—mobility is the symbol of modern industrial nations. And this trend can also be clearly seen in China. The development of the country's transportation infrastructure, in particular its rail network, will be a decisive factor in determining how fast China drives its economic growth and spreads it to all regions. Reliability, speed and feasible costs are the most critical factors here. Siemens offers solutions ranging from future-oriented high speed rail systems like the ICE to complete electrification, signaling and safety solutions for rail lines.

Modern societies and their economies also depend heavily on communications and data transmission systems. A high-performance information and communications infrastructure tailored to China's needs is the nerve system that links every part of the country. In many areas of daily life, the use of wired phones, cell phones and the Internet play a major role. A high-capacity information and communications system has become absolutely essential for the country.

Today's digital switching systems, high-speed fiber-optic transmission systems and mobile phones enable immense volumes of data to be transported everywhere, virtually instantly. And the high public acceptance of mobile communications in China not only improves the mobility and life quality of individuals: the technical know-how and ability to apply it also opens up enormous opportunities for China's economy to participate in the booming global market for telecommunications and information.

URBAN INFORMATION REVOLUTION

The second major field that will help decide China's future is urbanization. Worldwide, this is perhaps the greatest challenge of the 21st century. Right now, roughly half of the earth's population lives in cities. According to the United Nations, by 2025, two-thirds of the population will be clustered in urban centers. The number of megacities with over 10 million inhabitants will climb to 26 by 2015, from 17 at present. In China, Shanghai and Beijing already number among the world's megacities. Hangzhou and Tianjin will soon join this category. The consequences of this urban development will have a major impact on China.

"Sustainable development" was the theme of the 1992 Environmental Summit in Rio de Janeiro. And it could also provide a key answer as to how China's cities will develop in the future. It is not enough to meet the basic needs of people in cities and ensure adequate supplies or waste disposal. Cities have to be transformed, and not only because of their growing populations. In China's dynamically growing cities, powerful data and communication networks, intelligent transportation infrastructures, and efficient and decentralized energy supplies are the key factors determining urban development at the threshold of the third millennium. Holistic solutions have to be found for the complex questions and challenges posed by urbanization. This can be achieved only if all participants—urban planners, administrators, infrastructure experts and the industry—work hand in hand.

"Information for everyone, everywhere, at any time" is the best way to describe the steadily growing demand for communication in urban centers. In addition to traditional wired telephone networks, mobile networks are highly viable communication solutions and offer enormous advantages in urban areas. Streets don't have to be torn up, cable ducts needn't be laid, homes and businesses don't require wiring. Public life and traffic isn't disturbed, and the costs for setting up a communications system are kept low.

The incredible pace of the mobile revolution can best be seen in Hong Kong, where every second resident now uses a cell phone. Experts predict that within three years at the latest, there will be more cell phone subscribers than wired network users.

Special solutions are required for the administration's great variety of information and communication needs. In the planning and operation of highways, power supplies and urban railway systems, for instance, constant data exchanges and complex transactions must be made among various city departments and agencies. For example, the Land Management Information System Shanghai—installed by Siemens and its partners—manages the enormous amount of data compiled and used by Shanghai's land surveying office. This office maintains the city's official inventory of property, including its users and all associated maps.

TRANSPORTATION ON COMMUNICATIONS

Urban mobility also requires high-capacity passenger rail systems—metros, light rail systems and elevated trains. Millions of people use these systems daily to get to work. In Shanghai alone, two to three million people depend on reliable transportation.

This is just one facet of urban transportation. In megacities worldwide, mobility is often a synonym for countless cars filling the streets, for noise, and for polluted air. Inner-city traffic often is near a complete collapse. OECD countries currently spend some €450 million a year as a consequence of urban traffic accidents. In Hong Kong, traffic jams cause the loss of some €300 million in work time every year. And in Bangkok, the average speed for cars has dropped to only two kilometers per hour. Statistically seen, every resident of the city stands 44 hours a year in traffic. And it is feared that the situation will continue to worsen. The number of vehicles worldwide will keep growing from year to year. In China alone, around 80 million people plan to buy a new car by 2010. The consequences for people, the environment and the economy are threatening.

The only way to prevent total urban gridlock is to optimize the networking of existing urban transportation systems and traffic. Cars, trains, ships and planes have to be linked and coordinated electronically with intelligent guidance systems. Combined sensor, data and communication technologies—called telematics—can effectively monitor traffic in urban zones and keep it flowing. Navigation systems in cars, for example, help drivers find their way around unfamiliar areas and avoid unnecessary travel. Traffic management systems can also help coordinate private and public transportation. The schedules of buses, light rail systems and metros can be linked to traffic control and systems and public garage guidance systems to eliminate delays and jams.

Yet even the most advanced communications networks and most intelligent traffic management systems can't function without electricity. A major challenge for the urban environment is to provide efficient, decentralized power supplies. This means generating electricity where it is needed. This is particularly practical when power and heat are generated simultaneously and distributed. Shorter transmission distances, from the point of generation to end-users, also help reduce power losses and costs. Such decentralized energy concepts are particularly well suited for supplying high-rises, factories or entire city neighborhoods.

China's future has already begun, as can be seen by the positive developments in many areas of the economy, government and society. Above all, China's strength is its combination of tradition, an excellent sense for business, and an optimistic view of its future role within the global community. The 21st century may well go down in China's history as a century of remarkable renaissance. The signs for this are favorable.

DON H. DAVIS

Don H. Davis became chairman and chief executive officer of Rockwell International Corporation, a global electronic controls and communications company, in 1998. Davis, who joined Allen-Bradley in 1963 (acquired by Rockwell in 1985) as an engineering sales trainee, has held a series of key corporate and business unit executive positions culminating with being named Rockwell's president and chief executive officer in 1997. Prior to being named CEO, Davis had been president and chief operating officer since 1995. He also served as executive vice president and chief operating officer with responsibility for Rockwell's automation and former semiconductor systems and automotive components businesses. In addition to the Rockwell board and others, Davis is a member of the Business Council, the Business Roundtable, The Conference Board and is past chairman of the Board of Governors of the National Electrical Manufacturers Association, Washington, DC.

Rockwell International is a world leader in electronic controls and communication technologies and systems, with global leadership positions in the industrial automation, aviation electronics and electronic commerce markets. Rockwell has two primary businesses—Rockwell Automation (industrial automation) and Rockwell Collins (avionics and communications). Other businesses include Rockwell Electronic Commerce and the Rockwell Science Center. Rockwell, with its world headquarters in Milwaukee, Wisconsin, is a US$7 billion company with more than 40,000 employees at over 450 facilities in 40 countries, serving customers in more than 80 countries. Premier product brands include Rockwell, Collins, Allen-Bradley, Reliance Electric, Dodge, and Rockwell Software.

Rockwell Automation was established in China in 1986 and currently has approximately 240 employees in 11 facilities in nine cities with an annual turnover of approximately US$50 million. Major industries served include: metals, water, electric power, consumer products, paper and transportation.

In the following chapter, Mr. Davis will discuss the important role that advanced industrial automation technology will play in driving sustained development growth in China's future.

INDUSTRIAL AUTOMATION AND CHINA'S FUTURE DEVELOPMENT

Don H. Davis

Chairman & Chief Executive Officer, Rockwell International

CRITICAL TECHNOLOGY FOR DEVELOPMENT

China is in the midst of a developmental stage where advanced management knowledge and techniques and advanced industrial automation technology and solutions are fundamental and necessary elements for China's sustained growth and global competitiveness.

Industrial automation is a critical technology for developing countries such as China that hope to ensure domestic economic growth and the ability to compete in the global market place. While there are many steps that China must take to ensure the appropriate development of its industrial base and supporting infrastructure, the utilization of advanced industrial automation is a critical step. Increases in productivity and efficiency are not possible without a high level of industrial automation.

If we were to look at the growth in productivity of U.S. industry from the mid-1980s to the mid-1990s, two pivotal factors stand out. The first is a revolution in management techniques and consequent restructuring of the American corporation. Management became results-focused, flatter and more distributed, with great participation by the work force. The second pivotal factor was the infusion of advanced industrial automation into manufacturing and other automated processes. Together these two elements led to significant increases in productivity and efficiency. These increases led the way to sustained growth in the U.S. economy, so that by the late 1980s and early 1990s the U.S. economy was growing faster than that of Japan for the first time in several decades. China, which is now at its own critical industrial and management systems crossroads, can borrow from some of these experiences.

China has an unparalleled opportunity to adopt advanced industrial automation as this technology moves into the new millennium and into the information era. The future of industrial automation will be a networked future with a great reliance on wireless connectivity. Utilization of effective and open networks such as DeviceNet, ControlNet and Ethernet/IP, with their ability to connect to the Internet, allow for continuous control and feedback from the factory floor to the management office and beyond. The factory floor and the management office can be linked continuously and in real time with suppliers, sales force and customers. Every part of this chain will be able to monitor, input to and adjust the manufacturing process and supporting activities.

The future of industrial automation will also very much be linked to software that is an open platform and that is multifunctional. The right software package provides tremendous flexibility and agility in the manufacturing process. Industrial software provides the operator interface and gateway from the factory floor to the Enterprise Resource Planning (ERP) system and even to the Internet to provide a seamless flow of data and information so that the "Information Enabled Enterprise" can be managed in a more flexible, integrated, and efficient manner.

WHAT IS INDUSTRIAL AUTOMATION?

In order to understand how industrial automation will play a critical role in the future of China's industrial restructuring and infrastructure development, one must understand the various fields and complex applications that lay behind the concept of industrial automation.

There is no one good definition of what industrial automation is or what it does. Perhaps the best definition is a simple one—industrial automation is the use of electronics to control and monitor a process or machinery. In a practical sense, industrial automation makes machines run together at a controlled rate of speed, time duration and motion. Industrial automation allows processes to operate at higher efficiency, to produce higher quality products of standard consistency in shorter time with less interruptions of the process. Consistency in quality and improving efficiency are critical issues that China's domestic industry needs to overcome.

Industrial automation has changed significantly from a mechanical control process, to an analog electronic control, to a digital networked process that is highly reliant on open software systems. Industrial automation is constantly changing to take advantage of the latest technology developments. The introduction of new technology in computing power, networking, software, and communications has enabled automation to continuously in improve manufacturing or process flexibility and agility. Flexibility refers to the capability to manufacture to customer specifications and manufacture just in time. Agility in manufacturing means the ability to switch from one product line to another or producing a mix of products on the same line with minimal capital expenditures and time delays.

ADVANCED AUTOMATION SYSTEMS

All contemporary automations systems include three competencies: intelligent control, communication networks and visualization. The intelligent control portion of the system functions as the "brain" for the machine or process it controls—linking input from the machine/process (push buttons, proximity sensors, flow meters, limit switches, temperature switches, safety switches); to the logic performed by programmable logic controllers; to actuators and output devices (motor starters, variable speed drives, control valves, solenoids). With contemporary open architecture automation systems, programmable logic controllers (PLCs) can be deployed as software-based controllers on personal computer platforms or as dedicated, environmentally hardened platforms.

Communication networks in the factory are deployed at multiple levels of functionality. Device networks link sensors and actuators located around the machine or process equipment to the controllers. Mid-level networks pass control data between machine/process controllers within precise time frames to ensure deterministic communication. Ethernet has become the information backbone in the factory just as it has in the office. Factory floor Ethernet adds a level of ruggedness to the physical media as well as to the communication protocols that run on the network to ensure interoperability to the automation networks.

Visualization software is required in advanced automation systems to keep operators informed of machine/process status; to keep maintenance personnel informed of faults if repair is necessary; and to keep production supervisors informed of output. Operator interfaces can be in the form of low cost, machine-mounted information appliances, hardened personal computer-based displays, or monitors in a centralized control room. Supervisory software is also deployed at this level to coordinate entire process areas and share manufacturing information with business systems higher up the information chain.

These three competencies; logic, networks, and visualization, allow modern advanced automation systems to integrate control and information from "the shop floor to the top floor" of a manufacturing enterprise.

WHAT CAN INDUSTRIAL AUTOMATION DO FOR CHINA?

As noted previously, world class industrial automation technologies and solutions are critical to China during its current stage of development. Successful state-owned enterprise (SOE) reform requires a combination of modern management techniques and advanced automation technology and solutions. Making SOEs efficient, productive, and globally competitive requires the right mix of managerial expertise and world class industrial automation. World class automation insures production that is of consistent high quality, that is efficient in the use of energy and material resources, that is flexible and timely, and that is environmentally friendly and protective of worker safety. To be competitive globally, China's manufacturers must rely on the right tools. The right mix of management and advanced automation will afford China's domestic industry the opportunity to reduce the total cost of ownership for the customers' factory or process.

INFRASTRUCTURE

As China increasingly engages in the development of infrastructure, automation is needed to ensure infrastructure processes operate in a continuous and standard manner. Infrastructure uses for advanced automation include control of material handling, natural gas and oil pipeline management, water treatment and distribution, airport and seaport operations and light rail and subway control functions.

With the advent of the Internet and growth in personal consumption, and the consequent development of e-commerce, automated warehousing and distribution will become increasingly important so as to achieve the throughput of product and quality of services that will be demanded. Logistics suppliers such as Fedex, UPS, and Maersk, as well as manufacturers themselves, will invest in automated material handling to lower cost and improve service. Again, similar growing services in China will need to do so as well in order to sustain competitiveness.

In recent years, China has witnessed a massive overhaul of air traffic facilities with many new airports both completed and now under construction. In airports, automation is used to control the conveyors, which deliver luggage to and from the planes using bar codes to automatically identify the correct point of delivery. Similarly, automation is used to control the storage and retrieval of airline cargo. Automation is used to control the airfield lighting system, adjusting lighting intensity automatically to compensate for changes in weather. Automation is also used to deliver and monitor the flow of jet fuel to the aircraft. There are many other uses for automation at airports, which are analogous to small cities.

International trade, which accounts for 20% of China's GDP growth, will place increasing pressure on the infrastructure of China's docks and harbors, especially following WTO entry. At shipping terminals, automation is primarily used on the cranes, which unload and load containers or bulk material from vessels and store containers or distribute bulk material within the terminal or yard. Sophisticated software is used to automatically dampen the sway of the cable as an operator moves out over a ship to load or unload a container, reducing mechanical stress, thus lowering maintenance cost and improving equipment life. This improves the throughput of the operation significantly. Automation can also monitor the performance of each crane and the status of its control system and report this information to a centralized terminal control room.

Automation is also used extensively in mass transit systems for automatic train control, train scheduling, ticketing, signaling, and the control of the facilities including air flow, drainage, fire safety, lifts and escalators, lighting, and even advertising panels. Given the massive mass transit infrastructure investments underway both within and linking China's urban population centers, it is critical that these systems are integrated at the outset.

ENVIRONMENTAL PROTECTION

Many of the advantages of automation bear very directly on environmental protection and energy efficiency. In the environmental area, automation is very effective in waste water recovery operations, coal washing, and clean combustion, issues that China is now grappling with. Natural gas is a more environmentally friendly fossil fuel and as China moves towards natural gas for heating, cooking, and power generation, automation will be required to deliver and monitor the delivery of natural gas from deposits to points of use. Similar processes apply to oil exploration, production, and refining. Automation is used to control the onshore and offshore production of oil and gas to process the hydrocarbon fluids to a degree that they can be used for combustion processes, distilled to extract petroleum products, and used as the raw materials for plastics manufacture. Without automation, it is impossible to safely control and monitor the large refineries, and petrochemical plants being run and built in China today.

China has been plagued for centuries with droughts and floods. Water resource management is one of China's critical concerns for both industry as well as agriculture. Automation is used to control and monitor the flow of water from reservoirs and collection points to points of use, in many cases using radio telemetry due to the distances involved (that is, wireless communications). Clean water is essential to economic development for personal consumption, as well as use in farming and manufacturing. Automation provides precise control and monitoring of water quality as well as the efficient distribution of the water supply to points of use. Automation is also used to treat wastewater. One of the derivatives of this process is fertilizer, which can then be recycled and used in farming. In general, automation can provide China with an efficient and environmentally friendly approach to dealing with the byproducts of economic growth.

In the extraction and washing of coal, automation is essential to separate out the higher grade coking coals, which China uses for steel production from the lower grade coals used for coal-fired power stations. This is a task that is impossible to perform manually, as it requires specialized electronic coal scanners to be put in line with the automation equipment, to control the flow of the various streams of coal throughout the wash plant. Whether the coal is used for steel manufacture or power production, it is important to ensure the coal delivery matches the specification of the blast furnace or power station it is to be used in. Automation enables all these functions.

In countries such as China, it is important to ensure that the combustion processes for power stations, furnaces, and industrial boilers operate in the most efficient manner possible. This needs to be done to make the best use of scarce hydrocarbon resources such as oil, gas, and coal. Also, the most efficient combustion ensures the minimum emissions of greenhouse gases. Automation can provide China with a means of controlling the combustion processes such that the right amount of fuel is burned to match the demand, the minimal emissions of pollutant gases such as CO, CO_2, SO_2 and NO_x. Automation is a key driver in the development of new technologies such as combined cycle power plants, solar power and wind energy, all which can provide practical solutions to China's energy needs.

ENERGY EFFICIENCY

In the energy efficiency area, automation contributes to efficient industrial power management and power distribution and to substantially lower factory and infrastructure costs through the use of high efficiency motors, power control drives, and power monitoring technology. One of China's greatest opportunities for large energy saving gains is the utilization of variable frequency drives (VFDs) within the industrial and power generation sectors. VFDs provide complete and precise control of the speed of a motor. This control allows a motor to operate at the most efficient speed required by the process and can result in an energy efficiency savings which permits payback in as little as one year on high horsepower installations.

AC VFD products, especially at the medium voltage level, are already making an impact in power industry applications in China and around the world. A prime application of VFDs' drive technology to provide both energy savings and address environmental concerns is in boiler-induced draft fan control in the power generation industry.

VFDs are able to provide precise speed and torque control to the motors that control the induced draft fans on the boilers. Emission monitoring equipment on the flue output of the boilers feeds a process signal back to a distributed control system that determines the optimum input draft requirements to the boiler, which results in a highly optimized burn cycle in the coal-fired boiler. Facilities equipped with this technology enjoy the benefits of high cost savings, more efficient and complete fuel utilization, a cleaner flue discharge and a cleaner environment for all.

Energy efficiency includes minimizing process losses by using VFDs and high efficiency motors as well as effectively using energy by controlling how and when it's used and reducing equipment damage caused by voltage sags (under-voltage) and swells (over-voltage). One important point is that the same control system used to automate a process or plant may be utilized to "automate" energy usage.

Power monitoring devices connected to networked intelligent systems can provide real energy savings. Stand-alone power monitors can provide real-time information as an aid to troubleshooting system problems such as motors drawing excessive current due to low voltage. Stand-alone power monitors can also provide relay outputs for warning of power anomalies or control of devices based on power set points. An example would be dropping out a VFD or motor starter based on high or low voltage to avoid motor related problems. Networking of power monitors may be used for a variety of applications, including load profiling (collecting and logging power information), cost allocation (assigning energy costs to a department, process, facility, cost center, etc.) and demand management (monitoring and controlling demand to protect generating capacity). Software such as Rockwell Automation's RSEnergy is an example of a software application that can be used to collect data for load profiling and cost allocation, or RSPower32/RSView32 for demand management.

Advanced industrial automation providers like Rockwell Automation can contribute greatly to the process of infrastructure and industrial development in China. As China moves into the 21st century and the global economy, advanced automation technologies and solutions are necessary ingredients for economic competitiveness and success. Not only is advanced industrial automation required for China's entry into the global economy, it is necessary for the effective implementation of environmental protection and energy efficiency strategies.

Dr. Charles W. Pryor, Jr.

Dr. Charles W. Pryor, Jr. is president and chief executive officer of Westinghouse Electric Company, which is wholly owned by BNFL plc. In this position, he is responsible for all of the commercial nuclear operations of Westinghouse as well as the Fuel Group of BNFL in the United Kingdom. Before joining Westinghouse in 1997, Dr. Pryor owned and operated a management consulting firm in Lynchburg, Virginia in the United States. Prior to that, he was president and chief executive of B&W Nuclear Technologies.

Westinghouse, the world's pioneering commercial nuclear power company, offers a wide range of nuclear plant products and services to utilities throughout the world, including fuel, spent fuel management, service and maintenance, instrumentation and control, and advanced nuclear plant designs. Westinghouse supplied the world's first commercial pressurized water reactor (PWR) nuclear power plant in 1957 and has designed the world's largest installed base of operating nuclear power plants. Currently, approximately one half of the world's operating plants were supplied by either Westinghouse or its licensees.

In the following chapter, Dr. Pryor will draw upon his own knowledge and the extensive experiences of Westinghouse worldwide, in discussing the need to develop green sources of energy to fuel China's future mega-growth.

Fueling China's Growth

Dr. Charles W. Pryor, Jr.
President and CEO, Westinghouse Electric Company

Unprecedented Economic Growth

China finally has come to be recognized for creating one of Asia's, if not the world's, most vigorous and dynamic economies. After more than a decade of unprecedented economic growth and development, due in large measure to realistic planning and steadfast implementation of its plans, China today can stand as a model for emulation by countries struggling to overcome economic stagnation.

Having engineered one of the 20th century's most widespread economic recoveries and achieving economic growth results that are nothing short of spectacular, China's leadership today faces the challenge of continuing to grow the nation's economy at something approaching the record results of the past few years.

Fortunately, with its successive five-year plans, China's leadership has built a strong and durable foundation for future growth. Already it has in place plans and programs designed to reinforce earlier plans and program—these are continually reviewed and analyzed for their effectiveness and their realistic potential for helping achieve long-term growth goals.

Energy as the Critical Component

Energy is a critical component of all such plans and programs. The generation and distribution of electric power that is sufficient, reliable, and economical enough to fuel and sustain growth is key to both the establishment and the continued success of every developed nation's economic planning. Indeed, under China's Ninth Five-Year Plan (1996–2000) and the 2010 Long-Term Targets for China's National Economy and Social Development program, the electric power industry is identified as the center of the nation's energy development efforts.

But generating and distributing electric power that is sufficient enough to meet an economy's needs, reliable enough to ensure an uninterrupted supply, and economical enough not to be a deterrent to widespread consumption is merely a first step in the process of enhancing economic growth and development. The modern world and modern world concerns have added another ingredient to the mix. Now, in order to address and satisfy real and pressing worldwide environmental concerns, power generation and distribution must be carried out in a manner that will protect the environment and not only maintain but improve air quality. This is an enormous challenge in China, the third largest energy producer and consumer in the world. It is, however, a challenge that China has already demonstrated it is willing to meet.

Environmental concerns are rooted in the fact that most of China's and most of the world's energy is derived from fossil fuels: coal, oil and natural gas. But burning fossil fuels produces large amounts of carbon dioxide, or CO_2, and other gases that trap infrared radiation from the sun. As a result of the world's reliance on fossil fuels to power electric generation plants, the earth's atmosphere is heating up like the inside of a greenhouse. According to leading scientists, unless we reduce the rate of CO_2 gas emissions, the earth's temperature will rise by as much as six degrees Fahrenheit in the next one hundred years. The likely result of that level of warming would be widespread floods, droughts and changes in ocean currents, among other disastrous calamities.

To prevent such dangerous climate changes from occurring, worldwide CO_2 gas emissions must be kept at current levels at most and, ideally, reduced significantly. So in order for increased energy demands to be met without destroying the environment, the world will have to consume less oil, coal, and natural gas and rely more on non-fossil sources for fuel and on renewable energy sources like solar, hydro and wind.

NUCLEAR POWER COMMITMENT

Even though there are considerable technical and reliability problems associated with renewable energy sources, the Chinese have demonstrated some success with hydroelectric power and are to be commended for making a commitment to this non-fossil energy source.

China has made an even more significant commitment to another non-fossil fuel source: nuclear power. It is a sensible commitment to make, because nuclear energy, produced in properly designed, constructed, and operated power plants, can supply China and the world with the cleanest electricity available for continued development.

That is not an empty promise. Nuclear power has proven that it can be as environmentally friendly as it is efficient and economical. In the United States, for example, where one-fifth of the country's electricity is produced by more than 100 nuclear power plants, the generating plants are deemed to be one of the single most effective resources in the electricity sector to reduce harmful air pollutants. According to the U.S. Department of Energy, improved efficiencies at nuclear power plants in 1998 accounted for nearly half of all voluntary greenhouse gas reductions by American business and industry that year. In France, fully 75% of the country's electricity is produced in about 60 nuclear power plants that are virtually pollution-free.

China embarked on its nuclear program in 1974. It began construction of its first nuclear power plant in Qinshan in 1985. That facility went online in December 1991. As this is written, there are three nuclear plants operating in the country with eight more under construction. Those numbers are indicative of a healthy nuclear industry. According to an article in China's *People's Daily* in July 2000, construction of the units to be built during the Ninth Five-Year Plan is expected to be completed during the Tenth Five-Year Plan—that is, before 2005. The newspaper article quoted Zhang Huazhu, director of the China Atomic Energy Authority, as saying that construction of the projects signifies that China is out of the preliminary stages of nuclear power construction.

Without question, China has progressed far beyond those preliminary stages and is well on its way to developing a vitally important industry that will contribute mightily to the nation's stated goals of environmentally friendly energy efficiency, energy economy, and energy self-sufficiency. That is not to suggest that China will some day rely exclusively on nuclear power for energy production. A key consideration in its long-term planning is energy diversity and that is a sensible and realistic consideration. China's energy picture likely will continue to be dominated by coal and hydropower for any number of reasons. And hard decisions must be made on the extent of future government investment in nuclear, on reactor design, and on the design of a domestic infrastructure to deliver power. But it is safe to say that nuclear can and will play an increasingly important role in electric power generation in China in the years ahead.

COST EFFECTIVE GREEN TECHNOLOGY

Many feel that nuclear can be—and should be—categorized as a green technology because it fits the definition as an environmentally friendly energy source. Increased reliance on nuclear power will help, not harm, the environment. Nuclear reactors produce virtually no greenhouse gases, so they do not contribute to global warming like power plants that burn fossil fuels, and their operation does not produce acid rain. That is why they are uniquely suited to produce electricity for the densely populated areas of eastern China, where air pollution and methods to control and improve it are critical concerns.

Besides their enviable environmental record, nuclear power plants also are noted for their ability to produce electricity with a high degree of reliability and safety. Nuclear power plants in many parts of the world are setting new production records almost every year they operate and they do so without compromising the safety of either the public or those working in the plants. Indeed, the operating performance of the Daya Bay station near Hong Kong, under Chinese management, has steadily improved its reliability and load factors year-by-year. It now operates comparably with other plants of its age and design.

One of the identified aims of China's energy policies is cost reduction. Unfortunately, many of the country's people as well as some industrial plants in more remote areas cannot afford electricity because it is still relatively expensive. The government is attacking this problem in earnest because the leadership recognizes that continued economic growth can be achieved only by making reasonably priced electric power available to all areas of the country. Nuclear can be a potentially powerful weapon in that attack. With continual improvements being made in reactor technology, significant extensions of fuel and plant life, and dramatic reductions in plant outage downtimes, the cost of generating electricity with nuclear power is falling steadily and significantly. For example, in the United States in 1998, 16 nuclear plants achieved production costs of less than a cent-and-a-half per kilowatt-hour.

Another contributor to falling electricity costs is improved operating efficiency. Nuclear power has put up some impressive figures in this area as well. The energy produced per amount of material consumed is the highest of any fuel source. And the amount of waste produced in a nuclear power generating plant is the least of any major energy production process.

Towards Self Sufficiency

Nuclear power also can help the Chinese government achieve another of its stated energy goals, that of self-sufficiency. By forming Sino-foreign cooperative ventures to attract the newest technology, China should set a goal of being able to design, construct, manufacture, and operate nuclear power plants by itself. And at the Sixth China International Nuclear Industry Exhibition in Beijing in March 2000, officials of the Commission of Science, Technology, and Industry for National Defense indicated that China wants its nuclear power industry to be totally self-reliant by 2010.

That is a goal that is both admirable and attainable. There is sufficient evidence to indicate that the Chinese have developed a nuclear industry that is well on its way to self- sufficiency. And China's joint-venture partners, especially those based in the United States, have demonstrated that they stand ready to help the Chinese achieve that goal. The 1998 bilateral trade agreement for commercial nuclear power plant technology opened the China market to the world's pre-eminent nuclear power plant designs. The United States is the global leader in commercial reactor technology and the vast majority of the world's best and most efficient nuclear power plants are based on U.S. reactor technology. Unquestionably, American design and manufacturing capabilities can help the Chinese reach the level of self-sufficiency that is appropriate for a major nuclear energy program, just as they helped other countries, notably France, Japan and South Korea, become self-sufficient through technology transfers and partnerships.

At this juncture in the industry's development in China, there are critical skills in several areas, particularly project management and technology development, that require the involvement of a foreign partner. And while the Chinese have steadily increased their involvement and their contributions to successive nuclear projects, it is critical that they continue at this time to have access to the entire design basis and other project information. This aspect of technology transfer is characteristic of American nuclear plant designers and builders.

TRANSFERRING TECHNOLOGY AND SELF-RELIANCE

Westinghouse and others in the U.S. nuclear industry are committed to technology transfer and mutually beneficial business arrangements because nuclear power is among the most logical technologies to transfer in a manner that benefits everyone. Over the past 30 years, Westinghouse has established more than 30 international licensees and has implemented the transfer of technology to thirteen different countries.

Another reason why the Chinese are agreeable to continue working with foreign partners as they seek to achieve eventual full self-sufficiency is because doing so gives them access to design advancements. Westinghouse, for example, has a number of advanced designs that likely will prove to be the standard by which future plant designs are measured.

These designs include:

- the System 80+ Advanced Light Water Reactor (ALWR) licensed in the U.S. and the technology basis for the Korea Next Generation Reactor.
- The Westinghouse AP600 Passive ALWR, the first licensed in the world, which relies on passive safety systems.
- the Pebble Bed Modular Reactor (PBMR) which is being developed in South Africa by Eskom with support by BNFL, Westinghouse's parent company.

The Westinghouse AP600 is a simple, licensed, mature design using already proven components. It has the lowest projected cost of any licensed nuclear plant in the world, based on solid cost estimates. It has a verified construction schedule that is at least a year shorter than other plants on the market. Westinghouse also has begun to develop a next generation plant, the AP1000, which applies economies of scale to passive safety plants in an effort to reduce kilowatt-hour costs. It should be noted that working partnerships are not one-way affairs, with the foreign partner making all the decisions and the contributions while the domestic partner stands idly by. Westinghouse's development of the AP600 is a case in point. About a hundred Chinese engineers and technicians visited the Westinghouse headquarters near Pittsburgh, Pennsylvania in the U.S., while the unit was being designed and some 30 of them assisted in it's development.

No matter how China ultimately chooses to move its nuclear power program forward, Westinghouse and other U.S. suppliers are committed to helping China expands its domestic capabilities to become totally self-reliant. We believe sincerely that working in partnership with experienced global nuclear suppliers will be truly rewarding for the Chinese government and, most importantly, for the people of China, who ultimately will benefit by having more power, more affordable power, and cleaner power.

Dr. Manfred Schneider

Dr. Manfred Schneider has been chairman of the board of management of Bayer AG since April 27, 1992. He studied business management at the universities of Freiburg, Hamburg and Cologne. Upon earning his diploma in business studies, he obtained his doctorate at the Aachen Technical University. He joined Bayer AG in 1966.

Bayer is one of the largest diversified international chemicals and health care groups with annual sales of €27.3 billion and a net income of €2 billion (1999). The company's activities are divided into four segments—health care, agriculture, polymers and chemicals, comprising a total of 15 business groups. Bayer markets more than 10,000 products ranging from pharmaceuticals and diagnostic systems through crop protection agents, plastics, synthetic rubber to pigments, organic and inorganic intermediates.

Bayer is research-based and aims for technological leadership in its core activities. Research and development (R&D) have always played a key role at Bayer and they are the cornerstones of its growth strategy, along with capital investment, acquisitions and cooperations.

Bayer's ties with China date back as far as 1882, when Bayer dyes were first sold in the Chinese market. Today the Bayer Group in China has grown to 15 companies including the main trading entity, Bayer China, Co, Ltd., Hong Kong, which maintains liaison offices in Beijing, Shanghai, Guangzhou and Chengdu.

Bayer employs over 1,900 people in China. With total sales in the range of $US535 million, the country is Bayer's second largest individual market in Asia since 1998.

In the following chapter, Dr. Schneider discusses the future development of China's chemical industry in the new century, focusing on the key areas of health care, agriculture, fine chemicals, and polymers, where Bayer has substantial investments and expansive experience.

CHEMICALS — A KEY PILLAR FOR CHINA'S ECONOMIC DEVELOPMENT IN THE NEW CENTURY

Dr. Manfred Schneider
Chairman, Bayer AG

Over the past two decades, China's economy has seen increasing growth rates and a substantial expansion of the manufacturing sector. With rising production and strengthened economic conditions, the consumer base has broadened substantially over the years as well. This process of growth and transformation has brought overall better living conditions and significant improvements in the quality of life. As a result, China has evolved as a major economic force and it is clear that the current transition will have far reaching implications on the world's future economic landscape.

This development is based on the creation of a modern economy through economic integration with the outside world. The reduction of the role of central planning and increased reliance on market forces has obviously been the elements of economic reform. The "open door policy" has gradually opened up the economy to competition, new technologies and new markets. Determining the long-term future of China's economic development, ongoing reforms need to resolve the contradiction between centralized control and an evolving free market system.

Even more crucial to China's economic success are greater transparency and legislation targeted at better intellectual copyright protection. The entry into the WTO will see the gradual introduction and application of the set of laws and rules that governs international economic relations. In light of this, numerous sectors of Chinese economy have already undergone changes, including restructuring and decentralization of the foreign trade system, tariff reduction and liberalization of controls on foreign exchange.

The path into the future holds many challenges for China's political leaders. The main task is the creation of a strong industrial economy while at the same time providing and ensuring both political and social stability. Past successes indicate that China is on the right track: In the last 22 years, business-to-business transactions have risen from nearly zero to the highest in the world. Foreign trade rose from US$21 billion in 1978 to US$360 billion in 1999. Contractual foreign direct investment went from zero in 1978 to a high of US$91 billion in 1995 to levels in the range of US$40 to 50 billion over the past several years. In the last ten years, China has become a commercial borrower of note and has participated in international capital markets by issuing both stocks and bonds overseas. All are unequivocal signs that the Chinese business society is adeptly embracing and adapting to an existing global economic system.

Given this dynamic development of the Chinese economy, the chemical industry is set to play an even greater role in a future China as consumer demand and markets expand with further reforms. Chemistry provides the building blocks of human life. From a human cell that regulates body activity, to the chemical elements that make up our world, chemistry is omnipresent in virtually every aspect of life: in modern medicine, to ensure that we stay healthy; in advanced crop protection to guarantee our food supply; but also in products and goods that make our life comfortable, such as beds, refrigerators, cars and planes. Modern society today would be inconceivable without the contributions of the chemical industry.

The chemical sector will be one of the key pillars of industry in China, the indisputable engine for rapid economic growth and development. This expectation is also reflected in China's current Five-Year Plan (2001–2005), which sees chemicals as a key driving force for growth and development.

Bayer, being a broadly diversified health care and chemicals group, observes and is actively participating in China's future development through the paradigm of its own core competencies which include health care, agriculture, chemicals and polymers. These are all key areas that have a profound impact on the direction of future economic development.

HEALTH CARE

Health, quite obviously, forms the base for any kind of human activity. It is our most important asset and needs constant care and attention. Modern health care provides the means for preventing and curing disease, improving the accuracy of diagnosis and relieving common ailments with over-the-counter (OTC) drugs. It encompasses pharmaceuticals, diagnostics and consumer care.

Along with a rising quality of life, people put more emphasis on good health care services and information. Based on a public health system that has succeeded in making accessible primary care, control of infectious diseases and improved nutrition, the Chinese health care industry is set to expand further with innovative health care solutions.

Experience makes it clear that a major factor in the future of health care development depends on improving the domestic healthcare infrastructure to allow physicians, patients and consumers access to high quality, innovative and life saving medicines developed outside of China.

At Bayer, active research is ongoing to develop the products of the future. We are building a position at the leading edge of technology through a worldwide network of research alliances in genomics, bioinfomatics, high-throughput screening and combinatorial chemistry that will benefit health care and the life sciences as a whole.

In China, Bayer has made substantial investments in the areas of pharmaceuticals, diagnostics and consumer care, including the construction of a Good Manufacturing Practice approved manufacturing facility in Beijing designed according to Bayer's worldwide standards. The aim is to provide high quality and innovative drugs to Chinese consumers. More progress can be accomplished in the form of adopting a free pricing policy, better development and enforcement of strong and reliable intellectual property laws and conditions for the processing and approval of pharmaceutical and OTC imports to bolster these aims.

In the health care sector, Bayer continues to bring to Chinese society the benefits of state-of-the art manufacturing, employment and training for local employees and most important access to leading edge technologies developed throughout it's worldwide network of research alliances which also includes China. One example for this is the research cooperation with the Kunming Institute of Botany, where Bayer conducts research into plant-based active ingredients for the development of new medicines.

AGRICULTURE

Going hand in hand with improved health care, agriculture is where chemistry plays a key role in healthy nutrition. With modern agricultural methods and animal health products, advanced agricultural chemicals and veterinary drugs improve the productivity of farmland and livestock, which are vital for feeding a vast and growing population.

Significant changes in the agricultural sector can be observed in China. Take, for example, the production capacity of the Chinese agricultural chemical industry in 1987, when the total actual output of China's feed additives industry was less than 60,000 tons per annum. In 1998, China ranked according to statistics second largest in the world regarding this industry. And today the annual output has reached one million tons—evidence of remarkable growth in this sector.

Looking beyond these achievements, this sector is plagued by relatively low standards—small production facilities, old technology, inconsistent quality and high production costs. The challenge that faces the agrochemical sector, for example, is to adjust the product structure and to utilize and develop new products with high efficiency and low toxicity. The animal health industry faces similar problems, addressing the increasing demand for improved medicinal agents to protect food animals against disease while ensuring an adequate and safe food supply.

In China, Bayer's cooperation in the area of R&D with the Shanghai Institute of Agricultural Chemical Research is just one example that demonstrates active participation in achieving the goal to develop new products with new technology. Also Bayer's investment projects in agrochemicals in Shanghai and in animal health in Chengdu, Sichuan, are the basis for future success in cooperation with Chinese partners. The objective is to offer products that introduce new technologies, have a high added value, cut down production costs, improve environmental conditions and above all are highly effective. In this sector, WTO entry promises to open markets and strengthen protection of intellectual property rights, both critical areas marked for needed improvement.

FINE CHEMICALS

Chemicals, especially fine chemicals, are another key segment for China's future development where Bayer is actively engaged through investments and business in many diversified areas.

China's fine chemicals sector has made considerable progress and has achieved great development in production in recent years. The degree of self-sufficiency is constantly on the rise and the dependence on imports steadily decreasing. This positive picture has its downside because production is still not sufficient to meet the needs brought on by a rapidly growing industry in China.

This was addressed by extensive reforms to restructure the chemical industry implemented by the Chinese government in 1988. The aim was to achieve greater economies of scale, optimize costs, and to create synergies from shared and concentrated operations and to further reduce the role of government intervention. This was targeted at the increasing pressures on economic performance mainly brought on by the opening up of the market. One of the conglomerates that emerged from this restructuring, the Shanghai Huayi Group, has become a key partner for Bayer's future development and investment in the industry.

Bayer has observed with interest the continuous growth of chemical consumption, which has attracted a substantial amount of foreign investment. The broad spectrum of products flowing into the chemical process industries such as pharmaceuticals, food and beverages, consumer goods, textiles, leather and paper sparked Bayer's decisions to establish investment projects for flavor and fragrances as well as pigments in Shanghai and for leather chemicals and dyestuffs in Wuxi.

In addition to chemical products used in the environmental sector to ensure safe and clean water, Bayer's world class operating practices and its health, safety and environment management are being transferred to China via its joint ventures and business activities. High growth rates have been accompanied in China by severe environmental degradation in both rural and urban areas. Air pollution, loss of farmland to industrialization and challenges concerning the atmosphere and water supply are extensive. Bayer wants to set standards for environmental protection and safety and sees global commitment as global responsibility. Working within the framework of the worldwide "Responsible Care" initiative, Bayer believes it can only operate successfully if its activities and products are environmentally compatible and safe to handle, and if, during production, we take every opportunity to conserve scarce resources. This key corporate objective is best reflected in Bayer's slogan "Expertise with Responsibility." This is Bayer's commitment to a comprehensive management system for safety and environmental protection at all sites and for all employees including those in China. In the next century, Responsible Care is the watchword for the future, not just in chemical manufacturing, but in all human activities that have an impact on our natural environment and our resources

POLYMERS

The Chinese polymers sector has undergone far-reaching changes as well. With the petro-chemical industry playing an ever-increasing role in the overall development of the industry, this has resulted in a restructuring of the industry that targeted production adjustments, structural improvements, headcount reductions and better efficiency, paving the way for productivity increases.

Still, a majority of the high grade, specialized synthetic resins and synthetic fibers currently need to be imported. Foreign products—with their advantages in variety, brand and quality—dominate the market. WTO entry will allow multinational companies to have trade and distribution rights, which should increase the share of imported products when greater access to the market is achieved.

Given the dynamic development of the manufacturing, automotive and construction industries, China has developed into a key market for Bayer's polymer products. With a product range including thermoplastics, synthetic fibers, synthetic rubber, coatings and polyurethane raw materials, this sector has become the main focus of Bayer's plans to create a large scale integrated chemical site in the Shanghai Chemical Industrial Park in Caojing. The project includes a world-scale polycarbonate plant, which is planned to start up by the year 2003. The proposed integrated chemical site will be an investment of US\$3.1 billion for which completion is estimated in the year 2008.

In addition to polycarbonate production and compounding, production facilities are planned for isocyanates, styrenics, coatings, raw materials and synthetic rubber. The benefits of such an integrated site are economies of scale, organizational efficiency, implementation of advanced technologies, and more efficient utilization of resources. This project ranks among the largest investment plans in China and is a clear sign of our confidence in the growth perspective of the chemical industry in China and the manufacturing and construction sectors as a whole.

I believe that success is based on alliances, the pooling of ideas, know-how, core competencies and talent. Bayer's willingness to take a dynamic and constructive role in the future development of the chemical industry in China is one commitment that I can make with complete certainty and confidence. The interaction of both sides in this endeavor has demonstrated that win-win solutions are not only desirable but also achievable. Having arrived at the threshold of the new century, a quote from Carl Jung comes to mind as a very apt description for how China and Bayer are interacting as they move into this century clearly marked for China: "The meeting of two personalities is like the contact of two chemical substances; if there is any reaction, both are transformed."

Part V

GOVERNMENT AND LAW

"RULE OF MAN" VERSUS "RULE OF LAW"

Balancing the concepts of *ren zhi*, "rule of man," against *fa zhi*, "rule of law," has been an age-old contradiction within China's system of law and rule. In imperial China, the executive and judicial functions were fused. So, when the Chinese Communist Party with Mao Zedong as Chairman came to power in 1949, they inherited a tradition in which political power was the source of law. Just as imperial households had done before, they put in place an elaborate bureaucratic system with the power base at the center. For Mao and the early revolutionary leaders who were born in the shadows of the Qing Dynasty, it was one thing to create a new system of government. It was, however, quite another psychologically to completely depart from the traditional collective system of governance the Chinese people had known for 4,000 years.

Since launching the reforms and open policy at the Third Session of the 11th Party Congress in 1978, China has embarked on an ambitious program of building a legal-based system of governance. The "Chinese-Foreign Equity Joint Venture Law" adopted by the National People's Congress (NPC) in 1979 was the first in a long sequence of legislation permitting and protecting foreign investment. For those pioneer investors coming to China in the early 1980s, with a skeleton of legislation governing commercial practice, it seemed as if every time they drafted a contract, that they were effectively drafting law.

Legislation for both foreign investment and domestic rules of commerce has developed in a piecemeal manner ever since. However, there is a great deal of logic underlying this process. China, in the course of its rapid development and transformation from a planned to a market economy, is exploring new legal territory, trying to study and select legislation proven in other systems, and to adapt, rewrite and adopt those aspects that can be applied to the realities in China. The legislative process in China reflects the reform process. As Deng Xiaoping said, "We must cross the river by stepping on the rocks, taking one step at a time, observing the rocks carefully as we go along."

The legislative process that has emerged in China is one of a law being adopted by the highest governing body, the NPC, which is China's parliament. Often a law will present only a framework of broad principles, lacking substantive details to the distress of Western lawyers. There is a logic to this however. Details may need to be changed over time, as both the economic system and social structure inevitably change. The State Council, various ministries and bureaus underneath, as well as local governments, will issue specific rules, regulations and notices to supplement the law. This becomes the body of legislation that is developing and constantly changing.

For a developing country undergoing major structural economic change, this system makes sense as it allows for administrative legislation to be tested in practice before becoming law in substance. Often experimental legislation will be tested in regions before being adopted nationally. Legislation governing real property rights, securities and corporations was tested in both the special economic zone of Shenzhen and the progressive commercial center of Shanghai before being incorporated into national legislation.

The drawback to this system is that it is constantly changing and its application and implementation are subject to the interpretation of individuals administering it. As administrative legislation may be issued by various government departments having varying degrees of administrative authority over a particular subject, competing legislation will often be issued by the various ministries and bureaus, at times containing conflicting stipulations. Consequently, issues of administration fall back on personal interpretation and the dilemma of balancing *ren zhi* against *fa zhi* reoccurs.

COLLECTIVE CONSULTATION

Collective consultation underpins the government decision-making process in China today. Using the legislative process as an example, when a law is drafted, each department concerned will be involved in the drafting process, adding its opinions. Session after session of drafting and reviews will take place so that the final product is a reflection of the various ideas of all departments affected by this law or involved in its implementation. This may be interpreted as a democratic consultative process in that when the concerned legislation is finally promulgated, all departments involved in its drafting will be responsible equally for its enforcement.

Opposite to the western concept of a parliament or congress adopting legislation on the basis of a simple majority, in China, all concerned departments of government have been consulted and have participated in the creation of legislation which they must all live with and feel committed to uphold. From a totally Chinese perspective, in a straight democratic vote, if 51% agree on one issue or political candidate, then why should the other 49% have to suffer from a situation which they cannot accept and are unwilling to uphold.

This concept of concensus can be seen operating at the highest levels of government. The State Council has four vice premiers working alongside the premier and half a dozen State councilors (each responsible for a separate portfolio) to whom the various ministers report.

This concept is rooted in the Chinese people's 4,000-year collective unconscious, the root of which lies in the villages, which in ancient times were often huge extended families. Consequently China's system of governing by consensus is actually a part of the Chinese collective unconscious which often cannot be understood in the West where social conditions similar to China's have been historically different.

REFORMS BY CONSENSUS

As with the development of legislation, government reforms in China cannot be seen in such simple terms as the development of a one-man, one-vote democracy being a panacea, as some critics in the West insist. First, this approach is irrelevant when China's own traditions of government are considered, which have always demanded strong centralism. Second, the government reforms that are taking place in China address different issues altogether, which are far more relevant specific to the transitional questions that China is facing today.

Returning first to the strong centralism that characterizes China's traditional system of government, the very concept of *ren zhi* derives from the traditional emperor's "right" to rule, a "mandate" granted from heaven or effectively from China's masses, who themselves were often the source of uprising, toppling one dynasty and replacing it with another. In the 20th Century, the chaos surrounding the disintegration of Kuomintang rule prior to 1949, in the minds of China's rural masses at the time, effectively transferred this traditional mandate of heaven to the Chinese Communist Party.

The ability of the Chinese Communist Party to retain power into the 21st Century depends upon its ability to fuse economic progress with an ethos representing its symbolic mandate. This means upholding the banner of Chinese nationalism, which in itself provides a spiritual legitimacy to rule, while preventing chaos, which translates today as raising economic conditions generally and the standard of living of the people specifically.

Moving on to the government reforms underway today, it is important to note that the impetus for China's government reforms began with Deng Xiaoping. Deng inherited the problem of untangling the mesh of party-government-military authority left over from the turbulence and disintegration of law during the Culture Revolution. In addressing this problem, Deng introduced reforms aimed at addressing certain concrete realities facing China, which are being carried on today. Attempts are being made to coordinate the relationship between Party and Government and to determine the appropriate areas in which the authority of one should take precedence over the other. This has involved re-categorizing the authority and specific roles to be played by and between the Chinese Communist Party and the government.

POLITICAL DEVELOPMENTS IN CHINA

Today, political developments in China are moving towards a more formal balance of power between official bodies. This involves a clear strengthening of the role of the National People's Congress. Once criticized by Western analysts as being a "rubber stamp" for the Party, it has developed over recent years, asserting its role as national parliament, formulator and passer of laws. In turn, the Party and Government are both moving towards a more legally-based and systematic structure. The development of a complete and effective legal system is a matter of priority and a pre-condition to developing a higher level of consensual democracy.

A separation of the judiciary has been underway, involving the clarification of political policy versus statutory law. The role of the judiciary has also been strengthened and the implementation of law has become more systematic and procedural. In March 1996, the National People's Congress adopted new legislation providing protection for individuals in criminal prosecutions, including rights to legal defense and protection against detention without adequate cause.

This process has witnessed the search for an appropriate delineation between Party policy directives and legal procedures in the judicial arena. Similarly the balance of power and authority between the central and local government levels is being redefined. To restructure the relationship between government and state-owned enterprises has been one of the most complicated parts of this process.

From the Party's point of view, these reforms involve changing its own function from that of government to the former of ideological parameters and policy platforms, and not getting involved in specific government tasks, which have now been transferred to the government and the judiciary. The Party's role has been redefined to consider policy issues from a macro perspective and to not engage in daily administrative and government work.

From the Government's point of view, the reforms underway which will give greater independent decision making and self-reliance to state-owned enterprises, focus more on policy decision making and less on bureaucratic detail and change the Government's previous pattern of making direct investments and governing business too directly. The Government will refrain from trying to control markets, prices and commercial decision making, and focus on allowing the economy to flourish on free-market terms with defined policy parameters and intervention only when necessary.

Simultaneously, cadre and political personnel functions have undergone change. A system is being introduced nationwide calling for the bureaucracy to take examinations with official recruitment based on contracts and quali-fications—not relationships. A true civil service is in the making. Today, regardless of who is in power, the bureaucracy or administrative system will remain intact to provide continuity regardless of change in policy.

The selection of officials at the village and some urban levels is now being carried out through a direct election system. The clear direction is to gradually develop and expand this system. There is also a clear policy on the retirement of officials, to prevent a concentration of power in the hands of an elderly elite for too long a period, as happened in the past.

A SYSTEM REFLECTING CHINA'S SPECIFIC NEEDS

Clearly, China's system cannot be exactly like a Western system—the cul-tural, historical, social and economic factors in China are simply not the same. While the leadership recognizes a need to absorb Western principles that have been proven effective in other countries and to adapt them to China's own specific needs, China cannot entirely copy another system. Leadership will still be leadership under the Party, the Party being the strongest leadership group in China, and the only one that can provide direction and organization in a country that badly needs both.

What the Chinese people and the Party fear most is political unrest. China has known its greatest periods of peace under strong central as leadership, such as that during the Tang and Ming dynasties. Most Chinese in China today recognize the necessity for maintaining a consistently strong central leadership, especially in view of local protectionism and growing problems of corruption: chaos does not benefit anyone, therefore change must come gradually, as Deng said "step by step."

China does not want a Western model of democracy it observes in some countries, such as those of Latin America, where numerous parties are in constant struggle and have no unity of direction. The recent history of the Soviet Union is a perfect example of what China and the Chinese people clearly and unequivocally do not want. China believes that democracy is unanimity, the collective pursuit of ideas and the achievement of targets that have been selected through a process of internal consultation, not external conflict, where 49% of the population must endure the decision of the other 51%. China is not a culture of black and white as understood in the West where religion dictates contradiction, but a culture of yin and yang which calls for balance and harmony.

China's concerns over Western democracy are based not on a lack of understanding of the concepts, but rather on the recognition of the administrative limitations they present in China. Warlord infighting predated communism in the 1920s and 1930s, the direct result of Western democracy as introduced by Sun Yat-sen, which created a vacuum in the central authority of the imperial household he overthrew. The "pure" democracy of the masses, unleashed during the Cultural Revolution, created widespread factionalism, resulting in a breakdown and in turn messy merging of party-military-security and government functions, which have taken 20 years to undo. Chaotic small interest groups fighting among each other, leaving the country without a direction is one of the greatest fears and concerns in China today, as with the enormous reform agenda at hand. Nobody wants to end up with a government unable to make decisions because it is paralyzed by interest groups. (The American budget freeze of 1996 provides an example of exactly what China does not want and cannot afford to have).

Building a modern legal system administered in a manner perceived as fair by an increasingly educated and sophisticated populace is one of the challenges being faced by the Party. In doing so, the Party must now find a way to take the ideals upon which it was founded, and translate these to the cultural and social values of a new generation driven by conspicuous consumption in a thoroughly market-oriented society.

Jiang Zemin's efforts to develop the ideology of the Party through such concepts as "spiritual civilization" (intended as a balance against "materialist civilization" or pure materialism) and the "three representations"—which call upon the Party to represent the "interests of the masses" (Mao's order), the "interests of productive forces" (Deng's vision), and now the interests of "new advanced culture" (the reality which Jiang is facing today) are fundamental to understanding both China's government and legal reforms as they unfold—"step by step" in the century ahead.

In the following chapters, Chief Justice Xiao Yang of the People's Supreme Court of the People's Republic of China presents a detailed explanation of China's ongoing program of legal reform and roadmap for government and legal institutions in the century ahead. Professor Donald Lewis, who heads the China Legal Studies and China Law LLM programs of Hong Kong University, examines China's developing administrative system as related to foreign commercial issues. Michael Moser, a partner of the international law firm Freshfields and one of the most renown among China legal practitioners, discusses the role of mediation and arbitration in solving both current and future commercial disputes. Dr. Kam C Wong, Director of the China Legal Research Center of Chinese University of Hong Kong, explores the development of enforcement through a detailed examination of the evolutionary changes in Hong Kong's police force, post-1997.

XIAO YANG

Xiao Yang is the chief justice of the People's Supreme Court of the People's Republic of China, the highest body in China's judicial system. Between 1993–1998, he served as Minister of Justice, prior to which he held the position of Deputy Procurator General of the People's Supreme Procuratorate, and Chief Procurator of the Guangdong Provincial People's Procuratorate. Xiao Yang has proved bold and creative in pushing forward China's legal system reforms.

In the following chapter, Justice Yang outlines the roadmap of changes being planned and clarifies issues related to reforms in both the legal system and apparatus of China's government administration.

A New Chapter in Constructing China's Legal System

Xiao Yang

*Chief Justice, People's Supreme Court of
the People's Republic of China*

From the Rising to Halting,
From Destruction to Development

During the course of more than half a century since the founding of the People's Republic of China, the construction of our legal system has been full of twists and turns. It has experienced the tortuous process of rising, halting, destruction and development. Today, China has finally stepped onto the correct track of socialism ruled by law, in writing a new chapter in the construction of a modern legal system.

In the middle of the 20th century, the newborn People's Republic was like a rising sun, full of vigor and vitality. While abolishing all of the old legal systems of the Kuomintang government, at the same time, new China started the work of preparing to construct the people's new legal system. A judicial system with Chinese characteristics was initially formed through the adoption of the "Common Program." The Common Program functioned as a provisional constitution and enabled the promulgation of a series of laws, including: laws governing state power and the construction of government organs; laws for organizing trade unions; laws for penalizing certain conduct endangering the state; and laws penalizing corrupt conduct of government officials. Thus, the program thereby created new legal organs and initially formed a justice system with Chinese characteristics.

In 1954, the first session of the first National People's Congress was convened, during which the first Constitution of new China was adopted. This Constitution established the people's representative congress system, which was viewed as the basic political system of China. It confirmed the various freedoms and rights of citizens and defined the principles of our legal system, that among citizens, everybody is equal before the law. It also defined the independent trial principle of the People's Court and the justice system with opening trial, people serving as prosecutor and defense.*

Along with the establishment and promulgation of the Constitution, new China started the systematic process of legal system development and standardization. The drafting of certain important basic laws such as the Criminal Law and Criminal Procedure Law commenced. The whole country started to emphasize compliance with the law. In order to promote the enhancement of legal consciousness, during the 1950s China launched two large-scale activities for promoting a legal education system. The emergence of China's legal system construction could be clearly seen.

Regretfully, starting from the later part of the 1950s, failure to recognize the importance of law and order caused rampant legal nihilism. Legal system principles were criticized and negated. The authority of both the Constitution and law in general were greatly damaged. The legal consciousness of citizens, which had been initially cultivated, was almost eliminated. The process of legal system standardization was terminated. During the later part of the 1960s, the "ten year turmoil" (Cultural Revolution) began and legal system construction broke down altogether. At that time, the legislative departments of our government had no function at all and the number of drafted laws was very few. Judicial departments were destroyed, judicial workers suffered persecution, citizen rights were no longer protected and a great deal of injustice, framing and unjust cases emerged. The construction of China's socialist legal system underwent a great calamity.

In 1978, the Communist Party of China convened the Third Session of its 11th Congress, which symbolized the beginning of the new epoch of reform and openness for China. It also symbolized the resurrection of legal system construction in China. Based on the summing up of historic lessons, this Congress reached a basic conclusion: in order to realize socialist democracy and protect the long-term governance and stability of the country, the nation must be under the protection of a socialist legal system. Democracy must be systematized and legalized. This system must contain elements of stability, continuance and extremely high authority. The 11th Congress posed the historical tasks of "intensifying socialist democracy" and "perfecting socialist legal system," setting out a 16-character policy of legal system construction for China as follows: "There are laws to be complied with and they must be complied with, enforcement of the law must be strict and the

---

* The judicial system of a prosecutor and defense is western and not traditional, having been introduced to China only after 1954.

people violating law must be penalized." Since then, the legal system construction of China has grown vigorously, bringing about new changes day after day.

MAKING COMPLETE LAWS AND REALIZING THAT THERE ARE LAWS TO BE COMPLIED WITH

To carry out the construction of a legal system, we should understand that we must start with legislation as the basis. Without good and complete laws, modern legal system construction simply cannot even be discussed. After the Cultural Revolution, known in China as "Ten Years' Turmoil," China faced a legal field which was in ruins. Therefore, the resolution of the Third Session of the 11th Congress of the Communist Party of China proposed was that legislation work must immediately be put high on the agenda of the NPC and its Standing Committee.

In 1979, the NPC, China's highest legislative body, adopted seven laws including, the:

(1)   Organization Law and Electoral Laws, which were drafted to establish th e national legislative, administrative and judicial bodies;
(2)   Criminal Law and Criminal Procedure Law, which were drafted for penalizing committing crime, protecting citizen's personal rights, freedom and property, and guaranteeing citizens' litigation rights; and
(3)   China-Foreign Equity Joint Venture Law, which was drafted for implementing our policy opening to the outside and absorbing foreign investments.

The adoption of those laws shows that China had undertaken important steps in the area of legal system construction and the people saw, nationwide, the hope of carrying out a system of rule by the socialist laws.

In order to systematize and legalize democracy, we must have a Constitution that records and guarantees the democratic rights of the people. The 1954 Constitution was a very good constitution, which paid a great deal of attention to citizen's democratic rights. It also provided articles guaranteeing the realization of citizen's democratic rights. However, under the influence of legal nihilism, the stipulations of the Constitution regarding democratic rights of citizens became a mere scrap of paper and the Constitution itself was abandoned.

In 1975, 21 years after that Constitution was promulgated, a new Constitution replaced it. The 1975 Constitution only contains the provisions of the liabilities of the citizen and fails to provide special chapters dealing with the rights of citizens. Three years later, the provisions relating to democratic rights of citizens in the Constitution of 1978 were still imperfect and were hard to adapt to the needs of systematization and legalization of democracy. Thus, after the systematization and legalization of democracy was established by the Third Session of the 11th Congress of the Communist Party of China, drafting a new constitution became a task of top priority. After two years of deliberation and four months of nationwide discussion, in December of 1982, the fourth Constitution of new China was finally promulgated.

This Constitution satisfies the needs of reform and openness, reflects the achievement of political and economic reform in China, embodies the current features of reform and openness of China and accords with the aspiration and demands of the masses. As for various basic rights of citizens, including the basic rights of politics, economy, culture and society, the Constitution in particular provides detailed stipulations. The Constitution of 1982 was granted the highest supreme authority. It stipulates that all the political parties, state organs, social organizations and all citizens must comply with the Constitution. It also stipulates the protection system implemented by the Constitution. The Constitution of 1982 sets out the general regulations for guaranteeing democracy and running the country well and giving people peace and security during this new historical period of China.

In China, as reform and openness is being implemented, economic construction shall always be the focus of nationwide endeavor. During the process of economic system transition from a planned economy to a commodity economy, we are urgently required to intensify legal system construction in the economic field and further set economic relationships and guiding principles of economic activities in the form of laws. This is also a necessity in protecting the economic rights of citizens, legal persons and other economic organizations. In view of this, the NPC and its Standing Committee have viewed civil and economic legislation work as a top priority on their agenda and are speeding up the steps establishing legislation for a commodity economy. Laws such as the "General Principles of Civil Law," "Enterprise Bankruptcy Law," "Economic Contract Law Involving Foreign Interests," "Foreign Investment Enterprise Law," and "Patent Law," among others, have been promulgated in succession, through China's commodity economic legal system under planning was initially formed during this period extending through the later part of the 1980s.

Following the 1990s, as we enter the 21st century, China has further clarified its target of undertaking economic system reform in establishing a "socialist market economic system." This raised even higher China's requirements for construction of an economic legal system. Under the conditions of a market economy, the market's main players have broad productive and operative decision-making powers. The government is no longer participating in economic activities directly; however, this does not mean that the government is indifferent to the market. Only the method of administration has changed from that of direct management to indirect management and from management through mainly relying on administrative orders, to management through mainly relying on economic measures and legal measures.

The standards of development in the world economy prove that in the operation of an economy, the maintenance of market order, macro-control and management exercised by the state over economic activities—and between various links such as production, exchange, distribution, and consumption, among others—all require guidance and regulation under law. In the course of international economic exchanges, handling matters in compliance with international customs and rules agreed between countries is necessary. This has become an inherent requirement of the market. For this purpose, we must intensify socialist market economy legal system construction enact and perfect laws and regulations so as to guarantee reform and openness, strengthen management of the macro economy and regulate microeconomics.

After 1992, in accordance with the urgent need to establish a socialist market economic system, China accelerated the pace of constructing legislation for a socialist market economy. First, China intensified legislative efforts in connection with regulating the main elements of the socialist market, such as drafting a Company Law. Second, China intensified the legislation in connection with regulating the socialist market order, such as drafting a Contract Law, Anti-Unfair Competition Law, Securities Law, Foreign Trade Law, Arbitration Law, Negotiable Instruments Law, and Security Interests Law. Third, China intensified legislation in connection with regulating macro-controls, such as drafting a Commercial Banking Law. Fourth, China intensified legislation in connection with social protection, such as drafting an Insurance Law, a Consumer's Rights and Interests Protection Law, among others. The enacting and promulgation of those laws provided necessary legal system conditions for the cultivation and development of a socialist market economy and formulated a basic framework of the legal system of a socialist market economy.

ESTABLISHING THE AUTHORITY OF LAW, GUARANTEEING THE ENFORCEMENT OF THE LAW

Enacting law is the premise of legal system construction and the enforcement of law is the crux of legal system construction. Only by turning the stipulations of law into the practice of law and ensuring the unimpeded implementation of law, can legal system construction obtain final success.

In China, as a ruling party, the Communist Party's attitude towards law will directly affect the enforcement of law. In order to redress such past phenomena as existed within the Party—such as negating the law, making light of the legal system, using the Party to replace governance, using power to override the law and not complying with the law—we must demonstrate our determination to carry out legal system construction and guarantee strict enforcement of the law.

In September 1979, the Central Committee of the Chinese Communist Party issued an "Instruction Regarding Resolutely Guaranteeing the Full Implementation of the Criminal Law, and Criminal Procedure Law." This "Instruction" clearly reflects the spirit that the ruling party—the Communist Party of China—respects the concept of law and the legal system. The "Instruction" requires that all the party and government leaders at different levels, regardless of their position and authority, shall not and are now forbidden to over-rule written law with verbal orders. They must respect the law and the authority of the judicial departments. This "Instruction" expounds profoundly that the most important requirement in intensifying the leadership of the Party in undertaking judicial work is to truly guarantee the enforcement of the law, put into full play the function of the judicial departments and ensure that judicial departments exercise authority. It provides important, immediate, practical and profound historical significance in guaranteeing true law enforcement in China.

The implementation of law involves enormous system engineering. It requires the whole society to strictly observe the law and treat matters in accordance with the law. Specifically, three aspects will be included in the enforcement of the law:

1. Citizens and social organizations must strictly observe the law;
2. Administrative departments must strictly implement their administrative functions in compliance with the law; and
3. The judicial departments must strictly handle their cases in accordance with the law.

Strict observance of the law by citizens and social organizations is an important part of law enforcement. The prior condition for observance of law is that citizens must possess an understanding of modern legal concepts and possess a determined spirit to observe the law. In the past, China lacked the tradition of a legal system for a long time, and the concepts of legal consciousness and legal system among citizens fell into relative apathy. Especially, citizens lack the spirit to observe the law and they do not possess the consciousness of unifying their rights and liabilities, which are required by modern legal consciousness. The habit of respecting law and observing law has not been completely formed. This is the major obstacle for China in implementing its legal system.

In view of this, intensifying all national legal consciousness and legal system concepts has become the basic guarantee to the success of building up a legal system. However, China lacks the tradition of a legal system. Therefore, the formation of citizen's legal consciousness and legal system concept cannot be completely spontaneous and conscientious. It is necessary for the state to energetically lead, advocate and intensify legal system dissemination and education. In accordance with the national conditions of China beginning in 1985, China has launched a large-scale education program for the popularization of legal common knowledge. A program series of three "Five Years Popularization of Legal Knowledge" (that is, 15 years) of education has been launched since then. During that period, more than several million citizens are to receive legal system education through various forms and methods. The spirit of observing law, the consciousness of rights and liabilities and the concept of the main body of the broad citizens have obviously strengthened. It laid a relatively solid social and mass foundation for legal system construction in China.

Although observing law by citizens and social organizations is one basic aspect for law enforcement, for the strict implementation of the law, we require that the administrators shall strictly observe the law by themselves. The administrators must realize that in undertaking management in accordance with law they must change the previous management style with which they rely mainly on administrative orders. The administrative departments have the most direct and broad influence in the realization of citizen's rights. For protecting citizen's rights and preventing an unjust exercise of administrative power to invade the citizen's right, the exercise of administrative power must be strictly limited to the scope of the law and carried out in accordance with the stipulations of the law. During the course of carrying out the socialist market economy and democratic politics in China, exercising administrative power in line with the law has become a trend and the common demand of society.

In order to exercise administrative power in accordance with the law, to prevent citizens' legal rights from being invaded and to protect the formal social economic order, the highest legislative and administrative organs of China have enacted thousands of administrative laws, regulations and rules, and provided a legal basis for the administrative departments at different levels to exercise administrative power since the reform and openness. This is the systematic basis for exercising administrative power in accordance with the law. Especially since 1992, China has enacted the laws and regulations that include the: "Administrative

Penalty Law," "Administrative Supervisory Law," "National Compensation Law," and "Interim Regulations Regarding National Functions," among others, in further pushing the course of legalization of administrative governance in China.

In the meantime, intensifying the consciousness of leading cadres and state functionaries to exercise administrative power in accordance with the law has become the ideological basis of realizing the exercise of administrative power in accordance with law. To this end, during the course of national education and popularization of legal knowledge, the legal system education of leading cadres and functionaries has been stressed. From the central level to the local level, the leading cadres' legal education, legal knowledge, observation of law and utilization of law have become the order of the day. Especially within the Central Committee of the Communist Party, many legal system seminars have been held. The highest national leaders, including Jiang Zemin among others, have taken the lead in studying the law, which has played a tremendous role in pushing forward and promoting leading cadres nationwide at different levels to study law and enhance their legal system consciousness.

The exercise of power requires supervision, and the exercise of administrative power makes no exception. In order to protect the legal rights of citizens, legal persons and other organizations, supervise and promote administrative departments in exercising their administrative power in accordance with the law, and in addition to intensifying the (NPC's exercise) of supervisory in administrative power, China has also established an administrative review system and administrative litigation system, forming an efficient supervisory and control mechanism.

As an outside supervisory mechanism, the administrative litigation system of China began at an early period of reform and openness. In 1980, the "China-Foreign Equity Joint Venture Enterprise Income Tax Law" enacted by the Standing Committee of the NPC stipulated that if a foreign joint venture enterprise disagreed with a tax department decision regarding the issue of taxation, it may bring suit in the People's Court. This is first time that Chinese law has stipulated that if a citizenry, or legal person, disagrees with the decision of an administrative department, it may bring suit against the administrative department in the People's Court. In 1982, the Civil Procedure Law of China incorporated administrative litigation into its scope of regulation and the administrative litigation in turn became practice.

Along with the further development of administrative litigation, in 1989 China promulgated a specialized "Administrative Procedure Law," which went into effect starting from 1990. It standardized administrative litigation, further promoting the development of administrative trials.

During the ten years after the promulgation of "Administrative Procedure Law," the nationwide courts of China have tried about 500,000 administrative litigation cases, thereby vigorously promoting the exercise of administrative powers by administrative departments in accordance with the law, so as to protect the legal rights and interests of citizens, legal person and other organizations.

The third aspect for enforcement of law is that the judicial departments shall handle cases in compliance with the law. The Judiciary is the legal forum for resolving disputes and the last line of defense for protecting social justice. It is also the last resort for protecting the legal rights and interests of citizens and safeguarding normal social order.

Together with the continued deepening of social reforms in China and continued expansion of openness, all kinds of social contradictions and disputes have emerged sharply. Due to the intensification of people's consciousness of the developing legal system, the traditional concepts of "disliking litigation," or "non-litigation" have begun to change. The previous means of resolving disputes by mainly relying on administrative orders, non-governmental stop-gap measures, and moral education, can no longer meet the demands of society. Resolving disputes through litigation has become a new social trend in Chinese society. Legalizing various methods of dispute resolution has become an important task for legal system construction in China. In turn, the judiciary has become a new hot topic and focus of Chinese society. This type of phenomenon has never happened in Chinese history before. In this situation, the judicial function of the court has been constantly intensified and expanded, turning to focus mainly on regulating civil relationships, economic relationships, administrative relationships and other various legal relationships from the previous function, which was only to penalize those committing crimes and protecting society. Judicial activities have penetrated into the all of the areas and aspects of social life.

Since the twenty years of reform and openness began, the types and numbers of cases treated by the Chinese courts have increased constantly. From 1979 to 1999, the Chinese courts at different levels have handled about 50 million various first trial cases which were involved in criminal, civil, economic and administrative matters. The average annual rate of growth for these cases was 13%. The intensification of judicial functions has become one important aspect of building a socialist country run by law.

Along with the intensification of the judiciary function, the phenomenon of corruption has surfaced in the judicial system. A series of problems such as perverting justice for bribes, perverting justice for private affairs, perverting justice for relations have caused general concern throughout the whole society. The demands of the people for judicial fairness, efficiency, honesty and cleanliness have become ever more urgent. For this purpose, China has adopted a series of powerful measures such as undertaking internal education and rectification in judicial departments, implementing a system of ascertaining those persons involved in handling cases illegally or evading justice, and strictly penalize the person who handles the case illegally.

China is also carrying out judicial reform and guaranteeing that judicial departments exercise judicial power independently and impartially in line with the law based on the system. Through implementing these measures, the judicial situation in China has been further improved and is improving. The extent of satisfaction of the masses has increased constantly and trust worthiness of the public in the judiciary has been continually enhanced.

STRENGTHENING STATE POWER AND PERFECTING THE SUPERVISORY MECHANISM

In terms of our political system, there is a marked difference between China and western countries. Western countries adopt the principle of separating power through a system of checks and balances. China provides the People's Congress System with the separation of power under the leadership of the Communist Party of China. This political road was selected by the Chinese people, based on the nature of China's traditions. Under this political system, the People's Congress is the organ of highest power in the nation. It creates and supervises the state administrative organs, military organs, trial organs and procuratorial organs. In this regard, the National People's Congress and its Standing Committee are not only the highest legislation organs, but also the highest power supervisory organs.

After practicing a democratic legal system for twenty years, China has gradually realized that the rational disposition and scientific operation of state power and all powers have been perfected and intensified. The leading authority of the ruling party has been strengthened. The leadership of the Party is mainly applied in the areas of ideology, politics and organization. The power of the People's Congress and its Standing Committee has been strengthened and they truly exercise the legislative and supervisory rights vested by the Constitution. The power of administrative organs has been strengthened through implementing administration and control throughout society in accordance with the law. The power of judicial organs has also been strengthened with the independent exercise of right to trial and the procuratorate in accordance with the law. In a nutshell, through the operating process of the state power, all kinds of powers have been disposed of rationally, scientifically and in line with the rules. Therefore, it prevents vagueness of duties and liabilities, taking on what ought to be done by others, and shifting responsibilities onto others. It mobilizes the activeness of all parties and becomes the "socialist political system with Chinese characteristics."

The exercise of power cannot be done without efficient and powerful supervision. If there is no supervision, it will be very hard to prevent the occurrence of abuse of power and corruption. In China, the intervening supervisory network imposed on the exercise of power has been formed. In accordance with the Constitution and the Party Constitution, as a ruling party, the Communist Party of China must act within the scope of the Constitution and law. The Communist Party of China undertakes discipline checking and monitoring of all party members, of the state organs and of social organizations.

One of the important items of concern is to urge party members to observe the Constitution and law. The People's Congress and its Standing Committee carries out the supervision and monitoring of the work of the administrative, military and judicial organs through listening to the reports, making inquiries, questioning, and appointing and dismissing of officers. The Chinese People's Political Consultative Conference exercises democratic supervision over the work of the ruling party and government organs. The administrative organs themselves establish special administrative supervisory departments to carry out the supervision of conduct within these departments. The People's Court exercises supervision over the administrative powers through the means of administrative trial As a legal supervisory organ, the People's Procuratorate exercises special legal supervision over all the positions and conduct of state workers. Besides, there are multiple types of supervision such as media supervision and supervision by the masses. Since the twenty years of reform and openness, the system of power supervision in China has constantly improved, strengthening continually, the results of which have become more noticeable.

The enforcement of law cannot be accomplished without efficient surveillance. In China, undertaking enforcement of the Constitution is a special responsibility of the National People's Congress and its Standing Committee. Based on the stipulations of the Constitution, and the National People's Congress and its Standing Committee, the NPC and its Standing Committee are entitled to revoke administrative regulations, decisions and orders enacted by the State Council that conflict with the Constitution and legislation. It is also entitled to revoke local regulations and resolutions issued by local government authorities and organs which are in conflict with the Constitution, laws and administrative regulations.

Except when implementing surveillance to enforce the Constitution, the National People's Congress Standing Committee also implements surveillance to enforce other laws. This type of surveillance has become systematized through years of practice. From 1993 to 1999, the National People's Congress Standing Committee had examined the enforcement status of more than twenty laws and strongly promotes proper enforcement of these laws.

GOVERNING THE COUNTRY IN ACCORDANCE WITH THE LAW AND CONSTRUCTING A COUNTRY RULED BY LAW

In Chinese history, the ideology of rule by man has been dominant for more than two thousand years. Historically there were occasional sparks of rule by law, which always disappeared rapidly in the broad and deep ocean of rule by man.

After the Communist Party took power, the issue of adopting which way to run the country and the society, that is, either adopting a system of rule by man or rule by law became a significant theoretical and practical problem from the beginning. During the earlier period after the founding of new China, this problem was solved relatively smoothly. Regretfully, starting from the later part of the 1950s, due to the influence of all kinds of subjective and objective factors, the answer to this problem had changed. The ideology and phenomenon of rule by man dominated throughout the country and over life and society.

As Deng Xiaoping said, in the past, due to the influence of feudal tradition, the words spoken by leaders were always viewed as "law" in the life of the state and the party. Disagreeing with the words said by the leaders was regarded as "violating the law." As the leaders changed their words, the "law" would also be changed accordingly. This phenomenon mentioned by Deng Xiaoping actually reflects the rule by man. Under a situation of rule by man, man is higher than law, power is superior to law and law is enacted when the man in power speaks. In view of this, Deng Xiaoping consistently emphasized that we "must be careful to deal with the relationship between rule by man and rule by law, and in turn deal with the relationship between the party and government." The new generation of leaders around Jiang Zemin have expressly made commitments to the whole world to the effect: "We certainly will observe the policy of rule by law."

From 1978—when the historical task of "perfecting the socialist legal system" was put forward and the construction of a legal system began—to 1997 when the basic strategy and struggle toward "governing the country in complying with the law and building a socialist country of rule by law" was completely put forward by the Fifteenth Congress of the Communist Party, the construction of a socialist legal system entered a new stage and rule by law became the basic policy of the Communist

Party of China and the Chinese government to manage the country and the social affairs.

Under this policy, all the legal work of the State shall be gradually legal systemized and regularized. Socialist democracy shall be gradually systemized and legalized. In particular, imposing the task of building a socialist country ruled by law has raised higher the requirements in all aspects including legislation, law enforcement, judiciary, and law observation. It requires that the law itself must be complete and sound, reflecting the people's will. The Constitution and the laws must have extremely high authority and be observed properly. The power of the government must be restricted by the law. The rights of the citizen must be strictly protected by the law. The state power and the rights of citizens must maintain an organic balance. Posing the task of building a socialist country ruled by law symbolizes that the concept of ruling the country, as held by the Communist Party of China and Chinese Government, as a concept has entered into a new stage of development.

Certainly, any country that wants to establish a society ruled by law must focus on the specific situation of the country. The situation of China is the same. What we want to establish is a socialist country ruled by law with Chinese characteristics. The experiences of other advanced countries may be used as reference, even to some extent to be absorbed and used for our own purpose. However, those experiences absolutely cannot be copied without any analysis. In China, which is such a big country, copying the experiences of other countries will be doomed to failure. China must, based on own historical tradition, cultural background and social realities, walk on the road of building up a socialist country of rule by law. In contemporary China, in order to implement socialist rule by law, we must stick with the basic political system of the People's Congress under the leadership of the Communist Party of China. Only based on this, can the road of rule by law accord with the specific Chinese situation.

During the process of implementing the basic strategy of ruling the country in accordance with law, we must solve the issue of relationships, insisting that the leadership of the party rule the country in accordance with law. Based on China's own history and reality, the position of the Communist Party of China as a leading party and ruling party is unshakable. The basic strategy of ruling the country in accordance with the law is also unshakable. Therefore, the question is how to ensure that the leadership of the party ruling the country in accordance with the law is an issue which needs a design for the system. This design is to turn the views of the party into the will of the country through a procedure stipulated by law. This will realize the cardinal leadership of the party in a country where social life must be governed by law. If the views of the party are correct, they well certainly obtain agreement of the people and thereby be stipulated as law which will ascend to the position of will of the country and be observed by people unanimously. If the views of the party turn out to be wrong, it can also be discovered and corrected on time through the discussions among the people and avoid causing losses to the country and society.

The enactment of the Constitution of 1982 in China and thereafter the adoption of three amendment drafts were achieved through the drafting and amending of the Constitution put forward by the Central Committee of the Communist Party of China to the National People's Congress Standing Committee. It was then confirmed by discussions taken through legal procedure. This fully reflects the steadfast resolution and belief of the Communist Party of China to respect the law and implement rule by law.

This half century of the Party ruling the country in China has witnessed a historical transition from mainly relying on the policies in the past, to the present mainly relying on law and striding onto the correct track of socialist rule by law in the present. Over the course of fifty years, China's legal system construction fully proved that rule by law is the only way to develop a modern society. By not implementing rule by law, the country cannot be prosperous. If rule by law is not implemented, the people cannot be happy. Not implementing rule by law would mean that society would find it hard to realize long-term stability over the country. As Jiang Zemin, State Chairman of China pointed out: "Ruling the country in accordance with the law is the objective requirement of developing a market economy, it is the important symbol of civilization and progress of society, it is an important guarantee for long-term rule and stability of the country."

To some extent, the country will thrive through the implementation of rule by law, but will be weak when rule by law is not adopted. People are happy to see, learning the lessons of experience—both positive and negative—over fifty years, that China finally has found a road leading to prosperity through implementing rule by law. At the transition period between the two centuries, magnificent prospects are emerging in China: the legal consciousness and the concept of the legal system of all citizens are continually being intensified. The powers of all kinds of legal organs are gradually being rationalized, and the democratic supervision and restrictions on each other have become part of the current system. All sections of social life have entered or are entering the track of rule by law.

Today, while stepping onto the starting line of the new century, Chinese people have confidence that they are bound to win. People have reasons to believe that, as long as they insist on a strategy of ruling the country in compliance with law and making every effort to achieve the target of building a socialist country through rule by law. China certainly will be able to become a prosperous and strong, democratic and civilized socialist country with rule by law, and realize the great revival of the Chinese nation.

DONALD J. LEWIS

Donald J. Lewis is a Professor on the Faculty of Law at the University of Hong Kong. He is also currently a Visiting Scholar in the East Asian Legal Studies program, Harvard Law School. Professor Lewis has served as a consultant, expert witness, and leading authority on Chinese law to a host of international law firms and major multinational corporations. From 1984–86, he was a Fulbright law professor in China. He has lectured widely on Chinese law in Europe, Asia and North America. He is an accomplished author and his numerous publications on Chinese law include *China Investment Manual, 2nd Edition* (1998), *PRC Joint Ventures — Drafting and Negotiating Contracts* (1997), and *The Life and Death of a Joint Venture in China* (1996).

In the following chapter, Professor Lewis discusses the development of administrative law in China providing a prognosis for China's evolving system of legal governance.

GOVERNANCE IN CHINA: THE PRESENT AND FUTURE TENSE

Donald J. Lewis

Professor, Department of Law, University of Hong Kong

ACCOMMODATING CIRCUMSTANCES

The People's Republic of China stands on the threshold of a new century of great promise and opportunity. Yet China still stands apart from the Western world in multifarious ways. One of the great questions for the current Chinese and Western leadership is how and to what extent will China truly bridge the gap that separates it from the West. This question looms particularly large as China faces a milestone in its history: namely, accession to the World Trade Organization (WTO).

Like it or not, the Chinese find themselves on the brink of a millennial age of globalization. On account of Western systemic development and consequent technological advance, the world has shrunk dramatically. It is really no longer possible for any country, even one as large as China, to remain isolated from external forces of change, the phenomenon of what is now called globalization, and what used to be called in Asia, Westernization.

China needs to be able to accommodate itself to these new and historic international circumstances. It can no longer turn its back on the West or the world at large, as it did in previous centuries. The long era of splendid isolation for China has come to an end. China must be able to perceive the benefits of this new historical situation, and take an active, beneficial role in the affairs of the East Asian region and of the world. In this sense, I believe, China can and will make lasting positive contributions.

Yet, at this juncture, China seems to still define itself by reference to its differences, rather than its commonalities, with the West. This is perhaps understandable as China *is* very different from the West—and that may be a very good thing—something worth conserving. However, this tendency to stress the "China difference" by some Chinese can also be seen as but a further aspect of an outdated isolationism. Moreover, this differentiation appears to be couched in ideological terms, specifically, the theory of contradictions. This emphasis on contradictions, while perhaps ideologically correct, breeds hostility, antipathy and xenophobia—negative values that are not conducive to China's future positive international role. Importantly, this emphasis on differences and contradictions also runs counter to a strong and culturally sophisticated current throughout China's imperial past, namely, that all people should be able to benefit from the fruits of Chinese civilization and, further, that those who embrace Chinese culture may become themselves Chinese. I would submit that these are the sorts of attitudes that ought to guide a strong and forward-looking China.

At present, the differences that separate China from the West *are* fundamental and manifold. These differences encompass culture, social organization, ideology, and political and economic governance, to name but a few. Yet, there are forces both within and outside of China which have been narrowing and transforming the distinctive features of the Chinese landscape.

One of the areas of fundamental difference—that of ideology— needs to be more clearly understood by those in the West. Ideology continues to play an important role in directing the leadership of socialist China. In particular, ideology provides guidance to the Chinese leadership on issues of political and economic governance of the country.

I have already referred to the theory of contradictions. From an ideological perspective, the primary contradiction facing socialist China at this point in history is that of "economic development." Hence, the primary focus of Party and State activity is geared towards building up the Chinese economy. Such an orientation has characterized Chinese governance since 1978 when Deng Xiaoping launched the "Four Modernizations" in an effort to make China a modern nation-state. This emphasis on economics is also consistent with Marxist-Leninist Thought. Perhaps even more interesting is that this preoccupation with things economic has also been the key focus of Western political thinking for the past 200 years. Accordingly, one may say that both China and the West have the same essential political orientation at this point in time, although they differ with respect to the means to achieve similar ends.

Yet, even with respect to the means to be employed to achieve economic development, we have witnessed since at least 1992 convergence between China and the West. In 1992, the Chinese Communist Party launched its "Socialist Market Economy" program in an effort to create Western-styled markets and thereby strengthen horizontal economic relations, while diminishing vertical administrative controls over economic actors. Such economic reforms have as their goal the creation of an economic system that is basically compatible with Western and WTO capitalist norms.

Yet, the Chinese leadership may wish to question whether an entirely economic orientation will bring into play China's great strengths and comparative advantages. China's historic future contributions to the emerging global order are likely to be non-economic in nature, and more profound as a result. China may wish to think of itself more in terms of a civilization, rather than as a Western nation-state. Certainly, this would be more consistent with its illustrious past. It would also provide a "new" model for governance—not only for China, but also for the West and for a "world of the regions."

China has always been a civilization. A civilization is firstly a moral universe—this has always been appreciated by the Chinese both in the past and present—hence, the continuing importance of ideology in China. One of the greatest of all Chinese inventions may be ascribed to Confucius: the creation of a moral superstructure for Chinese society not connected to any religion. The liberal West of today, having secularized society, operates systems which are largely amoral, predicated on economic value, rather than moral values. In this sense, the West may be said to fail the test of a civilization as it lacks a moral superstructure. This also points out the fallacy of organizing society primarily for economic purposes.

To some extent, the Chinese Communist Party (CCP) has recognized the inadequacies of governance solely to achieve economic ends, at least in their critiques of capitalism. "Politics in command" has been a distinguishing feature of CCP thinking at various times. However, I would submit that it is neither economics nor politics which should drive a civilization. Rather, the driver of a civilization must be culture, broadly speaking. Mao Zedong seems to have appreciated this fundamental principle.

If you like, the primary contradiction should be *cultural*, not *economic*, development. This is because culture, not economics, determines the forms and patterns of societal organization and governance. In this sense, I would submit that Marx was not entirely correct. Marx maintained that the political and legal superstructures of any given society are determined by the economic base. What Marx failed to realize is that there is something more fundamental than economics, which gives rise to all societal systems, including political and economic systems. That something is—culture.

What is most likely to provide the impetus to innovation and social advance in Chinese civilization is the free cultural expression of the Chinese people. What this will entail for the CCP is a de-politicization of the Chinese culture and society. In other words, the CCP should consider stepping back from its heretofore active role of political guidance of the masses in certain ways. In this regard, it may some day be said that:

Mao liberated the *political* forces of the Chinese people,
Deng liberated the *economic* forces of the Chinese people, and
Jiang and Zhu liberated the *cultural* forces of the Chinese people.

In this sense, the Chinese people should be encouraged to rediscover a fabulously rich treasure: the Chinese past. It should be remembered that the modern West owes its global ascendancy to the rediscovery of its classical past during the Renaissance. China has yet to experience its own Renaissance, despite a much longer and richer history than the West.

In this rediscovery, the Chinese may find that certain aspects of their own science/philosophy are more real and profound than Western counterparts, including certain tenets of Marxist–Leninist Thought. In this regard, I would mention only one example, but one which could entirely change China's approach to the world in a post-Cold War era. Again, I return to the theory of contradictions. The theory of contradictions, like most Marxian ideology, is predicated on a conflictual Hegelian dialectical model of thesis, anti-thesis and synthesis. The Hegelian model postulates that opposite forces will naturally arise, will contend with each other for supremacy and that out of this conflict a synthesis or some combination will result. Compare this model with that of the earlier, original Taoist theory of *yin-yang*. According to *yin-yang*, opposite forces exist, but they are not involved in conflict; rather, as true opposites, they co-exist and cannot overcome each other. Instead, true opposites only interact with each other, and from such interaction all change flows. What is most important with *yin-yang* is striking the proper balance between opposites so as to achieve the Tao (the Way).

Moving from a conflictual model of change to a positive interactive model as postulated by Taoism would greatly alter the dynamic of contemporary international relations, and it would be consonant with true Chinese thinking, not Western ideas. Again, this could be a model not just for China, but for the world, in a nascent Age of Peace and emerging Global Civilization.

ADMINISTRATIVE SYSTEM EVOLVES

Let me dwell further on China's current systems of political and economic governance. The Chinese systems of governance diverge widely from Western systems. Culture, politics and ideology may be said to account for such divergence from the West. In this regard, I describe the Chinese systems of governance as "administrative" systems. This is to be contrasted with Western governance, which is primarily "legal."

The Chinese administrative system is not a new phenomenon. Its antecedents date back perhaps two millennia and the current socialist incarnation is consonant with Ming and Qing imperial bureaucratic traditions of governance. This is not surprising for it may be noted that another of the great Chinese inventions was bureaucracy. Again, there is a contrast with the West: the great invention of European civilization was law.

The current Chinese administrative system is more broadly based than its predecessors, and encompasses not only purely political aspects of governance, but also a wide range of economic activity. In this sense, China has both an "administrative polity" and an "administrative economy." Moreover, it may be said that China has dual administrative systems: State and Party.

There are numerous features of the Chinese administrative system which distinguish it from Western legal systems of governance. Among the most important systemic differences is the unification of powers in a very powerful central executive branch, namely the State Council and its subordinate Ministries and Commissions. The legislative and judicial branches of the Central People's Government are very weak by comparison. It should be further noted that the Chinese executive or administrative organs have been most active in the promulgation of laws and regulations since the foundation of the People's Republic. Moreover, these same administrative organs practice, in a unified manner, not only law-making and law-implementation, but also law-interpretation, often to the total exclusion of the judiciary. Consequently, in stark contrast with the West, the primary legal institutions, namely the legislature and the courts, are weak and largely marginalized.

Another very important feature of the Chinese administrative system is the subordinate role of law in the governance process. The Chinese practice what is called "legal instrumentalism". Law is but one of an array of instruments available to administrators, and is frequently subordinated to policy. In other words, the Chinese system is characterized by "rule by law," rather than "rule of law." This arrangement can and does lead to wide and unchecked administrative discretion and, in some cases, abuse and corruption.

These characteristics, among others, of the Chinese administrative system raise troubling dissonances for China's imminent WTO accession. The WTO, as a Western creation, is perhaps most importantly a legal institution. The WTO is a rule-based system, predicated on strict legal principles and procedures. The WTO presumes, and may be said to require, that all WTO members have functional legal systems and practice "rule of law." Importantly, many of the WTO agreements stress the importance of judicial review as a check on administrative action.

It is clear that China's current administrative systems of governance are not yet compatible with WTO prescriptive norms. The question arises, as mentioned at the outset of this chapter, whether China can bridge the gap, which separates itself from the West and implement the changes required by WTO membership. A related question is: will the WTO change China or will China change the WTO?

Towards Rule of Law

It is equally clear that the Chinese leadership recognizes the enormous challenges posed by its WTO accession. Significant and sustained efforts have already been made to move China in the direction of eventual WTO compliance.

In this regard, it must be noted that China has, since 1979, vigorously embarked on the truly historic task of constructing a legal system. Literally thousands of laws and administrative regulations have been promulgated in the interim in pursuit of this national priority. At the 15th Communist Party Congress, in 1997, Secretary-General Jiang Zemin declared 2010 as the year in which the construction of the Chinese legal system would be completed. Moreover, in March 1999, the 1982 Chinese Constitution was amended to include the principle *of yi fazhi guo*—"to rule the country according to law." Some commentators have suggested that this potentially historic constitutional amendment represents a commitment of the Chinese leadership to achieve an eventual "rule of law" State, while others have argued that the concept is too vaguely framed and may comprehend either "rule of law" or "rule by law."

The Chinese legal system is still under construction, although remarkable progress has been made in the space of some 20 years. However, it is one thing to promulgate a law, and quite another to comply with it, or to enforce it. China is still faced with major problems of "legal formalism," propagating "legal consciousness" and law enforcement. Legal systems are not constructed overnight, particularly in an environment devoid of an historical legal tradition.

However, what is perhaps even more potentially delimiting for the nascent Chinese legal system is that China already has an alternative and indigenous system of governance: the administrative system. It seems clear that the developing legal system in China is not currently intended to supplant the administrative system. Rather, the legal system would appear to be subordinate to the predominant administrative system. Particularly poignant in this regard is the weak position of the key legal institutions in China: the National People's Congress and the People's Courts.

The position of the legal system is perhaps at its most discouraging when we look at that most fundamental of legal institutions—the judiciary or People's Courts. The Chinese courts are currently hedged about by various monitoring administrative organs. Inside each People's Court there exists a Communist Party Committee. Externally, there is also a supervising Party Committee: the Committee of Politics and Law (*zhengfa weiyuanhui*).

In addition, the People's Courts have relatively limited powers of judicial interpretation and, importantly, are essentially excluded from hearing cases involving administrative rules and regulations—the interpretation of such enactments being vested with administrative departments, such as Ministries and Commissions under the State Council. Judicial review of administrative action is also very restricted, notwithstanding the promulgation in recent years of some important pioneering administrative laws, including the *Administrative Litigation Law* and the *Administrative Review Law*.

The Chinese judiciary also has to vie with a host of arbitration and administrative bodies with respect to dispute resolution. Many cases—particularly those of a commercial nature—never reach the People's Courts, but are funneled into a well developed, bifurcated arbitration system consisting of the China International Economic and Trade Arbitration Commission (CIETAC) and domestic arbitration commissions. In this sense, arbitration in China serves the administrative system, and retards the development of the legal system.

The People's Courts are characterized by judicial personnel who are poorly trained, poorly paid, and, as acknowledged even by Chinese national judicial officials, are susceptible to external influence and corruption. Local protectionism plays some role in the decrepit state of the Chinese judiciary, to be sure. However, there also seems to be some sort of "benign neglect" operating as well. Problems of enforcement of both judgments and arbitration awards are recognized as a growing concern by both Chinese and foreigners alike.

As China enters the 21ˢᵗ century, and faces the rigors of WTO membership, it is evident that major and continuing transformations of the Chinese systems of political and economic governance will be required. It remains to be seen how the tensions between the currently dominant administrative system and the developing legal system will play out. Can the Chinese leadership really expect law to perform its apparently intended function of regulating and promoting economic development in the absence of a "rule of law" State? Can law operate effectively if it occupies a subordinated, merely instrumental role in the governance of State and society? Can an administrative system with legal attributes meet the challenges of WTO compliance, particularly with respect to the enforcement of WTO legal norms and procedures? Is an Eastern administrative system ultimately compatible with an internationally-dominant Western legal order?

LOOKING TO THE FUTURE

Looking to the future, it would appear to this author that China would necessarily be required to further strengthen and develop its nascent legal system at a minimum. This will entail difficult transfers of real political power from the administrative organs of both the Party and the State to the true *legal* institutions of the Chinese government, the People's Congress and the People's Courts. It may perhaps be easier to initiate such power redistribution by beginning with the People's Courts.

Among the most important steps in this process is likely to be continuing administrative law reform. It may be that the administrative system is incrementally "legalized" in this way—in other words, brought gradually under the rule of law. Such a legal reform would entail, over time, a transfer of the law-interpretation powers of State administrative departments to the judicial system, and a general expansion of law-interpretation powers of the Chinese judiciary *per se*. At the same time, there should occur a substantial expansion in the judicial review power of the courts over administrative action.

Future legal reforms will most certainly require a very substantial strengthening of the People's Courts. The exigent need for far-reaching judicial reform is already appreciated by the Chinese leadership and tentative steps in this direction have been initiated, particularly by the Supreme People's Court. However, much more needs to be done. The negative effects of local protectionism should be concretely addressed as they are demonstrably responsible for many of the enforcement problems and corrupt tendencies currently associated with the Chinese courts. The most efficacious means of reducing local protectionism would be to bring the People's Courts directly under the control of the Central People's Government in Beijing. In other words, to create a system of "federal" courts similar to those that now operate in the United States. In this regard, it is noteworthy that the Beijing leadership has already begun a process of re-centralization, in whole or in part, for certain key administrative departments in the areas of customs, taxation and foreign exchange to alleviate the influence of local interests and the phenomenon of *dui ce* or local "counter-policy."

There are a multitude of other substantive measures which will need to be adopted and implemented if China is to achieve viable and effective systems of political and economic governance befitting its anticipated role in East Asia and the world in the 21st century. Larger patterns and currents of economic and political reform will no doubt influence the nature and direction of the legal and administrative reforms canvassed above. The implementation of Chinese democracy, as already presaged by President Jiang Zemin, is certain to change the dynamics of governance in China in profound and as yet unforseeable ways. If democracy is indeed the ultimate goal, it will prove infinitely fascinating to watch how the Chinese leadership manages to turn a culturally top-down model of governance literally on its head. In this regard, it can only be hoped that democracy in Chinese soil will comprehend *both* political *and* economic democracy, consonant with China's socialist heritage.

As the millennium turns, the Chinese future is perhaps brighter than its has been for over 300 years. The great Eastern dragon has awakened. However, many potential pitfalls and errors litter the road to greatness. There are many divergent paths to avoid, but also risks must be taken. What China will become remains a cipher of the future.

What can perhaps be said about the coming century is that China will arrive at a Chinese destination—which will be different and yet similar—to where the West is today. We may expect a form of governance, to be sure, but it will be "governance with Chinese characteristics." China should be encouraged to travel its own road, its own Way, for in the journey the Chinese may uncover something new and different, and of enduring benefit to us all.

MICHAEL J. MOSER

Michael Moser is a partner with the international law firm of Freshfields Bruckhaus Deringer. A member of the New York and Washington, D.C. bars, he obtained his J.D. from Harvard Law School and his Ph.D from Columbia University. A fluent Mandarin speaker, he is a leading China specialist and has worked in this area for over 20 years. A major focus of his practice is dispute settlement. Mr. Moser has substantial experience as arbitrator or counsel in international arbitration proceedings. He is a member of the Panel of Arbitrators of the China International Economic and Trade Arbitration Commission and a member of the Governing Council of the Hong Kong International Arbitration Centre. He is also a member of the panel of arbitrators of a number of other international arbitration bodies.

In the following chapter, Mr. Moser draws upon his extensive practical experience in analyzing China's present forums for dispute resolution and prognosis for their future development.

The Role of Arbitration in Resolving Chinese-Foreign Business Disputes: Past, Present and Future

Michael J. Moser
Partner, Freshfields Bruckhaus Deringer

Why Arbitration?

Disputes are a normal—and inevitable—part of business life everywhere. When disputes occur, business partners generally want to avail themselves of a dispute settlement mechanism which is fair, effective, fast and economical. In the context of Chinese-foreign business disputes, arbitration has become the dispute settlement mechanism of choice for most companies operating in China. Most observers agree that more disputes are dealt with by arbitration than by any other means including the courts.

Arbitration's key role in Chinese-foreign dispute settlement can be attributed to a number of factors. First, arbitration is strongly encouraged by Chinese law and policy. For example, China's principal laws and regulations dealing with contracts contain specific provisions supportive of arbitration as a preferred means for resolving contractual disputes. Other laws make arbitration mandatory in certain areas, such as certain types of securities disputes and labor disputes. The draft Build, Operate and Transfer (BOT) Law is also reported to make arbitration mandatory for the settlement of disputes between the parties to these projects.

A second and related reason for arbitration's appeal is that it is supported by a comprehensive domestic and international legal framework. The PRC Arbitration Law adopts many of the key principles found in international legislation and practice and provides a sound basis for the conduct of domestic and foreign-related arbitrations in China. China's membership of the New York Convention, to which it acceded in 1987, permits the recognition and enforcement of Chinese awards in more than 120 member states and vice versa.

Third, arbitration also receives significant support from the practices of Chinese state-owned corporations that conduct the bulk of China's international business. Virtually all of the foreign trade corporations require that business be conducted pursuant to a standard contract form that almost always requires the arbitration of disputes. Arbitration provisions are also found in the model contracts developed by China's state-owned oil and gas corporations and in the model joint venture contract developed by the Ministry of Foreign Trade and Economic Cooperation (MOFTEC).

Finally, arbitration receives strong support from both Chinese and foreign parties for the perceived advantages it brings as compared to litigation. These include greater party autonomy, more flexible procedures, greater cost effectiveness, finality and confidentiality.

ARBITRATION OPTIONS

Chinese law, in accordance with the principle of party auto-nomy, permits the parties to a Chinese-foreign business contract to choose both the situs of the arbitration and the procedural rules under which the arbitration proceedings are to be conducted. The most common options are: (1) arbitration outside China, (2) arbitration before a PRC arbitration body inside China and (3) arbitration in the Hong Kong Special Administrative Region (HKSAR).

Most foreign parties would generally prefer to arbitrate outside China in familiar international centres such as London, Zurich, Geneva, Paris or New York. In practice, Chinese parties have usually tried to insist upon arbitration in China.

Over the last decade, China's practice with respect to third country arbitration has become considerably more flexible than in the past. Most major investment contracts today contain a third country arbitration clause, and arbitration proceedings are regularly conducted either pursuant to institutional rules or on an ad hoc basis. Even the International Chamber of Commerce (ICC) in Paris, which was shunned by Chinese negotiators when Taiwan was a member of the ICC, has in recent years begun to handle a growing number of Chinese-foreign business disputes. The Chinese have traditionally preferred arbitration in Stockholm, Sweden under the Arbitration Rules of the Arbitration Institute of the Stockholm Chamber of Commerce. A vestige of the cold war, the long-standing Chinese preference for Stockholm has waned in recent years. Recently, Chinese parties have become increasingly reluctant to agree to arbitration in Europe or the United States and prefer proceedings be conducted in Singapore or Hong Kong, primarily on grounds of convenience and expense.

Notwithstanding the increasing acceptance by Chinese parties of third country arbitration, however, the fact remains that most Chinese-foreign contracts continue to provide for arbitration in China pursuant to Chinese arbitration law and Chinese arbitration rules.

Prior to the promulgation of the Arbitration Law in 1995, the arbitration system was bifurcated into two separate regimes: one dealing with international or "foreign-related" disputes and the other dealing with local or "domestic" disputes. International or foreign-related disputes fell within the exclusive domain of two arbitration bodies: the China International Economic and Trade Arbitration Commission (CIETAC), which was authorized to deal exclusively with foreign trade and investment disputes, and the China Maritime Arbitration Commission (CMAC) which dealt with maritime matters. Domestic disputes fell within the exclusive jurisdiction of a variety of local arbitration bodies. Ad hoc or non-institutional arbitration is not permitted.

The 1995 PRC Arbitration Law maintained the distinction between domestic and international arbitrations and continued to require that all arbitrations in China be conducted under the auspices of an approved arbitration institution. At the same time, the new law brought about a number of critical changes to China's arbitration system, including a complete reorganization of the domestic arbitration system. A new group of arbitration commissions was established under the China Arbitration Association (CAA), the umbrella organization for arbitration bodies in China. While CIETAC and CMAC were retained, the old domestic arbitration organs were replaced by local arbitration commissions established at the municipal level. By the end of the year 2000, more than 200 municipalities have qualified to establish arbitration commissions and 143 are in operation. The CAA, pursuant to the Arbitration Law, subsequently introduced model arbitration rules for adoption by local arbitration organizations.

Since the reorganization of the PRC arbitration system under the new Arbitration Law, the earlier bifurcation of the arbitration system into domestic and international or foreign-related regimes has broken down. In 1996, the State Council General Administrative Office issued a Notice permitting domestic arbitration tribunals to expand the scope of their jurisdiction beyond domestic disputes to "foreign-related" and international arbitration disputes as well. To counter this new competition, in May 1998, CIETAC amended its arbitration rules to permit it to hear not just international and foreign-related cases but also certain types of domestic disputes, principally those involving foreign investment enterprises such as joint ventures and wholly owned foreign enterprises in China.

As a result of these changes, domestic arbitration commissions may now hear all types of foreign-related or international disputes and all types of domestic arbitration disputes. International commissions such as CIETAC, which previously enjoyed a monopoly over international disputes, are now empowered to hear certain types of domestic disputes, previously the exclusive domain of domestic arbitration bodies.

As a result of the reformation of the Chinese arbitration system, arbitration in China today conforms closely to international practice. In most cases, the parties to an arbitration are able to appoint foreign nationals as arbitrators and the procedural rules adopted by the various arbitration commissions ensure for the most part that the proceedings will be conducted in a fair and efficient manner. Evidence of the growing confidence in China's arbitration regime can be seen from the fact that the number of international cases handled by PRC arbitration bodies has been increasing over the years. In particular, CIETAC's caseload has experienced dramatic growth, expanding from 37 cases in 1985 to more than 900 cases a decade later.

Arbitration in Hong Kong presents an option which is a half-way point between arbitration outside China and arbitration within the PRC. Since 1997, Hong Kong has been a part of the People's Republic of China, but its status as a special administrative region (SAR) ensures that it will continue to maintain its own English-based legal system for years to come. Arbitrations in Hong Kong are governed by the Hong Kong Arbitration Ordinance, which is one of the most progressive arbitration statutes in the world. Among other things, the Ordinance adopts the UNCITRAL Model Law on International Arbitration, providing parties with a high degree of flexibility as to the conduct of proceedings and minimizes the prospect of interference by the courts. Arbitration proceedings may either be conducted on an ad hoc basis or administered by the Hong Kong International Arbitration Centre (HKIAC). Arbitration awards made in Hong Kong are enforceable under the New York Convention and may be enforced within mainland China pursuant to an Enforcement Arrangement put into force in February 2000.

FUTURE PROSPECTS

As the above overview demonstrates, arbitration is well established in China. Over the past 20 years, significant efforts have been made to establish a modern and effective arbitration system. No doubt the progress made in this regard has contributed to China's attractiveness as a destination for foreign investment.

What of the future? Arbitration will certainly continue to play an important role in resolving Chinese-foreign business disputes. But its scope and methods are bound to change in the decades ahead.

One development which will have an impact on traditional approaches to dispute settlement is China's entry into the World Trade Organization (WTO), expected in late 2000 or early the following year. As a member of the WTO, China will have recourse to the body's dispute settlement regime which regulates international trade disputes. Other WTO members will also have access to the system and can be expected to resort to the arbitration panels set up under the WTO to ensure compliance with China's trade and tariff commitments made at the time of accession.

Another development to be expected is the use of the internet and related technology to deal with disputes "in cyberspace." The HKIAC is already establishing a pioneering "on-line" system to deal with domain name disputes and plans are afoot to expand the regime to cross-border trade contract disputes in future.

KAM C. WONG

Professor Kam C. Wong, J.D. (Indiana), Diploma (N.I.T.A.—Northwestern), M.A., Ph.D (State University of New York-Albany—Criminal Justice) is Professor of Criminal Law and Criminal Justice at the Department of Government and Public Administration and the Director of Chinese Law Program, Chinese University of Hong Kong, where he specializes in comparative policing, criminal law and criminal justice issues. Professor Wong was an Inspector of Police with the Hong Kong Police and was awarded the Commissioner's High Commendation. Professor Wong has a regular column with the *Hong Kong Standard* and *South China Morning Post* on law and order issues. He also has contributed to *Far Eastern Economic Review, Apple Daily* and other major newspapers in Hong Kong. He is a frequent commentator on Hong Kong law and justice issues with RTHK, on commercial radio, TVB, ATV and CNN.

In the following chapter, Professor Wong draws upon his own practical experience with police work, analyzing the difficulties in administering law enforcement during periods of systemic transition.

The Future of Law and Order in Hong Kong: Reinventing the Hong Kong Police

Professor Kam C. Wong

Director, Chinese Law Program, Chinese University of Hong Kong

Direction of Change—The Vision of the Hong Kong Police

Recently, on the anniversary of Hong Kong's reversion to Chinese rule, there was a lot of discussion about how the Hong Kong Special Administration Region's (HKSAR) political, legal, economic and social systems have changed. Surprisingly, there is virtually no attention being paid to the changes with the Hong Kong Police (HKP), one of the more important legal-political-social institutions affecting Hong Kong people's life.

The HKP is gradually being transformed in structure, process and values to accommodate the change in political sovereignty and adapt to evolving social conditions. While the transformation process is far from complete, the vision, direction, commitment and strategy for reform is clear.

Much western media efforts have slanted the development of impartial law and legal apparatus in post-colonial Hong Kong. It is time that somebody set the record straight.

This is an overview of the HKP's effort to redefine itself in the midst of revolutionary changes in political and social conditions in Hong Kong in the last three years.

In April of 1996, the Commissioner of Police Eddie Hui Ki-On and his chiefs of staff drafted a vision statement for the HKP. "The Hong Kong Police Force will strive to respond to the changing aspirations of our community, ensuring Hong Kong becomes a safer and more stable society." The vision statement informs what the Hong Kong Police stands for, where its ultimate values and interests lie—basically, maintaining needed political and social stability in Hong Kong while striving for desired organizational and cultural changes within the Force.

To realize the force vision, the commissioner and his chiefs have identified the following areas of concern, to:

(1) Examine, reassess and improve the way in which divisions work;
(2) Improve upon internal communication;
(3) Ensure that training at all levels reflects and reinforces force objectives;
(4) Assess internal and external customer needs with a view of developing service level agreements;
(5) Redefine the force's management role, building upon financial delegation and performance management;
(6) Establish consultant and support services to give police formations the necessary expertise and contacts to develop their own initiatives; and
(7) Measure performance through developing realistic indicators with input from staff and the public.

For the last three years, the commissioner and his senior managers (chiefs of staff) worked to make the vision a reality. Changes envisioned for the HKP follow.

CHANGES TO THE HKP

Living the Values

In order to change the old ways of thinking and doing things, HKP has insisted that its staff should "live the values" of the HKP and practice what they believe. Three waves of "live the values" sessions, involving the Commissioners to the police constables and everyone in between, were held. The "live the values" campaign is used both as a communication device and as a transformation tool. It clarifies Force values as it transforms staff attitude. As the Deputy Commissioner of Police Tsang Yam-pui said: "We must continually re-assess our performance to ensure that we are measuring up to and following the high ideals that we have set for ourselves."

Customer-Oriented Services

The HKP has taken upon itself to engage the citizens in its reform process at the management review and policy formulation stages. In order to make the HKP more informed of and receptive to the public and staff's needs and concerns, customer (public, staff and management) surveys were used as a basis of policy formulation and resources deployment.

The surveys, the first of their kind to be used at the HKP, also drew the public, staff, management into the reform process making them stakeholders in turn. This customer-oriented approach to policing represents a shift of paradigm in HKP policing strategy. It marks the end of colonial (top-down, control-denominated) policing with the introduction of democratic (bottom-up, service-oriented) policing. For example, the internal staff survey (3,500 random sample) shows that HKP staff are concerned with effectiveness of communication channels within the force, working relations among different categories of staff and job-related stress. All of these matters were deemed not important under the colonial administration.

Public Participation in Reform

The HKP has taken upon itself to engage citizens in its reform process at the grass root and implementation level. For example, 16 Eastern District Fight Crime Committee (EDFCC) members were invited to play an active role in the Customer Service Improvement Project of the Eastern Police District by contributing comments and suggestions through observation sessions on report room processes at North Point Police Station.

More Accountability to the Public

In the past, the Complaints Against the Police Office (CAPO) was solely responsible to the Commissioner of Police for investigating all complaints of police misconduct or allegations. A CAPO investigation was not open to the public nor were the results encouraging. Expectedly, the public has shown very little confidence in police investigating itself within a "black box."

In order to address this problem, the existing Independent Police Complaints Council (IPCCC) Observers Scheme was introduced in April of 1996. The scheme allows IPCCC members to be an observer to the investigation. In 1996, the IPCC Observers Scheme was expanded to include lay observers.

In July 1998, after HK's return to China, the office of the HKSAR approved adding 50 lay observers. The IPCC members, or lay observers, will be allowed a "scheduled observation" (pre-arranged), or "surprise observation" (walk-in).

MORE TRANSPARENT CRIMINAL INVESTIGATION PROCESS

Traditional criminal investigations have been conducted out of the public's view, and understandingly so. This has led to constant complaints of police abuse and resulted in many failed prosecutions. It has also given rise to occasional public outcry of lack of police accountability, leading to calls for public inquiry and legal reform. In order to avoid charges of police abuse of legal process and infringement of citizens' rights, the HKP police has introduced the video recording of a suspect program.

Video interview rooms provide openness and transparency while preserving the rights of those being interviewed and without unduly disrupting the police interview process (and in turn the court process). Video recording of suspect interviews by the Hong Kong Police began in 1993 as a pilot project. By the end of 1997, there were eleven tapes on file and at this writing, there are 60.

Doing More with Less

The HKP is committed to doing more (tasks/functions) with less (staff/resources). Technology is used to enhance performance or productivity. For example, the Police Study Team has saved 147 divisional sub-divisional cell guard posts with the installation of 427 intercoms in police detention cells at a total cost of HK$7 million. The intercoms do away with the need to guard low-risk prisoners.

Another manpower saving device is the installation of the Automated Station Security Pilot Scheme to enhance station security (first tested at Shatin). Lastly, the Computer Assisted Fingerprint Identification System (CAFIS) applies computer technology to fingerprint storage, search and identification procedures. CAFIS has greatly reduced the investigative workload of fingerprint specialists by quickly narrowing the field of suspects and allowing for more time to focus on prime suspects.

Projecting a Smarter and Caring Image

The HKP is trying to change its image from one of militancy and muscle, guns and authority—to one of professionalism—intelligent and caring. This rebuilding of image is warranted both by the daily reality of police work and the new mandate of democratic policing.

Street policing is more service-oriented than law enforcement in nature. Democratic policing is more about helping people to maintain peace than imposing on them a preconception of law and order. In this regard, Hong Kong needs thinking and caring police officers more than order takers and quick shooters. For example, in 1998 the HKP launched a television commercial as part of its new recruitment campaign with the slogan: "An Identity to be Proud of." The new television commercial shows a quick-witted police constable who climbs out to an upper-floor balcony and splashes water on two children trapped between a fire engulfing their apartment and the bars on their balcony.

MORE EDUCATED POLICE OFFICERS WITH MORE DIVERSE BACKGROUNDS

More and more graduates from tertiary institutions with diverse backgrounds are joining the Force at both the probationary inspector and constable levels. Enhanced education is required because the police are called upon to deal with a more sophisticated public (one in four is now a university graduate and more and more people are informed of the law and their rights) and a more complex society (witness the right-of-abode dispute). For example, in a recent recruit class, 14 out of 420 recruit constables were university graduates with one holding a M.S. from Yale University. Overall, the number of applicants who are academically qualified to be appointed as inspector has increased from 8.4% of the total number of applicants in 1988–1989 to 14% in 1996–1997. A full 90% of the inspector recruits are now university educated. The incoming officers have such diverse backgrounds as teacher, banker, nurse, artist, and U.S. Army Reserve officer.

MORE SOCIALLY RELEVANT AND COMMUNITY–BASED POLICE TRAINING

In the past, police training has focused on physical fitness, firearm use, internal security drills, and laws and procedures in court. This is not enough to prepare the police to deal with the complex society, variegated situations and diverse people they come in touch with. In order to overcome this difficulty the HKP has taken steps to make the police training at the Police Training School (PTS) more "street-wise" and "people-oriented."

Starting in June 1998, all police recruits at the PTS go through the Community Interface Program. The program is designed to provide the police recruits with a better understanding of how people from different sectors of community think, communicate and act. This will enable them to perform their duties more effectively.

EQUAL OPPORTUNITY FOR FEMALE OFFICERS

In the past, female police officers have played a more reserved and supportive role, for example, performing station duties versus handling mainstream police operations. The HKP is actively cutting down the male and female barriers in training and deployment. For example, in September of 1996, the Police Tactical Unit (PTU)—an all male outfit—started training female officers. In February 1998, Woman Superintendent of Police (WSP) Elsie Wong Mui-Kit was made PTU's first female company commander. PTU training opens doors to other field careers, such as the emergency Unit, which is necessary for police promotion.

Police promotion review boards look for well-rounded officers with field and operational experience, a qualification the female officers lacked in the past. On October 1, 1996, female Sergeant Lai Choi-King became one of the force's 200 and first female Uniform Branch firearms and tactics instructor. The full integration of female officers into the HKP is long overdue. It is required by law and is consistent with social trends.

SENSITIVITY TRAINING WITH SCIENTISTS TO SHARPEN SKILLS

Increasingly, HKP is asking its front-line staff to be more sensitive to human emotions and psychological needs. In this regard, the HKP is turning to social and human scientists to tell/train them how to do their jobs better. This is a sharp departure from the past where little attention was paid to the interpersonal dynamics between police and the public, except perhaps words of wisdom and advice from old timers.

For example, Wanchai Divisional Commander Eddie Ko Chi-Ming has organized a series of conflict management training sessions (designed by a clinical psychology student and supervised by the Senior Police Clinical Psychologist Eddie Li Kam-Wah.) in order to minimize unnecessary conflicts and improve upon the quality of service to the public.

COMPUTERIZATION OF HKP

The HKP is going all out to computerize as a way to increase productivity and reduce costs. In 1995, there were only 600 computers in the force. Now there are 7,000 computers and the number is growing. Recently, a HK$30 million Sybase system has been installed as the foundation of all database applications in the force.

Two major projects have been installed: First, the Formation Information Communal System (FICS), which allows for the storage and retrieval of information from four key areas of police work: reports from members of the public; processing crime complaints; handling lost and found property and managing people in police custody. Second, the Personnel Information Communal System (PICS), which will greatly improve the efficiency, and access to, personnel management information within the Force. It provides a computer personnel and training record for every one of the Force's 39,000 staff, with strategic information on the positions and cases undertaken as part of these responsibilities approved by Government, the jobs done and those planned.

The system includes functions on establishment and strength, redeployment, staff details, career management, action review scheduler, various reports, and security and audit trails. Office automation systems with interfaces to PICS include recruitment, quartering, discipline and health impairment. The first FICS was installed in Wong Tai Sin in October 1996. The rest of the force followed in the next 12 months.

PROACTIVE AND PROBLEM–ORIENTED POLICING

In the past, the HKP style of policing was one of reacting to reported crimes. Currently, the HKP is adopting a proactive and problem-oriented approach, that is, dealing with the root of a crime problem (for example, family discord) and not only the symptoms (for example, spousal abuse). For example, troubled youth living near the Tin Shui Wai Police Division are being placed in an individualized program of counseling, supervision and self-discipline training provided by their respective school's representatives and social workers from the local branch of the Evangelical Church of Hong Kong Social Service Center. The program, tailored for the students, involves house visits, family conferences, peer counseling, school monitoring and police supervision.

INCREASING PRODUCTIVITY WITH LESS WORK

The Rennie Report issued in the late 1980s found that a majority of police officers worked more than 48 hours per week. There were calls to make police work a 48-hour-per-week job by working more efficiently and productively, for example, by shortening the briefing and debriefing time before and after patrol. The impetus behind the reduction in working hours drive is based on the belief that a properly motivated person can achieve more in a shorter period of time than a person who is not motivated, which will improve service in the Force. A trial scheme began in April 1997 to reduce the working hours of Uniform Branch officers in seven land formations (Eastern District, Hung Hom Division, Sau Mau Ping District, Kwai Tsing District, Tai Hing Division and EU, NTS). Now, over 27,000 police officers are eligible to work three hours less per week.

AFTERTHOUGHTS

The HKP has a sterling reputation locally and abroad, and deservedly so. The latest round of self-initiated reform shows that that the HKP is a forward-looking and progressive force. This is not to say that the HKP does not make mistakes, for example, redefining the role of Auxiliary Police. It only means that the HKP has shown itself to be capable of taking the initiative to make things happen and learn in the process.

The manner in which the HKP has sought to initiate and follow-through on its own reforms after the HKSAR returned to China is an untold story of the system of *gang ren zhi gang*, "Hong Kong people administering Hong Kong," at work. It also highlights the way in which newer and higher standards of work efficiency and ethics have been introduced in the post-colonial era. Hong Kong's legal system has served as a model for the rest of China in such areas as property rights, securities law, and corporate law. As China's legal enforcement apparatus is itself now under pressure to rationalize functions to keep up with economic and socials reforms, the HKP may very well serve as a model in this regard as well.

Part VI

BANKING AND FINANCE

MACRO-CONTROL MONETARY ENGINEERING

Deng Xiaoping's "southern inspection tour" in 1992 removed major obstacles to China's economic liberalization process and led to the introduction of ground-breaking market reforms. The economy entered a new period of expansion, growing by 15% annually for three consecutive years. Inflation, however, at first matched, then exceeded, growth. By 1994, it had hit a dangerously high 27%, signaling an urgent need for tough action. Zhu Rongji, then vice premier carrying the portfolios for economy and finance, stepped in personally taking the reigns as acting central bank governor, appointing Dai Xianglong to work beside him.

Lacking the monetary tools at the disposal of central bankers like U.S. Federal Reserve Chairman Alan Greenspan, Zhu devised his own. He developed a system of "macro-economic control," cutting credit lines and money supply. Inflation began to fall. By 1995, it had dropped to 10%, barely higher than the rate of economic expansion. The following year, inflation declined again to 6%, slightly lower than growth. By 1997, Zhu had achieved a near miracle: inflation closed the year at 1.1%, while growth registered an impressive 9.7%. At the end of 1999, growth was still high at 7.6%, while inflation had turned to deflation at falling by negative 3.6%.

Besides fighting inflation, Zhu Rongji, soon dubbed China's "economic czar" by the international media, took on the task of modernizing his country's antiquated banking system. He oversaw reforms at the People's Bank of China, which transforming it into a real central bank. He also oversaw the separation of policy and commercial functions of the state-owned banks, converting them into commercial banks as new policy banks were created. Shareholding banks were formed. Credit cooperatives were separated from the giant Agricultural Bank. Investment and trust companies were hived off from commercial banks and their numbers (which had proliferated at every government level) pruned through tough regulatory measures. While pushing all those reforms, Zhu also brought China's currency, the renminbi, to the brink of convertibility.

A Decade of Financial Reforms

Under Zhu Rongji's supervision, China has undergone a series of critical reforms in the financial sector. These reforms have involved a three-stage implementation program, which began in 1993 and is still continuing today. The first stage of China's financial reforms began in 1993 with the overhaul of China's taxation system. The second set of reforms introduced in 1994, involved the reorganization of China's foreign exchange system. The last of the three reforms and the largest in scale, involves the complete restructuring of China's banking system organizationally and structurally, requiring the untangling or clearance of state-owned enterprise non-performing debts.

The most dramatic turning point for China's financial reforms occurred in 1994. At the time, the central government in Beijing was undergoing a period of introspection and reorganization. The People's Bank of China (PBOC), together with entities such as the State Commission for Reform of Economic Systems, the Ministry of Finance, and the State Administration of Foreign Exchange Control, underwent a period of coordination and adjustment, leading to both banking, foreign exchange and tax reforms, which brought China's financial system in line with international standards within a remarkably short period, with the PBOC emerging as the central bank, supervisory body, and policy think-tank.

In 1994, the three policy banks, the State Development Bank of China, the Agricultural Development Bank of China and the Import and Export Bank of China, formally commenced business. This represented the completion of the severance of policy banking from commercial banking. With policy banking business having been transferred, the State specialized banks accelerated their own transformation into commercial banks. As the State commercial banks still carry some of their old policy portfolios to date, this process is, in effect, continuing today. Recent moves underway to accelerate this commercialization process of China's state-owned commercial banks involves restructuring that will convert them into shareholding banks.

In 1995, urban cooperative banks were organized on a pilot basis. This involved new equity structures and the adoption of new operational mechanisms of the existing urban credit cooperatives, so that they could transform themselves and function as true cooperative financial organizations. Further reforms in the late 1990s witnessed the transformation of urban credit cooperatives into local city shareholding banks.

Reforms of the insurance system gained momentum in 1996, with the implementation of a separation of property and life insurance. Regional insurance companies and special insurance companies were established so as to facilitate the formation of orderly competition in the insurance market in China. Approval of foreign insurance companies to establish branches and joint ventures began.

The foreign exchange system has also undergone substantial reforms. The merger of the former dual exchange rate system has been realized. The implementation of a unitary, managed floating rate system on the basis of market demand and supply has been put into effect. In parallel, a successful bank settlement and surrender of foreign exchange system has been established. The former system of foreign exchange retention and turning over to the State has been abolished.

Even throughout the Asian financial crisis, China maintained its foreign exchange reserves, assuring exchange rate stability. Foreign exchange reserves were at US$153 billion in 2000, putting pressure on the renminbi to revalue upwards rather than devalue. As China moves into an export promotion policy in line with WTO entry, the growth rate of exports is expected to increase steadily, and with it China's foreign exchange reserves. Maintaining and exceeding this performance, it will be reasonable to expect in the years ahead paving the way towards eventual renminbi convertibility.

Monetary policy is not the only macro-economic policy regulation affecting the banking system as a whole. Other macro-economic policies such as: fiscal policy, income policy, investment policy, industrial policy and money supply, all affect monetary policy and all must continue to be coordinated together. Therefore, in implementing monetary policy, the PBOC together with the Ministry of Finance, State Economy and Trade Commission, and State Planning Commission together with the State Council are working in close cooperation to comprehensively coordinate all macro-economic policies.

COPING WITH CREDIT

China's overall credit policy will continue to give priority to key projects, optimizing the use of loan placements and liquidity. Priority will continue in the short term to be given to supporting agricultural production, key State construction projects, and the reform of State enterprises. As for working capital loans, borrowers will continue to be restricted from using funds in operating real estate, stocks and other securities, or in manipulating working capital for fixed asset investments. Instead borrowers will be encouraged to create liquidity, to limit production, hold down inventories, promote marketing, liquidate debts in arrears, accelerate the turnover of funds and increase the concrete results of using credit funds.

Many of Zhu Rongji's ambitious programs have, however, been threatened by massive debts that the state-owned enterprises owed the banks, but were unable to pay. Cross debts and complex layers of unrecoverable receivables further complicated the situation. In effect, the state corporations were undermining new reforms meant to revitalize the banking system. The enterprises' failure to repay their debts threatened to bring the banking system to the verge of collapse.

At Zhu's initiative, the government adopted key measures in 1996 to help overcome these difficulties. They involved expanding the liquidity of state enterprises by making low-interest policy loans available to them, and by reducing the lending rates offered by commercial banks. Corporations able to export their products were given accelerated tax rebates. The aim was to raise production standards, as these enterprises would be encouraged to focus on international, rather than purely domestic, markets.

During a 25-month-period between 1996 and 1998, interest rates were slashed half a dozen times. In June 1998, at the height of an Asia-wide financial crisis, China cut deposit rates by 1.1% and lending rates by 1.5%. The Zhu-inspired moves sought to ease the interest burden of state corporations, with a view toward slowly untying the knot of enterprise cross-debts. Through such initiatives, Zhu actually succeeded in reducing the interest burden of state companies by Rmb70 billion a year.

In December 1998, the People's Bank of China announced that interest rates would be cut again, with deposit rates declining 0.5% across the board. Financing loan interest rates were also slashed by 0.5%. The *People's Daily* explained why. "While the state-owned enterprise results are good, they basically remain not so good, so this measure must be taken," said the Communist Party's official newspaper. "Prices are dropping more slowly than before."

It was clear that China's central bank was embarking on an expansionary monetary policy, kicking more currency into circulation. It seemed bent on stimulating consumer demand, as too many enterprise products were sitting on store shelves and in warehouses. Inflation for the first three quarters of 1998 had been a negative 2.5%. Moreover, the government was evidently trying to relieve the state enterprises of their debt-servicing burden, as they remained stuck in a quagmire of cross-debts.

FROM DEBT TO EQUITY

The success of China's ambitious state-owned enterprise reforms will ultimately come to rest on current reforms in the banking sector, a problem underscored by the extensive bad assets which China's state-owned commercial banks are carrying. In fact China's state-owned enterprise and banking reforms are inextricably entwined. Consequently, one of the major tasks which the People's Bank of China set out to accomplish last year was to tackle the problem of state-owned enterprise bad debts which have left a historic black hole in China's State-owned commercial banks, where most of the nation's deposits are concentrated.

In 1999, the China Construction Bank established China Cinda Asset Management Company as a pioneer vehicle to "purchase" from the China Construction Bank its "bad assets" with the intention of "managing" these debts and turning them around. As banks are not permitted to hold equity directly in enterprises, Cinda was created as a subsidiary under the China Construction Bank for this very purpose. The concept underlying this move was to effectively convert bad debts to equity holdings, held by the management company. As shareholder, the management company's brief would be to turn around the loss-making enterprise.

On July 15, 1999 the State Economy and Trade Commission, which the central government has entrusted with supervising State-owned enterprise reform, and the People's Bank of China jointly issued guidelines on procedures for these asset management companies to undertake debt to equity conversions. In short, the State was instructing the new asset management companies as to which enterprises should be undertaking debt-to-equity swaps. The State Council has selected some 500 enterprises for this grand experiment, which in principle is based on models adopted in other countries (such as Sweden) but with Chinese characteristics.

Shortly after the establishment of Cinda, each of the other three state-owned commercial banks jumped on the bandwagon establishing asset management companies of their own. By the end, the Bank of China had established China Oriental Asset Management Corporation, which has to date undertaken debt-to-equity swaps in 19 enterprises involving asset conversions of Rmb18.8 billion; the Agricultural Bank of China had established China Great Wall Asset Management Corporation, which to date has managed to only swap debt to equity in two enterprises involving Rmb600 million; while the Industrial & Commercial Bank of China has undertaken swaps involving 16 enterprises and a massive Rmb15.4 billion in debt to equity swaps. Cinda for that matter has relieved its parent the China Construction Bank of some Rmb15 billion in bad assets spread across ten troubled enterprises.

To date, the experiment in its present stage of advancement has been hailed by China's official banking and finance publication *Jinrong Shibao Financial News* as the "most outstanding news in the financial area" reported at the outset of this year. In reality however, such judgements are premature. While the asset management companies consolidate the bad assets, cleaning them off of the portfolios of the commercial banks, there is as of yet no clear exit strategy for the asset management companies. While banks under law cannot become shareholders in enterprises, by creating asset management companies under the banks to become the shareholders, one could argue that the problem is being shifted from one hand to another, or from front burner to back burner.

Increasingly, the task of solving the enterprise question was falling into the basket of problems being handled by People's Bank of China. It was clear that the question of state-enterprise reform had become inextricably intertwined with the very viability of the country's banking system. Solving this critical problem is the key issue which China's central bank must tackle in order to push forward its ambitious program of rationalizing the banking system and financial service sector in the century ahead.

In the first chapter of this section, People's Bank of China Governor Dai Xianglong provides a very detailed overview of the key financial reforms in the new century. In the second chapter, Goldman Sachs International Chairman Peter Sutherland discusses the role that securities firms, investment banking and corporate finance will play in globalizing China's financial system. Dr. Alexander Hendrick George Rinnooy Kan, chairman of the executive committee of ING Asset Management, examines China's commercial banking sector, providing his prognosis for the future in the third chapter. In the fourth chapter, chief executive officer of Swiss Re, Walter B. Kielholz, discusses

China's growing insurance industry and the future role re-insurance will play. In the last chapter of this section, Mark L. Clifford, Asia regional editor of *Business Week*, draws attention to critical risks in China's financial system which must be addressed to assure China's financial stability in the century ahead.

DAI XIANGLONG

Dai Xianglong is governor of the People's Bank of China, the central bank of China. A professional banker by background, Dai graduated from the Institute of Banking and Finance in 1967 and served as vice governor of the Agricultural Bank between 1985–1989, following which he served as chairman of the Bank of Communications and then chairman of China Pacific Insurance Co. Ltd., before becoming first vice governor of the central bank in 1993, when Zhu Rongji was serving as acting governor. Dai has worked closely alongside Zhu Rongji in steering China through a critical inflationary period in 1993–1994 and through the Asian financial crisis of 1997–1999. He has overseen the implementation of dramatic reforms in China's banking and financial system.

In this chapter, Governor Dai presents a comprehensive overview of China's banking and financial sector reforms currently underway together with a roadmap for the future.

CHINA'S BANKING AND FINANCIAL SECTOR REFORMS IN THE NEW CENTURY

Dai Xianglong
Governor, People's Bank of China

Significant achievements have been attained since China adopted its reform and open door policy in 1978. During the years 1979–1999, China's annual GDP increased at an average rate of 9.6%, far faster than the annual GDP growth prior to our reforms, and at a higher rate than the world's average 3% growth rate for this same period. The living standards of the Chinese people have greatly improved, as have social and political stability.

China will soon enter into its tenth five-year development plan and will soon join the WTO, under the terms of which China will grant national treatment to foreign enterprises, especially foreign financial institutions after a five-year transition. This combination of events will bring both rare opportunities and severe challenges to China in the reform and opening of its financial sector. China will therefore need to speed up its pace of financial system reforms and improve the competitiveness of China's financial sector in entering the 21st century. The following tasks lay before us.

FINANCIAL ORGANIZATION SYSTEM REFORMS TO IMPROVE COMPREHENSIVE SERVICE FUNCTIONS

After 20 years of reform and opening, China has established a basic financial organization system with commercial financing serving as the base, with various financial institutions engaging in separate but cooperative work. By the end of 1999, the total domestic assets of all financial institutions under the supervision of the People's Bank of China (PBOC) amounted to Rmb17.2 trillion. A breakdown of this figure shows that the assets of the

267

state-owned commercial banks amounted to Rmb10.4 trillion, or 60.5%; the assets of various shareholding commercial banks amounted to Rmb2 trillion, or 11.6%; and urban and rural credit cooperatives and trust and investment financial institutions amounted to Rmb4.8 trillion, accounting for the remaining 27.9%.

In the future, the construction of our financial organization system will not mean just increasing the number of organizations and offices, it will rather focus on accelerating structural reorganization, transforming the operational mechanisms, and establishing a modern enterprise system, while improving comprehensive service. Forming various financial institutions and separating their work while enhancing cooperation, will adapt the system of financial organization under the new atmosphere of reform and openness. The following outlines various measures underway to enhance systemic reform among the different financing organizations in our system.

STATE–OWNED COMMERCIAL BANK REFORMS

In accelerating the reform of China's state-owned commercial banks, the question of how to reform the wholly state-owned commercial banks is the most critical issue we are facing in forming a new banking system. In the year 1999, China formed four financial asset management companies to purchase, manage and dispose of non-performing assets so as to separate these from the banking sector, through the implementation of debt-equity swaps for certain qualified state-owned enterprises. A sharp reduction in the non-performing loans in the portfolios of the four state-owned commercial banks was achieved through this separation process. In addition, through Ministry of Finance support, China will increase the capital funds of the state-owned commercial banks through various means, including the self-accumulation of funds by financial enterprises, increase in budgetary support, and the issuing of long-term financial instruments and securities.

In the future, certain qualified state-owned commercial banks will be transformed into state-held shareholding commercial banks. It is estimated that during the tenth five-year plan, the four state-owned commercial banks will increase their loan portfolio by Rmb5 trillion, which will require the banks to increase their capital funds by Rmb400 billion. Based on this, the state-owned commercial banks must undertake comprehensive reforms and transform operational systems according to the requirements of a modern banking system. This will involve reducing branches and offices, laying off redundant staff, and reforming personnel management and salary systems. The implementation of a precise accounting system, together with a five-category loan quality ranking system, will gradually lead toward the establishment of a complete financial information disclosure system.

Shareholding Bank Development

We need to aggressively support the development of shareholding banks. At present, there are 100 shareholding banks in China, of which one portion came from the urban commercial banks that were built upon the urban credit cooperative base, and the other portion came from cross-border shareholding commercial banks. The emergence of shareholding commercial banks imploded financial market competition, promoting the formation of a competitive environment within the banking sector, and in turn, supporting the development of small and medium-sized enterprises.

In order to support the development of small and medium-sized commercial shareholding banks, China must undertake the following measures: further regulate ownership structures; improve efficiency and profitability of operations; and support business cooperation according to market principals. Aside from the target of raising share capital, we must promote those qualified small and medium-sized shareholding commercial banks which meet the requisite conditions to list on the securities markets, and adopt various means which even include seeking foreign capital in order to enlarge their capital funds. Moreover, within a competitive environment, we must advocate proper mergers and acquisitions.

Credit Cooperative Reforms

We must further deepen urban and rural credit cooperative management system reforms. In China, there are more than 39,000 rural credit cooperatives, 2,000 of which are county-level urban credit cooperatives. In the future, better support will be provided for the development of urban and rural credit cooperatives to improve services provided to support the private individual economy. In order to meet the demands of farmers in developing the rural economy, rural credit cooperatives will be transformed into cooperative financial organizations along the principals of "independent operations, self-supervision, self responsibility in undertaking risks, self-development.

Non–Banking Financial Institutions

To better support the development of non-banking financial institutions, it is important to put into play various self-operating mechanisms. We must grasp the opportunity to complete restructuring of the 200 trust and investment companies that now exist. Of these trust and investment companies, some two-thirds will need to be abolished or merged, and the remaining one-third will need to be restructured along the principal of serving as "trustee financial agent."

On this basis, the trust and investment companies will be expected to manage a principal's money in developing financial business opportunities so as to meet the rational financing needs of state-owned enterprises. Special emphasis will be placed on developing financing companies and financial leasing companies in the sectors related to promoting technological modernization, investment and consumer activities.

SECURITIES AND EQUITY FINANCING

Direct equity financing will be expanded through developing our securities industry. At the end of 1999, China had 90 securities companies and 22 securities investment funds. In the future, the market will be managed on the principles of the market economy according to the direction of "law, supervision, self-discipline, and standardization." On the basis of standardization, we will accelerate the development of our securities market, and run the market according to the law in order to protect the legal rights of investors. In this manner, our securities markets will be put to better use in promoting both state-owned enterprise reform and the development of our national economy.

INSURANCE INDUSTRY DEVELOPMENT

Developing the insurance industry will be critical in assuring our ability to strengthen economic development. In 1999, income from insurance premiums was Rmb139.3 billion, insurance density was 1.67% and penetration was worth Rmb110.85. In the future, China will increase the number of insurance companies and branches, developing the insurance agencies to complete the development of our insurance market. This will involve opening up and expanding the insurance business to urban and rural areas so as to strengthen abilities in fighting natural calamities that both enterprises and individuals may face. In accordance with law, insurance companies will expand their capabilities and increase the value of their insurance funds, so as to improve the ability of insurance companies to provide compensation.

DEVELOPING FINANCIAL MARKETS AND IMPROVING FUND CIRCULATION SPEED AND EFFICIENCY

In recent years, we have established a monetary market management system, which, in essence, accords with China's actual situation. Market practices have been basically standardized through the establishment of a nationwide, interbank market and accompanying transaction networks, leading to the gradual expansion of the scale of financial institution transactions. At the initial stage of forming the nationwide interbank market and interest rate system, we have encountered a situation in which interbank market interest rates are essentially able to reflect the actual supply and demand of funds on the market. Through the opening and development of the money market, the central bank has continued to expand its effectiveness through open market operations.

In 1999, the volume of state bonds in circulation was Rmb1,054.2 billion, estimated to increase annually in the coming years. In the future, China will continue to utilize state bonds and financial debt instruments in developing the monetary market, and putting into play open market operations so as to facilitate basic money supply and market interest rate adjustments, to serve in the promotion of developing a money market. A primary transaction commercial system is being gradually perfected.

The number of interbank bond market members has increased. A secondary trust management system is being established so as to allow enterprises and individuals to conduct over-the-counter treasury bond transactions to expand transaction volume, and increase liquidity. A nationwide interbank electronic transaction system is being further perfected, pushing forward the establishment of a correspondent banking system. This will fully bring into play monetary market guidance for remaining short-term fund adjustments, forming a short-term fund interest rate base, which will increase the speed with which funds are circulated and utilized efficiently

Since 1990, China's securities markets have undergone, and will continue to undergo, further development and standardization. By the end of 1999, there were 949 domestic listed companies, totaling 308.8 billion shares, and the aggregate market share value was Rmb2.6 trillion, equivalent to 32% of GDP. Since the establishment of our securities markets, a total of Rmb447.9 billion in accumulated capital has been raised on the stock exchange, among which, Rmb94.1 billion in capital was raised in 1999 alone. This figure represents a 12% increase over the previous year, equivalent to 8.7% of total bank financing growth for the same year. When compared with the securities markets of developed nations, the scale of China's stock exchange market scale is relatively small, the direct fund-raising ratio relatively low, and the function of institutional investors has not been fully utilized, leaving an enormous opening for the potential development of China's securities market.

In the future, China must further standardize and develop the securities market. On the basis of a primary board for outstanding medium and large-sized state-owned enterprises, we must also speed up the pace of constructing and developing a secondary board, primarily for small and medium-sized high-technology start-up enterprises. Establishing a tiered level market structure will open up a direct financing channel for small and medium-sized enterprises including high-technology companies.

By gradually establishing a financial derivatives market, we will enhance the variety of market products, further improving the stock exchange market structure, thereby creating an attractive securities investment environment. Standardizing the operational behavior of securities companies will further perfect their internal control systems and enhance the actual strength of these companies by expanding their share capital, which will optimize the organizational structure of security companies.

Institutional investors must be actively cultivated so as to progressively enlarge the scale of funds, to develop and launch trial funds, and push forward pension and other long-term funds to steadily enter the securities market. We must fully develop the effectiveness of raising long-term capital from the securities market by assisting state-owned enterprises in separating from their losses, transforming their operational mechanisms, and strengthening their rational allocation of resources.

RAISING THE LEVEL OF FINANCIAL MACROCONTROLS

After 1999, China's broad money supply, M2, was Rmb12 trillion (M2 = cash + unit current deposit + unit fixed deposit + residence deposit), increasing by 14.7% over the previous year. Narrow money supply, M1, was Rmb4.6 trillion (M1 = cash + unit current deposit), increasing by 17.7% over the previous year. Money in circulation, M0, was Rmb1.35 trillion, increasing by 20.1% for the same period. At present, China's monetary control policy has basically realized the transition from direct control to indirect control. Finance is now increasingly affecting our national economy, with monetary policy playing a significant role in managing inflation and preventing deflation.

We will continue to maintain the stability of the renminbi while promoting economic growth as a monetary policy objective in the formulation and implementation of monetary policy. In order to realize this target, we must correctly manage the relationship between preventing financial risks and supporting economic growth, trying hard to improve monetary policy at the operational level, increasing the volume of monetary supply appropriately. Over the next five years, China's monetary supply will expand at a rate slightly higher than the aggregate rate of China's GDP growth and inflation rate. However, the lending growth rate will, to some extent, decrease, as there will be an obvious corresponding increase in direct financing through the capital markets.

Over the past several years, the PBOC has fully utilized the interest rate lever. Interest rates were increased twice in 1993, and lowered seven times between 1996 and 1999, playing an important role in bringing inflation under control and in overcoming deflation. Over the past few years, experiments and accumulated experience with the interbank money market rate, state bonds and the issuance of policy-backed financial treasury bonds, purchase back and discount rates, relaxation of central bank open market operation rates, and the margin and interest rate floatation on loans, have been gradually expanded, in order to promote reform of the interest rate market.

In the future, China will continue to conduct reforms of the interest rate management system, creating conditions that will gradually realize a situation where the deposit and lending rates of financial institutions are determined by the market. In the long run, China's interest rate management system reform will be based on supply and demand in the money market. A system of determining various interest rate levels will be based on the central bank base rate as the core, money market interest rates serving as an intermediary, money supply and demand. At the same time, use of the interbank union for forming interest rates will be put into play. The general strategy is: according to the principal of proceeding step-by-step in an orderly way, to firstly open up foreign currency deposit and lending rates in order to meet international financial market interest rates; and secondly, open up deposit and lending rates for rural credit cooperatives below the county level, in order to provide credibility among the people. And then, gradually expand the floating margin and scale of urban financial institutions' lending rates. Finally, the ceiling of lending rates and managed deposit rate elasticity will be relaxed.

ESTABLISH AN EFFECTIVE FINANCIAL SUPERVISION SYSTEM

Before 1984, China carried out a mixed operational banking system, without a specialized central bank. In 1984, the People's Bank of China began exercising the specialized functions of a central bank. In 1995, "The People's Republic of China Banking Law" was approved by the National People's Congress, establishing a legal basis for China's central bank system. In 1998, the China Securities Regulatory Commission (CSRC) and the China Insurance Regulatory Commission (CIRC) were established, which marked the separation of the supervisory system tentatively formed for the separate operations of banking, securities and the insurance industry.

In October 1998, there was an important reform carried out in the management system of the People's Bank of China, involving the abolishment of the former 32 provincial, autonomous region and municipality level branches directly under the central government. These 32 branches were replaced by nine cross-province branches, which in turn set up financial supervision offices in the provincial cities where no branch had existed, to replace the abolished branch organizations which formerly existed in the same city. These measures reinforced the independence and fairness of the central bank in fulfilling its responsibility.

According to the stipulations of "The People's Republic of China Commercial Banking Law," "The People's Republic of China Security Law" and "The People's Republic of China's Insurance Law," China has implemented separation of the management systems of the banking, securities, and insurance industries. This legal base and supervisory model will basically be adopted throughout the development stage of China's financial sector, and it is expected that this system will remain unchanged for a certain period of time. However, with the creation of new financial products and the development of electronic information technology, overlapping business will expand across the banking, securities and insurance sectors. Particularly due to the fact that there is no legal division in the boundaries between the various intermediary services available, such overlap will occur easily.

Over the next few years, we must encourage the creation of interagency services among commercial banks, security companies and insurance companies. As for any banking debt or invisible debt, business which has not yet arisen as long as the business is not forbidden—as stipulated in the financial supervisory regulations—financial institutions can conduct or proceed with after reporting to the relevant authority for registration. At the same time, in following and studying development trends in the international banking sector and new supervision technology, we will draft the supervisory countermeasures for new businesses, like electronic banking, in advance.

In accordance with the developing trend of consolidating a variety of financial services, financial supervision must also gradually move in the direction of consolidation. At present, the three large financial supervisory organs, the People's Bank of China, the China Securities Regulatory Commission, and the China Insurance Regulatory Commission, will strengthen their coordination and improve overall supervisory standards. A system of regular and timely discussions will be established to fix the boundaries of supervisory responsibility where services overlap and solve policy coordination problems where issues of separate supervision arise. A system of jointly sharing supervisory information will be established. Joint research of critical issues will mean that countermeasures may be put forward early so as to perfect China's financial supervision system.

The key point in supervising the banking industry in the future will be to continuously carry out plans for maintaining financial stability. Financial asset management companies will purchase and settle the nonperforming loans. High-risk financial institutions will undergo rectification, supported and helped or turned over to the market. Various measures will be adopted to replenish the capital funds of financial enterprises. Careful supervision will be carried out according to international standards. Transparency of information will be gradually improved. The system of strict effective financial supervision and self-discipline and industry union self-discipline will be further perfected. The People's Bank of China will supervise based on the law, and society in general will jointly supervise a strict and effective financial system. After more than two years of effort, the central bank supervisory structure and system has dissipated the risks associated with high-risk financial institutions, various kinds of banks and nonbanking financial institutions which are required to meet the targeted requirements of supervision.

PROACTIVELY PARTICIPATING IN FINANCIAL GLOBALIZATION

Since opening and reforms, China's financial sector has opened to new areas, gradually expanding its business scope. The ability to maintain an international balance has been strengthened and international exchanges and cooperation have been expanded.

By the end of 1999, there were 182 financial institutions in operation (not including insurance institutions), of which 87 were foreign financial institutions and group enterprises from 22 countries and regions established in China. The assets of foreign banks in China totalled US$318 million (Rmb263.3 billion), among which foreign exchange loans amounted to US$218 million, accounting for 20% of total foreign exchange loans domestically. At the same time, Chinese financial institutions have also aggressively entered the international market to explore business. By the end of 1999, there were 472 operational organizations set up overseas by Chinese banks with total assets of US$151 billion. In the future, China will push further the opening up of its financial sector and aggressively and safely participate in the process of financial globalization.

PUSH FORWARD CAPITAL ACCOUNT CONVERTIBILITY

At present, China's capital accounts are not yet freely convertible. This is due to two substantive reasons: the first is to control and approve the overseas borrowings of China's industrial enterprises; the second is that foreign capital is not allowed to enter into China's A share market. This is due to considerations over the small scale of the A share market relative to total market turnover, which valued only Rmb800 billion by the end of last year; the market and management ability need to be improved. If we allow short-term capital to flow in and out easily, it would not be safe for either domestic or overseas investors.

After joining WTO, China's economy will be further integrated into the global financial market. In the long run, realizing renminbi convertibility under capital accounts will be a coming force. But opening up the capital account will bring risks, which may attack the domestic financial market, causing international short-term speculation funds to threaten our national economy and financial stability.

Therefore, realizing renminbi capital account convertibility will be a medium-to long-term step-by-step process. China should adopt a careful and realistic attitude towards this. Over the next few years, we will speed up setting up a modern enterprise system, improve both the fiscal and financial situation, standardize and expand our securities markets, and improve our ability in balancing international revenues and expenditures, so as to create the conditions which will enable capital account convertibility.

PERFECTING THE RENMINBI EXCHANGE RATE MECHANISM

In January 1994, China successfully conducted foreign exchange management system reforms, realizing the merger of dual foreign exchange rates, establishing a single and manageable floating exchange rate system based on market supply and demand. In December 1996, renminbi convertibility under current accounts was realized.

Between the years 1994 to 1997, the renminbi was facing pressure to revalue, and foreign exchange supply exceeded demand. The People's Bank of China, through open market operations, purchased US$120 billion in foreign exchange, then rapidly increased foreign exchange reserves, and stabilizing the exchange rate. During 1998 and 1999, China was facing the effects of the Asian financial crisis. This time, through measures involving the sale of foreign exchange, combined with increased export rebates, we were able to maintain the renminbi exchange rate, preventing devaluation. From 2000, China's international balance of income and expenditures has been good, foreign exchange supply now exceeds demand, and the renminbi exchange rate has been stable.

The stability of the renminbi exchange rate has had a positive effect not only on improving China's economic development, but has played an active role in stabilizing the Asian financial crisis. In the future, we should further improve supply and demand by providing a basis for a single exchange rate system under a managed float. The important point will be to perfect the exchange rate formation mechanism, to increase encouragement for the main part of the economy to participate in the foreign exchange market. Such initiatives in counter-attacking exchange rate risk by using the market will improve the degree to which the market itself will become the renminbi exchange rate mechanism, protecting exchange rate stability while allowing a relative float. At the same time, we must expand foreign exchange forward transaction business, gradually forming rational mechanisms through which exchange rate risks may be avoided.

ACTIVELY PARTICIPATE IN INTERNATIONAL FINANCIAL AFFAIRS

In the future, based on the principals of fair competition and mutual benefit, we will strengthen cooperation among nations and among the central banks of Asian countries. We will continue to support a continuing role for international financial organizations such as the IMF in international financial affairs. We must actively seek mechanisms for maintaining currency stability in the Asian region, in order to create positive conditions for China's further economic integration into the world, so that we can play an ever-increasing role.

In addition, recognizing the problems of a lack of qualified financial management personnel and of the low level of electronic information systems, China must both train and introduce from elsewhere, senior level management and qualified supervision personnel. In accordance with the trends of the developing financial sector, which include Internet-based financing, consolidation and internationalization, we must strengthen unified planning for the construction of electronic financing networks, increase investment, and improve the modernization of technology, equipment and management standards of China's finance industry.

PETER D. SUTHERLAND SC

Peter D. Sutherland SC is chairman and managing director of Goldman Sachs International (1995–current). He is also non-executive chairman of BP Amoco plc. (1998–current) and from 1997, was non-executive chairman of British Petroleum Company plc. Of Irish nationality, he was born on April 25, 1946 and was educated at Gonzaga College, University College Dublin and the King's Inns. Mr. Sutherland graduated in Civil Law. He was also admitted to practice before the Supreme Court of the United States of America. From 1969 to 1981 he practiced at the Bar. Mr Sutherland currently serves on the board of directors of Telefonaktiebolaget LM, XXX and Ericsson.

Prior to his current position, Mr Sutherland served as Attorney General of Ireland (1981–1984), EC Commissioner responsible for Competition Policy (1985–1989), chairman of Allied Irish Banks (1989–1993), director general of the World Trade Organization, formerly GATT (1993–1995). He has received 11 honorary doctorates from universities in Europe and America. He was awarded an honorary fellowship of the London Business School in recognition of his contribution to business and trade (1997). His publications include the book, *Premier Janvier 1993 ce qui va Changer en Europe* (1989), and numerous articles in law journals. He chaired the committee that reported to the EEC Commission on the functioning of the Internal Market after 1992 (The Sutherland Report).

In the following section, Mr. Sutherland discusses the many challenges facing China's financial system and opportunities that can be forthcoming in respect of corporate finance, securities and investment banking.

CHINA: THE LONG MARCH TO CAPITAL MARKET REFORM

Peter D. Sutherland SC

Chairman and Managing Director, Goldman Sachs International

BUILDING FOUNDATIONS

China has traditionally been known as a closed country. Its history is largely that of a nation politically and economically separated from the rest of the world. However, the situation is very different today. China is now the ninth largest trading nation, ahead of Korea and Spain, for example, and is likely to become the second largest trading nation by 2025, exceeded solely by the United States. Furthermore, China is expected to achieve US$100 billion of foreign direct investment (FDI) and US$600 billion per annum in external trade by 2005. In new technologies also China is advancing. It has the world's fastest growing PC market, inspiring the capital and confidence needed to stimulate further China's emerging technology sector. Given the direction of economic reform, the outlook for China's growth is bright; the average growth rate for China's real GDP is estimated at 7% per annum between 2001 and 2025, well above the United States' 3–4% and Europe's 2–3% GDP growth rates.

However, one must not forget that China is in the course of implementing a dramatic series of changes that constitute formidable challenges. For example the country has to deal with the significant problem of non-performing loans (NPL's) and has to gradually lift capital controls, allowing foreign investors into the Shanghai and Shenzhen A-share stock exchanges. With accession into the World Trade Organization, it is imperative that China deals with these issues as quickly as possible. They will contribute significantly to providing the basis of sustainable economic growth. China must build a solid foundation for economic growth through four critical areas: banking reform, state-owned enterprise (SOE) restructuring, easing of capital controls, and capital markets development.

BANKING REFORM AND SOE RESTRUCTURING

In the past, banks in China often did not lend on the basis of proper risk evaluation. In effect they provided credit to loss-making SOEs. Many SOEs treated credit not as debt to be repaid, but effectively as a government grant. Inevitably this has led to a significant number of non-performing loans (NPLs). In essence, savings deposits served as another way to provide state subsidies. Credit problems were further exacerbated by poor regulation, supervision and management. Essentially, many SOEs had few incentives to make profits and little or no financial accountability. Inevitably this led to substantial credit problems with the banks. In some instances, SOEs effectively declared bankruptcy to avoid loan repayments to creditors, and the legal system was ineffective in providing effective bankruptcy proceedings and foreclosure rules. As a result, domestic credit outstanding amounted to 110% of GDP as of March 1999, with the Big Four Chinese banks (Industrial and Commercial Bank of China, Bank of China, China Construction Bank, and Agricultural Bank of China) accounting for 72% of total credits. The NPLs are estimated to be 30–45% of total loans outstanding.

Attempts to restructure the banking system and the NPL's took place in 1999, when China established the Cinda Asset Management Company, whose purpose was to take over NPL's from the China Construction Bank, and to collect loans and/or sell them to domestic and foreign investors. Three other asset management companies (AMCs) have also been established and are in the course of attempting to address the NPL problem of the other Big-Four state-owned commercial banks. In September 1999, the 15th Party Congress revealed the government's intentions to remove intervention from all competitive industries and activities, reducing the share of SOEs in the economy, either by leasing or selling the medium and small companies, while privatizing the largest SOEs such as China Telecom and PetroChina. The anticipated accession into the WTO makes these privatization plans more crucial than ever. Further privatizations over the next few years could raise a further US$21 billion.

REGULATORY FRAMEWORK AND EASING OF CAPITAL CONTROLS

Previously, a range of government organizations controlled listing decisions for companies through a quota system that favored SOEs. However, with the structural reform in 1998, the State Council Security Commission, the government representative for the People's Bank of China, the Ministry of Finance, State Development and Planning Commission, and the State Economic and Trade Commission, merged into the China Securities Regulatory Commission (CSRC) in the following manner:

Current Supervisory Structure

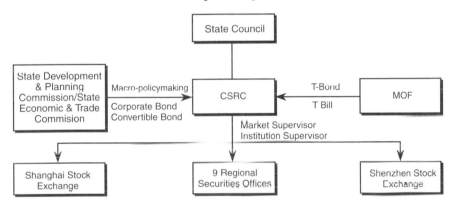

Formed in 1991, the CSRC effectively dismantled the awkward and inefficient governing board of the many government divisions, becoming the sole market and institution supervisor over nine regional securities offices and both stock exchanges, thereby significantly streamlining the regulatory process. Other significant reform decisions included changing the listing approval process from a quota system into a merit system complying with international standards. In addition, the Securities Law 23 for market reform (approved by the People's Congress in December 1999) prohibits insider-trading, misuse of clients' funds by brokerage firms, and other breaches of proper market procedure. This law also provides for transparent reporting. The law, in short, brings China's capital markets much more into line with established international practice and deserves to reduce concerns about China's commitment to capital markets and market reform. In my opinion, these reform measures support analyst predictions of significant growth in the coming years in China's market, especially after accession into the WTO.

The current government and banking reform will certainly boost the prodigious market performance that has already occurred, but it is nonetheless important to keep China's market in perspective. Relative to its economy, the stock market is small by international standards. The equity market, with two stock exchanges, has a total market capitalization of less than 50% of GDP, and the illiquid domestic debt market is limited to long-dated government bonds with few actively traded corporate bonds. Despite this the extent of the rapid growth of the Chinese market is remarkable. The Shanghai and Shenzhen stock exchanges were established in 1990 and 1991, with initial total market capitalization at US$2 billion. By the end of May 2000, there were over 47.7 million stock investors in China. The total market cap of A-shares (stocks issued by PRC enterprises in renminbi (Rmb) that can only be traded by PRC residents and institutions) amounted to US$483 billion, growing at the average annual rate of 200% over the past five years. Domestic savings have also increased about eight times from 1990, reaching US$724 billion. This establishes a considerable market for asset management. Furthermore, these growth indicators have signaled to investors the vast potential of China's capital markets.

Capital markets continue to be a positive influence on China's economy, rewarding companies on managerial performance. The Shanghai and Shenzhen stock markets are valued at US$486.9 billion, making them the world's best performing stock markets in the year 2000. The A-share market currently has an average P/E of 55x, with the Shenzhen A shares index up 48.6% since January. This is much higher than the 28x P/E valuations of the NYSE, and will continue to reach peak levels in the short and medium-term if China maintains its high economic growth rate. Because of a friendly market environment, low issuance costs and high P/E valuation, small to medium-sized domestic companies prefer to issue their stocks in the A-share markets, rather than in H-share or B-share markets, which represent companies' shares traded in Hong Kong or in China by Qualified Foreign Institutional Investors (QFIIs) respectively. Additionally, the anticipation of China's accession into the WTO is driving the A-share market even higher.

Unlike the A-share market, the B-share market has experienced problems since its inception. B-shares (stocks issued by the PRC enterprises in either US$ or HK$ that can be accessed solely by foreign investors) have only raised a total of US$4.38 billion since 1991 and have a total of 108 listed companies. Virtually from the beginning, the B-share markets have experienced a downward trend due to illiquidity and poor performance. Interestingly, 81 of the 108 B-share companies also have A-share listings with an average P/E ratio gap of 40x. There has been some discussion on possible solutions to this conundrum such as combining the A and B-share markets to enable foreign investors to join both markets and raise more capital. Another suggestion has been to permit domestic investors who collectively own over US$111 billion in foreign currency savings deposits to buy B-shares, but the government is apparently worried about its control over the foreign currency capital account.

Mutual funds and asset management are two significant potential growth areas. In March 1998, the first two securities investment funds were introduced to the Chinese market. Currently, there are 25 balanced and index funds with total assets of US$9.56 billion. Four of these have total assets of approximately US$1.93 billion. In the past, the CSRC has only licensed closed-end funds, with the ongoing capital markets development in China, the CSRC is now willing to approve open-end funds. There are currently 10 domestic fund management companies licensed by the CSRC to manage all funds and they are also considering a bill regarding joint venture (JV) asset management companies managing domestic funds and JV funds. Should this bill pass the State Council in 2001 as analysts predict, some of the most prominent fund managers will enter China's asset management companies. JV funds and Qualified Foreign Institutional Investors will offer foreign investors an entry into the Chinese market. Foreign shareholders may take no more than 33% interests, which is expected to change to 49% by 2003, and to fall away completely in five years. Despite the lack of convertibility of the renminbi, JV Funds and QFII's make it possible for foreign investors to directly enter into China's domestic market, allowing investments on behalf of Chinese customers as well as investments in Chinese domestic security markets.

The government has encouraged housing investment and private home ownership, including the privatization of existing stocks of public housing. The residential housing industry has great potential for growth given China's huge population and the abnormally low share of owner-occupied housing. The securitization of mortgages is an untapped potential resource and an essential area of growth. China's mortgage loans accounted for less than 3% of total banking lending as of 1998. Thus, the securitization of mortgages should help to deepen China's capital market by matching long-term savings with long-term borrowing. Hence, developments in the secondary mortgage markets parallel developments in the pension and insurance industries, as both combine to deepen equity as well as the debt capital markets.

China's Internet market is now growing rapidly. From its Internet user base of 8.5 million in January 2000, there were 17 million in July. Tight regulation and strict licensing of ISPs has kept the development of China's infrastructure market relatively slow, but the evidence suggests that the government is supporting the development of e-commerce in China. At central government level, laws are being enacted to encourage e-commerce and set standards, but individual ministries will also establish laws relating to their own particular areas of the economy. To date, the government has been the primary driver of systems integration projects as well as IT purchases.

KEY PLAYERS

In 1999, there were 90 securities companies and 203 trust investment companies operating in the securities markets. Currently, the CSRC is attempting to divide companies into two tiers: first tier companies operating in all business lines in the domestic capital markets and second tier companies focussing on brokerage. As this division is still being structured, ten securities companies have finished restructuring and capital expansion, and have received licenses as first tier firms from the CSRC, the top five being Guo Tai Jun An, Guo Tong, Zhong Xin, Guo Xin, and Guang Fa.

Some government-owned operations are taking advantage of market opportunities as well: China has privatized some of the leading SOEs, such as China Telecom (initial offering value of US$4 billion), PetroChina, and China Southern Airlines and is continuing to privatize other energy and media companies.

- *China Telecom.* Formed from an eclectic assortment of the state's telephone assets in the southern provinces, China Telecom became a cellular phone company with western standards of transparency and disclosure and financial reporting; the resulting company went to the global equity markets in late 1997. Today, China Telecom is the third largest cellular company in the world with a US$126 billion market cap and a growth rate approaching 50%. Its stock has more than tripled in value.
- *PetroChina.* China has taken some of its most productive domestic oil and gas assets and created the fourth largest integrated energy company in the world. Only one-third of the work force of the old China National Petroleum Corporation are employed by the new company. PetroChina has independent directors, a set of accounts sufficiently rigorous to satisfy the U.S. Securities and Exchange Commission, disclosure and corporate governance in line with

international standards and a management that will be compensated on how well the company performs financially, rather than on how much oil they produce.

Private and foreign joint venture companies are now responsible for 70% of China's industrial output, and are growing at an 11% per annum, creating more than 100 million jobs.

TRANSITION INTO THE WORLD TRADE ORGANIZATION

Although China has an impressive economic track record, it still has many hurdles to overcome, such as the NPL problem and banking reform. Essentially, China needs to build strong financial institutions. It requires a modern central bank that can supervise the banks and provide monetary control; a modern accounting system that can increase transparency in financial reporting; competition in line with international standards; and an enforceable legal system that will hold banks and companies accountable for breaches of contract or fiduciary duty. Moreover, China needs a liquid market to aid China's best companies' growth, allocating capital in the right places, creating jobs in growing industries and make good use of its huge pool of savings.

As is occurring with PetroChina and China Telecom, most SOEs need restructuring. These institutions employ over 50% of the urban working population. With SOE restructuring and market institutionalization, China has already experienced an increase in unemployment, reaching 9% in 1998 from the 2.5% in 1996. The vital need is to stimulate sufficient investment to provide jobs and growth.

The global economy is anticipating the landmark event of China's accession into the WTO. China's membership will boost productivity gains arising from tariff reductions, non-tariff barrier removals, and open markets. The November 15, 1999 agreement with the United States regarding China's accession into the WTO contained the following important changes for China's relationship with outside investors: not only will China remove most non-trade barriers and lift many tariffs, China will also open up many service sectors to foreign competition, such as the telecom industry, retail banking, and insurance industries. Furthermore, foreign companies will be granted rights to conduct wholesale, retail sale, distribution, and export and import businesses throughout China. This accord allows for foreign investment in Internet companies, doubles the number of foreign films allowed into Chinese theaters from ten, permits foreign banks to offer services in local currency to mainland companies within two years of WTO accession, and allows foreign auto companies full distribution and trading rights. China is expected to reduce tariffs on automobiles to 25% from the current 80 to 100%, and will cut tariffs on agricultural products to 14.5% from the present 15%.

The consequences of these changes are substantial for many multinational corporations. Industries are also expected to boom because of the tariff reductions and open markets, such as the technology industry. Although there are less than 10 million Internet users today in China, it is estimated that there will be 80 million users by 2003, warranting an increase in the need and use of a wide range of Internet services. The telecom industry will also open its markets, although currently foreign investors can only enter the telecom market through investing in or alongside one of the three existing domestic players: China Telecom Hong Kong, China Unicom, or China NetCom. Even in the retail industry, international companies such as Wal-Mart and Carrefour/Promodes are expected to expand into China, tripling revenues over the next three to five years. The airline industry is also expected to grow significantly and, as a regional market it will exceed the size of Japan's. Thus, overall, the projections for China's WTO accession are encouraging, not only for China but for many multinational corporations as well. However, before all this occurs, China must address a difficult but necessary adjustment process—inevitably, increasing bankruptcy filings will occur as foreign financial institutions expose China's financial institutions to competition. However, these short-term costs are ultimately a small price to pay for the long-term substantial growth that China should see in future years.

CHINA IN THE NEW MILLENNIUM

While much remains to be done to complete China's push towards efficient capital markets, the political leadership has taken significant steps to lay the foundations of the necessary reform process. As I have pointed out, measures such as SOE restructuring and privatization are key to the promotion of further capital inflow into the country. At the same time this capital flow will demand reform in corporate governance. Free markets and openness to foreign trade are vital for high economic growth so is good transparent corporate governance. China will not be able to maintain this high rate of economic growth. I believe that China's economic success will enable it to join the United States, Europe and Japan as global economic leaders, contributing to poverty alleviation and economic development in sub-Saharan Africa, South Africa, and other less-developed parts of the world, not least through the example that it will provide. As one of the major economic powers China must play an important role in safeguarding world peace and prosperity, and its on-going economic transformation will be judged as one of mankind's greatest triumphs. I am convinced that the successful integration of China into the global economic system is an immensely positive event that will result in substantial gains for global GDP growth. The natural dynamism and entrepreneurial flair of the Chinese people should ensure this success.

Dr. Alexander H.G. Rinnooy Kan

Dr. Alexander Hendrick George Rinnooy Kan is the chairman of the executive committee of ING Asset Management since 1997 and a member of the executive board of ING Group since 1996. He also holds the unique distinction of serving as advisor to the Guangdong Provincial Government on financial matters and advisor to the China Development Bank.

ING Group is a global financial institution of Dutch origin, active in the fields of banking, insurance and asset management in over 60 countries, employing over 90,000 staff. ING, is one of the largest integrated financial services groups in the world with total assets exceeding US$531 billion as of June 30, 2000. S & P has assigned a rating of AA-/As2 to ING Group and its major banking and insurance subsidiaries, ING Bank and Nationale-Nederlanden. Under ING, there are over 60 companies under their own brand names, including ING Bank, ING Barings, ING Insurance, BBL Bank, BHF Bank, Postbank, ING Real Estate, Baring Asset Management, Mercantile Mutual and ING Direct. In China, ING has established 17 offices in banking, insurance and asset management.

Drawing on the combined experiences of this impressive network of extensive financial service institutions, Dr. Rinnooy Kan provides a clear overview of the developments and reforms in China's banking and financial sector in the century ahead.

Banking and Finance in China

Dr. A.H.G. Rinnooy Kan
Member of the Board of ING Group

The Big Wave of Reforms Has Just Begun

With the imminent accession of China into the World Trade Organisation, the whole landscape of the Chinese banking and financial system faces a dramatic change. Obviously, the influx of big global players and the exploding application of Internet and e-commerce will have a significant impact. As foreign businesses are allowed to compete on a more level playing field in China's domestic markets, the policy makers have stepped up the pace of reforms ahead of new challenges whilst aiming at a soft landing for state-owned banks and enterprises after the market has opened up. While China has come a long way, the big wave of reforms and restructuring has just begun.

Banking Reform Overview

Banking reform has been moving forward slowly in the past decade, with structural impediments remaining. Over years of intimidation of looming collapse, China's fragile banking system has proved surprisingly resilient. China has not plunged into the deep banking crisis faced by Thailand, Indonesia and South Korea during the Asian financial crisis, mostly thanks to its closed capital account system, the high foreign exchange reserves and the strong liquidity in the domestic banking sector.

Although there is no immediate threat of a systematic banking failure, China must admit that its banking system remains inherently unstable given the serious State-Owned Enterprise (SOE) and Non-Performing Loan (NPL) problems. Either a major external economic shock or a sudden turn in macro-environment could explode the bomb. In the wake of the GITIC collapse and the impending WTO entry, the government is aware of the urgency of a major overhaul of the banking system.

REGULATORY REFORM

The first step in regulatory reform was the promulgation of the Central Bank Law in 1995, which legitimately named the People's Bank of China as the only government body to supervise and regulate the banking sector. In relation, China has split up three regulatory bodies to supervise three different financial services.

> People's Bank of China (PBOC)—banking sector
> China Insurance Regulatory Commission—insurance sector
> China Securities Regulatory Commission—securities sector

In 1998, the PBOC was restructured to enhance the independence and authority of the central bank. This led to the establishment of nine regional PBOC branches to replace the previous 31 provincial offices, which is a structure that is modelled after the U.S. Federal Reserve System. As we know, a key problem in China's banking sector has been the local political influence placed on provincial PBOCs and state-owned banks to lend to failing SOEs. The new regional PBOC branches are less susceptible to such local pressures as their senior officers are appointed by the PBOC head office directly instead of by the local governments. Each branch assumes supervisory responsibilities over three to five provinces and as a result, their widened geographical representation would free them to a large extent from the influence of one particular province.

Apparently, the newly found power of the restructured central bank was evidenced from the closures of some bad local financial institutions. Nonetheless, behind these closures, there were also political forces at work. Major financial institutions closures by the PBOC recently include:

- In June 1998, Hainan Development Bank and China Venturetech Corporation
- In October 1998, Guangdong International Trust and Investment Corporation
- In July 2000, three Wuhan trust and leasing companies, and three ministry level trust companies

Therefore, it is fair to say that the central bank is much more independent and powerful than before, but local governments still maintain some influence so that the central bank may have to compromise at times.

COMMERCIAL BANK REFORM

Since the establishment in 1994 of three policy banks—the China Development Bank, the Export/Import Bank of China (China Exim Bank) and the Agricultural Development Bank of China—all other Chinese banks are grouped under the commercial banking category despite the fact that nearly all of them are still government-owned. The "Big Four" state-owned commercial banks (Bank of China, Industrial & Commercial Bank of China, China Construction Bank and Agricultural Bank of China) account for about two-thirds of all the banks deposits and loan assets in China. Although the four banks are intended to act as commercial banks, they remain in reality the government policy tools to achieve its economic and social goals. After the credit quotas system was abolished in 1998, the four banks have gained more autonomy in making individual loans, but in general, they still have to comply with the government's development policies. As long as the banks are owned and controlled by the government, their policy role is unlikely to be changed fundamentally.

Arguably, the most critical problems in the banking sector are the high level of NPLs and the continued lending to bad SOEs. So what is the actual level of NPLs in China? Some estimates are as high as 30–40%. Nevertheless, PBOC had paid more attention to these problems since the enactment of the Commercial Banking Law in 1995. But the most aggressive attempt to address these issues were the re-capitalization program in 1998 and the asset management companies scheme initiated in 1999. In August 1998, the central government injected new capital for the amount of Rmb270 billion (US$33 billion) into the Big Four to more than double their capital base. In conjunction, the minimum statutory reserve ratio was cut from 13% to 8%, releasing about Rmb377 billion of liquid assets into the banking system.

ASSET MANAGEMENT COMPANIES—A SOLUTION OR A BURDEN?

Besides capital injections, the four newly formed AMCs are the most important tools of the Chinese government to resolve the huge NPL problem. Modelled after the US Resolution Trust Co, the first AMC (China Cinda) was established in April 1999 to take over the NPLs from China Construction Bank. Subsequently, three other AMCs were set up and put into operation in late 1999. The following four AMCs are attached to each of the four state-owned banks respectively to tackle their asset quality problems:

- China Cinda Asset Management Corp—China Construction Bank
- China Great Wall Asset Management Corp—Agricultural Bank of China

- China Hua Rong Asset Management Corp—Industrial & Commercial Bank of China
- China Orient Asset Management Corp—Bank of China

Under the scheme, the AMCs will issue long-term bonds (10–30 years) to the banks in exchange for the NPLs due from a list of SOEs at face value. According to the Chinese press, the AMCs have realized, by mid 2000, the initial target of taking on Rmb1.2 trillion of NPLs from the Big Four. The speed with which these AMCs have achieved this initial target was impressive, but this is not the end of the problems.

Establishing AMCs to clean up the long-overdue NPLs of the state-owned banks and to reduce the heavy interest burden of the SOEs is a move in the right direction. Although the bailout is extremely costly to the public purse, the benefits to the banks are enormous. The removal of the bad loans from the books of the banks has effectively increased their capital base considerably. With the AMCs' bonds, the banks' asset quality is much improved as is their cashflow and profitability, given the fact that the AMCs will make coupon payments to the banks. At an annual coupon rate of 2–4%, the bonds can generate substantial interest income for the banks for up to Rmb24–48 billion, which is a few times more than their reported net profits.

However, there remains a challenging task of how to dispose of or recover the NPLs. Although the AMCs have become major shareholders of these SOEs, it is slow in restructuring the SOEs and thus it will take a considerable amount of time to dispose of these SOE assets. The PBOC believes that the ultimate loss will be below 9% on an NPL ratio of 25%, implying a recovery ratio of 64%. This appears to be very ambitious given the large impairment of the loans assets (SOEs) that have been transferred to the AMCs. According to Moody's, the recovery rate would be very low and the final bailout cost to the Chinese government could easily reach Rmb1 trillion, which represents about 12% of China's 1998 GDP, or about 100% of its 1998 fiscal revenues. Clearly, the cost will no doubt put pressure on the government's fiscal resources, despite the fact that the major part of the costs will not be realized until the AMC bonds are redeemed in 10–30 years.

Now the question arises whether AMC will be a solution or a burden to China? Will the sense of accountability of the state-owned banks be inspired or will they continue to rely on government bailout and seek for another cleanup in the future? The policy makers must recognise that for these one-off benefits to be sustainable after the WTO entry, deeper reforms on management culture and other structural issues must be continued.

WTO CHALLENGES

China's long-awaited WTO entry will be good for China and good for the world. It will enlarge China's participation in the global economy that can lead to long term gain of 1–2% of GDP for China, although some of these benefits will take time to materialise. While there will be clear economic benefits, WTO membership will also pose challenges to China's financial system (banking & insurance sectors) and many industries like agriculture, automobiles, IT and telecom.

There has been much speculation on how Chinese financial institutions cope with the influx of global players who are both financially strong and efficient. Yet, the heightened competition these Chinese institutions have to face is partly mitigated by their funding advantage in the domestic market and the government support. Moreover, other structural barriers (such as lack of reliable data and opaque regulations) and the underdeveloped domestic market will continue to prevent foreign firms to capture more business immediately. Practically speaking, only a handful of the big global players can reap any material benefits in the short term after the WTO accession.

For the longer term, the Chinese bankers and insurers are still very concerned about the WTO impact. They understand that they lag far behind their counterparts in terms of capitalization, global network, efficiency, expertise, modern management system and culture. As the WTO pact allows a transitional period of two to five years, China has to adjust its financial system and to implement more initiatives very quickly to meet the post-WTO challenges.

MORE RAPID TRANSFORMATION REQUIRED

Reconfiguration of the largest state-owned banks should be encouraged to enhance the efficiency and competitiveness of the banks. Domestic banks have a huge burden due to their massive network and number of staff. The average cost to income ratio exceeds 80%, which is one of the highest in the banking world according to the calculation made by the Banker. To enhance operational efficiency and net profits, they must change the huge cost structure by largely cutting the redundant resources. This is a very delicate issue and the process has been modest and slow in the past decade.

As disclosed by the former president of the Bank of China, his informal statement of intending to reduce half of its 200,000 workforce had nearly paralyzed the bank, as staff feared for their jobs. Though difficult, the banks must not slow down their pace to reduce its high cost/income ratio. This could take the form of early retirement of elderly staff or the sale of some branches to newer institutions (local or foreign) that wish to expand.

DEPOSIT INSURANCE

Deposit insurance is a way to maintain the financial system's stability against financial institution failures. With the Asian financial crisis and some domestic financial failures, a stabilising mechanism has become increasingly necessary. A moderate capital flight has already occurred in the months after the closures of GITIC and Hainan Development Bank, as depositors shifted their accounts from smaller banks to bigger state-owned banks.

A deposit insurance scheme has its pros, but the big four may argue that they hardly need such protection since they are enjoying a degree of public confidence. On the other hand, such scheme may also encourage financial institutions to take on more risks or ignore the importance of prudent management, which may work against the whole idea of banking reform. Nonetheless, a deposit insurance scheme should not be treated as a remedy to China's financial illness, as it cannot prevent a bank collapse in itself. Only a sound financial system and prudent management can sustain public confidence.

CULTURE RESHAPE

No matter how good the regulatory or supervisory system is, it cannot guarantee that a financial institution is managed properly. Competent management is the first line of defense. But a lack of sense of accountability is deeply rooted in the culture of the domestic banking sector, in particular for state-owned banks. In this respect, the reform dimension should focus on loan officers' accountability and the related credit approval and risk control process. The accountability should somehow be tied to appropriate incentives.

In general, salaries of bank officers are relatively low and unrelated to their performance, while fringe benefits make up a considerable part of the compensation. Formal incentives should be introduced like options (for listed banks), bonuses and promotion, based on individual performance that are measurable.

MORE FOREIGN PARTICIPATION

Healthy competition is a prerequisite to the successful commercialization of the Chinese banks. PBOC should allow more foreign financial institutions to expand their business scope by further easing the constraints it imposes on the limited number of foreign banks that are allowed to deal in local currency transactions. Although the WTO pact allows more liberalization in this area in two to five years, the central bank is said to be putting up new barriers to re-regulate foreign banks' access to local currency business in order to protect the interests of Chinese banks. The measure currently under consideration is to cap renminbi lending to a multiple of 12.5 times of the Rmb30 million capital base of most foreign banks. Should this re-regulation be implemented, it will be a major setback for the entire banking reform. It is important to get the balance right and over-protection will only prolong the reform progress.

Other forms of foreign participation should also be considered like lifting the ban of foreign interests in a local Chinese financial institution. So far only China Everbright Bank and Ping An Insurance Company have a small percentage of foreign interest. If the scale of foreign participation is increased, it will greatly enhance the reform progress with more healthy competition and higher capitalization of local financial institutions.

UNIVERSAL FINANCIAL SERVICES

The current segmentation of financial activities (banking, insurance and securities) will have to adapt to a global trend of universal financial services after the WTO entry. Citigroup and ING Group are two leading examples in the global financial services field. In China, CITIC and China Everbright are currently the only two Chinese entities allowed to undertake diversified banking, securities and insurance activities. They have the competitive advantage to enjoy the greater synergy effects over other financial institutions.

MOVING TOWARDS IPOs

Raising money from the equity market is the most effective way to recapitalize China's banking system and other financial institutions without using fiscal resources. The equity raising exercise is virtually a proxy to China's banking reform, as listed financial institutions are automatically subject to the scrutiny of the market forces. On the other hand, the government considers the stock market a socialist tool for raising capital to revitalise SOEs but inclines to maintain majority ownership in strategic firms. Although the scale of privatization is still pretty small, it will eventually end the primacy of state-ownership and release the heavy burden of the government.

Driven by the WTO entry, the government has been actively privatizing (or selling minority shares of) some of the major SOEs like the successful listing of China Telecom (now renamed as China Mobile), China Unicom and PetroChina in the HK Stock Exchange since last year. Yet, the initial public offering (IPO) progress of Chinese banks has been much slower. Pudong Development Bank, listed earlier this year on the Shanghai Stock Exchange, is only the second Chinese bank being listed, with Shenzhen Development Bank having been quoted on the Shenzhen Stock Exchange since 1990. China Minsheng Bank, the only non-government owned commercial bank in China, has been scheduled to raise funds in the Shanghai stock market later this year. Many other smaller Chinese banks are said to be planning for listing in the near future.

The other major market on which China can raise capital is Hong Kong. The recent acquisition by ICBC of the 51% stake in Union Bank, a small retail bank in HK, is considered an important step for the continued restructuring of this giant state-owned bank as more asset injections and restructuring will follow. China International Trust & Investment Corporation (better known as CITIC) and one of the largest financial institutions in China owns 55% of CITIC Ka Wah, another HK-listed bank. Besides, China Everbright Bank has a 20% interest in International Bank of Asia, which is also listed in HK. Other than that, the HK stock market has not been actively used by Chinese banks, in particular the Big Four, for fund-raising and reform purposes.

At least two issues have to be addressed along with the privatization of financial institutions—tax reform and securities market reform. Tax reform is critical to the Chinese banks that are currently subject to an unusually high tax rate of 55%, compared to the 15–33% rate for foreign banks. Without tax reform, the Chinese banks will never make a respectable return on investments and therefore cannot be expected to run on a purely commercial basis.

Swift changes in the stock market are gathering pace, as the Chinese leaders understand the urgency of a deep, liquid and sophisticated market to support the task of privatization. China needs a stock market that is attractive enough to encourage people to invest their savings and liquid enough to dispose of state assets to fund their social liabilities. Besides, the stock market is also a key to economic efficiency as well as economic growth.

There are now debates on the merger of the Shanghai and Shenzhen stock exchanges and the merger of the A-share market with the hard currency B-share market. The latter is particular difficult since China at present has a closed capital account. The CSRC also wants to set up the "second board" for hi-tech hi-growth companies as early as the first quarter of 2001. It wants to introduce index futures and other options, which are required by institutional investors for hedging risks.

On the Rise

China's banking transformation is indeed interlocked with the entire chain of reforms in insurance, securities market, pension, and other currency or interest rate liberalisation. All these efforts have led to some improvements in transparency, efficiency, corporate governance, management, and shareholder value, which will lead to higher investor demand for new IPOs, thus facilitating the privatisation and reform process. Virtually, a self-sustained reform cycle is emerging. There is no quick fix but the good news is that China is committed to all these economic reforms. All the facts point out that China's complex and huge economy is on the rise, and that the long-cherished goal is in view.

WALTER B. KIELHOLZ

Walter B. Kielholz (born 1951) studied business administration at the University of St. Gall, graduating in 1976 with a degree in business finance and accounting.

His professional career began with the General Reinsurance Corporation where, after spending some time in the USA, the UK and Italy, he assumed responsibility for marketing tasks in Europe. In 1986 he moved to Credit Suisse, where he was responsible for customer relations with large insurance groups within the Multinational Services department.

He joined Swiss Re at the beginning of 1989 as head of the Japan and Far East sector, taking charge of marketing coordination in these markets and of underwriting property and casualty business. At the beginning of 1992 he was also assigned responsibility for the head office's reinsurance business in the USA and the UK.

In January 1993 he became a member of the executive board of Swiss Re, Zurich. Since April 1995 he has been a member of the Executive Board Committee, responsible for the Alternative Risk Transfer division, which comprises worldwide activities in business with major industrial clients and in the field of financial products and covers for insurers, as well as the services associated with these areas.

On January 1, 1997, he became chief executive officer of Swiss Re. At the annual general meeting of June 26, 1998, the shareholders elected him to the board of directors of Swiss Re. The same day, the board of directors appointed him managing director.

Walter Kielholz serves on several boards of other financial service companies such as Credit Suisse Group and the credit insurer EULER (Paris).

In the following chapter Mr. Kielholz provides an overview of developments in China's insurance sector examining the challenges, opportunities, and role that re-insurance will play in the future.

China's Insurance Industry—Facing a New Era of Opportunities and Challenges

Walter B. Kielholz

Chief Executive Officer, Swiss Reinsurance Company

Overview of China's Insurance Industry

China's insurance industry is characterized by a short but eventful history. The People's Insurance Company of China (PICC) was established in 1949, following the nationalization of all insurance business. All domestic insurance business was suspended from 1959 to 1979 with only international insurance remaining. The importance of the insurance industry was only recognized in 1980 when domestic insurance resumed. For the next six years the PICC continued to monopolize the market. It was only in 1986 that the authorities licensed a second provider, putting an end to the PICC's monopolistic position. The 1990s saw the industry blossom. Not only did premiums more than quadruple over the decade in real terms, but more insurers entered the market too, offering a significantly broader range of products and services. In 1992, the doors were opened to the first foreign insurer, marking a milestone in the liberalization of the market.

In 1986, total premiums in the Chinese insurance market amounted to a mere US$1.2 billion. At this time, per-capita spending on insurance was as little as US$1 and the share of insurance premiums in GDP amounted to a mere 0.4%. Commercial life insurance was virtually non-existent prior to 1986. Since then the Chinese insurance market has grown into Asia's fourth largest, recording a total premium volume of US$16.8 billion in 1999. Coupled with strong economic growth, over the past 13 years, the market has enjoyed a real average growth rate of 27% per annum. The number of market participants has increased from one to 22, including 11 domestic insurers, six foreign branches and five joint ventures. A further six operating licenses have been granted to foreign insurers and these are expected to start underwriting in the near future. In 1997, life insurance surpassed non-life insurance to account for a 56% share of total premiums. This dynamic development and the obvious market potential has not failed to attract foreign insurers: some 113 global insurers from 17 countries have established their presence in China hoping to benefit from the industry's upturn.

The astonishing achievement of the insurance industry in such a short time was brought about by the economic and socio-cultural developments taking place over the last two decades. Since adopting market-oriented economic reform and open-door policies in 1978, the Chinese economy has unleashed enormous vitality. Over the past 20 years, the economy grew at a real average rate of 10% per annum. Economic activity was given a significant boost and assets accumulated quickly. Annual disposable income per household has increased 15-fold over the past two decades. Living standards in China have been rising at a rate that is almost unprecedented in world economic history. Total foreign trade volume increased from US$20 billion in 1978 to US$320 billion in 1998, securing China's position as the ninth largest trading nation in the world.

Economic reforms and developments have brought gradual but profound socio-cultural trend shifts to an otherwise agrarian, state-centred, closely-knit and largely homogenous society. These trend shifts have had far-reaching implications for the development of insurance markets. The most important developments comprise industrialization and urbanization and the transition from a centrally-planned economy to a market-oriented one.

With market mechanisms being introduced sector by sector, the government has been gradually retreating from its role as the ultimate bearer of risk in Chinese society. Under the planned economy, state-owned enterprises (SOEs) were operated directly by the government while their employees enjoyed cradle-to-grave welfare benefits including such as free housing, medical care and pensions. In 1978, SOEs accounted for nearly 80% of the economy's total industrial output, employed 80% of the total urban labor force and accounted for more than 80% of the country's total fixed investments. Though the SOEs' share of total industrial output fell to 40% in 1998, they still employed around 45% of the total urban labor force and accounted for more than 50% of total fixed investments. Over the past decades, the dominance of SOEs in economic activities dampened incentive for the purchase of commercial property and life and health insurance covers.

The market-oriented economic reforms and the gradual withdrawal of the government as a "last-stop" lender, though still incomplete, has already begun to change the way enterprises and individuals deal with risks. Reform of the SOEs, the social security system, health care systems and housing all point towards a move in economic and social responsibility away from the government and towards individuals and enterprises. As a result, these developments have boosted the demand for commercial insurance from enterprises and individuals seeking to protect themselves against risks.

A New Era of Challenges and Opportunities

Over the past decade, the non-life insurance market has been growing at a real rate of 12.0% per annum while the life insurance market has been growing at 25.5% per annum. Despite such impressive rates of growth, current market volume is still viewed as being far below that which the economy may yet provide. In terms of insurance penetration (that is, premiums per GDP) and density (ie premiums per capita), China lags far behind the developed markets and many emerging Asian economies. In 1998, insurance density amounted to US$11, while that of the U.S. was more than US$2700 and that of Thailand US$41. Insurance penetration was 1.5%, far less than the level of the western countries' average of approximately 8% and less than Thailand's 2.3%. Of course, for a country where significant disparity in regional growth exists, China's figures should be interpreted with care. For example, in 1998, Shanghai's insurance density and penetration were US$95 and 2.8% respectively, considerably higher than the national average.

Nevertheless, the statistics reveal that although the potential of this huge market of 1.3 billion people, keen to avoid risk and having a high savings ratio, is obvious, the question remains as to whether and how soon it can be realized. By all measures, the Chinese insurance market is still in its infancy. With one of the world's lowest levels of insurance spending, public awareness of insurance and risk protection concepts is still very low. Until recently, for example, buying life insurance was generally regarded as bringing bad luck since it involves the issues of mortality and death. The wide gaps in incomes existing between urban and rural areas and between coastal regions and parts of the underdeveloped interior mean that the most of the population have no insurance cover. On the other hand, domestic insurers who dominate 99% of the total market are undercapitalised and, having been around on average for less than ten years, generally lack the necessary technical, investment and organizational expertise.

Despite displaying an overall impressive growth rate over the last decade, the non-life insurance market has slowed down significantly since 1995. Predatory price setting aimed at competing for market share and the withdrawal from insurance programs by the loss-making SOEs have taken a toll on premium growth in recent years. From 1995–1999, the non-life insurance market only recorded a real rate of growth of 3.2% per annum, a fraction of the rate recorded in previous years. For years, innovation was maintained at an extremely slow pace with little improvement in customer services.

Life insurance products in China traditionally emphasize savings rather than risk protection. Following seven consecutive interest rate cuts between May 1996 and June 1999, traditional life insurance products have lost much of their attraction due to the interest rates promised in the policies having fallen substantially. Life insurance premium growth has consequently slowed since 1998. On the other hand, interest rate cuts have left life insurers with considerable exposure to liability risks, resulting from a negative interest rate spread.

A related issue is the limited investment opportunities faced by insurers. Prior to July 1999, all insurers in China were only allowed to invest in government bonds apart from bank deposits. This poses serious problems for companies' asset-liability management and depresses their overall profitability in an environment with declining interest rates. Since July 1999, insurers have been allowed to invest in corporate bonds with a credit rating of AA+ or better with a limit of 2% of assets and, via mutual funds, in equities with a limit of 5% to 15% of assets. Despite the relaxation of investment restrictions, an immature capital market continues to limit insurers' investment opportunities.

Though usually perceived by domestic insurers as another challenge, foreign entry into the local market has actually proved to be positive to the market's development. Besides bringing in capital and technical expertise, foreign insurers have also helped promote public awareness of insurance. The entry of the American Insurance Association (AIA), for example, has stimulated the Shanghai life insurance market by introducing the agency system into the industry; agency sales currently being the dominant distribution channel for life insurance in China. This innovation has benefited domestic insurers as well.

Further market liberalization as a result of China's WTO accession should provide fresh impetus to the fledgling industry. The commitments China has made to the bilateral trade agreements with the US and the EU, if implemented, would have far-reaching implications for the local insurance industry. The prospect of effective management control by foreigners in life insurance joint ventures, foreign majority ownership in non-life insurers, the removal of geographical and line-of-business related underwriting restrictions and the granting of licenses based on "prudential criteria" suggest a sea change in China's insurance market.

From the domestic insurers' point of view, the influx of more foreign insurers may pose a threat in the short term while in the longer term, the capital, expertise and innovations being brought in by foreign insurers should prove beneficial to the whole market. More important, the perceived fiercer competition may create pressures for local insurers to step up moves towards innovation, improve services and enhance internal management, all of which are crucial elements for the further growth of the industry.

Being fully aware of the implications of the country's WTO accession, the domestic insurance industry has already begun to respond to the potential challenges. The China Insurance Regulatory Authority (CIRC) has stepped up regulatory control of the industry, setting up regional offices and passing two new regulations on insurance company management and rates and forms control for property insurance. More regulations are planned, including some applying to foreign insurance companies and reinsurance. Domestic insurers, on the other hand, are actively looking for ways to strengthen their capitalization, speed up innovation and improve services.

Domestic structural reforms will continue to act as insurance market growth drivers. With the loss-making SOEs being turned around and the large and medium-sized SOEs being further corporatized, demand for industrial insurance should be stimulated. Housing reform will create more private ownership of properties, which together with the increasing ownership of other private assets such as cars may serve to boost the development of personal lines in the medium to long term. Furthermore, proper functioning of the market mechanism requires the rule of law. As legal standards are raised, casualty lines are also likely to enjoy considerable growth.

On the other hand, social security system and medical care reforms may raise the demand for additional pension and health care insurance cover. The rapidly aging population and falling size of the average family as a result of the rigorous one-child-per-family policy have also created greater long-term incentives for life and health insurance.

THE DEVELOPMENT OF THE REINSURANCE INDUSTRY

Unlike the direct insurance market, the Chinese reinsurance market has not seen much development over recent decades. In 1985, a provisional regulation stipulated a 30% compulsory cession to the then reinsurance department of the PICC. This ratio was revised to 20% when China's Insurance Law came into effect in 1995. The PICC's reinsurance department evolved to PICC Re in 1996 as the first national professional reinsurer. In 1999, with the disbanding of the PICC Group, PICC Re was reorganized as China Re, the first independent domestic reinsurer. Except for compulsory cessions, local insurers retain the bulk of their business so that the commercial, non-compulsory reinsurance volume is very small. Business available to foreign reinsurers is limited to foreign-currency denominated business and does not exceed a few hundred million US dollars.

Against the backdrop of the enormous challenges facing local insurers, particularly in the light of the impending accession to the WTO, the government is becoming increasingly aware of the importance of reinsurance to the operation of the whole insurance industry and as a means of helping local insurers hold their own against fiercer competition. The development of a commercial reinsurance market currently ranks high on the political agenda. Besides the establishment of China Re as an independent provider, there is also a call for the establishment of reinsurance exchange centres and commercial reinsurers.

Indeed, the lack of capacity and technical know-how among domestic insurers calls for support by professional reinsurance, especially international support. Such support could benefit the domestic insurance industry by boosting underwriting capacity, strengthening solvency and improving risk management. Reinsurance would therefore help local insurers position themselves in the face of increased foreign competition.

The severity of domestic capacity constraints is most conspicuous with regard to infrastructure projects and natural catastrophe risks. Across China, tremendous resources have been spent on or committed to such projects. In many cases, the schemes are too sizable for one or two insurers alone— or even all domestic insurers combined—to provide adequate cover. A recent engineering project scheduled for completion by 2009 is expected to cost a total of Rmb200 billion (around US$24 billion), which is four times the total volume of non-life premiums in China and twice the current value of Chinese non-life insurers' total assets.

China exhibits one of the world's most serious exposures to natural perils. However, mainly due to inadequate capacity, there is at present cover for only a tiny share of these natural catastrophe risks. As an example, the economic loss from the 1998 summer floods in China amounted to Rmb200 billion, while insured losses came to a mere Rmb5 billion.

Professional reinsurers could narrow the capacity gap—reliably and cost-effectively. This in turn would facilitate economic growth and technological progress in China. In a broader sense, business's willingness to take risks, which itself enhances the efficient utilization of resources and economic growth, largely depends on the availability of insurance covers. The same applies to foreign direct investments and the associated influx of external capital and technological know-how.

Closely related to inadequate capacity, weak capitalization is an issue for most local Chinese insurers. CIRC has identified solvency as one of the key challenges facing the industry, and has stipulated clearer solvency requirements in the Insurance Company Management Regulations which came into effect in March 2000. With fiercer competition, solvency control is expected to be further tightened and more strictly enforced. Against this backdrop, reinsurance protection is set to become an effective means for local insurers to strengthen solvency.

Increasingly, the role of a reinsurer is moving from that of being merely a capacity provider to that of a client service provider, offering services such as claims management, risk restructing, pricing and management advice, consultancy and asset management. This may greatly improve the risk management skills of local insurers, especially when they lack the required expertise.

The development of the Chinese reinsurance market and its opening up to foreign participation are not separate issues. This is because reinsurance, by definition, is an international business. Large risks need to be diversified over a wide geographical scope and across lines of business. There are risks which are so large that a single loss might account for a substantial part of the total premium income of all domestic insurers. And if a country is highly exposed to natural perils, a single event could severely affect an area of production and other resources. It therefore pays to spread these risks over the international market since doing so can help remove the heavy financial burden and incalculable solvency risk from domestic insurers and decrease the domestic economy's vulnerability to catastrophic events.

TAKING OFF

In the short space of two decades, China has created an economic miracle. Its insurance industry has undergone a revolution all of its own. Though faced with considerable challenges, the forces at work in China's insurance markets suggest that the industry is headed for continued growth. Besides economic growth, a gradually diminishing role of the state as the ultimate bearer of risk, as well as opportunities deriving from China's WTO membership will be the key market drivers.

In line with the dynamic developments in direct insurance markets, commercial reinsurance in China is similarly poised to take off. The proposed establishment of new domestic commercial reinsurers and the opening up of the market to international reinsurers will significantly boost reinsurance growth—to the ultimate benefit of China's direct insurance companies, their policyholders and the nation's economic development in general.

MARK L. CLIFFORD

Mark L. Clifford is the Hong Kong-based Asia regional editor for *Business Week*. He joined the magazine in 1995 and won an Overseas Press Club award for his 1997 coverage of the Asian financial crisis. Previously he was business editor at the *Far Eastern Economic Review*.

He is author of the widely acclaimed book *Troubled Tiger: An Unauthorized Biography of Korea Inc.* and co-author of *Meltdown: Asia's Boom, Bust and Beyond*. He appears regularly on StarTV and has been a frequent contributor to BBC World Service, CNBC and other radio and television networks.

Business Week is the world's largest business magazine, with a worldwide publication of more than 1,100,000 copies and more than six million readers in more than 130 countries. *Business Week* has bureaus in Beijing, Shanghai and Hong Kong.

In the following chapter, Mr. Clifford provides sharp insight into the fundamental friction points in China's financial reforms drawing attention to critical weak points, which must be addressed in order for China to avoid the problems which have other fast growing Asian economies in recent years.

CHINA'S FINANCIAL SYSTEM NEEDS TRANSPARENCY AND ACCOUNTABILITY

Mark L. Clifford
Asia Regional Editor, Business Week

FINANCIAL REFORM AT THE CROSSROADS

It's become commonplace to say that financial reform is one of the keys to enduring economic progress in China. Almost as often, it's said that financial reform is approaching a watershed. Though these two statements are repeated with a mantra-like intensity, they're worth repeating again. For if China can't manage to get its financial system sorted out, there's little hope that reform will move forward. Instead, the economy will continue to be hobbled by money that flows to the wrong businesses for the wrong reasons. Conversely, if China does move convincingly toward a modern, market-oriented financial system within the next decade, it will lay the foundation for a huge burst of growth and cement the country's claim to be one of Asia's most important and dynamic economies.

Despite a decade of substantial progress, especially in securities markets development, the toughest work still lies ahead. Real reform of the banking sector lies at the heart of the challenge. But sweeping changes lie ahead in securities, insurance and non-bank financial institutions as well. China, like every country that's undergoing the transition from a repressed financial system to a more market-oriented one, will have to make some tough political choices as part of the reform process. For there most certainly will be losers, especially among the sprawling state-owned enterprises that gobble up the lion's share of credit and do so at below-market interest rates—even though they often have little ability to repay debt. The government will have to provide some protection for the less fortunate among those people who are whipsawed by the changes ahead, especially the

307

tens of millions of workers who are likely to be displaced as part of this process of cleaning up the financial sector and the related massive restructuring of state-owned enterprises.

A cautious, step-by-step approach to financial reform has served China well for more than a decade. Capital controls and a tightly managed financial sector helped insulate China from the worst of the financial typhoon that swept through Asia and much of the developing world in 1997–98. The currency held its value and unemployment has been kept within politically tolerable limits. But this caution may be an impediment in the decade ahead. China's best companies, rather than its best-connected, need access to capital so that they can compete in what promises to be a much tougher market after WTO accession. WTO will mean a more ruthless environment both for Chinese financial institutions and, at least as important, for their customers, the Chinese companies that are trying to carve out profitable positions at home and abroad. To shackle these companies, especially the dynamic private companies that are China's best hope, will mean to surrender a good part of China's economic sovereignty before the game has even begun.

State-owned banks, given their size, are inevitably at the heart of the hopes for and worries about change. Important regulatory reforms, particularly the strengthening of the regional branches of the central People's Bank of China in 1998, hold out the promise of more oversight over often chaotic local banking operations. Though there has been much talk about reform at the largest state banks, particularly in the form of tougher credit standards, the good intentions have yet to translate into measurable results. Little lending is extended to private firms or small and medium-sized enterprises, the most dynamic sector of the economy. Indeed, the threat to punish loan officers who extend credit to companies that ultimately cannot repay, understandable though those warnings may have been, has resulted in the paradox of a credit squeeze at a time when banks are flush with liquidity. As with other distressed financial systems around the region, notably Thailand, this excess liquidity is a sign not of health but distress.

THE REFORM AGENDA

The reform agenda in banking alone is a full one. The most dramatic move may be the emerging consensus to allow one or more of the large state-owned banks to list on the New York and Hong Kong stock exchanges. If a listing occurs, and it is unlikely to be before 2002, it will usher in a dramatically different era. A listing will require adherence to U.S. standards of financial disclosure and, to some degree, corporate governance. That, in turn, will require a dramatic change in management culture. In order to sell such share offerings to eagle-eyed foreign money managers, Chinese banks will have to open themselves to an unprecedented level of scrutiny. But it's not just the scrutiny that will be difficult: internal operations need to be cleaned up so that the bank will beckon as an attractive investment. Most obviously, bad loans will have to be recognized and dealt with.

But the change needed is far more fundamental. Banks will have to set up an internal credit culture that embraces a set of self-policing measures to manage risk and ensure that loans are made on a commercial basis. It's not simply a matter of being cautious about making loans. It involves an entire culture, where risks are measured against rewards. Even with the best of intentions, the difficulty of moving from a state-owned mentality, where bureaucratic procedures are often more important than profitability, to one in which returns on capital are the guiding principle, cannot be overstated. The limits of a top-down centralized control system are apparent now that the economy has reached a new level of complexity. The often harsh logic of the stock market will act as an overseer, in conjunction with regulators who must be better-trained to assess risk, rewarding or punishing management for its ability (or inability) to articulate and execute its business strategy and goals.

The move to partially privatize the banks reflects a sea-change in thinking among China's financial policy makers. As recently as the end of 1999, leaders decided that privatization for everything except the banks should get the go-ahead. The decision to approve one or two large banks for privatization reflects a belief that well modulated corporate governance can be an ally of regulators as they try to nurture the development of a more market-oriented economy.

The successful listing of PetroChina on the New York and Hong Kong exchanges in early 2000 marked a major step forward and gave confidence to top leaders that foreign stock market investment could be an ally rather than an adversary in the reform process. Significantly, the PetroChina listing marked the first time senior management at a Chinese state-owned company received performance-linked compensation. Three hundred of the company's top managers have up to 75% of their pay linked to performance. Other companies are following suit, including Sinopec and China Mobile, and the trend is expected to accelerate as increasing numbers of leading state companies seek overseas stock listings. This shift to more of a meritocracy, coupled with market discipline and oversight, marks a sharp departure from the ways of the past. It also marks a recognition that the market can complement the role of the many government auditors, inspectors and examiners who look at both financial and non-financial institutions. There still remains a role for strong government institutions, but the recognition that investors are not just quick-hit speculators but valuable partners in corporate development reflects a newfound maturity among China's leadership.

REALITY VS. EXPECTATIONS

The establishment of asset management corporations in 1999 marked a milestone in attempts to resolve the massive problem of bad debt in the Chinese system. Modeled loosely on the Resolution Trust Corporation in the U.S., the asset management corporations took bad debts off the books of major state-owned banks. The banks in turn took bonds from the asset management corporations as payment for the debts. This effectively allowed the banks to clean up and recapitalize their balance sheets. Just as important, by disposing of bad loans, the banks could start afresh with a new attitude toward deciding which customers it lent to and which it would turn down. Meanwhile, the asset management corporations would be tasked with raising what cash they could through assets sales and debt-for-equity swaps among the troubled creditors who made up their loan portfolios. That would allow them to service the interest on the bonds and eventually repay the principal. That, at least, was the theory.

The reality has fallen well short of expectations. First, it's not clear that the asset management corporations took all the banks bad loans. Well-sourced estimates are that they actually took only one-third to one-half of the bad loans, although absolutely no one knows for certain. Moreover, the asset management corporations have been slow to sell assets. This slowness results in part from inexperience and in part from the difficulty of breaking longstanding banking relationships that are woven tightly into the very economic fabric of the country. Although the asset management corporations are nominally independent, in practice they have been staffed by former employees of the very banks from which they are buying assets. Naturally, this has raised institutional difficulties and prompted questions about their autonomy.

As a result of the slow asset disposal, the asset management corporations have had little cash coming in and difficulty servicing their bonds. That has left the banks in a bind. Despite initial high hopes, the debt-for-equity swaps have also been a disappointment. Too many companies saw the swaps as a cost-free way of reducing debt. Although companies surrendered equity in return for erasing bad debt, many firms have been unwilling to change their corporate governance practices in return. For too many, it has been business as usual. Given that those very same business practices resulted in non-performing loans, that's not good enough.

The disappointing record of the asset management corporations can be salvaged and these problems may go down as the initial growing pains of young institutions. But it is going to require a good deal of political and institutional will to ensure that these well-meaning institutions do not become hollow vessels. Given the massive size of China's non-performing loans, which are generally estimated at 25–40% of bank assets (and Gross Domestic Product), the stakes are too high for China to get this wrong. But simply setting up institutions is not enough. Given the scale of the problem, and the way it is inextricably linked to troubled state-owned enterprises, a resolution of the bad-debt overhang will only occur in tandem with broader reform of the state sector.

The scale and scope of problems in the non-bank sector remains unclear. News that the People's Bank of China will provide about US$4 billion (33.3 billion yuan) in support facilities to rural credit cooperatives highlights the difficulties that this troubled corner of the financial world is undergoing. Many of the more than 40,000 rural credit cooperatives are in deep financial distress. Poorly-regulated, many have engaged in highly dubious lending decisions, ranging from speculative property developments to distressed township and village enterprises. The central bank acknowledges that the rural credit cooperatives as a group are insolvent. The September 2000 infusion of funds, which doubles the Rmb30 billion spent from end-March 2000 to end-August 2000, will provide needed short-term stimulus for the rural economy. But it may lay the groundwork for more serious long-term problems, by encouraging further lending to questionable projects.

KEY INNOVATIVE REFORMS NEEDED

Many of the most important reforms are now occurring in the securities area. The China Securities Regulatory Commission has dropped listing quotas, ending the cumbersome system that was designed to ensure an orderly stock listing process but all too often only resulted in well-connected companies getting approval to list while denying the same opportunity to companies that had better prospects. If it occurs in reality as well as theory, the end of quotas will usher in a new era in securities market development. It will go a long way toward eliminating the artificial scarcity engendered by the quota system. It will also, for the first time, put the burden of vetting companies and launching issues at market-driven prices squarely on the shoulders of the underwriters. The advent of a NASDAQ style second board, designed to encourage younger companies, will also be an important indicator of change. Although these sorts of boards have mixed records, at best, in the rest of Asia, this innovation could be one way in which China funnels money to more innovative and entrepreneurial companies.

A review of the company law, which came into force in 1994, is underway and should result in a strengthened corporate governance system and much better protection for minority investors. The reforms will allow lawsuits against directors and provide legal aid for these sorts of lawsuits, an important step in the effort to instill more accountability among management and boards. To back up the stick of lawsuits is a carrot, in the form of a slew of training programs underway to teach senior management the many responsibilities that go with a public listing. Revised regulations for mergers and acquisitions, which are due out shortly, will also make it easier to engage in much-needed corporate rationalization.

The introduction of a system to allow foreign investment in A shares, most likely in 2001, will be another big step forward for reform. Foreign investment in the local market will mean more money for domestic companies, of course, but it will also help to improve corporate governance, just as it will in overseas-listed companies. The system will have to be carefully calibrated to ensure that it does not undermine China's capital controls while at the same time allowing foreign investors enough flexibility to feel comfortable in investing. Taiwan, which has run a similar system, has attracted US$32 billion in foreign capital in ten years. China's ambition is to surpass that amount in a far shorter period of time. A number of foreign asset management firms have already announced joint ventures. Whether these really result in enhanced foreign participation in the market—and thus better corporate governance and a more efficient capital market—will await the test of time.

The move to bring in foreign equity investors marks one of the most hopeful signs in China's financial system. Along with openings in other parts of the financial system, including banking and insurance, it offers the possibility of a very different financial market emerging over the next decade. But to truly realize the promise that foreign investment brings, Chinese authorities at all levels of the government are going to have to take the risk that working with foreign investors as true partners—rather than trying to limit foreign involvement as much as possible out of a misguided conception of what constitutes national interest—will be to China's advantage. The next decade will be a tumultuous one for the Chinese economy, as the easy stage of reform passes and much tougher work begins. The challenge is to align China's interests with those of foreign investors, rather than imagining that finance is a zero-sum game in which one side's profits represent the other side's loss. Foreign capital and, just as important, the transparency and accountability that comes with more developed capital markets, will be key for China to extract the most benefit from its opening to the world.

Part VII

TECHNOLOGY AND INTERNET

CHINA GOES DIGITAL

Enter Beijing's China World Hotel on any day of the week, smell the pungent waft of coffee, and you will most likely find yourself amidst the bubbly atmosphere of yet another Internet technology conference. "The numbers are phenomenal," you will hear the speakers repeatedly say at such events. Not surprising: the Ministry of Information Industry predicts that there will be easily 30 million Internet users in China by the year 2003; the Chinese Academy of Social Sciences predicts there will be 60 million!

The China National Network Information Center published its updated "China Network Development Situation Statistic Report" on July 27, 2000 in Beijing. The report indicates that by June 30, 2000, Internet users in China had reached 16.9 million, increasing about four times over the previously recorded four million as of June 30, 1999. The total domain names registered under "cn" (for China) reportedly reached 99,743, indicating that the application of Internet use by enterprises, government departments and private persons in China has increased drastically over a remarkably short time span. The report also showed that most Internet users concentrated in the three regions of Beijing, Guangdong and Shanghai. These three cities alone represent 43.33% of the total numbers of Internet users in China at the start of this century.

The Ministry of Information Industry has explained that "China's information industry has already initially established a relatively complete relative scale of industry," pointing out "in the 1990s, China's information industry growth rates averaged three times higher than the national economy. Annual growth rates have been maintained at over

20%, among which the electronic industry products manufacturing total output has already reached Rmb778.2 billion from only Rmb245.7 billion in 1995," adding that its contribution to the national economy has already provided a stimulus to other industries as well.

China's fixed telephone network scale now stands as the second largest in the world. China's mobile phone network scale is now the third largest in the world. China's broadcasting and television network is the single largest in the world with 80 million cable television users. China is the largest single producer of televisions in the world.

REGULATING INTERNET

It should, therefore, be no surprise that when Premier Zhu Rongji convened the 31st Standing Meeting of the State Council in the autumn of 2000, the first item on his agenda was to adopt two draft regulations: the "Telecommunications Regulations of the PRC" and the "Internet Content Service Management Administrative Measures of the PRC."

The Telecommunications Regulations are intended to: "regulate the telecom market order, protect the legal rights and interests of telecom users and telecom business operators, protect the safety of the telecom network and information, and promote the sound development of telecom business." The purpose of the Internet Content Service Management Administrative Measures are to "intensify supervision and administration over the content of Internet services so as to prevent against dangerous information affecting society, especially affecting the security of the State, social stability, and public order."

The speed with which these regulations were adopted indicates that while telecommunications and Internet are contributing to China's economic growth, they may also be developing in an irrational manner. Customers are complaining about shoddy services and often, fraud. Also, the Internet is full of pornography and other kinds of materials viewed by the government as disruptive within the framework of China's social structure.

On October 1, 2000, when the Internet Content Service Management Administrative Measures came into effect, it was reported in China's Economic Daily that, "These measures are regarded as the basic frame- work and policy of China addressing international competition and information security issues for the next period of management and administration of the information industry in China." Moreover, China's "Internet management will gradually transform to regulatory standardized management."

These measures are critical in connection with China's WTO entry, as they provide a long-awaited legal framework for ICPs, and at the same time permit existing unstructured dotcom businesses—such as Sohu.com and

Sina.com that have been floating in a legal void—to at least have the assurance that they can continue to exist without undergoing major legal structural adjustments at this time. The new measures allow for money to be provided to domestic Internet service providers without such funds necessarily being counted as equity or loans. The new Internet Content Service Management Measures contain several key segments as outlined below:

- Private enterprises may enter the arena of Internet content providers meaning that China will allow private domestic enterprises to legally operate Internet content and other value-added telecom services and businesses.
- "ICPs" will be clearly defined in China under the two separate categories of: "business operations," which provide services for a fee which will fall under a licensing system; and "non-business operations" which provide services for free and only require filing for the record rather than actual licensing.
- China will adopt a "multi-department joint management system" over the Internet content service sector with the following government departments cutting in on the act: the Ministry of Information Industry, the State Administration of Industry and Commerce, together with other departments.
- Without the Ministry of Information Industry's approval, Internet companies may not seek stock exchange listings either in China or overseas. Likewise, foreign investments in Internet information service providers also requires approval according to the existing legislation concerning foreign investment with equity ratios determined accordingly.

As it is impractical to close down all existing Internet companies that already have foreign capital that has not been legally invested, the question of capital structure has been glossed over in the measures as an issue to be addressed. To some extent this is a practical and maybe a very Chinese way of addressing the issue, that is to say, it does nothing at all. In short, venture capital financing can still be provided on the basis of promise and vision. There will be more money for start-ups with an idea to burn.

CHINA'S GOVERNMENT GOES DIGITAL

When the State Science and Technology Education Leading Group convened a "Scientific Technology Seminar" in Beijing in mid-2000, State Council Premier Zhu Rongji spoke at the seminar concerning "adopting modern scientific technical measures especially advanced information technology" to "speed up the informationalization process of the government administration."

Premier Zhu called upon "all government bureaus to push forward the informationalization process" pointing out that "customs, taxation, banking, foreign exchange management administrations and law enforcement agencies must raise their quality to a new level."

Premier Zhu Rongji's appearance at this event sent an important signal concerning how his administration is viewing the importance of developing information technology. Underlying this motivation, clearly, is the need to wire the financial system that is connecting foreign exchange administration issues with the banks, and in turn, the taxation and customs departments, as together these organs form a critical network in surveying foreign exchange inflows and outflows as well as gray market arbitrage activities.

Premier Zhu also used the "Scientific Technology Seminar" at the State Science and Technology Education Leading Group as an opportunity to stress the need to adopt information technology in various government departments and introducing policy measures to achieve this. The following highlights from Zhu's talk reveal much:

- "Last year's anti-smuggling effort indicated that without advanced measures and modern information technology, it would be difficult to attack criminal groups efficiently and protect the economic and legal system in the interests of the nation;"
- "Two construction projects are to be initiated—one is the 'golden customs project' and the second is the 'gold taxation project'" which will put much of the work of these two departments on-line followed by the foreign exchange and banking departments;"
- "Government functions should be law enforcement and administration, not interfering in the economy and undertaking projects to give a nice image. All comrades should personally grasp the work of informationalization and Internet in every department".

Chinese government bodies are in a bit of a dilemma. On the one hand, they are anxious to push forward the development of the Internet as a means of driving the economy and stimulating consumption through all the excitement generated from Internet. On the other hand, they realize that it is hard to tax transactions online. Last year's total volume of transactions on line reached Rmb55 million, which is a meager sum amounting to only 0.02% of the total national consumption output. It is hoped that Internet transactions in China will reach Rmb10 billion by the year 2002. This waits to be seen.

The Ministry of Finance announced that methods to be applied in taxing Internet businesses are now under study, adding that the State Taxation General Bureau has established a special research group to plan the taxation policies to be applied next year to the collection of taxes from Internet income. A number of concerned departments of the government are now drafting and issuing "Internet Taxation Detailed Regulations." A policy framework for taxing Internet companies may be expected to kick in sometime soon.

PROMOTING HIGH TECHNOLOGY INVESTMENTS

China's State Development Planning Commission and the State Economy and Trade Commission jointly issued a list of the "State's Major Current Development Industry and Products Technology Categories," a catalogue of projects that are being encouraged as of September 1, 2000. This mega-list of categorized high technology investment projects is intended to "provide a main base for China's State economy structural strategic adjustment aimed at improving the investment structure, and investment projects," the official *Economic Daily* reported.

The government initially determined that there should be 28 areas within which some 526 types of products and technology would be listed. Infrastructure and services are also listed within. The reason for issuing these guidelines is to avoid duplicated construction and duplicated projects, a problem that is now deeply affecting China's economy by creating oversupply gluts in many products sectors and in turn forcing price wars. The "State Major Current Development Industry and Products Technology Categories" are determined based on five key principles listed as follows:

- "according to market requirements future development will require expansion of the domestic market;"
- "higher technology content will be required" and "enterprise equipment updates and industrial technology progress" will be requirements;
- "conducive to the creation of technology, a new economic increment point will be formed;"
- "conducive to the savings resources" and "improve the ecological environment;"
- "promote the rationalization of the economic structure" and "keep the national economy consistent, speedily and with sound development."

The State Council in parallel issued regulations to promote and encourage software and integrated circuit production. The "Several Policies to Encourage the Development of Software and Integrated Circuit Industry" are aimed at assuring the rapid growth of China's information industry. The target is to assure that China's software industry research and development capacity can reach an "international advanced level" and "domestic produced software and integrated circuits cannot meet the needs of the domestic market."

The aim is to fulfill, through domestic production, the needs of domestic demand for software and integrated circuits by the year 2010.

International standards need to be adopted. Research and development is required to achieve this calling for regulatory measures to encourage the industry so that tax and other officials do not drive researchers and developers crazy with the normal plethora of taxes and fines dished out by officials throughout China. The underlying objective of the State is certainly through research and development to develop quality products that can be exported and competed internationally. Local companies exporting their software products may be included in the scope for Export–Import bank loans.

The policies adopted are also aimed at luring foreign venture capital as well. As foreign venture capitalists (VCs) tend to be more naive than serious industrial investors, these measures are aimed at enticing them. The terms are even more marvelous than anything offered in California. For instance, a VC that invests in a software or circuit board producer is now allowed to sell its shares immediately upon the moment the producer company is listed.

The ownership categories applied to other enterprises will not apply to software companies, which means if they are state-owned, then this does not matter. (Previously, it was really only the state-owned enterprises that were permitted to list). As long as it is a software company, it can be listed, provided that its categories meet the requirements of the security market. This is a high sign for the beginning of a China NASDAQ or GEM market. Capital and profit will no longer be required as these can be replaced by "quality of management," "invisible assets," and other vague notions that helped make NASDAQ what it is today.

A GREAT LEAP IN TECHNOLOGY

China's current program of developing the information industry involves the promotion of an industrial strategy to activate information industry product manufacturing, software production, network and telecom facilities, and network technology applications. There is no question that China is now adopting an aggressive program to promote the information industry, a fact emphasized by State Chairman Jiang Zemin's own presence at the opening of the 16th World Computer Congress in Beijing, an event that under normal circumstances would call for no more than a minister-ranking official to be present.

The year 2000 at the opening of the new century also marked the first time in 30 years that the World Computer Congress has convened its annual event in a developing country. Jiang Zemin spoke at the opening ceremony emphasizing that, "China will focus on developing high technology and push forward the informationalization of the domestic economy and society." He noted that "China is a developing country and the tasks of industrialization are yet uncompleted. Now we are facing a hard task to realize informationalization."

Jiang noted that, "Our strategy is that during the process of completing industrialization, we will bring in information technology to enhance the level of industrialization, and during the process of pushing forward informationalization, use information technology to reform traditional industries, and use informationalization to lead industrialization. We must endeavor to achieve a big technology leap."

In the first chapter of this section Minister Wu Jichuan of the Ministry of Information Industry elaborates on China's plans to develop and promote Internet technology in the new century. In the second chapter, Peter Yip, CEO of chinadotcom, the first successfully listed China Internet player discusses the evolution of the industry and the role which China dotcom companies will play in the development of the information age in China. In the third chapter, Thomas Lewis, chairman of the Boston Consulting Group, looks at the development of the telecommunications and information industries as a whole, the role that they will play in fueling China's continued economic development, and explores creative financing packages that will energize this sector in the years to come. Jon Eichelberger, China partner of the Silicon Valley law firm Coie & Perkins, presents China's developing legal structure, which will provide a critical framework for the healthy and progressive growth of this exciting industry.

WU JICHUAN

Minister Wu Jichuan heads the Ministry of Information Industry, formed in March 1998 when the former Ministry of Posts and Telecommunications, Ministry of Electronics Industry, Ministry of Radio Film and Broadcasting, and information departments of the National Aeronautics and Aviation Corporation and State Aviation Bureau were merged into a single ministry to oversee China's both emerging and thriving information and telecommunications sectors.

Before assuming this new position, Minister Wu headed the Ministry of Posts and Telecommunications from 1993 to 1997, during which he oversaw the transformation of China's telecommunications sector to a wireless dominated system and the evolution of the Internet industry. Wu has an excellent background in the telecommunications sector, having himself specialized in wire communication engineering at the Beijing Institute of Posts and Telecommunications. He then held key positions in the Ministry of Posts and Telecommunications, serving as division chief and deputy director of the Materials and Equipment Bureau and deputy director of the Planning Bureau before assuming the position of vice minister in 1984.

In the following chapter, minister Wu draws upon his insights into the information and telecommunications sectors in explaining the policies and programs for development in the century ahead which will bring China to become a leader of the information age.

THE DEVELOPMENT OF THE INFORMATION AND NETWORK TECHNOLOGY INDUSTRY OF CHINA

Wu Jichuan
Minister, Ministry of Information Industry

INFORMATION AND NETWORK TECHNOLOGY— OPPORTUNITIES AND CHALLENGES

The new technology revolution of our contemporary world, represented by information and network technology, is vigorously pushing forward the development of social productive forces and changing the appearance of human society. First, the rapid development of microelectronics and software technology is causing the ratio between the operation capacity of chips, computers, performance and price to continue to increase in accordance with the rule of geometric progression, thus creating conditions for large scale and highly efficient collection, storage and processing of digitized information.

Second, under the impetus of three technologies—microelectronics, software, and laser—telecommunication network technology has realized the transfer from simulation to digital, from low speed to high speed and from single media to multimedia. In particular, the broad application of Internet and IP technology brought another leap of telecom network technology, promoting the emergence of a new generation of public network systems.

Third, the technologies of computer, telecom and media technology are undergoing reciprocal penetration and merging into each other. They are pushing the development of information and network technology into a brand new epoch.

Rapid development of information and network technology is speeding up the process of information online, leading to the rise of a network economy. While raw material suppliers, producers and consumers are commonly connected through the network, the means of connection (telecom) in the productive activities of mankind will be greatly improved. Due to unimpeded information between the supply and demand chain and the reduced role of the middleman and resultant savings in operating costs, the economic operating efficiency of our entire society will be greatly enhanced. For this very reason, at present, enterprises throughout the world will spend hundreds of billions of U.S. dollars on computers, software and networks aimed at coping with the ever-growing challenges of the network economy now on the rise.

The network economy is the direct embodiment of electronic commercialization, reflecting in fact, the progressive organizational and structural adjustment of enterprise productivity. It is the reflection of the contemporary progress of technology in economic life. Meanwhile, online social services, which include government online, education online, medical treatment online and media-entertainment online, are becoming a reality.

The Network Economy has now gone beyond just theory. Its realization has come upon us.

INDUSTRIAL DEVELOPMENT AND CHINA'S INFORMATION NETWORK TECHNOLOGY

China is planning to revive the manufacturing, telecommunications and software industries in relation to electronic information products, and to promote the informationalization of the national economy and social services. These are all aspects referred to under the name "information industry."

At present, the information product manufacturing industry of China has formed a relatively complete industrial system. In 1999, the electronic industry's total sales volume reached Rmb300 billion. Family household appliances such as tape recorders, telephone sets, color TVs, color tubes, sonic apparatus and VCDs have achieved standardized production and these products' output ranks number one in the world. China possesses standardized production capacity (including joint venture production) for the first-generation of telecom network products represented by fiber optics transmission and program control switchboards, which can basically satisfy the demands of network development. The research and development of technology and equipment in connection with the wireless mobile telecom and Internet are also speeding up in China.

The telecom service industry of China has developed drastically. During the 10 years from 1989 to 1999, the total quantity of telecom business and the total assets of the telecom networks have all increased by 35 times. The average annual growth rate is 43%. The scale of public telephone networks expanded by 15 times. The volume of switchboards reached 150 million households. The total number of users reached 110 million. Mobile phone use has emerged and the number of users has reached 55 million. During these past 10 years, the popularity of telephone use increased by a rate of 13% from the previous 1% (including mobile phones). Over the last two years, the growth rate of Internet use has doubled every six months on average. Currently, Internet users number around 15 million.

CHINA'S INFORMATION NETWORK
TECHNOLOGY INDUSTRY PROSPECTS

It is now a known fact that the information industry is the leading industry of our national economy. It is a catalyst and multiplier of economic growth. Over the past 10 years, the average growth rate of the information industry has been more than three times the growth rate of the national GDP. Its contribution to national economic growth and the leading role it plays in affecting other industries increases daily. Over the next 10 years, it is expected that China's information industry will continue to maintain a growth speed three times over that of GDP growth. In comparison with 1999, the proportion of China's information industry out of total national GDP has increased to 7.6% from 3.3% and the information industry's direct contribution to GDP growth is expected to rise to around 40% from the current 10.5%.

Our plan for speeding up the industrial development of information and network technology includes the following four-point strategy.

1. Activating the Electronic Information Product Manufacturing Industry

The electronic information product manufacturing industry represents the major technology and material basis for the construction of information networks. In the future, the State will place electronic information products into the major industry category in the national economy, accelerating its development. The marketing prospects for Chinese electronic information products are significant. Total sales value is estimated to reach around Rmb3000 billion in 2010. Under this scenario, we will continue to intensify the industrial structure adjustments, vigorously develop basic industries including microelectronics, and cultivate certain state-level development and production bases. We will also assist the large-scale enterprise groups that have international competitive capacity, thereby forming a pattern by which large corporations will be the main bodies, while leading the medium and small-size enterprises in joint development.

Through enterprise reform and integration, the strength of enterprises' creative development will be intensified into a highly efficient mechanism. A set of high-tech enterprises that possess its own intellectual property rights and competitive advantages has emerged in areas such as chip design and manufacturing networks and telecom, software and information household appliances among others. Products such as personal computers, mobile telephones, fiber optics telecommunications, network equipment, network tools, digital TV and information household appliances among others—which apparently have promising prospects of development—will be treated as key developing products for which large scale standardized production will be formed.

2. Vigorously Develop the Software Industry

The key element behind developing the software industry is human intellect. China possesses huge potential advantages in respect of talented software personnel. China will regard the software industry as a national strategic industry and undertake research to set out and put into play a long-term 21st century development strategy and development way of thinking. In the meantime, China will draft policies and measures to promote the development of the software industry.

China will establish mechanisms to absorb and provide stable working conditions for outstanding software talent, thereby allowing them to fully put into play their creativity and proactive energy. In compliance with the standards and rules of a market economy, China will absorb common investments from every aspect of society and intensify investment in software industry. Meanwhile, by relying on the force of the market, China will also develop the venture capital industry and create a group of venture capital investors who can organize capital, technology and personnel talent to lead the rapid development of China's software industry.

3. Speed up Construction of Network-Based Facilities

The realization of the information network requires speeding up the construction of network-based facilities. We will expand and perfect the existing base transmission network with fiber optics as the main pillar and push forward basic, general telecom services. At the same time, we will vigorously develop and utilize the most updated contemporary telecom and information, scientific and technical achievements and accelerate the building up of a new generation public information network which contains super capacities, is highly flexible and secure, and reliably covers the entire country. Facing the 21st century, we will also build up the State information infrastructure facilities. The construction of information infrastructure facilities must be carried out under the government's unified plan and guidance. We must organize various forces in the society and rationally distribute the resources to avoid duplicated construction based on the divisions of work, coordination and fair competition. Eventually, we will form a modern network layout adapting to the requirements of network information.

4. Using Competition Mechanisms to Implode the Telecom and Information Services Market

Over the next 10 years, China's telecom and information service industry will continue to maintain high-growth momentum. Firstly, the public telephone network will continue to develop rapidly. The scale of the network will more than double. The number of users will reach two to three hundred million. Secondly, wireless mobile telecommunications will become even more developed. Within the next 10 years, the users of mobile sound, voice and data services will also reach two to three hundred million. Thirdly, the Internet and related services will undergo dramatic development. Users of the Internet and information flows will catch up or exceed those using the telephone network. China's telecom service has undertaken a series of major reforms over the past two years, seeing that the new generation of wide-band high speed public information network of new IP technology will consistently mature during this development process and the online economy and social service methods of this type of network will be broadly promoted and adopted, in order to meet the telecom industry's even greater development.

At present, we have realized the separation between the government and enterprises and initially established a competitive telecom marketing structure. We will further perfect the telecom legislative system and telecom supervisory and administrative system. These will be used for safeguarding fair and orderly competition and fully utilizing the force of the market as well as speeding up the development of telecom and information services.

INFORMATIONALIZATION OF SOCIAL SERVICES IN PROMOTING THE ECONOMY

While speeding up the development of information technology and information network infrastructure facilities, we will emphasize the spread and application of information and network technology in all trades and professions. At present, we will focus on the online projects in connection with government, enterprise and family, spread information knowledge and promote the development and utilization of information resources.

We will vigorously support all kinds of public departments and government institutions including finance, accounting and taxation, customs, scientific research, education, culture and hygiene. We will actively utilize information technology and telecom networks to establish and perfect highly efficient and reliable social service information systems that must face specialized application. In addition, we will also encourage enterprises, in particular the large and medium-sized enterprises, to utilize the spread and application of information and network technology as a tool to push forward the upgrade of traditional industries, improve enterprise management and enhance the quality of products and the efficiency of enterprises.

We will put into play enterprise activities encouraging enterprises to develop online electronic services. The government shall closely cooperate with enterprises and jointly promote the development of a network economy in order to create a proper environment of law and regulation, information security environment and commercial environment for developing online commerce.

We will continue to adhere to the policy of reform and openness. Under the principle of mutual benefit and interest, we will continue to intensify economic and technical cooperation with countries all over the world. We will jointly develop information and network technology and industry and push forward national informationalization and the cause of modernization.

PETER YIP

Peter Yip, chief executive officer of chinadotcom Corporation, has over two decades of successful entrepreneurial experience in media and telecommunications, technology investment and technology transfer. Prior to forming chinadotcom Corporation, Peter Yip founded a systems integration company which eventually was sold to SHL Systemshouse, a company since acquired by MCI. Mr. Yip previously held management positions at KPMG and Wharton Applied Research. Mr. Yip serves on the boards of Softbank Strategic Internet, e2Capital, and several joint ventures established under the auspices of the Chinese government, in addition to that of chinadotcom Corporation. Mr. Yip received his MBA from the Wharton School and both his masters in science and bachelors in science in electrical engineering from the University of Pennsylvania.

chinadotcom Corporation is a leading pan-Asian integrated Internet company with businesses ranging from portals, online marketing and e-business solutions, to an investment program that includes incubation, acceleration and partnership. The first Asian Internet company to list its shares on NASDAQ, chinadotcom offers a full range of Internet services across more than 10 markets in the U.S. and the Asia Pacific region, including Japan, Korea, Australia, China, Hong Kong, Taiwan, Singapore, Thailand, and Malaysia.

In the following chapter, Mr. Yip explores the boundless potential of the Internet in a wireless China, and as a force in shaping China's future.

How the Internet Will Shape China

Peter Yip

Chief Executive Officer, chinadotcom Corporation

Impressive Potential

At current growth rates, China's 1.3 billion population will theoretically pass three billion come 2,100, an increase of 145%. In contrast, the mainland's Internet user community, now standing at about 17 million, is expected to increase by the same percentage within the next 12 months.

A contrived comparison maybe, but one that vividly illustrates how fast the Chinese Internet is evolving and how vast its long-term potential is. Just as impressive, using the same rate of growth, Internet penetration in China, now at only 1.3%, will match the present United States level of just over 50% within the next ten years.

By then this vast nation will be a full member of the World Trade Organization. No doubt, it will have cycled through several more rounds of economic reform programs and its infrastructure—technical and otherwise—will be on a par with that of its competitors and trade partners in the West.

Trends Predict the Future

Trying to predict any technology developments over the next 100 years, let alone the changes on the Internet in a fast-changing country like China, would be a fruitless exercise. Better then to look at the trends that were brewing in the closing years of the last century that are now in full swing, propelling the world's most populous country into the ranks of free trade and global economies.

327

While figures vary from source to source, China's on-line community is expected to top 300 million by 2005. Compare this to the total population of the United States, which stands at 275 million, or the combined 15 states of the European Union, with 375 million citizens. Add to this China's growing technical prowess and the academic and industrial initiatives underway to create a home-grown Chinese-language computing industry, and it is not hard to imagine the day when the Net is dominated by Chinese-language content, Websites and e-commerce sites. Analysts predict this could happen as soon as 2010.

INCREASING ACCESS

Driving growth of the Internet communities is a combination of factors creating a virtuous, self-fuelling circle. Firstly, economic reforms are leading to a gradual shift in social attitudes, expectations and purchasing power. Secondly, the country's growing major infrastructure investments are literally coming on-line, enabling easier and quicker communications—locally, provincially and internationally. Add to this the central government's policy initiatives to lower the cost of phone and Internet connect charges and one can understand the impetus behind the remarkable growth in Internet usage.

Like the rest of the Internet world, China is sufficiently advanced in its metropolitan centers and special economic zones to already be looking at new ways to access the Net. Convergence and change point to the "post-PC" period arriving closely in step with the rest of the world. Mobile phones, Personal Digital Assistants (PDAs) and dedicated Internet appliances will proliferate, and the environment will become increasingly fertile for consumers, Netpreneurs and big businesses alike.

By entering the on-line era a few years later, China has the opportunity to leapfrog the popular wired technologies and rely more heavily on wireless technologies, facilitating rapid conversion of its mobile phone users to Internet users once the enabling equipment become widely available. Some products already on the horizon include "Set-Top Boxes" and "Game Machines," which will both be extremely popular for a number of reasons, including: price, the penetration of television, the popularity of gaming, and the familiarity factor. Others include Internet Appliances (IAs) and PDA-MP3 music players, already on the street in some countries. A wave of new devices is expected to ripple around the world within the next 12 months.

While most businesses may not have an immediate need to equip their staff with IAs, unless they have a mobile workforce working in the field for instance, these types of devices are expected to stimulate the global Internet end-game—that of business-to-consumer (B2C) e-commerce. According to a recent study, worldwide sales of IAs will boom from 29 million units in 2000 to 302 million units in 2005, with much of that growth in Asia and China.

A WIRELESS WORLD

Wireless—The impact of wireless on the Internet and for mobile Internet access (m-commerce) is already being felt, and by the end of 2002 it will likely dominate wireline connections as the way to access the Net, as it already does in Japan. China has not been slow off-the-mark either, with more than 8,000 subscribers to Beijing Telecom recently signing up for the new phones as soon as they became available. Waiting in the wings are the 3G standards slated for introduction in 2001 and 2002.

Combining this new technology with the mobile phone of the future—a hybrid phone, IA/PDA—and new voice recognition systems, will foster the birth of yet another generation of applications. This is of particular relevance to China which will be freed from the inconvenient and laborious task of inputting Chinese characters through an unsuitable input device—the keyboard.

The wireless world is integral to the evolution of the Internet and m-commerce and is expected to deliver on the long-hyped prediction that the way we work, rest and play is going to radically change. China is poised as a leading adopter of these new devices and techniques—described as "the boom technology of tomorrow"—for connecting its citizens to each other and the rest of the world, in the process fundamentally changing its society in ways unimaginable now.

The mainland already sports the largest population of mobile phone users in Asia, with 51.7 million subscribers as at August 2000 three-times greater than the number of current Internet users, ignoring users in both groups. As convergence bites, the mobile community will no doubt form the majority of China's 300 million Net users come 2005. As a regional Internet analyst recently said in a report, "We believe mobile Internet access—or m-commerce—to be the single most important development for the Internet in Asia."

BEYOND ACCESS: E-COMMERCE

Business-to-business (B2B) e-commerce is expected to grow rapidly because of its promised benefits of lowering costs of doing business and increasing markets at low incremental cost. Already, major initiatives are under way, with the strong support of the central government, to develop business-to-business application service providers (B2B-ASP's), which will facilitate the growth of B2B e-commerce by providing low cost, user-friendly software for major industries nationwide.

Based on experience in the West, it was widely believed that the lack of credit cards in China would hamper the development of B2C e-commerce. This has turned out not to be the case. While consumers may not actually complete many cash transactions on-line at this stage, finding and choosing products and services, making price comparisons and the placing of an order are all carried out on the Net through the browser. This is e-commerce, Chinese-style, as it stands at the moment, with consumers and e-tailers readily accepting delivery times and cash-on-delivery (COD) as administered by the Post Office.

Research and numerous reports indicate a steady increase in on-line buying and although only five percent of Internet users, as of May 2000, have made on-line purchases. This is expected to climb sharply. A survey in July 2000 by the China Internet Network Information Centre (CINIC), an official body that releases twice-yearly assessments of Internet subscriber demographics, indicated that 14% of Internet users are willing to try on-line shopping. The Post Office currently delivers more than 1,000 goods on behalf of on-line merchants each day, plus numerous private courier companies are setting up to tap into this market.

Moreover, technology vendors and systems integrators are engaged in various mammoth projects with numerous Chinese banks that will enable a nationwide upgrade of the financial services industry. Holders of credit cards, smart cards and bank account debit cards are increasingly commonplace in the industrialized areas, particularly the South Eastern seaboard where the new rising middle-classes live, so e-commerce in China will move ahead just as fast as anywhere else.

In June 2000 a significant step towards completing transactions on-line was taken when a new payment processing platform was introduced in Shanghai. Before this initiative, there was no universal on-line payment platform accessible to all credit cardholders issued by the multitude of banks. Other major cities are expected to implement the system by the end of 2000.

E-commerce should be hitting its second growth phase by 2002 when, in terms of technology, China will be facing the same issues, such as security, as any other country on the way to its New Economy. Additionally, it may well be at an advantage, having leapfrogged many mature economies to implement the latest in technology-based banking and communications systems.

With these significant developments emerging from the pipeline, it helps to put things into perspective by looking at the U.S. market. On-line shopping in the States has been a reality for almost a decade, and while it only accounted for 1.4% of all retail purchases made in 1999, this still gave a total-spend of US$80.5 billion. If e-commerce and m-commerce spreads as predicted, China will be a trillion-dollar market and the Internet could become the country's prime income generator.

Forecasters, and even central government, concur. While projections vary, China's Ministry of Information Industry (MII) has predicted that e-commerce transactions for 2000 will reach US$96.6 million and could go as high as US$1.2 billion by 2002. Other forecasters agree with the 2002 figure and suggest it will rise to $3.8 billion by 2003. Both B2B and B2C will be prime revenue generators within five years and Forrester Research believes that Asia-Pacific will become a "dominant player in e-commerce when it hits hypergrowth in the next two years."

China's entry into the WTO, its increasing move to a market-driven economy and its ability to provide less expensive manufacturing centers for international businesses, point towards it being a major force in both regional and global Internet commerce.

GOVERNMENT

Despite the negative perceptions associated with the recent issue of laws and directives to control the activities of ISPs and websites, the Chinese government is necessarily developing a raft of new systems, checks and balances for a nation in transition. This is change management on a vast scale.

While central authorities have been seen as hesitant towards the Internet and have at times sent out mixed messages, this is simply a function of the emergence of a new and powerful economy. The fact that the government is paying attention and becoming involved is proof that it is taking the Internet seriously—as any government should. In step with pushing through economic reforms, policies and opinions need to be formulated to reflect the reality of what is happening as the Internet flows from the industrial centers and cascades across the provinces.

The Internet presents many of the same challenges and opportunities the world over, and government concerns are by no means unique to China or other Asian destinations. The U.S. government is currently drafting nationwide laws covering e-commerce, and the Federal Bureau of Investigations (FBI) is set to introduce an extensive email surveillance system called Carnivore. The Australian state security agency, ASIO, has already introduced email surveillance that employs sophisticated satellite tracking.

Political leaders in China fully realize the potential benefits and pitfalls of technology and the future for e-commerce in their country, which is exactly why there is such major investment projects underway to transform roads, cities, telecommunications systems, banking systems... the list goes on. The apex for many of these initiatives is to unite people, businesses and services using the Internet. The consequent growth of business and consumer Internet communities will promote greater communication and trade both at home and abroad. Non-monetary benefits are also seen from greater Internet usage—the equalization of social relationships through the power of information, the bridging of the gap between rich and poor, and greater two-way communication with the outside world.

According to recent reports, the government has decided to make "e-commerce the cornerstone of its drive for economic development." While still in its early stages, movement on the ground backs this up. In August of 2000, at the opening of an international computer conference, President Jiang Zemin said, "The melding of the traditional economy and information technology will provide the engine for development of the economy and society in the 21st century." He then added, "We should deeply recognize the tremendous power of information technology and vigorously promote its development." With this more open view, the government can be seen as both encouraging local use of the Internet, as well as China's membership of a global community linked through cyberspace.

The recent historical decision by the U.S. to grant permanent normal trade status, marking one of the final steps in clearing China's entry into the World Trade Organization (WTO), can only add to the impetus for developing the Internet that is already evident. Removing trade barriers will inevitably permeate China offline and on-line, attracting more businesses to venture into the world's largest potential consumer market. In turn, China will look increasingly outwards to myriad new international business opportunities that will arise for its own Netpreneurs and business communities.

In summary, China's modernization is now inextricably linked with the global phenomenon of the Internet. And while it shares the same aspirations of every nation to play a rewarding role in an increasingly complex world, it finds itself in a unique position. Twenty percent of the world's population lives within its borders and two-fifths share the same language. The next 100 years will see every nation having to cooperate to face many new challenges, the environment and sharing of global resources being the most important. With a vast pool of human talent and a modern technology-supported economy, China is poised to play a crucial role in shaping the fortunes of humankind.

Thomas G. Lewis

Thomas Lewis is regional chairman of The Boston Consulting Group's Asia-Pacific practice and a member of the firm's world-wide executive committee. He joined The Boston Consulting Group in 1975 and prior to moving to Hong Kong in early 1996 had been based in BCG's Boston, London and Germany offices.

In his professional practice within The Boston Consulting Group, Lewis has focused on several areas: working with companies to increase their growth and profits by sharpening their corporate strategies, including addressing broad ranging issues of general corporate direction and portfolio and regional focus and the capabilities on which they should be based; assisting companies in implementing detailed measures for pursuing these goals, such as merger and acquisition strategies and managing the post-merger integration process; and designing the structure and key processes through which the corporate center directs the corporation and adds value.

He has authored numerous articles on corporate development, which have been published in the *Financial Times* and various German and Asian journals. In 1994, he published a book in Germany on the topic of value management. Mr. Lewis received his undergraduate degree in agricultural economics and his MBA in Southern and Central Africa.

In the following chapter, Mr. Lewis analyzes the impact of the Internet and mobile technology revolution on communications as a driving force behind China's economy in the information age, and the role which entrepreneurs will play in shaping China's future.

WIRING CHINA FOR THE NEW CENTURY

Thomas G. Lewis
Regional Chairman, The Boston Consulting Group

CHINA ENTERS THE INTERNET REVOLUTION

With the coming of the Internet and other new communications technologies, we are witnessing a revolution as fundamental in its way as the coming of the railroad or the telegraph. As Philip Evans and Thomas Wurster say in their book about this phenomenon, *Blown to Bits*, the new economics of information is blowing apart the foundations of traditional business strategy.

In China, we expect the ground-shaking effects of these changes in the way we communicate, exchange goods, and conduct other forms of commerce, to have dramatic effects on business, the economy and everyday life. But, equally, the reach of these effects, or the speed at which they occur, is far from assured. Many variables, some global, but many within the mandate of the Chinese people and its government, will affect how, and how fast, this e-commerce and telecommunications revolution transforms life in China.

In essence, this global revolution is being driven by two forces: the explosion of connectivity and the adoption of common information standards. These forces will apply equally in China as they do in the rest of the world. The growth in connectivity through electronic networks is exceeding most predictions in the United States and Europe and is also likely to do so in China. Connectivity means information can flow with next to zero cost or delay. This connectivity growth is combining with the transition from proprietary to open communications standards: the Internet, extranets, intranets and so on. This rapid emergence of universal technical standards, which allows everybody to communicate with everybody else at essentially zero cost, will constitute a sea change in the way China communicates with itself and in the way it communicates, and does business, with the rest of the world.

Aside from these global factors, we see several major trends driving the revolution in China. These are: the introduction and rapid adoption of mobile telephony; the process of deregulation in the telecommunications sector and the opening up of the sector to international operators; the rise in consumer incomes and the rapid uptake of mobile technology; the emergence of a new breed of Chinese entrepreneurs and the growth of private companies: and the continuing expansion and growing importance of China in the global e-commerce market. Not all of these factors are having an equal influence, some are partly dependent on others as pre-conditions, but clearly all are inter-linked.

Let us look at each of these trends in turn.

THE INTRODUCTION AND RAPID ADOPTION OF MOBILE TELEPHONY

Mobile telephony holds the key to China being able to leapfrog the long lead times, which will otherwise be required for this vast country to install the wired infrastructure necessary for even the most simple telecommunications capability. While between 15 million and 20 million new lines are being installed across China every year, it will take many years for fixed line telephones to reach penetration rates similar to those in the United States, Europe or Japan. Still, the total subscriber base is now more than 200 million and about 50 million of those subscribers are mobile users. The potential for mobile telephony to accelerate the process, even off China's currently low overall density (about 18% according to the Ministry of Information Industries), is clearly seen in the expansion of telephone use in China since the creation of China Telecom in 1994 as shown in chart 1 on the next page.

Major potential for growth lies in China's large east coast cities, many of which are aspiring to become international commercial centers. These cities are where wealth, commerce, education, and infrastructure are concentrated. They are part of the global and new economies already, and mobile phone users are increasing at a very rapid rate. Despite the relatively low penetration rates, China's fixed and mobile networks are among the world's largest in terms of

Chart 1

Rapid Growth of Mobile Subscribers

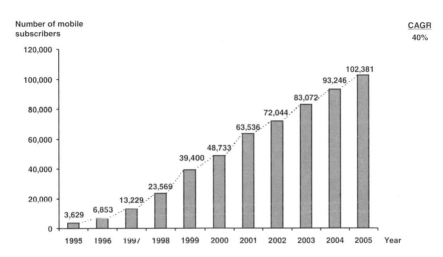

Number of mobile
subscribers

CAGR
40%

Source: China P&T Annual Reports (1995, 1996 real numbers).   MILL (1998 real number);   Paul Budde Communications 1999, Warburg Dillon Read 1999;   Lehman Brothers 1999

both scale and subscriber base. And this trend towards accelerating telephone use is evidence in itself that China appears to be skipping interim development stages otherwise dependent on fixed line infra structure.

Furthermore, mobile telephony is also contributing to a dramatic fall in overall telecommunications costs for both domestic and business users. The price of long distance calls has dropped by 70% in the past five years, while phone installation fees and mobile subscription fees have been reduced by 80% and 75% respectively.

The trend is continuing, and the latest leap forward promises to be just the beginning. The coming of so-called third generation (3G) mobile telephony is expected, as long as participants can operate in a certain environment, to change dramatically the Chinese model for the telecommunications business. 3G, and the availability of new spectrum and bandwidth on the network, will mean a multitude of follow-on effects: virtual networks; the further proliferation of mobile phones; new efficiencies for business through mobile sales forces, and business and personal management systems; multimedia via mobile telephones and more.

In voice, we can expect to see a dramatic change in the relationship between customer and carrier. Whereas in the past a few monopolistic carriers dictated prices and "services" to customers, customers in the future will choose a wide variety of services from several fiercely competing companies. In data, existing and new carriers will find relationships are a vital component in their new paradigm. Relationships with international firms will deliver new data capabilities, while other alliances and arrangements will deliver new customer relationships.

While at the time of this writing, the choice of a 3G standard is still the subject of considerable uncertainty, it is expected to be based on some more advanced version of code division multiple access (CDMA), i.e., wide band code division multiple access WCDMA, cdma2000, or China's own proposed standard—time division synchronized code division multiple access TD-SCDMA. The biggest mobile operator in China, China Mobile, uses global systems mobile communications GSM, and GSM's market share is currently more than 90%. However, the WCDMA model provides a feasible migration path from GSM.

Approval for this international standard would lead to immediate benefits to consumers as well as significant opportunities for domestic and international equipment providers and international carriers, whether those opportunities are in the areas of content, the provision of regional services, or marketing. Against the rapidly evolving face of the mobile market, we do not see a strong future for current generation wireless application protocol WAP in China. Its content is limited, costs are high and connection speeds frustrate users.

DEREGULATION OF THE TELECOMMUNICATIONS SECTOR AND OPENING UP TO INTERNATIONAL OPERATORS

Despite some reservations, and sometimes contradictory signals from regulators, we remain confident that the government's regulatory trend will favor a more open telecommunications market in China. Although today's competitive landscape in basic-telecom services is dominated by two major full-service providers (China Telecom and China United Technologies), a number of strong new players have emerged providing broadband (China NetCom) and Value Added Services (Jilong). In 1999, in a first step towards creating a new regulatory and competitive environment, the government divided China

Telecom into four entities, covering fixed line operations (China Telecom), mobile (China Mobile), satellite (China Satellite Communications Corp.), and paging services (folded into China Unicom).

With China's entry to the WTO will come a commitment to open any major telecommunications company to up to 50% foreign investment by 2006. But current foreign investment is low (even in the mobile sector where Nokia has invested several billion dollars), and funding is largely dependent on relatively scarce internal resources. We expect two scenarios to develop out of this landscape. The primary drivers of these scenarios will be the degree of competition (determined by the speed of implementation of pro-competitive regulation), and the level of foreign direct investment into the sector. The most likely outcome, from our perspective, is that China Telecom will be further broken into six regional operating companies (each with operating autonomy), with these regional operators and a couple of other major new entrants competing in a range of business and residential segments. The most likely outcome, from our perspective, is that China Telecom's regional operating subsidiaries will be given more autonomy, competing with a couple of other new entrants in a range of business and residential segments. On the value-added services side, it is likely that the market will see the adoption of new standards and the possibility of foreign players investing up to 49% in local operators after one year. This will lead to new, multiple players in the cellular, internet service provider ISP, internet service re-seller ISR, internet phone I-phone, paging and broadband areas.

It seems to us that there is significant value in a single large subscriber base that will allow China Mobile (now the second-largest mobile operator—next to Vodafone—in the world) to develop and create a true value-added mobile portal that will have strong brand equity (by virtue of being the first on the handset, especially with the introduction of 3G), potential for fees through listing, e-commerce and so on, and possible extension to other Chinese speaking-markets as a MVNO [Mobile Virtual Network Operator]. It is likely that it is this potential that encouraged Vodafone to pay such a high premium for just two percent of the company.

However, significant concerns remain regarding the persistence of some regulations that act as a strong break on capital flows into the industry and slow development of the Internet and telecommunications as economic drivers in China. In the Internet environment, the government currently requires all businesses with an Internet site to register their encryption software, and Chinese companies are prohibited from buying overseas-designed encryption software. New rules for Chinese Internet content providers mean they must seek government approval for joint or co-operative ventures with foreign companies. All Internet and telecommunications companies must also apply for licensing from the government.

THE RISE IN PERSONAL INCOMES — DOMESTIC UPTAKE OF THE INTERNET AND MOBILE TELEPHONY

China is one of the poorest countries in Asia, and its GNP per capita is around just US$750. However, in recent years, urban incomes have grown dramatically, and in 1999 urban per capita incomes were about US$2,600, three times the national average. This is having a strong positive effect on the rate of domestic uptake of the Internet and mobile telephones. Xinhua, China's official news agency, has said that the average Internet user in Beijing spends almost 35% of his salary gaining access to the Internet compared with about one percent in the United State—a remarkable contrast.

According to China's Academy of Social Sciences, Internet users now number about 10 million, and are expected to rise to 60 million by 2003. Some forecasters even suggest that Internet users will reach 100 million by 2003. While the price of personal computers remains relatively high, compared with countries such as Singapore, Taiwan and Hong Kong, it is falling rapidly. This trend towards accelerating uptake of the Internet is also being encouraged by the rapidly falling prices of user terminals. According to official figures, prices for desktop PCs fell between 18% and 22% between 1994 and 1998. This trend has accelerated over 1999–2000 with prices falling a further 30% to 40%. Some household models have even fallen by as much as 50% in price in this period. Internet access charges, too, have fallen rapidly, as shown in the bar graph (Chart 2). Access fees were halved in 1999–2000, and fell further in 2000 through fierce competition among Internet service providers. Prices are now likely to stabilize with competition in the future centering on service quality and bandwidth.

The average price of mobile handsets has also fallen dramatically— 50–70% in the past five years. Mobile phones are now affordable for China's urban young, as product life cycles shorten and prices come down even further within those cycles. Again, while GDP growth per capita in China lags behind most other countries in the region, this does not prevent teenagers in Beijing, Shanghai, or dozens of other coastal cities, from buying and using a mobile phone.

Chart 2

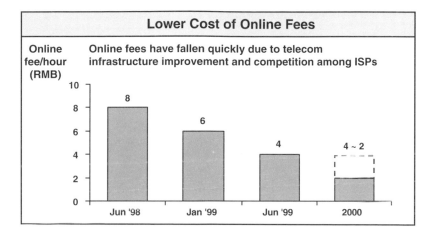

Still, it is becoming clear that patterns of use for the Internet and mobile phone technology are significantly different in many Asian countries, including China, than in the United States or Europe.

E-commerce is still in a nascent stage in China, and is likely to remain so for some time. Most domestic users of the Internet use it for e-mail and information search, and uses such as online shopping and online brokerage are tiny compared with the United States. In our recent study, *E-tail of the Tiger: Retail E-commerce in Asia-Pacific*, we noted several major obstacles to the proliferation of the Internet as a retail channel in China. These obstacles persist, and include: concerns about online security, the high costs of access (including both the high prices of PCs and charges for users to be online), slow order processing times, and the often slow and unreliable nature of fulfillment.

However, the retail base is massive and, moreover, the existing retail market is fragmented, inefficient, and ineffective. E-commerce, over the long term, will be a catalyst to radically transform these retail supply chains, rather than a tool to simply patch them up. For example, China, like many other Asian countries, is a large supply base of consumer products (apparel, gifts and home décor to name a few) to major U.S. buyers such as Pier 1 Imports and Wal-Mart. E-commerce exchanges are being set up to help buyers to greatly improve efficiency in sourcing and order processing, resulting in great cost savings. Similarly, e-commerce opens up tremendous opportunities for good quality producers that would otherwise have difficulty in tapping into international demand.

Clearly, significant cultural shifts related to the communications revolution are also taking place in China. The e-economy is pushing the boundaries of cultural and social change, and it is becoming obvious that these changes, at a personal, business, and social level, will become significant factors in shaping the country's communications future.

For example, the rapid penetration of mobile telephony, compared with the rate of fixed line infrastructure growth, is being partly driven by young urban consumers—including those who are prepared to spend a third of their salaries on Internet access. While overall consumer costs of mobile technology are higher in Asia than in Europe and North America, mobile uptake is also significantly higher overall in Asia. For example, in September 1999, Japan had a mobile penetration rate of about 42% compared with about 28% in the U.S. Mobile phones are part of the clothing—a fashion accessory—for teenagers in urban Asia, including China. These teenagers are prepared to pay a high proportion of their monthly income on such "must have" accessories.

However, The Boston Consulting Group does not expect that mobile technology will replace the personal computer as the primary entry point to the Internet. In the near term, at least, mobile devices will remain limited in their ability to display the richness of information available on the Internet. We expect it will be voice-enabling technologies that will further drive mobile technology penetration rates.

While Internet penetration is often seen as the international communications benchmark, in China, as in other Asian countries, it is highly likely that new models, more appropriate to the Chinese environment, will emerge. For example, high mobile telephony penetration, combined with the coming convergence of the Internet, telecommunications, and data communications, opens up new opportunities for new applications and models. These new models will be terminal and user driven—PDAs, trimmed down personal computers, and other devices are already being developed in China for the Chinese market. Models similar to that of Japan's NTT DoCoMo are likely to develop, as users seek high-end service. I-mode has demonstrated the huge market potential of short messaging using mobile devices. NTT DoCoMo's world class I-mode technology, in tune with young users' interests and apparently insatiable need for message exchanging and mobile Internet (both driving major traffic and revenue growth for NTT) is already attracting strong interest in China. True 3G solutions will deliver multimedia messages, and revenue streams, which are likely to be strong enough for operators to develop robust business models.

Home grown solutions and enhancements will also surface. Chinese enterprises have improved personal handheld (PHS) fixed-line technology for secondary city markets, and multiple trials are already being under way. These phones (using technology similar to cordless phones and a network of urban base stations) are one quarter the size of a GSM phone and just one fifth of the price. They not only combine much currently available capability, but they can also be linked to personal computers to surf the net. Voice over the Internet (VoIP), too, will play a growing role in telecommunications in China, and provide strong competition for local and long-distance calling, once issues related to pricing, licensing, and quality have been addressed.

THE EMERGENCE OF A NEW CLASS OF ENTREPRENEURS AND THE GROWTH OF PRIVATE COMPANIES

Capital and entrepreneurial flair in the form of returning Chinese are now flowing back to China. It is this group of returning Chinese, now numbering many thousands, which is pushing much of the innovative change in China's new economy. Many of these returning Chinese—entrepreneurs who have formed their own companies, information technology specialists, telecommunications and Internet experts, managers and infrastructure designers, bankers, and venture capitalists—have seen Silicon Valley and know the oppor-tunities of the new economy. They have the mindsets required for success.

These returning Chinese will drive more than the ideas and the new ventures. China's new economy needs large capital injections, and these entrepreneurs also hold the potential to lead new venture funding from the capital markets and bring much needed new man-agement skills. For example, The Boston Consulting Group has formed an e-commerce venture, China eLabs, with a Shanghai-based venture capital firm, Shanghai New Margin (led by returning Chinese entre-preneurs and professionals). China eLabs is currently leading several enabling technologies and business-to-business related initiatives to market, and these pioneers will lead growth in a field that has so far lagged that in other Asian countries.

China's stock market capitalization is just over 30% of GDP. However, alongside the growing importance of venture capital funds as a major source of growth for e-commerce and telecommunications, we also expect to see a similar increase in the role of the stock market. Weighting towards technology stocks has surged in recent times, and the authorities plan a second board for small, high technology stocks. Recent high technology alliances between companies such as News Corp and the People's Daily, and China Unicom, Softbank Corp, and Unitech Telecom, are also indicative of a global trend spreading to China. However, significant reform in the banking and financial services sector in general will be needed before the stock exchanges in China become true avenues for channelling funds for development of business as we see in Europe and the U.S.

THE INCREASING IMPORTANCE OF CHINA AS A GLOBAL E-COMMERCE MARKET

Business-to-business e-commerce holds much stronger short and medium-term potential for China than business-to-consumer growth. Business-to-business transactions are still small compared with the United States, Europe and even other Asian countries, but traditional business— such as petroleum, textiles, and automobiles—can capture very significant cost savings and efficiencies through development of vertical and horizontal portals similar to those now springing up around the world. Portals such as YourImporter, e-Marketplace, and ChinaMallUSA are establishing the models for the future.

The benefits to China's industry will be clear and dramatic when strong models are established and running. They will include improved supply chain efficiency, enhanced data processing, and much-improved infrastructure. However, we expect it will take five to ten years before business-to-business is a big component of China's economy. Vast chunks of China's existing industry base do not yet have the pre-conditions to go to this next step. It will take time for businesses, especially state-owned-enterprises, to gear up and, more importantly, address the fundamental cultural, managerial, and skills issues that currently act as factors limiting change.

Private companies on the other hand, are more likely to be able to take advantage of business-to-business initiatives in the short term. In this segment, private companies are already setting up exchanges and business-to-business consolidation is taking place. For example, in the white goods industry, Haier, Chunlan, Little Swan and others have invested billions of renminbi in an industry business-to-business exchange.

And perhaps the biggest current potential lies in tapping into the vast trade that occurs between China and the west. The Internet makes possible much more efficient search engines and methods of contracting for western buyers and Chinese sellers. Such models already exist offline, with middlemen making significant margins, or buyers from western markets wasting significant time and energy in finding the right factory or supplier. The key will be to take these processes online and drive significant new cost savings and efficiencies.

Success Not Assured

Against these compelling trends, we see an absolute imperative for China to come to grips with several significant impediments to the establishment of a strong and sustainable telecommunications and high-technology sector. As already noted, uncertainties over copyright, intellectual property rights, patents and privacy protection remain as a significant brake on the inflow of ideas, capital, and technology into the sector.

While the Chinese government has repeatedly reiterated its promise to open its telecommunications market to foreign investment following its coming entry to the World Trade Organization, some signals still leave potential investors uncertain of its commitment. For example, draft regulations governing foreign investment in Chinese telecommunications infrastructure appear likely to force foreign investors into partnerships with a handful of state-owned firms which meet significant annual revenue requirements (these can be as high as US$350 million for at least two years) and have a long operating history. Clearly, these requirements will effectively force foreign investors to team up with existing government-dominated players. Regulation might also oblige foreign investors to accept chairmen of such joint ventures appointed by the Chinese side. In the face of this uncertainty, foreign investors also worry that such limiting regulations might also be extended to the Internet. And as mentioned earlier, similar uncertainty surrounds when and how China will act on its plan to adopt a version of code division multiple access technology for 3G mobile telephones.

From our perspective, the underlying objective of the regulators must be to create an open and certain environment which encourages innovative and effective penetration of communications-related technologies for private and business use. It is only through the creation of such an environment that China will establish the underlying pre-conditions for it to take full advantage of this global communications revolution. It is only through the creation of such an environment that China will attract the investment, knowledge and talent required to give the revolution the impetus needed to compete internationally.

We also see advances in business education as a potential accelerator of this revolution. While China is significantly ahead of its rival India in development of its physical telecommunications infrastructure, it certainly lags in this vital field. Today, just 3.5% of China's 1.2 billion people have a tertiary education, and most of China's top graduates leave the country. Contrast this with India, where the schools of the Indian Institutes of Technology and Management consistently produce outstanding technicians and business innovators who are contributing to that country's economic development. There is, as yet, no Chinese business education equivalent, although the government recognizes the vital importance of rapidly accelerating business education standards. The announcement of the government's "211 project" involving the establishment of 100 world-class universities to meet China's future high technology needs provides a vision for the future. Clearly, talented people are the scarcest commodity in the new economy. A concerted effort to build educational capability will pay handsome dividends in future, especially in the field of the Internet and telecommunications.

Furthermore, the concentration of talent attracts more talent in a virtuous circle, as we can see in the examples of Bangalore in India, and Silicon Valley in the United States. Create world class universities and centers of intellectual creativity, and further industry and technology will be drawn to drink at the well. Consider, too, how the communications revolution might benefit western China. While major growth will happen in the major cities and in eastern china, the Internet and new telecommunications holds huge potential for accelerated growth in western China through new data processing, financial services, medical research and academic institutions. The adaptability of new service sectors to new locations, and their ability to service customers from almost anywhere, means new opportunities can emerge in many locations.

AND WHAT MIGHT CHINA'S CONNECTED FUTURE LOOK LIKE?

Perhaps the Olympics of 2008 will provide a window on that future? Beijing and China are making a determined bid for the 2008 Games after having missed out to Sydney in 2000. Despite the overblown claims of marketers that often accompany the Games, they hold significant potential to accelerate the telecommunications revolution in China. The Olympics in Tokyo in 1964 and in Seoul in 1988 served to bring both Japan and Korea into the global mainstream. As a one-off showcase, the Olympics encourage the hosts to accelerate infrastructure development and to present their best side to the rest of the world. Will millions of Chinese watch their own sporting heroes win gold on their personal 3G communications devices which deliver pictures through broadband internet connections? Will 20,000 internationally accredited journalists instantly file their stories through voice-enabled technology using their mobile phones? Will spectators be guided to their stadium seats, or the nearest restaurant, using displays on their DPAs or mobile phones? Will the 2008 Olympics be the opportunity for China, with new models and unique solutions, to show it is fast-becoming a world leader in the communications revolution?

JON EICHELBERGER

Jon Eichelberger is a partner based in the Hong Kong office of the law firm Perkins Coie LLP. For the past nine years, he has focused his practice on foreign investment and trade matters related to China and has advised clients on their China-related investments and operations, particularly in the areas of company formation and structuring, tax planning, technology licensing, contract law, government regulation, foreign exchange control, real estate and employment. As Internet-related businesses have taken off in China, his practice has increasingly involved clients from this sector. He serves as the firm's representative on the E-Commerce China Forum and as co-chair of the American Bar Association's China E-Commerce Working Group.

Perkins Coie LLP, founded in 1912, is an international law firm that has, over the past decade, achieved a strong reputation in the areas of high technology, Internet and electronic commerce, and in 2000 was named one of the top 10 technology law firms in the United States by the industry magazine *Red Herring*. Perkins Coie's Electronic Commerce and Internet Law Resource Center (www.perkinscoie.com) is the Web's most comprehensive compilation of Internet-related case law. The firm's clients in these areas include such well-known companies as Amazon.com and Yahoo!. Perkins Coie expanded its Asian practice at the beginning of 2000 with the addition of a group of lawyers highly experienced in China trade and investment. A particular focus of the China Practice Group of Perkins Coie has been to integrate its lawyers' many years of China experience with the firm's broader telecommunications, Internet and e-commerce expertise.

Mr. Eichelberger obtained a bachelor's degree in International Relations from Stanford University in 1981 and a J.D. from Harvard Law School in 1990. He was admitted to practice in New York State in 1991. Mr. Eichelberger has resided in mainland China for more than 13 years and is fluent in Mandarin Chinese.

In the following chapter, Mr. Eichelberger reviews the evolution of Chinese law and regulation as it will pertain to the creation of e-business in China.

Internet/E-Business in China: Development of a Legal Framework

Jon Eichelberger
Partner, Perkins Coie LLP

One of the most exciting developments in China in recent years has been the growth of the Internet and the beginnings of e-business. Although at a comparatively early stage of evolution now, Internet-related business holds great promise for China's further economic reform and modernization in the first part of the 21st century.

Law will be crucial to the growth of this sector. Government regulation of Internet access, online content, advertising and foreign investment, protection of property rights, electronic contracting, taxation of online transactions, mechanisms for financing new businesses—all are examples of legal issues that will have a direct and significant impact on the development of e-business in China.

The principal dynamic of legal development in this sector will be the effort by lawmakers to balance two goals: facilitating the growth of Internet businesses while regulating Internet content and technology. Strong government support for the Internet and e-business was expressed as early as 1998 in speeches by President Jiang and other senior leaders, and transformation into an information-based economy will occupy a key place in the 10th Five-Year Plan that will be adopted when the National People's Congress meets in March 2001. At the same time, recent legislation and statements by leading policymakers also reflect the government's keen desire to regulate the dissemination of information via the Internet and to control Internet technology.

Perspectives on Legal Development in China: Implications for Internet/E-Business

The emerging legal framework for the Internet and e-business in China is better understood when viewed from the perspective of legal development over the past two decades. The fundamental task of the State has been to reform and modernize the economy by means of an orderly transition from a predominantly state-owned, planned economy to a socialist market economy with a significant degree of private ownership. Construction of a legal system is viewed as an essential part of this transition and the idea that law is a key regulator of relationships in a market economy is well accepted.

Impressive gains in building a legal system have been achieved, in the enactment of laws and regulations, the creation of legal institutions and the training of legal professionals. At the same time, law has remained primarily a tool for economic reform and transition, and the needs of this process have largely determined the nature and development of law. In the absence of historical precedent to guide the transition to a socialist market economy, the process requires experimentation and flexibility. Two further requirements are widely viewed within China as essential: social stability and a high degree of guidance from the State. These various factors lend certain characteristics to the law: (i) a tendency for laws and regulations to state general principles that are open to a range of interpretations and therefore flexible in application, (ii) a large number of administrative regulations, often provisional regulations, which can be modified more easily than laws in order to adjust to changing circumstances or experience, and (iii) a high degree of administrative discretion in implementing laws and regulations.

In developed, capitalist countries, law is also viewed as a tool for regulating economic relationships, both between the state and economic actors, and among economic actors. Emphasis is placed on creating laws that are transparent in meaning and implementation and thereby provide a relatively high degree of certainty or predictability to economic actors. This view of law is also recognized in China and will gain importance over time in response to further economic development, as well as to the requirements of the WTO. Plainly, however, a tension remains between legal certainty and predictability and the need for experimentation and flexibility during the present stage of China's economic reform. Both sides of this tension are evident in the emerging legal framework for Internet and e-business.

Government Regulation of Internet/E-Business

Government regulation of the Internet began in earnest with the State Council's promulgation of regulations concerning Internet access in early 1996. Over the ensuing four years, central government departments issued a variety of Internet-related regulations, but in some cases with an apparent lack of coordination. The regulatory framework advanced significantly in the latter part of 2000 with the promulgation of the *Telecommunications Regulations of the People's Republic of China* (Telecom Regulations) and several companion regulations. These regulations marked the beginning of a more ordered system of government regulation and established *the Ministry of Information Industry* (MII) as the principal, though not the only, regulator of the Internet and related businesses.

Internet Access (ISPs)

Starting in February 1996, the State Council issued a series of regulations that mandated a four-tier system for Internet access. The first tier is a "gateway" of international telecommunications lines under the control of MII. The second tier comprises the "interconnected networks," which connect to the global Internet via this international gateway. To date, the government has authorized five commercial interconnected networks, each of which is linked to a major telecommunications operator, and two non-commercial interconnected networks, one established by the Ministry of Education and the other by the Chinese Academy of Sciences. The third tier is made up of "access units" that provide Internet access directly to users through the access units' connections to the interconnected networks. The fourth tier comprises the users of the Internet.

In practice, the interconnected networks have offered Internet access directly to users, in addition to providing interconnection services to the access units. Thus, the term "Internet Service Provider" or "ISP" is often used to refer to both the interconnected networks and the access units. One further result of this practice is that the access units, of which there are scores throughout China, must compete in some markets with the interconnected networks on which they depend for their connections to the Internet.

For businesses, a significant exception to the Internet access system is that multinational companies, whether incorporated in China or abroad, have been permitted to establish company intranets using international leased lines without going through the four-tier system.

In September 1998, the State Council implemented an operating permit system for access units and interconnected networks. It appears that this system will be continued under the Telecom Regulations, which require all providers of telecommunications services in China to be licensed by the MII or its local counterparts. Based on the classification scheme set forth in the Telecom Regulations, the interconnected networks will be viewed as providers of basic telecommunications services, while most access units will be classified as providers of value-added telecommunications services.

At present, the high price for Internet access is an important problem, but one which stems more from the stage of development of the telecommunications infrastructure and related pricing regulation than from the Internet access system itself. One part of this system that deserves further consideration in terms of its potential relationship to prices, however, is the terms of competition between the interconnected networks and the access units.

Internet Information Services

The basic framework for the regulation of information services over the Internet was set out in a series of regulations issued in the autumn of 2000. These included the *Measures for the Administration of Internet Information Services* (IIS Measures), promulgated by the State Council, the *Provisions for the Administration of Internet Electronic Bulletin Services* (EBS Provisions), issued by MII, and the *Interim Provisions for the Administration of Web Sites Engaged in the Business of Publishing News* (Internet News Provisions), issued jointly by the State Council's Press Office and MII. Further regulations are expected to provide more detail and address other sub-categories of Internet information services, but the main direction is apparent from these regulations and the Telecom Regulations.

The IIS Measures broadly define Internet information services as the "provision of information services to online users via the Internet." They cite a few general examples of information services, such as the "provision of information," "web page creation" and the provision of "public and shared information" over the Internet. Web site businesses will need to watch for more elaborate definitions that will develop through practice and in detailed implementing rules and interpretations. For example, it is not yet clear whether a manufacturer's or an off-line service provider's web site that only releases information about the enterprise's own products and services will come within the scope of the IIS Measures.

Electronic bulletin services are a sub-category of Internet information services and are defined more precisely in the EBS Provisions as the "provision to online users of the conditions for release of information through such interactive forms as electronic bulletin boards, electronic white boards, Internet forums, online chat rooms and message boards." Some of these terms also will require more detailed definition. For instance, the term "electronic white boards" reportedly includes technology that allows a company's personnel in different locations to hold private meetings using the Internet.

Publication of news on web sites is another sub-category of Internet information services. Although the term "news" is not defined in the Internet News Provisions, reference may be made to existing laws and regulations governing the press. The Internet News Provisions regulate publication of news on the web sites of news organizations and on portal sites of non-news organizations. Portal sites of non-news organizations may apply for approval to republish news from Chinese news organizations or, with special approval, from foreign news organizations, but are prohibited from gathering or writing their own news.

The main features of the emerging regulatory framework for Internet information services include:

Internet Information Services Operating Licenses

The Telecom Regulations classify Internet information services as one form of value-added telecommunications service. Those who provide telecommunications services as a business are required to obtain an operating license from the competent licensing authority, which is either MII or a provincial telecommunications authority depending on the geographic scope of the services. Consistent with these requirements, the IIS Measures distinguish "commercial" Internet information services provided for compensation from "non-commercial" Internet information services provided without charge. Providers of commercial Internet information services must apply to the competent licensing authority for a value-added telecommunications operating license for Internet information services. Those who provide non-commercial Internet information services are only required to complete filing procedures with the licensing authority. The license or the filing number must be displayed prominently on the web site's home page.

Under the EBS Provisions, a provider of electronic bulletin services must make a special application to the licensing authority and obtain a specific notation on its Internet information services operating license or filing document before it begins to provide these services.

Clarification of the delineation between commercial and non-commercial information services would be beneficial to Internet businesses, particularly as to web sites that generate revenue from sources other than the site's subscribers or viewers, such as through advertising, links to other web sites or sales commissions. Although some guidance may be gleaned from earlier regulations issued by other government departments, it is not conclusive.

Other Approvals and Permits

The IIS Measures require providers of Internet information services in areas such as news, publishing, education, medical treatment, healthcare, pharmaceuticals or medical apparatus to obtain approvals from other relevant government authorities before applying for an Internet information services operating license. For the most part, these approval requirements are based on existing laws and regulations applicable to those industries. Therefore, the role of government authorities such as the State Press and Publications Administration, the Ministry of Education, the Ministry of Public Health and the State Drug Administration in regulating certain types of Internet businesses appears to be largely the same as their role with respect to off-line businesses.

The Internet News Provisions establish a licensing system under the authority of the Press Office of the State Council for publishers of news on the Internet.

Content Restrictions

The Telecom Regulations, IIS Measures, EBS Provisions and Internet News Provisions each state a uniform list of prohibited Internet content. The list includes information that (i) is contrary to the basic principles laid down in the Constitution, (ii) endangers state security, discloses state secrets, subverts state power or disrupts the unity of the State, (iii) infringes upon the honor or interests of the State, (iv) incites ethnic hostility or racial discrimination, or disrupts ethnic unity, (v) disrupts the religious policy of the State, or propagates heresies and feudal superstitions, (vi) spreads rumors, disrupts the social order or breaks down social stability, (vii) disseminates obscenity, pornography, gambling, violence, murder or terror, or instigates others to commit offences, (viii) insults or defames others or infringes upon the lawful rights and interests of others, or (ix) contains other content prohibited under laws or regulations. This list seems virtually identical in meaning with the list of prohibited content published in 1997 by the Ministry of Public Security. Those directly responsible for releasing prohibited content on the Internet may face administrative, civil or criminal penalties depending on the circumstances.

The issuance of a uniform list of prohibited content provides better guidance to Internet businesses and facilitates a more orderly marketplace. At the same time, clarification regarding the scope of certain items would be extremely helpful for businesses as they seek to comply with these regulations.

Record-keeping, Monitoring and Reporting

The IIS Measures require ISPs to maintain records for 60 days of the log on times, account numbers, Internet addresses or domain names, and originating telephone numbers of online users. These records must be made available to relevant State authorities when they make inquiries in accordance with law.

Web sites that provide information services such as news, publications or electronic bulletin services are required to record the content they make available, the time of release of such content, and the related Internet addresses or domain names. These records also must be maintained for 60 days and made available to relevant State authorities when they make inquiries in accordance with law.

The IIS Measures require any Internet information service provider that discovers prohibited content on its web site to cease transmitting it, keep relevant records and report it to the relevant State authorities. The EBS Provisions contain the same requirement for electronic bulletin service providers. Web site businesses will need more detailed guidance from the authorities as to the monitoring requirements that may be implied by these provisions. For instance, it would be useful for businesses to know if they will be required to meet certain technical standards for monitoring content, as well as whether they will be protected from liability if they comply with these standards.

Web Site Name Registration

Under interim measures issued in September 2000, the State Administration for Industry and Commerce designated the Beijing Municipal Administration for Industry and Commerce as the registration authority for web site names throughout China. This is part of an experimental program to establish a national filing and registration system.

An applicant for web site name registration must be the owner or licensee of the web site's registered domain name and a legal person, a lawful organization or an individual citizen of China. A web site may apply for up to three names using Chinese characters, Roman letters, numerals or a combination of these. Following preliminary approval, the names will be published for a period of 90 days, during which another person may object based on a name being identical to that person's enterprise or organization name, confusingly similar to that person's registered web site name, or otherwise misleading. Web site names that survive this 90 day period without successful objections will be granted registration and issued a registration certificate.

A key issue that the measures do not fully address is the relationship between registered web site names and potentially competing forms of intellectual property rights, such as domain names and trade marks. The measures deal with some of the relevant questions, but not with many others that are likely to arise in practice. For example, it is not clear how rules concerning internationally well-known trade marks will be applied in disputes over web site names that arise after the granting of registration.

Commercial Web Site Filing and Registration

Interim measures concerning the registration of commercial web sites were issued together with the web site name registration measures, and likewise designated the Beijing Municipal Administration for Industry and Commerce as the nationwide registration authority. Commercial web sites are defined as electronic platforms for releasing information, advertising, maintaining electronic mail boxes or conducting commercial activities on the Internet, or for providing space for doing any of these activities, that are owned by an enterprise and operated for profit. The applicant for commercial web site registration must have an authorized scope of business that corresponds to the commercial activity for which it seeks registration. After having been approved for registration, the enterprise is given an electronic identification for display on its web site and permitted to begin commercial web site operations for a trial period, pending final registration of its web site name. If name registration is rejected, the enterprise may apply for a different name and continue trial operations, up to a maximum period of 12 months.

Advertising

Advertising is an important source of revenue for many Internet businesses. Some merely publish advertisements on their web sites, while others also provide advertising design and related services. The existing regulatory system for advertising in China requires separate government approvals or filing procedures for each of these two types of activities.

In view of the importance of advertising to *e-business*, the State Administration for Industry and Commerce has started pilot projects in three cities, Beijing, Shanghai and *Guangzhou*, for the registration and licensing of online advertising. Based on the experience gained through these pilot projects, the government intends to formulate a system for implementation nationwide.

The Beijing Municipal Administration for Industry and Commerce issued a notice in May 2000 that may serve as a precursor of future regulations. Under the notice, which is only effective in Beijing, business entities that already possess advertising operations licenses are permitted to engage in design, production and agency for online advertising, and to publish advertisements online. Other lawfully established Internet entities will be permitted to publish advertisements from authorized advertising agencies after having completed the procedures to become authorized publishers of advertisements. Such entities may also apply for advertising operations licenses, which, if granted, will allow them to engage in advertising design, production and agency services.

Thus, the main direction of regulation appears to be to require Internet businesses to comply with the existing regulatory framework for the advertising industry. To obtain the required approvals or licenses, these businesses may have to meet special requirements related to personnel, equipment, accounting and similar matters.

Security

Regulators have been intensely concerned about the security of information communicated via the Internet. This concern has focused on general security issues related to such problems as hacking, viruses or violations of privacy, as well as on particular security issues regarding the protection of state secrets.

The Ministry of Public Security promulgated measures at the end of 1997 regarding security in the international networking of computer information systems. These measures contained anti-hacking and anti-virus provisions, stated the principle of legal protection for privacy of correspondence over the Internet, and imposed on the interconnected networks, access units and users of the Internet certain responsibilities in regard to network security. Among other things, all such entities and individuals are required to submit a recordal form to the public security authorities within 30 days of connecting to the Internet.

Regulations were issued in January 2000 concerning the protection of state secrets on the Internet. These regulations established the principle that whoever releases information over the Internet must take responsibility if any state secrets are disclosed or state security is threatened by that release. They also prohibit the storage, processing or transmission of state secrets over computer systems connected to the Internet, require all providers of information for release on a web site to establish internal review and approval procedures based on the requirements of state secrecy regulations, and require web site operators to obtain the express agreement of information providers before releasing any information (other than news that has already been published by authorized news organizations).

Regulations concerning commercial encryption technology and products have also drawn much attention in the Internet sector, particularly in so far as they purport to restrict the use and sale of imported encryption products in China.

Security issues are among the most difficult to address in terms of the balance between facilitating Internet growth and regulating Internet content and technology. In one sense, the regulatory framework regarding state secrecy and security is long standing and relatively well understood in China, and its extension into the Internet and e-business sector is unsurprising. At the same time, rapid exchange of information is central to the Internet and the transformation into an information-based economy. This factor heightens the importance of making the rules regulating Internet content well-defined and easily understood for businesses.

Database Protection

The obligations of Internet businesses to maintain the privacy of personal information and correspondence has been expressed in a number of regulations, including the Telecom Regulations, the IIS Measures, the EBS Provisions and regulations promulgated by the Ministry of Public Security in 1997. The EBS Provisions state that personal information may not be disclosed without the user's consent, apparently permitting web sites to request user consent online as is commonly done in other countries. However, in the course of a government effort to reduce spamming that began in late 2000, it was announced that all sales of database information are illegal. As the licensing or sale of database information can be an important revenue generator for Internet businesses, the authorities may wish to consider whether regulating the disclosure of such information rather than banning it outright would better facilitate the growth of e-business in China. The substantial body of law that has developed on this subject in the United States, the European Union and other jurisdictions would be a useful reference for further study.

Conclusion

The emerging framework for government regulation facilitates the growth of the Internet and e-business by better defining Internet-specific requirements and by addressing the applicability to the Internet of pre-existing regulation in areas such as advertising or security. Regulation is moving in the direction of providing greater certainty and predictability to economic players, of creating a more orderly marketplace and a more level playing field. This should enable Internet businesses to adopt more rational business models and make businesses easier to finance.

At the same time, regulation potentially over-burdens new businesses with an array of requirements and restrictions. One example is the number of registrations and approvals that an Internet business must obtain from different government authorities: company registration, domain name registration, web site name registration, commercial web site registration, a value-added telecommunications operating license, special approvals related to information services and sector-specific approvals or licenses related to advertising, pharmaceuticals, healthcare and so on. A streamlined process involving more coordination among government departments, as, for example, the "one-window" approach that some of the special investment zones have adopted for the establishment of foreign invested enterprises, would better facilitate growth.

More generally, in seeking a balance between facilitating growth and regulating content and technology, government regulators may consider several principles that would further improve transparency and decrease the regulatory burden on businesses:

- Regulatory requirements should be well-defined. A trend in this direction is evident in many newer regulations, which contain more defined terms and more precise definitions than older regulations. At the same time, a number of the points where more clarity is needed have been suggested in this chapter and more will arise in practice.

- Regulatory requirements should be held to the minimum level required to achieve the goals of regulation. Greater coordination among government authorities would help in realizing this principle.
- Substantive requirements should be technologically feasible and the costs of compliance should be reasonable. For example, Internet business have raised these questions in regard to content monitoring and reporting requirements.
- Regulatory procedures should be applied equally to all businesses and administrative discretion should be limited when possible. Many of the newer regulations evidence these principles by requiring regulatory authorities to provide written responses to applicants within fixed time periods, and to state reasons for denying applications. More precise definitions of qualifying criteria would also further these principles.
- The regulatory process should stimulate the development of well defined interpretations and detailed rules that respond to the tremendous variety of actual business situations. Regulatory authorities need to be aggressive in understanding the industry and the market, and in translating that understanding into appropriate regulations.

Many positive trends are evident in recent legal and regulatory developments for Internet and e-business. One hopes that the great importance of the Internet and e-business to China in the information age of the 21st century will spur the continued development of a more transparent legal and regulatory system for this sector.

Part VIII

MEDIA AND COMMUNICATIONS

CHINA'S MEDIA EVOLUTION

In 1948, Chairman Mao Zedong set the framework of China's official media function when he expressed, "To establish well, newspapers, and to establish newspapers which are interesting, to correctly propagate the direction of the Party in the newspapers and through newspapers to strengthen the relationship between the Party and the masses, this is an aspect of the Party's work which should not be underestimated in importance as it carries with it issues of great significance." Mao added that, "The strength and function of newspapers will enable the Party's program, lines, guidance and working style to swiftly and most broadly meet the masses."

During China's epic civil war of the last century, the media organs under the Communist Party of China served as critical tools in mobilizing people, issuing policies governing the Soviet or "liberated" areas, and propagating the principal direction and ideological platform of the Party. This pattern of functions soon became trademarks of China's official media. Since the founding of the Communist Party of China, its media organs have served as the "throat" or "tongue" of the Party.

The *People's Daily* was established on June 15, 1948 when the *Shanxi-Hebei Liberated Area Daily* and the *Shanxi-Hebei-Shandong-Henan Liberated Area People's Daily* were merged in the final days of the civil war. In March 1949, the *People's Daily* shifted headquarters to Beijing when the Kuomintang surrendered the city. In August 1949, the *People's Daily* became the official voice of the Central Committee of the Communist Party of China, two months prior to the establishment of the People's Republic on October 1st of that year.

In China, the media has served as a tool for disseminating information. Newspapers, magazines and radio soon became the key communication

361

tools of a new nation short of material resources, and trying to reconstruct itself. Daily newspapers were pasted on billboards so that the broad
public could read them. Loudspeakers on farms and factories projected
national radio broadcasts and announcements. The official Chinese media
became the source of policy dissemination and administrative guidelines
covering industry, agriculture, politics and society.

Following the reforms and open policies, China's media continued to
operate within its established framework. Newspapers and magazines, however, became increasingly specialized, functioning as communication
vehicles representing the various government departments under which they
may be established. For instance, the *People's Daily* belongs to the Central
Committee of the Communist Party of China. Its headline news reflects
the current political atmosphere and policy directions of the Party. The
Financial Times, however, belongs to a consortium of state-owned banks
which includes the People's Bank of China and People's Insurance Corporation, along with six other banks, and therefore serves as a key source in
disseminating financial and banking policy information. The *International
Business Daily* belongs to the Ministry of Foreign Trade and Economic
Cooperation, reflecting trade and foreign investment concerns. The Ministry
of Justice's *Legal Daily* is a main source of new legislation, and so on.

For a Chinese person who has grown up in China, there is an understood meaning to much of the reporting in the Chinese press. Chinese
people have learned to read news between the lines. Much can be understood concerning shifts in political and economic policy from the way in
which certain information is reported and often from what has not been
reported at all. For example, a report on the economy may begin with several
paragraphs praising the successes of certain economic policies. Maybe mid-
way through the article after the litany of praises, the word "however" will
appear. A Chinese reader will automatically know that the real news starts
here, with an explanation of those exceptions to the successes. In fact, the
purpose of an article discussing the exceptions is to discuss the real problems.

Likewise, political shifts are often indicated by the line-up of officials
at meetings, seminars, banquets or events reported in China's official
media. Who was present, where their name is positioned in the overall
order of names mentioned, who delivers which speech and who says what,
are points which carry clear symbolism and often specific indications of
the political rise, fall and shift of personalities juxtaposed against others,
and in turn the policies associated with these individuals.

Against this pattern, several developments are now occurring between
the Chinese press and its readers.

First, a plethora of local newspapers has appeared focusing on social
issues alongside news. Th ese newspapers do not necessarily belong to
government organs and therefore can be labeled as unofficial press. Some,
which do belong to government-sponsored associations, are yet one step

removed from the official media and often also select their own editorial line. Consequently, a semi-independent press is emerging, which is identified as not being the official media. While not necessarily challenging the official media politically, this press is competing with it commercially by attracting larger readership segments, which find the unofficial press's new reporting more interesting and engaging than that of the official press.

Secondly, the general readership is tired of the old pattern of reading between the lines and searching for answers. Again, a competitive press and the introduction of Internet access is causing an increasing number of Chinese readers to seek more engaging, analytical and comprehensive news reporting. In short, China's educated urban populace is outgrowing the Chinese media's old framework of official news reporting at Internet speed.

Thirdly, China's leadership itself is realizing that old style news reporting is now out-dated and less effective domestically, if not ineffective altogether in terms of international news dissemination. In short, there is a tendency to drop the word "propaganda" from the vocabulary of officials seeking more persuasive manners of presenting news in a way which will be more acceptable to both an international audience and a domestic readership. Again, both groups, through the Internet, are increasingly able to access international news reporting and make their own comparisons.

In a first attempt at addressing this development, a nationwide overhaul of domestic newspapers and magazines commenced in August 2000 involving two principal measures:

- those excessive newspapers and magazines are to be consolidated under or merged into local newspapers or magazines following which their old names will be changed or removed;
- those which cannot be consolidated or merged will simply be cancelled and operations closed down altogether.

The effect of these moves is to require more than 400 newspapers and magazines to face market realities by the end of this year. This press overhaul is aimed at achieving two specific objectives.

The first is to transfer many of the newspapers under control of various government organizations to the market and let them survive on their own commercially, a move also intended to break up the monopoly controlled by certain newspapers under these government departments, essentially creating an environment of competition.

The second is to force periodicals to seek real subscribers who are private individuals, rather than having the newspaper or magazine owned and controlled by a government department force all the sub-departments to use that government department's money to subscribe to it as has been the case in the past. China's official press is being forced to come to terms with the market.

RESTRUCTURING THE FILM INDUSTRY

Chinese films are now winning international awards in Cannes and other film festivals. Chinese directors and actors are being acclaimed internationally and, in turn, at home. At the same time, many western movies have been restricted in the past from entering the China market, more often due to concerns over their competitive impact on the local industry rather than over any particular ideological issue.

In a landmark decision in 2000, the State Broadcasting, Film and Television Bureau and the Ministry of Culture jointly announced "Certain Opinions Concerning Deepening the Movie Industry Reforms," a decision aimed at promoting the further development of China's film industry through a set of reform measures.

The Central Committee Propaganda Department simultaneously issued a notice requiring "all local Party committee propaganda departments to completely recognize the importance of emergency and necessary actions" and to "completely recognize that the film industry development is a critical part of developing socialism."

One might ask on first glance what these two announcements mean? Simply put, China's entry into WTO has forced a reassessment of its own television broadcasting and film-making industry. Where official film-making has been a monopoly of the state film studios in the past and inquisitive popular interest films the endeavor of smaller unofficial low-budget efforts, the two are coming together. A merger of interest has arisen out of commercial interests sparked by competitive pressures.

The objective of China's film industry reforms is to develop several large and internationally competitive movie production "group" companies. These companies would have control over production and distribution, and even theaters, a system modeled after that of Hollywood, where several companies have vast financial resources at their disposal and a virtual monopoly over the entire industry. Previously, China's movie industry was characterized by a separation between film production, distribution, and the theatres themselves.

Under the reforms being put into play, the movie production companies will be restructured into shareholding companies, but the majority equity must be controlled by the State. Within this structure, however, foreign investment may enter with a minority position, making this a long-awaited breakthrough decision.

While this framework will apply to the major movie production studios, even further flexibility is now being provided for companies established to produce a one-off production. In other words, a movie company established privately on a small scale to produce only one movie may be privately dominated and have foreign equity participation. Apparently foreign-dominated equity is permitted for these one-off production companies.

The structure of distribution companies, however, will require State-dominated equity control with domestic non-state equity participation in the minority. As for the theatre companies, these may have both domestic private and foreign equity participation as well, on the condition that domestic equity control (which can be state or private) be retained.

WESTERN MEDIA PERCEPTIONS

China's official media often reacts to the excessive negativism in Western reporting on China, which in turn stimulates more negative reporting. In turn, as China enters a new century and era, probably the single greatest handicap to western business decision-makers and politicians in making informed decisions concerning China, is the lack of balanced and clear information—reflecting in the western press—the reality of developments in China. To a great extent, this is due to the fact that western perceptions of China have been formed within a framework of self-perpetuating misperceptions and prejudices, which more often than not serve as convenient political ammunition for domestic voter consumption where the electorate itself remains ill-informed on the subject. Unfortunately, this framework is not easy to dismantle, as it stems from over a century of misleading reporting.

In the 1800s, dogmatic foreign missionaries reported China as a vast population of "heathens" to convert into a "harvest of souls;" western politicians supported this premise as it coincided with the political objectives of the day, that being to colonize Asia economically. During the cold war period, nascent American policies of containing China were premised on the domino theory of John Foster Dulles, who hyped a "red threat" consuming Asia and threatening American security interests. Journalist reports from the field by the likes of Edgar Snow and Theodore White attempting to explain what communism meant for "New China," were suppressed by editors who sought to adhere to the Washington, D.C. line. The framework for western media coverage of China had by that time more or less been set.

The tendency of the Western media is to cover China through the framework of stereotype, focusing on the exotic oddity or extreme situation. Often the Western press relies on rumors generated among the diplomatic or foreign business communities in China, not on actual circumstances.

These rumors or examples of situations which can be repackaged to fulfill preconceived ideas of China are the substance of news, which is absorbed by the western public as fact. This situation is extremely dangerous when one thinks that key business and political decision-makers are relying on speculation and recycled stereotypes when making policy which concerns the most populous nation on earth and the fastest-growing developing economy in the world today.

In fact, there is nothing new about blinkered reporting on China, a tradition in the western media which dates back to the old Treaty Port era. Author Sterling Seagrave, in his biography of the Empress Dowager Ci Xi, described the tenor of China reporting at the end of the Qing Dynasty as follows:

> Little historical background was understood by westerners in China, who were dependent upon what they could learn from Treaty Port compradors or hired interpreters, who were themselves ill-informed and far from disinterested. Such people filled in the gaps in their knowledge with colorful inventions, because it was important to seem to know what was going on. Over drinks at the Long Bar in Shanghai or gossiping at the new racetrack, they mingled misinformation and supposition and passed it on by letter, diary, memoir, travelogue, diplomatic report, and journalism to the far corners of the earth, where it was accepted as fact.

The above in fact, serves as a good description of the reporting situation as it exists today. Much of what is reported in the Western press, and in turn accepted as fact about China, is derived in very much the same way. The Shanghai Treaty Port atmosphere of speculation and hype described by Seagrave could very well be applied to Beijing, Shanghai, or Hong Kong where most journalists' China scoops originate. The analysis provided in the Western media is often flat, viewing China's political dynamics as a struggle between extreme factions (conservative-hard-liner vs. liberal-reformist). Such extreme factions do not really exist. Deeper analysis of China's complicated politics is hard to find in the Western media, which tends to reduce everything to Hollywood bad guy—good guy simplicity. As William Overholt, who wrote *China: The Next Economic Superpower*, has commented:

> For any historian of Chinese–American relations, the mystery is why the outside world has failed to appreciate the positive aspects of China's course. Whereas any East European leadership that recorded one or two of China's achievements in 1994–1995 would have been hailed for its genius, most of China's accomplishments attracted no attention in the Western press. As far as the average American could tell [from the media] China did little in this period except oppress its people and plan an invasion of Taiwan.

While there is nothing wrong with reporting negative events in China, to simply focus exclusively on them and to blow them up, painting them out of context, does not help westerners coming to China, or their governments, to usefully comprehend those events and to place the economic, social and political transitions occurring here today in their correct con text or perspective.

There is little attempt to understand the workings of the Chinese government, or the reasons underlying certain policies, or the psychology of the Chinese populace and their subsequent reactions. More often then not, the western media seems to be forced to find stories to match the requirements of editorial boards in New York City or Washington, D.C., which need to keep fulfilling what they believe or imagine to be the state of affairs in China. When reading China press reporting in the major American newspapers, it seems as if these reports could be coming straight from the desk of the U.S. State Department, not from the cities or countryside of China. Little wonder Chinese officials—together with many from other Asian countries as well—tend to see western media coverage as part of a conspiracy to retard China's economic growth and coming of age as a superpower. Whether correct or not, when somebody living or travelling regularly to China reads the western press coverage of China, it is easy to come up with such rationale as a logical explanation.

On August 15, 2000, in commenting on differing perceptions between the western and Chinese media concerning coverage of China, State Chairman and Party General Secretary Jiang Zemin explained to CBS reporter Mike Wallace that, "We insist on 'one hundred flowers blooming and one hundred schools of thought contending'. China's news has freedom. But this freedom must obey and serve the interest of protecting the state and the public. In fact, in the west there is no exception to this situation. China's news, in particular the *People's Daily*, are followed closely by the people. If information is reported which is false, then the people will react. It is different from your press which can write a lot of things regardless of whether it is true or false, and nobody really cares."

Jiang went on to comment on the Internet's effect on China's media pointing out that, "Internet is the same. We feel that Internet should collect information conducive to the development of China. We also want to restrict information which is counter productive to our development and unhealthy information such as pornography which effects young people."

In summary Jiang explained, "You have your choice. We have our choice. Look at your choices. You choose to restrict reporting on developments in China. There is very little about the real situation in China which is reported in the American press."

This section explores developments in China's media, the impact of digital technology, and the relaxation of past restrictions on press freedoms. In the first chapter of this section, Minister Zhao Qizheng of the State Council News and Information Office, examines the evolution of China's media in light of the Internet revolution and how it will effect change in the years to come. In the second chapter, StarTV CEO James Murdoch analyzes the future developments of China's media sector in the digital age, predicting its future evolution and advancement of China's media sector in light of technology developments now underway. Ta Kung Pao, special commentator, and senior journalist Ma Ling, discuss the need for greater competition and in turn for changes in style and approach within the Chinese domestic press in the third chapter. In the final chapter, nationally acclaimed media expert and author Professor Li Xiguang of Qsinghua University discusses the gradual relaxation and greater openness of the Chinese press.

ZHAO QIZHENG

Zhao Qizheng is minister of the State Council News and Information Office, the department of the State Council responsible for the dissemination of information, news, press conferences and releases, and coordination of media and news related issues.

Minister Zhao previously served as vice mayor of Shanghai, with particular responsibility for the Pudong New Economic Area, spearheading the new growth and revival of Shanghai as China's business and finance center. He served in the Shanghai Municipality from 1982–1998, holding a range of positions in the Industrial Work Committee, the CPC Shanghai Municipal Committee and the Organization Department. He graduated from the Modern Physics Department of the Chinese University of Science and Technology in 1963.

In the following chapter, Minister Zhao discusses how China's media intends to enter the Internet age, taking a front row position in utilizing digital technology in driving forward the globalization of China's media networks.

CHINA'S MEDIA IS WELCOMING
NETWORK TIME

Zhao Qizheng
Minister, State Council News & Information Office

A NEW MEASUREMENT OF TIME

In the last week of June 2000, I visited America's Silicon Valley again and was told of a new saying: In Silicon Valley, the time is counted by "dog years" (the life of a human being is counted by a hundred years and the life of a dog is counted by ten years). This means that at present, the progress of information technology is so big and so fast that the progress during each ten-year period is now much greater than that of a hundred years in the past. In comparison with any century in the past, the 21st century will conceptually be a long time.

Although history is not divided by the demarcation line of the century, while entering the dividing line which marks this century, human civilization is being characterized by rapid development of information technology, with the Internet becoming the symbol for this epoch. Rapid progress stimulates world civilization.

With extreme warmness, the Chinese government and Chinese people welcome the arrival of Internet time and are considering how to utilize it to promote the development of China's media.

Up to the end of 1999, China has more than 2,200 types of openly published newspapers and more than 8,000 types of journals and magazines. Each year there are over 100,000 types of books published. China now has 743 medium and short-wave broadcast launching stations with a population coverage rate of 90.4%. China now has 1,283 television transmission stations and relay stations (exceeding 1,000 watts) with a population coverage rate of 91.6%. At present, China has 77 million cable television users.

In terms of the time period from the introduction of one type of new electronic medium to the formation of 5,000 users, it takes 38 years for broadcasting, 13 years for wireless television and 10 years for cable television. It only takes four years for Internet.

In China, Internet users at the end of 1999 are four times the number at the end of 1998. At the end of 2000, Internet users will exceed 20 million. Many institutions have forecasted that in 2004, the number of Internet users in China will be ranked second largest in the world.

Most of China's major news units started their on-line services at the end of 1996 and the beginning of 1997. At present, there are more than 700 news units in China that have established their independent domain names. The web sites of Xinhua News Agency, *People's Daily*, China International Broadcasting Station, and *China Daily*, and more, have begun to take shape. The China International Internet Information Center (CIIC) has opened comprehensive and special subject web pages with independent domain names such as China, China Human Rights, China Tibet, China Taiwan, 50 years of New China, Macao 1999, '99 Global Fortune Forum, Shanghai, '99 Paris, Chinese Cultural Week, and so on. CIIC has also opened overseas image sites such as China News and China Guidance.

CHINA IN THE INTERNET EPOCH

Reviewing past epochs, which were symbolized by technical progress by the people—the steam engine epoch, electric epoch, radio epoch, atomic energy epoch, computer epoch (although they are not strictly divided)—we find that China has always fallen behind the "epoch" for dozens of years. However, if we take the time in which people have started using public commercial Internet as the mark, there is no big time difference in entering the network epoch or the initiation of the so-called information epoch between China and developed countries. The news web sites of China started at almost the same time as those of the foreign media.

In any case, there are still some big disparities, whether in terms of news quantity or quality, between the on-line units of China and their foreign counterparts. Basically, the information updating speed of 70% of the media web sites is the same as the publishing cycle of the original media. Some minor web sites are even laid behind the original media. The updating speed of about only 9% of the web sites is faster than the updating cycle of the original media. The news content published by most of the media is a copy of the traditional media (newspapers and magazines, broadcasting and television). Only 10% of the web sites have reorganized and enriched their information.

Judging only from the fact that we are starting to apply the Internet, it is fair to say that China has entered the Internet epoch. However, there are several difficulties that exist in terms of how to develop the Internet in China:

1. The network infrastructure is relatively backward. The domestic network spreading density and bandwidth are not large enough. The bandwidth of the across-continent network is too narrow.
2. Like many other Asian countries, China has not mastered the related core technology of hardware and software and is in a position of follower in terms of technology development.
3. The on-line storage of Chinese information is inadequate. The share of Chinese information amounts to a very small proportion among the total information import and export flow of the Internet. It is much lower than in the developed countries, such as the United States.

China shall overcome those difficulties and needs to intensify the cultivation of talented personnel as well as increase capital input into infrastructure. In time counted by "dog years," these are all urgent and major projects.

China's Networks Online

China plans to take around three years to make the online rate of State news units reach 100%. The on-line rate of the major news units of all provinces, autonomous regions and the cities directly under the central government's administration shall reach 90% and the on-line rate of embassies abroad shall reach 80% during that time. Especially, we shall concentrate our strength on constructing a set of major web sites, including the foreign language web sites with English as the main language. We should ensure that those web sites contain a large quantity of information, have broad coverage, maintain strong service functions and become well-known. They shall also link to all the web sites of news units of China, provide search engines and provide guide service for domestic and international visitors.

All the new web sites (pages) shall fully use the information accumulated by the traditional media and all aspects of the society over the years. Through planning and organizing methods, they shall develop and utilize this information rationally and comprehensively. In developing news information resources, the news web sites shall stress the immediate news and background materials with the supplement of other information services. To enable domestic and international visitors to understand and recognize the published news easily, the web sites shall also publish more broad material covering the areas of society, history and culture. All the individual news units must be based on their own specialized areas and regional characteristics, foster strengths and circumvent weakness, and intensify strategic link-ups and cooperation. Thus, we can gradually form a close cooperative system between the State and local news networks, realize the utilization of mutual advantages and form a broad effect of network news.

NEW TECHNOLOGY BRINGS NEW CHALLENGES

Network information technology receives much close attention in all countries of the world, because people recognize its important function in pushing forward social politics, economy, scientific technology and the culture of the human race. Anything has two sides. The advantages of surpassing the time and space and the interchanges of network information transmission provide convenient conditions for transmitting information across the boundaries of countries and regions. However, in the meantime, it also brings in unfavorable factors.

Each user of the Internet is both the receiver of information and the disseminator of information. Some people vividly analogize this free receipt and dissemination of on-line information as navigation on the network. They think this type of on-line navigation provides an exciting and free soaring feeling. It is just like walking into a huge candy store packed with goods: a child without the restraint of an adult suddenly feels faced with a situation where you can take anything freely. Some Internet users have this type of feeling, as well as lack restraint to the transmission of network information. This can lead to unsound Internet practices by some Internet users with low moral self-discipline and moral concepts, resulting in the disclosure and invasion of individual privacy, the flow of unhealthy information and the consistent invasion of hackers.

It is now easy for all kinds of unhealthy and harmful information to become mixed with news information of various media, often leading to situations where information and even news shams are passed off as genuine, thereby lowering the trustworthiness and safeness of news information. This is a new problem and new challenge faced by various media of the world as well as the Chinese news media. The Chinese news media will welcome the challenge of technical development of network dissemination by relying on increasing the truthfulness, efficiency and enhanced competitiveness of news dissemination.

Along with the continual deepening of the market economy in China, the industrialized nature of news media will be confirmed. The "Content Industry" will be able to play its function to the full.

China will enter WTO, and the development of Chinese Internet industry and network news industry will face a tremendous challenge. During the process of opening the market, the dual relationship of cooperation and competition between China and foreign counterparts will exist. I trust that international investors will share in the opportunities provided by China during its development. They will also carry out fine cooperation with Chinese counterparts and jointly accomplish achievements satisfactory to both sides.

JAMES MURDOCH

James Murdoch is chairman and chief executive officer of STAR TV, News Corporation's Asian satellite television and multi-media service. He is a member of News Corporation's Executive Committee.

Mr. Murdoch founded News Corporation's U.S.-based interactive publishing subsidiary, News Digital Media, in November 1997, and was its president until September 1999. In that position, Mr. Murdoch established and oversaw the strategy, business initiatives and daily operations of News Digital Media's interactive properties as well as made investments in various new media companies. Currently, Mr. Murdoch also oversees the company's international music businesses. News Corporation's music operations include: Rawkus Entertainment, founded by Mr. Murdoch in August 1995, and the Festival and Mushroom records groups based in Australia and in the U.K. Mr. Murdoch serves on the board of News Corporation subsidiary News Digital Systems (NDS), as well as on the boards of the YankeeNets, Inner City Scholarship Fund, and Jump Start, and on the board of trustees of the Harvard Lampoon.

STAR is a wholly-owned subsidiary of News Corporation and is Asia's leading multiplatform content and service provider. STAR's 30 distributed services, in seven languages, reach more than 300 million viewers across 53 Asian countries. STAR will become a subsidiary of Sky Global Networks, the world's leading distributor of pay television via satellite through its owned and affiliated platforms, before Sky Global Networks' anticipated initial public offering.

STAR TV channels include *STAR Chinese Channel, Phoenix Chinese Channel, STAR Plus, STAR World, Channel [V], ESPN, STAR Sports, STAR Movies, STAR Gold, Phoenix Movies, VIVA Cinema, STAR News*, in addition to distributed channels *Fox News, Sky News* and *National Geographic Channel*. STAR has also invested in cable systems such as Hathway in India, and Internet portals and services companies, including netease.com, renren.com, Indya.com. In the following chapter, James Murdoch discusses his vision for the future growth opportunities for China's media sector.

THE NEW MILLENNIUM: CHINA IN THE CONNECTED WORLD

James Murdoch
Chairman & CEO, STAR

Any attempt to contribute to the body of thinking on China's development at the convenient, but not inherently significant, cusp of the next century, is fraught with dangers. From the outset: I am not a sinologist, nor even particularly expert. Furthermore, the essay is written from the perspective of an interested, and intrigued, observer. As a broadcaster, of course, my area of expertise is limited, but it is an area (in the broader sense of media, and telecommunications) that will have a profound impact on the daily lives and consumption patterns of the substantial constituency of the growing Chinese "consumer class."

THE EMERGENCE OF A NETWORKED SOCIETY

This impact of media and telecommunications will be remarkably acute as China enters the 21st century, riding a wave of innovation that has only just begun to engulf the developed world. In particular, it is this emergence of a networked environment, across all walks of life and fields of endeavor, that is transforming the way we consume information, disseminate ideas, and nurture our communities. And this phenomenon will contribute markedly to what I believe is China's very likely preeminence on the growing stage of global enterprise.

The simple premise that we start with will be that a combination of factors and forces are coming together at this critical time, and that they collectively, in ways both causal and not, are compounding and accelerating China's inevitable development as the model of a networked society in the 21st century.

First and foremost on the list of positive indicators is recent (and current) policy in China. There can be no doubt that the pro-active financial policy of China's leadership is creating an unprecedented number of new productive members of a large and growing consumer class in the world's largest country. Culminating in entry to the WTO, this policy arch has, and will be, rightfully recognized as a watershed, not just within China, but around the world.

What will happen, as this consumer class grows, when 300 million new international travelers start spending on hotel rooms, airplane flights, holiday gifts, and the like? Already the extraordinary growth in international voice traffic between the mainland and the rest of the world is fueling a boom in Pacific and South-East Asian fiber carriers.

As the Chinese market continues to open, and Chinese spending power starts to impact more severely the global economy, the dogged and thorough approach to economic reform taken by China's leadership, and by those nations with whom it shares its vision of global economic cooperation, will have paid off in spades.

China's Uniqueness

Moreover, as East and South-East Asia enters the 21st century, China's position is unique. Premier *Zhu Rongji*, in his foreword to this volume, is absolutely correct in asserting that Asia's and China's prosperity are inextricable. Advantageously for China, current political instability in Indonesia and the Philippines, combined with an ebbing Japanese economic potency, creates a leadership vacuum in the region that is begging to be stepped in to. Market reform and a continued, muscular, economic strategy are the keys to filling this vacuum.

But importantly, a Chinese economic powerhouse today is going to be very different than it might have been twenty, or even ten years ago. Technology does change things, and markedly in China, Internet usage growth creates a positive environment for economic growth as well as international economic integration. Indeed, it is this growth in connectivity on a mass scale that has seeded the ground for an unprecedented acceleration of development—an acceleration that is necessary in a country as large and diverse as China.

Simply look at what mobile equipment giant *Nokia Corp.*, of Finland, calls the emergence of the "mobile information society." It is this kind of consumer connectivity, woven into the fabric of people's everyday lives, that reinforces community, allows for the easy flow of communications and information, and equips the beneficiaries, the consumers, as fully connected participants in the cultural and economic society of which they are a part.

Mass Connectivity

Mass connectivity feeds on itself. The simple nature of a network external-ity impacts the uptake of these new communications products in a pro-found way. And it is particularly relevant in a market the size of China. One telephone, connected to nothing, is worthless. Two telephones, connected to each other, are each worth a bit more. But any one phone of a million, interconnected, is priceless. And interestingly, the price of that phone is inversely related to its inherent value to its users, as the more are in the market, the cheaper the unit price. This same effect takes part in the uptake of Internet services, and of all kinds of connectivity. In China, it means that rapid deployment of new communications and media services across vast swathes of the population is not only quite possible, but is probably at this point inevitable.

Much of the basic infrastructure of a connected society is already being put in place. China's cable television industry, for example, is one of the world's most extensive and impressive. However, an accelerated liberaliza-tion in this area, with respect to "value-added services" in particular, is critical if the range of services envisioned by policy makers is to be a reality. Foreign and independent investment in the production of media services, the development of media related technologies, and the build-out of new media-delivery systems, such as satellite, fiber, and digital terrestrial broad-casting, would contribute enormously to the effective deployment of new and affordable media and communications products to Chinese families across the nation.

These new services can undoubtedly be affordable to this new Chinese consumer class. Urban households' disposable income grew to $US650 per year in 1998, which represents seven times growth since 1985. And urban households represent some 30% of China's population, with incomes three times as high as the average, at a Purchasing Power Parity adjusted US$3,275. And China is demographically young, though not as dramatically young as India, but far younger than the U.S. or Japan—boding well for future growth. Most interestingly though, is the percentage of living expenses being spent on communications and recreation activity, growing to 20% by 1998.

Moreover, the rise in connectivity and media penetration, through mobile networks, cable television, et cetera, leads to other opportunities. Credit networks, billing systems, and the like, to name just a few, are made exponentially more practical in a networked environment in which consum-ers and families use their mobile phones to buy goods and services, organize their utility payments through their set-top box, and so on. The networked environment enables a society to quite literally leapfrog and then outpace historically more developed countries.

Meeting the Challenges

So these factors—economic policy, politics, and technology—are clear positive indicators of an extraordinary period of growth and prominence for China in the new century. That said, there are many obstacles that lie in the path towards prolonged prosperity.

First—law. The recent, firm, crackdown on corruption within the State must be extended to encompass the private sector, as the latter grows larger. A fair business environment, guided by law as well as by the market, is obviously an essential element in the expansion of economic productivity. Furthermore, in order to take full advantage of imminent WTO accession, the foreign investors that will in large part accelerate the development of new services and catalyze the modernization of a wide number of industries, must be made to feel that the crony-ism of many developing business communities is at least kept at a minimum in China.

In addition to bribery and fraud laws, strong and fair anti-trust guidelines are needed to ensure competition in emerging industries and to lay down a fair field of play for new entrants into various markets.

The second obstacle, and perhaps most important, is the risk of intra-national instability as the potential for increased income-gap widening becomes a more urgent reality. Current policies regarding the development of the west of China must continue while a strong hand guides the economic ship of state through what are sure to be turbulent waters, in this regard.

The Counselor

China at this moment in history stands on the cusp of tremendous advancement, but with the risk of destabilization, economically and politically, looming large as its leadership tackles head-on the challenges of integration into the global economic community. But as much of the world has struggled with the same problems, with both notable successes and failures to learn from, China has the extraordinary opportunity to enter a new phase of growth, equipped with the industrial wherewithal, the technology, and the single-mindedness that no previous state has enjoyed simultaneously on such a grand scale. As Pericles famously advised: "Wait for the wisest of all counselors—time."

China has just such a counselor, and by all indications, is listening. And given the successful handling of manifold risk-scenarios, the consumer class of China will continue to grow, and will continue to adopt new communications and media technologies at a brisk pace. In the waxing years of the 21st century, I believe, we will see in China an astonishing example and paragon of managed, sustainable, growth. As the members of this huge consumer class enter their most productive phase (in terms of family, wealth creation, and output) in what promises to be a "next generation" environment of near-ubiquitous connectivity. This confluence of a variety of reforms, demographic trends, scientific advances, and macro-economic factors stands to create a potent cultural and economic dynamism which will have intra-national, regional, and global ramifications.

Ma Ling

Ma Ling, born in Beijing, is a senior journalist and special column commentator of Hong Kong's *Ta Gong Bao*. She has personally covered numerous on-the-scene breaking news stories in China and Hong Kong concerning key political and economic events.

Ma Ling is also an accomplished author, having written *Within and Outside the Red Wall: An Exclusive Report* and contributed to *Behind the "Mistaken" Bombing*. She regularly comments on current events in "Ma Ling's Special Column" of *Ta Gong Bao*.

Ta Gong Bao is the earliest of Chinese language newspapers still going strong today. It was founded during the Qing Dynasty in 1902 by a Manchurian named Ying Jianzhi in Tianjin, carrying on after the 1911 Revolution of Sun Yat-sen, and continuing after the liberation of China in 1949 by the Communist Party. This background gives the newspaper a critical position of importance in the history of modern China, covering over one hundred years of tumultuous events and rapid changes. *Ta Gong Bao* received worldwide acclaim—the first Chinese newspaper to be recognized internationally—upon receiving the American Minnesota University Award for Journalism in 1941. During the Cultural Revolution, *Ta Gong Bao* changed its center of operations from Beijing to Hong Kong, which is where the newspaper is still based today.

In the following chapter, Ms. Ma examines the competitive pressures that China's official state-owned media is now facing in an environment which has become intensely commercial, calling for changes in style and approach.

THIRD EYE TO READ CHINA'S NEWS

Ma Ling

Senior Journalist, Special Column Commentator, Ta Gong Bao

NEWS WITH CHINESE CHARACTERISTICS

China's news broadcasting, in certain respects, has characteristics different from the commonly used international news-broadcasting model.

The human being in the world only has two eyes, which is enough to watch news broadcasting. However, to read the unique sector of Chinese news broadcasting you would need to have a third eye.

The so-called using of "the third eye" to watch the "unique" points of Chinese news refers to the content with "Chinese characteristics." Let's use the 7:00 p.m. China Central Television (CCTV) news broadcast, which enjoys the largest viewing audience in China, as an example. During this half-hour news report, the editorial acceptance and rejection of which news headlines to broadcast basically are determined by political guidelines. Sometimes state leaders are shown receiving visitors; sometimes the opening of an important state meeting is highlighted; sometimes a hero or model worker is introduced; sometimes it exposes and criticizes the organizational activities of Fa Lun Gong.... In this author's impression, in recent years, there was only instance of an event such as the American aerospace shuttle "Challenger" explosion in 1986 used as the lead international news report in CCTV's "news broadcasting."

"News Broadcasting's" broadcasting model is to place Chinese news as the priority, which takes about 20 minutes, while international news is left to the end and usually allocated less than 10 minutes. When there is the occurrence of a significant affair, the regularly scheduled half hour news broadcast will be extended; sometimes international news may be omitted, or sometimes one or two pieces of international news is reported within an extremely short time frame.

All Chinese local television stations are requested to relay the 7:00 p.m. most authoritative "News Broadcasting" on scheduled time. The major characteristic of "News Broadcasting" is that all kinds of political propaganda and a series of receptions and meetings are grandly pushed out in the news. This socialistic country's special style has never changed over the past 50 years, since the establishment of the new People's Republic of China. Obviously, this style of news broadcasting—of highlighting politics —is different from the international, generally accepted news-broadcasting model, this one containing "Chinese characteristics."

Changes are Happening

Certainly, changes in news broadcasting are happening. Let's use the same example of CCTV. Besides the 7:00 p.m. "News Broadcasting," some other news reporting of CCTV has begun to pay attention to and follow the international approach. On one hand, CCTV carries out reports several times a day adopting the news broadcasting rolling model; on the other hand, various news shows, such as, "Morning News," "Noon News," "Current Reporting," "Evening News," and so on, have continuously improved truthful news reporting. These programs are not restricted by the two main criteria:

1. They do not need to generally report political propaganda information, as they are only required to mention its key points in the news headlines; and
2. They are allowed to set the order of reporting based on news elements, with the added benefit that all local television stations are not required to relay at the same time.

However, despite the current "Morning News," "Noon News," "Current Reporting," and "Evening News" having attracted and dispersed some of CCTV's audience, due to old habits or some other reason we do not know, the survey shows that the 7:00 p.m. "News Broadcasting" of CCTV is still its most popular program.

Let's take the *People's Daily*—the official newspaper of Chinese Communist Party—as an example, this being the most influential major newspaper, having gone through 20 years of open reform testing, has never changed its traditional style. Nowadays, it still operates restrictively, following the principal of politicians running a newspaper" put forward by China's current state leader Jiang Zemin. This newspaper is facing the problem of shrinking circulation year after year. Seldom do ordinary people read this newspaper. However, *Global Times*, a small newspaper that was derived from the *People's Daily* and covering hot international developments, is warmly received by common people.

The Chinese newspaper readers have shown a tendency to deliberately distance themselves from the stereotypical political propaganda newspapers, preferring the intimacy of small newspapers possessing a human touch and readability. It may be seen throughout the entire nation. Not only has the circulation of the small newspapers derived from central government official newspapers increased greatly, but also the official newspapers of local party committee have been facing the same situation. For example, the Henan Provincial government official newspaper, *Henan Daily*, is having a hard time with circulation; readers have been decreasing daily. However, *Da He Daily*, derived from *Henan Daily*, is very popular.

In the current Chinese newspaper field, such situations as "small newspapers being superior to large newspapers" and "small newspapers supporting large newspapers" are a very common phenomena worth paying attention to. Why does this situation occur? This is mainly caused by management reasons. The big newspapers' difficulties are caused by their traditional restrictive management, which always follows closely to the Party line, taking it as their own, while the small newspapers have flexibility, arising from their relatively relaxed environment, following closely the common people as their target.

THE FOURTH MEDIUM

The *People's Daily* is under current severe attack from the fourth medium and is determined not to be outdone, using its strength and enormous publicity, establishing a web site to reflect its actual strength. The Internet version of *People's Daily* is not only limited to the contents of its paper edition, but also uses the contents of Internet journalists. Quick information and a vivid web site Internet version, combined with special discussions of hot points, makes it far superior to the newspaper version of *People's Daily*, and in turn, it is more warmly received by Internet users. *People's Forum*, started by the *People's Daily* web site, changed the high-handed style of the old newspaper version, using joint publishing methods to bring in active Internet user participation. For example, in May 1999 when the Chinese Embassy in Yugoslavia was attacked by the NATO bombing, this *People's Forum* was very active, which made its name very famous. Now, the *Strong Countries Forum* and *Sports On-Line* web sites of *People's Daily* are very favorable to Internet users. *People's Daily* in print and *People's Daily* on-line have given people two different impressions, and the *People's Daily* in print seemed to transfer its approach to getting closer to common people.

Based on the statistics for the end of 1999, there were over 2,200 various comprehensive or professional newspapers in China. With every newspaper trying to achieve social impact and economic profits, competition is heated. This competition consists of changing black and white newspapers to color newspapers, establishing and promoting Internet web sites, exploring various exclusive news besides sensitive political news, and so on. This now includes such stories as revealing the local, tyrannical style of government officials. For example, a Henan public security official escaped from his car accident; a Hebei public security official was protected after he shot a person to death; and so on—these were published in the small, local newspapers first, and then in the big newspaper or on CCTV, and then went further to do follow-up reporting, attracting central government leaders' attention, after which heavy punishment for the public security officials was approved. Criticizing improper measures or unfair behavior of government organizations—for example, the State Civil Aviation Bureau forcing set prices of flight tickets by breaking the rules of market operation, the low efficiency but high fees collected by China telecommunications organizations, and so on—were all publicly criticized and attacked by many media. So in addition to many local television stations, CCTV has also begun starting up special programs exposing various social problems.

Chinese audiences have gained and benefited increasingly from all this media competition. Without doubt, the effectiveness of the electronic media platform is embodied in its supervisory effect upon daily news reporting. So far, in the newspaper sector, there does not seem to be any hot nationwide newspaper that can take the upper hand in China. The central level, official, large newspapers are too orthodox to be able to establish wide circulation among the general population. However in some provinces, many local newspapers are heavily competing with each other and are gaining a somewhat front-runner position. In the television sector, at present there is only one television station that can challenge China's only state-level television station, CCTV, and that is the Phoenix Star TV station, controlled by China and established in Hong Kong. The other newly rising television station is Hunan Star TV. The Hong Kong Phoenix Star TV, by using its international model for news reporting, has attracted a large news audience. Hunan Star TV has attracted a large leisure audience through its special and active entertainment programs.

UNAVOIDABLE INTERNATIONALIZATION

There are two official news agencies in China: one is the official "mouth throat," Xinhua News Agency; the other is the China News Agency, which provides information for the overseas Chinese language media. The position of Xinhua News Agency is still exclusive and unshakable. Things concerning significant political affairs or central leaders' important activities must be drafted and released by Xinhua News Agency to determine a general tone; other media are not allowed to give free rein to their work. Though other major television or newspaper's journalists cover these important political affairs or central leaders' activities, they still need to adopt or follow the standard drafting of Xinhua News Agency. For instance, when President Jiang Zemin or Premier Zhu Rongji visits abroad, although many Chinese journalists accompanied them during interviews, the news manuscript released by the thousands of media in China look as though they came from one person's hand.

According to the statistics of the China Internet Information Center, by the end of June 2000, there were 16.9 million Internet users when compared with only four million at the end of June last year, showing a sharp increase in the number of Internet users. According to a news research organization survey, people who read Internet news as their main purpose for getting on-line was listed as number one. The same forecast shows that the number of Chinese Internet users will definitely lead the world and China will become a major Internet country. Consequently, reading news on-line will become the main source for people to obtain information.

No matter domestic or overseas, news information via the Internet, will drive straight into ordinary Chinese people's eyes. It seems difficult to draw borderlines. Click the mouse, and the country's borderline is broken through immediately. All kinds of domestic and overseas news is easily known to everyone. Despite the State Council News Office's efforts to continuously strengthen the management of Chinese Internet news releases, the people on-line can easily jump out of Chinese web sites and enter into overseas spaces directly. Hence, in the third eye, as China seeks to move in the direction of globalization at the same time, I'm afraid that internationalization of Chinese news is unavoidable.

LI XIGUANG

Li Xiguang, professor of journalism and American studies, is the director of the Center for International Communications Studies, and academic dean of the Department of Communications, Qinghua University, Beijing, China.

He was a research fellow at the Joan Shorenstein Center on the Press, Politics and Public Policy at Harvard University (1999), senior editor and director of the political and cultural desk of Xinhua News Agency (1996–1998), visiting journalist with the *Washington Post* (1995), and a Young Scholar of the UNESCO Silk Road Project (1990–1992).

He was the author or co-author of the following books: *Search for a Lost Buddhist Kingdom* (1995, Beijing); *Hunger* (1996, Beijing); *Discovering China from Sand and Dirt* (1996, Beijing); *Behind Demonizing China* (1996, Beijing); *How Bad Is China?* (1998, Nanjing); *Media Bombardment* (1999, Nanjing); *Online* (May 2000, Beijing); *Collapsing News House* (October 2000, Chengdu); and *Follow Me to Lop Nur* (October 2000, Beijing).

He has also been awarded numerous literary prizes by Chinese authorities and journalists.

In the following chapter, Professor Li draws upon his years of experience as a journalist in chronicling the liberalization of the Chinese press and calling attention to changes expected in the future.

CREEPING FREEDOMS IN CHINA'S PRESS

Li Xiguang

Director, Center for International Communications Studies,
Qinghua University

"TO CHANGE A BRAIN"

If we want to see the reality of China's press today, we should not discuss it in the frame of Tiananmen. When we examine the change of the Chinese press, we should go beyond the frame of Tiananmen and the preexisting assumptions concerning a communist nation. Based on their familiar historical and conceptual knowledge, many people in the West are expecting a bad communist, never a good communist. They do not expect that anything good is happening in a communist country, that the government is more confident and gaining the trust of the people, and that the government's rule is enhanced instead of being weakened.

The American public feels upset at disclosure and news reports of such positive changes. All they expect is a cruel, ruthless government on the brink of collapse. If positive changes happen, they think that must be brought by a handful of exiled political activists with support from the West. Like the U.S.' mass media's coverage of China, if it is A, it must act A. They never expect A can act as B or A can change to AI or AII. But in an informed and knowledgeable academic discussion, we must avoid analysis based on narrow preexisting values and conceptual knowledge. And if we limit our sources to some biased media and publications, it only reinforces stereotypes and we will never be able to see the true face of the Chinese press, politics, the society and the people.

In contrast to recent Western criticism of China's tightened social control and the crackdown on dissent, a liberalizing tendency has rippled in the most dangerous water in China: the press. The birth and growth of a freer press was inconceivable ten years ago. Since the spring of 1998, "a quiet revolution" has been taking place in the Chinese media. As China is embracing a free market economy, its press has begun to embrace a new journalism, which is not a planned move on the agenda of China studies programs and the Western media at large. The new journalism is becoming a media for the communications of news and formations of new ideas. The rise of such a new journalism and its influence on Chinese society and China's politics cannot be ignored.

The creeping freedoms, which have slowly come into being as a result of radical economic and social changes in China, can also be seen as the inevitable and unplanned result of social and economic forces unleashed by the Chinese Communist Party itself. In a sense, these freedoms and changes are not simply added spice to the dull format and content of the Party media nor are they intended to meet insatiable demand for information from the public. By analyzing the content of the new media and studying their effects, we will discover that they are functioning as media of mass communications, unlike the Party journalism which served as a means of mass propaganda.

An orthodox Marxist ideologue would find himself living on another planet after waking up from a 20-year coma in China. Reading today's Chinese press, he will find that more than half of the vocabulary the press currently uses is alien to him. For example, the most popular clichés to be found in the Party press are:

> With Chinese characteristics; tertiary industry; market economy; fast food; capital operation; crack-down on fake products; sideline job; lowering saving interest rates; resign for another job; capital regrouping; reorganization of state-owned enterprises; rehabilitation of political purges; bonus; sponsor; disco; white-collar workers; leisure life; re-employment, fired from job; karaoke; seafood; knowledge-based economy; computer; taxi, home-mover, pager, mobile phone, bar, Internet, T-shirt, driving school, multi-media, white collar pollution, green food, TV shopping, Miss Public Relations; hour-worker; VCD; DVD; information society; information highway; bull market; bear market; AA (going "Dutch"); starting a business; credit card; multi-media; and "Ku"(cool!).

In the realm of China's new journalism, the ideologue will be more surprised by the popular political slogans printed in the Party papers, which he might consider dangerous politically and even poisonous:

> Practice is the sole criteria of judging truth; Let some people get rich first; It's good to have one child; Time is money; Long live understanding; Poverty is not socialism; Science and technology is top productivity; Development is hard theory; Join the international track; Invigorate China with science and technology; One nation, two systems; Build socialism with Chinese characteristics.

The changes of terminology in the press and the daily life of the Chinese people and the freedom not to use hackneyed Party phrases and clichés can be seen as the obvious signs of a liberalizing press or a new openness in China. Studies show that the Chinese press is adding at least 800 new words and phrases to the Chinese vocabulary each year. And a total of 5,000 new words and phrases have been created over the past 20 years since the country opened up to the world.

Serious researchers are not Hollywood film producers who tend to see the Chinese as hapless victims or lawless villains. Academics are not media people who are manipulated by a down-market. In our discussion, I will try to avoid two falsehoods in my observations of the Chinese press. First, we cannot examine the Chinese press within the still picture of Tiananmen. Secondly, we should avoid another false impression—that the Chinese press is moving toward American-style freedom. Using the American yardstick to measure Chinese press freedom could be misleading.

The conventional wisdom that a communist government would not loosen control of the press is not supported by empirical evidence. As a Chinese journalist notes, the control of the media in China has shifted from a "visible hand" to "an invisible hand." "As a reflection of market economy by the means of news, the gravity of news media is shifting from a government behavior to a market behavior, from the area of production to the area of circulation. In a market economy, in order to guarantee a rational use of resources, an important link is information gathering, communications and their applications. As a result, the main function of news media has evolved from releasing government information to that of gathering and spreading information, communications and providing services to the society."

Deng Xiaoping once asked Chinese officials at all levels to have "a change of brain" in order to adapt to the new situation of China's reform and opening to the outside world. An updating of our thoughts of journalism is actually "a change of brain" for press thinking, for news topics, for news structure and for news style. If we do not to a new brain and do not update our concepts, we will by no means push forward the press reform in China. "Updating concepts is the pilot of behavior. Updating our press thought is the key link to implement a smooth press reform and to set up a new press system and a new journalism model which will be consistent with the socialist market economy."

So, in this chapter, I will try to use a "new brain" to look at the change of the Chinese press today.

"A Pretty Woman is a Bad Woman"

Before delving into the new journalism, I will take you to have a look at the propaganda journalism China has practiced over the past decades. We will not see a clear picture of China's burgeoning freedoms of press without a brief retrospective look at China's press over the last decade. We cannot start a serious discussion of China's new journalism without considering the role played by the Party propaganda and press policy in the past and today. It may not be "new journalism" by Western standards. But it is "new" in China considering the decades of dominance of propaganda journalism.

First let us read a story told by columnist Ma La:

> After the Spring Festival, I saw my neighbor's daughter, who is a first year pupil, reciting her Chinese textbook. Lesson One is "I am a Chinese." Lesson Two is "I love teachers". Lesson Three is "I love daddy and mom."
>
> But 30 years ago, when I was her age and opened my first Chinese textbook: Lesson One was "Long Live Chairman Mao;" Lesson Two was "Long Live the Chinese Communist Party;" Lesson Three was "Long Live the undefeatable Mao Zedong Thought." These three slogans were pasted all the way along my road to school. I heard the comrade heroes shouting the three slogans in movies and on stage. When I moved to a higher grade, I read in my textbook a lesson of a hero of a people's commune. My lady teacher wrote on the blackboard the central idea of the story: The hero defeated attacks of money, pretty women and sugar-coated bullets launched by the class enemies. At that time, even though we were all poor children, we all understood the meaning of "money." Growing up with the little red book, we all had vague ideas of "class enemies" and "sugar coated bullets." But 'pretty women' was a new phrase to us. A bold classmate shouted to the teacher, "what is 'pretty women?'" The lady teacher dumbfound for a moment, then replied, "Pretty women are 'bad' women."
>
> In 1980, I went to college in Sichuan. In my Chinese textbook, there was a romantic poem titled "the light in the office of Premier Zhou" which sings sentimental praise of the hard-working spirit of the Chinese leader. On our campus, I met an American teacher at a restaurant. He said, "Why did your country's poet write poems about your government leader? In the United States, it is unthinkable for romantic poets to write eulogies praising the hard-working sprit of Secretary of State Henry Kissinger. The Secretary of State probably worked very hard and sometimes forgot turning off the light. But wasn't he a top public servant? The poets in your country are beyond my understanding. The Sichuan girls are so pretty and there are so many pretty women here. Why don't you write for a pretty woman instead of writing for the premier? Since you already know your premier does not have time to turn off the light, how could he find time reading your poem?"

The story illustrates vividly how the country's propaganda worked for the best part over the last half a century. The wry propaganda model which still persists in some of the Party papers has much to do with a language environment that many of an older generation of Chinese journalists grew up with.

A photo editor of the *People's Daily* told a story that took place before 1978. A photo journalist came to the newsroom with a photo and asked the editor,

> "What kind of caption should I write on the picture?" The picture shows a group of people having a meeting.
> "Should I write it is a meeting denouncing capitalism or a meeting of studying of Chairman Mao's works?"

China does not have a law to govern the press. The government controls press through various press and publication policies as well as administrative measures. For the most part of the last 50 years, not only newspapers and broadcasts were under the strict control of the State; the public did not even have the right to read newspapers and listen to radio freely. Before 1978, the Chinese public listened to news from loudspeakers, which were set up to transmit news and circulars at a certain time of the day and night. It was a crime of "counter-revolution" if you tuned to broadcasts from *Radio Moscow, VOA, BBC* and Taiwan over a radio. And on Saturday afternoons, cadres, farmers, workers, students, soldiers would be organized into different political study groups reading newspapers. Reading and listening to news was not a personal choice. It was "a grave issue of right or wrong" and "a problem of your political attitude towards the Party and the government."

For many years in China, covering difficulties and problems of the country was a taboo for journalists. When the media reported that "the overall situation is good," it really meant "the situation is grave." When the media reported "a prosperity of market," it really meant "a shortage of materials." At a meeting of a selection committee for the best news photos of 1979, there were three pictures showing the poor housing conditions of a primary school. Some members of the selection committee opposed, "No, it is not appropriate to let so many dark-side pictures get the prize?" In those days of lying, of empty words and high-sounding slogans, an editor would kill a photo if he saw a person in rags or farm cattle in the picture. He would regard this kind of picture as damaging to the image of socialism. Zhang Dongping wrote in the *Beijing Daily* on November 16, 1998, "there was absolutely no way at all to report the sufferings of the common folks. At that time no one had the guts to speak the truth. But once you were bitten by a snake, you will be carried by a rope in the following ten years. After 20 years of reform, a huge change has taken place in Chinese press. But the old frame comes back to us from time to time. To photo journalists, the liberalization of thought will always remain a fresh topic."

The long-practiced propaganda is characterized by a writing style which is known as "good news is news, bad news is not news" and "always making bad news look like good news." The following paragraphs in a column appearing in *Southern Weekend* in the summer of 1998 really hits the nail on the head:

> "I often read such a news story: a natural disaster takes place somewhere, whether it is an earthquake, a flood or a fire. The local government tirelessly organizes rescue work and arranges the life of disaster-stricken people, who, having survived despite all of those sufferings, say gratefully, "It is the Party and the government who have saved me. Socialism is good." Such reports are frivolous.

For many years, there has been a pattern in news reporting that writes little about the cause of disaster, descriptions of the disaster scenes, casualties of people, loss of properties. All the sources, quotes and focus in these reports seem to be an endless verification of the truth that "socialism is good."

The same patterns are also followed in such news reports: public security department rescues kidnapped women; social welfare department extends regards to poverty-stricken families; government official hands out alms to laid-off workers and so on.

Day after day our media never felt tired of using shallow cases to prove a deep truth. Isn't it too artificial? Nowadays, the public, who is well informed and vastly knowledgeable, will likely question the logic of such reporting: Can it be that the governments in the capitalist countries would leave things as they are?

Facing a natural disaster, both the socialist and the capitalist countries will spare no efforts in disaster relief. Particularly with the developed countries who have a strong economy and advanced technologies, in some cases they could do better than what we are doing here. But I have never heard the media there run such reports quoting a tearful and grateful citizen as saying "Capitalism is good."

Regrettably, some of our propaganda departments are fixed in their way of thinking, a legacy of the extreme leftist period, which considers "anything good is socialism and anything bad is capitalism."

This is a graphic description of what news the Chinese had been reading, watching and listening from the Chinese media over the past decades.

But how could such reports like "feeling grateful" to the "concern of Party and government leaders" always fill headlines of news? How could journalists never feel tired of writing these kind of "grateful stories"? Chinese political scientist Liu Junning says that this problem has been caused and rooted in the public consciousness of the Chinese people. In tradition, he writes, "The Chinese are always expecting a benevolent leader but not expecting a system to protect their rights and freedom. There are tens of thousands of cases like this in China. The people are always surrounding and kneeling in front of an outgoing governor seated in a sedan chair, expressing their gratefulness in tears. The people only know to feel deeply grateful to the government officials but they never know that any good deeds performed by these officials are their obligations." And with this kind of public consciousness, the public for a long time did not feel it natural for the press to take as a top priority the writing of unflattering stories.

Even after the end of the Cultural Revolution, when China decided to reform and open up to the West, the traditional press policy of treating the media as part of the revolutionary machinery has remained almost unchanged.

POSITIVE PROPAGANDA

"Positive propaganda" is supposed to be the guiding principle of action for all Chinese journalists. This propaganda and press policy has remained unchanged for almost half a century, without even an insignificant deviation from the pronounced policy.

Explaining "positive propaganda," Yang Weiguang, president of CCTV, wrote that relying on positive propaganda means "unity, stability, encouragement and advocating the main theme. While practicing diversity in our programs, we must timely, comprehensively and accurately propagandize the lines, policies and decisions of the Central Committee; reflecting the life and the demands and wishes of the people and masses; educating people with patriotism, collectivism and socialism and enrich the cultural life of the masses with civilized and healthy arts and entertainment programs."

If you follow closely the Party media's coverage of China's battle against the country's worst floods in decades in 1998, you will see a clear picture of how the propaganda journalism and the new journalism work differently.

Speaking to a national meeting of the country's propaganda chiefs, Ding Guangen, minister of the Propaganda Department of the Central Committee of the Chinese Communist Party, instructed the major media of the Party and the government to place the coverage of battling floods as top priority. "You must follow the request of the Party Central Committee and the State Council, report the flood-control-related decisions of the Central Committee timely and accurately, reporting the information released by the central flood control headquarters, publicizing the heroic deeds of the unity between the army and the people and their hard struggle against the floods. The coverage must firm people's confidence, boost their fighting spirit. It must provide a powerful opinion support to the overall victory in the war against floods."

As described in a report on the state press coverage of the floods, the *Washington Post* wrote: "With a propaganda campaign worthy of the Maoist era, the People's Liberation Army is using China's worst floods in 44 years to improve the military's battered image. The state-run media have blanketed China with disaster coverage focusing on the strenuous efforts of soldiers wearing fatigues and bright-orange life preservers. Troops are frequently shown shoveling dirt and saving children in the floods, which the government said today have killed more than 3,000 people. Soldiers are videotaped using their bodies as human sandbags when earthen dikes burst. They work until their fingernails literally 'lift off' their fingers," the radio reported, and they "even vanquish waterborne poisonous snakes."

It will be more illustrative if we make a comparative study on how the propaganda journalism "provides opinion support to the war against the floods" and how the new journalism exposes corrupt party and government officials abusing power in the floods. How the propaganda journalism glorifies the victory over the floods? How the new journalism exposes the suffering of the flood victims? How the new journalism differs from the communist-hero image-building in the party press?

On midnight of November 13, 1998, the night shift editor of the *People's Daily* was busy for the final reading of the next day's newspaper. But a story stopped him from sending the newspaper for printing. It was a story of the summit meeting between Chinese President Jiang and South Korean President Kim. There were no problems with Jiang and Kim. But the problem was how to rank two Chinese senior officials who were present at the meeting: Qian Qichen and Jiang Chunyun. The editor was not sure who should go before whom. So the editor started making phone calls to seek a solution to this problem. It was not until 3:10 in the morning before he got the right answer. "This is extremely necessary for running a newspaper," Xu Zhongtian, editor-in-chief of the *People's Daily* writes in an article praising the night shift editor.

As a Xinhua editor observes, "The common problem of the official news media was that there were no quotes, no human faces, no sources and no stories. There were also too many clichés, emotional words and too many political jargons and too much editorializing. When the news report is full of political jargon, it is not the true political news. There are too many meeting and achievement stories. Most of them were ineffective news. As a result, the media has lost its function of communications, because no one wants to read it."

A NEW MIRROR

But for many Chinese journalists, this bad style of cliché-ridden propaganda has been deeply rooted in their blood. In this environment, you have to fight your way to becoming a good journalist. This frustrating situation must be changed. The Party line of the communists is mass line. That is to say, you must really serve the people. Even Deng Xiaoping was unhappy about this propaganda journalism. He blamed the press for being full of meetings, conferences and formality. Articles and speeches of leaders were always too long and the contents of different newspapers are often totally the same.

China's President Jiang Zemin was also frustrated with the ineffectiveness of the press and he called the media to get rid of articles that lack news value and pay attention to the art of propaganda; emphasizing politics doesn't mean to carry out some empty thing but to pay attention to the art of propaganda and enhance attractiveness and make newspapers newsworthy. It is the people, not the propagandists or the interviewees that we journalists should serve.

At a national meeting of propaganda officials on February 26, 1999, President Jiang Zemin elaborated the image-building role of the Chinese official media as displaying to the world an image of a socialist modernization; an image of reform and opening to the outside world; an image of a peace-loving Chinese people; an image of struggling for stability, university and prosperity; and an image of a democratic and legal country.

Jiang's idea of building an image for China is actually a reflection of many Chinese intellectual journalists over the last 100 years. Ever since the beginning of the 20th century, threatened by Western powers, when the last imperial dynasty was on the brink of collapse, many patriotic and freedom-loving intellectuals have been looking for a new identity of China. They have used such imageries as "New China," "a chaotic country," "a civil village," "a morning mist" and "a sleeping lion" in their writings. During the May 4th Movement of 1919, Hu Shi, a leading intellectual of that period, described China as "a sleeping beauty," meaning that she is so pretty and so weak that she needs to be wakened by a Western warrior. Lu Xun, a leading writer of that time, uses such metaphors as "a nightmare" and "an iron house" to imply China's decadent image. Guo Moruo, a writer of the same period, compared China to "a young girl" to express his passionate love toward his home country.

In the 1930s and 1940s, most Chinese intellectuals were disappointed with the country's development and they used such phrases as "dead water" to describe China. But in the 1950s and 1960s, the Chinese found a new point of imagination and used the images of "railroads" and "coal mines" to display the country's efforts toward nationalization and industrialization. China image-building has been a tradition of Chinese intellectuals.

But today, some Chinese intellectuals and journalists have realized that a complete and accurate China image can only be reflected from a mirror and the mirror is its image in the eyes of the Western world. The classical image of China in the Chinese eyes before the Opium War of 1840 was a glorious image of being the center of the world. But after the classical mirror was broken by the Western powers, China needs a new mirror to reflect its modernity.

BOTTOM LINE NOT PARTY LINE

China's transition to a market economy is pushing official media organizations to promote reforms in content, style and management. Press reform is underway in China's mass media at all levels, in response to the market economy, and in the hope of attracting a wider audience with a new face. Advertisements began to appear in the mass media after China began focusing on economic development in 1978, and now the Chinese media presents its readers and viewers with dynamic choices, from matchmaking to the stock exchange, from street gossip to academic opinions. Market forces also call for the role of a watchdog and muckraking reportage.

Most editors of Chinese media have focused their interest on selling newspapers and advertisements, which almost means a single-minded pursuit of journalism while the journalism has a clear-cut defined function: a strong sense of propaganda responsibility to reinforcing the leading position of the Party. "Commercialism is eroding the traditional supremacy of the Party press," Jaime A. Flor Cruz, former Beijing Bureau Chief for *Time* magazine observes. "Continual market reform over the past decade has eroded the dominant position of the official media as the media have become increasingly open and responsive to public demand. To the people in China, the press, the broadcasts are now a real source of information and food for thought, rather than a skimpy compendium of sterile polemic abstruse dogma. The vibrancy, diversity and enterprise of newspapers, magazines and television reflect growing pluralism—and Beijing's inability to control it."

Now let us discuss the interrelationship between economics of the newspapers and the news consumption of the public.

Before 1978, all news organizations in China were under the complete control of the Party and the government. The management of a news organization had little power from personnel to finances. But since the 1980s, the government has reduced and gradually stopped subsidies to most of the news organizations, allowing the news organization to undergo a structural reform which has made most of the news organizations economically independent, which means the newspapers have to feed themselves. As a result, the news organizations have gained power, personnel and finances from the government. But an unintended consequence of this reform is that the news organizations must actively respond to the demand of audiences. Otherwise, they will be dead.

In the meantime, the market has weakened government's effective editorial control of the press. The reasons are simple: (1) the government wants to control the press; (2) the government refuses to give money to the press but lets the press make money from the market; and, (3) the market shares the control of the press.

After 20 years of reform, a substantial change has taken place in the government's monopoly control of the publishing industry. The control power of publications is invisibly and irreversibly shifting to the public. Today, the government and the readers have shared control power of the publishing industry. Of course, the foundation and means for the government and the readers to exercise power are vastly different. The power foundation of the government is state machinery, while the power foundation of the reader is the market. The government governs the publications through punishment and encouragement, while the readers promote the publishing industry through appreciation. In the market of the press, you need to sell your papers and make a profit in order to survive.

A newspaper or the government cannot force newsstands and readers to sell and buy a certain newspaper or force people to watch a certain TV show (but this was true during the Cultural Revolution). And they cannot force a businessman to buy an advertising page from a certain paper. The profits come from readers and advertisers. As a result, the top priority of a newspaper or a TV station is to meet the interests and inclinations of the audiences. Under such a circumstance, many Chinese newspapers have no choice but to print detailed and even graphic reports of Clinton's sex scandal, the death of Pol Pot, the real situation in North Korea and the killing of ethnic Chinese in Indonesia, despite the unhappiness of some government officials. The newspapers and TV stations understand very well that "the audiences have no duty to let their reading interest follow an administrative order from a government department. A blind command often means heavy economic losses. And at this moment, a resistance form the controlled is inevitable."

A close look at the process of the marketization of the Chinese press and the reform of Chinese media's personnel system, financial management, journalists' income system and ownership structure "suggest that the Chinese press is undergoing a liberalizing experience in some areas, which serves to dilute its mouthpiece function." In China today, 2,163 daily newspapers, 1,416 radio stations, 943 TV stations, 1,270 cable television stations and thousands of magazines are competing for readership and advertisements throughout the country.

Heated competition has resulted in the emergence of media conglomerates with economic clout and a wide range of business interests. "Fierce news competition is pushing Chinese press, including party newspapers to develop in the direction of quality, efficiency and the industrialization," said Yu Youxian, director of the State Administration of the Press and Publications. By 2010, Chinese newspapers will have formed some conglomerates and some of these will join in the international news competition, according to the administration. As an observer notes, the Chinese media are changing "from the propaganda organs of the Chinese Communist Party into modern firms." The latest statistics show that the number of news groups had grown from six in 1998 to 11 by March of 1999. The most successful new firms among them include the *Southern News* Group and *Guangzhou Daily*

News Group in Guangdong province, the *Jiefang Daily News* Group, *the Beijing Daily News* Group and *Guangming Daily News* Group in Beijing, *Harbin Daily News* in northernmost province Heilongjiang. Observers believe that this is likely to be just the beginning of a trend.

"It is not accidental that news groups are emerging in the frontiers and the highly developed province of Guangdong. Some new organizations are starting to register as industrial and commercial enterprises like a state-invested news corp. In theory and principle, these news organizations have become different from the old news organizations. It shows that it is a trend of marketizing Chinese press and to turn them into enterprises," comments Zhang Jian, a journalist from Xinhua.

Li Zhuren, senior editor of Xinhua News Agency, writes that despite the attempts by the Party and government to have a tight grip of the news organizations, "they are at the same time to operate the same way as business entities. Even the state-run Xinhua now is covering 40% of its own operational expenses."

With the marketization, journalists with the popular newspapers and TV shows, such as *Beijing Youth Daily*, *Southern Weekend* and *Daily Focus* are well-paid and they become respected for their bylines. So they have motivation to pursue their trade.

Toward Transparency

Even Zhao Qizheng, the minister of information of the State Council, calls for *tou ming* (transparency) in the *People's Daily*. "Under today's situation, the best method of letting the people of the world to have a timely and correct understanding of China is to enhance the accuracy, transparency and timeliness of our news reporting. The live coverage of U.S. President Clinton's visit to China won wide applause from home and abroad."

The new journalism stresses that bad news is news, problems are news and selling points are news, while the propaganda journalism stresses progress is news, good news is news. Progress reports and positive coverage are what the propaganda journalism exists for, while problem and negative stories are what the new journalism strives for.

Observers agree that publishing stories exposing worsening pollution problems, failures of government policy and sometimes even stories of embarrassing episodes in the history of communists may sound unflattering to the government, but they serve the ultimate goal of maintaining political stability, as such exposes serve as social safety valves.

Why do the official propagandists show their tolerance of negative reporting?

A senior party propaganda official admits that the public is getting frustrated with "positive reporting" and the Party is worried about the negative effect caused by "positive reporting." Xu Guangchun, vice-minister of the Propaganda Department of the Chinese Communist Party explains in an article titled "Pay Attention to the Negative Effect of Positive Propaganda:"

> The readers are frustrated with the press when it does not report what the readers want to know and always reports what the readers do not want to know. The readers are thinking they are being fooled by the press. For example, facing a profit-losing enterprise and the lay-off of workers, the readers are very concerned about the reviving of the state-owned enterprises. But, if some newspapers, sticking to positive propaganda display only the achievements of some state-owned enterprises or repeatedly report the stories of the few enterprises with brand names, the readers will raise a question: why can't we get our paycheck when the situation of the state-owned enterprises is so good?
>
> A few years ago, there was a flood in Sichuan that washed away a village. An army officer jumped into the flood and rescued several people including old and young. The deeds of the army officer caught the attention of the Party organization, which requested the press to publicize his lofty character. A journalist came to take a picture of the scene showing the officer saving people. The journalist brought an old man from the village. The reporter asked the officer to carry him across the river while he was taking a picture. The picture was published in some of the national newspapers. When it was exposed that it was a fake, the reporter was condemned by readers. As a consequence, the heroic image of the army officer was severely damaged, causing a grave negative effect.

PROBING NEWS

"Daily Focus" on China Central TV network, hosted by Fang Hongjin, is a popular program attracting 300 million viewers every night and getting over 1,000 phone calls from the audience every day, Fang believes that his show "has spoken the true works of the common people." Both the public and the Chinese leaders believe that media supervision of government is the best way to curb corruption. A few years ago, it was unthinkable to read extensive and detailed exposés of high-level Party and government officials in the Chinese media. Such exposes would be banned by some propagandists because they believe such writings damage the image of the Party. The Party would not allow negative stories about upper echelons of power, such as officials at ministerial or provincial governor level.

Elisabeth Rosenthal, the correspondent of the *New York Times* writes, "Every evening at 7:38 more than 300 million people tune in to the 15-minute program whose hard-hitting investigations and interviews show just how far the Chinese media have come since the days when they provided little more than Communist Party dogma. The program, which was first broadcast in 1994, is sophisticated, offers great drama, and confronts a wide range of topics that would have been deemed too sensitive for exploration only a few years ago: domestic violence, corruption in the courts, state factories flouting pollution laws, nuclear proliferation in Asia. Last month, Israeli Prime Minister Benjamin Netanyahu appeared on the program during his visit to China. The program's investigations and choice of topics clearly reflect China's new openness about certain types of problems, particularly official corruption." But as Elisabeth observes that "some less prominent programs and certain publications with looser government ties, like *Southern Weekend* and *Beijing Youth Daily*, have pushed the boundaries of discourse a bit further."

Observers believe that such exposés serve as social safety valves that release pent-up frustration. At the beginning, the exposés targeted only petty officials. But since last year, there appears a tendency of exposing senior Party and government officials at or above provincial and ministerial levels. According to Xiao Yang, chief judge of the People's Supreme Court, in 1998, more than two-thirds of the 40,000 officials investigated on corruption charges were indicted in cases in which more than US$534 million in bribes was involved. Notable cases involved three officials equal in rank to provincial governors, 103 provincial department chiefs, and 1,714 county leaders.

An American observer notes, "Westerners often decry human rights conditions in China, citing political restrictions on writers and intellectuals in the large cities. But for hundreds of millions of ordinary Chinese who live in towns and villages, it is the unrestrained authority of a local party chief that is usually most oppressive. The Chinese press is moving into this uncharted water: to dig dirt of local government officials."

In September 1998, China's two most influential media outlets, the *People's Daily* or organ of the ruling communist Party, and China Central Television (CCTV), have worked out a plan to jointly criticize government corruption. Reporters from the two press organizations will probe into hot topics and difficult issues and report them simultaneously in an effort to arouse greater attention from top leaders and the public. As a trial run, the two media giants reported on a serious case on September 16 in their "Society Weekly" and "Daily Focus" segments, respectively. The case concerned illegal fund-raising activities during the law enforcement process at a local anti-corruption bureau in Fuzhou Prefecture in east China's Jiangsi province. "This cooperation demonstrates our determination to carrying out supervision of the government in an all-round way and at a higher level," says Sun Jie, producer of the "Daily Focus." Li Youcan, director of the Public Opinions Department of the *People's Daily*, says that as the Party's organ, the paper's function of supervising the government has not yet been fully displayed, and its operation with CCTV will help push the paper's reform in this respect.

Lu Mingjun, a *People's Daily* reporter participating in the joint project, notes that the media usually encounters many obstacles created by various sectors and persons when they prepare to criticize a government department for its wrongdoing. "The cooperation between several news organizations will undoubtedly strengthen their ability to endure the pressure."

As early as in the spring of 1998, when the National People's Congress convened its annual meeting, many deputies called for stronger supervision of the government by the media to eradicate corruption and ensure that the country is governed by law. Top Chinese leaders have recently repeatedly urged that media watch be enhanced, particularly, that cooperation between news organizations create a healthier social environment.

Researchers believe the survival and development of the exposing stories in Chinese press has been the consequence of moving towards a democratic society. "The supervision of the government by the media has become a mega-trend of the Chinese press and China is entering a period of stronger confidence, freer speech and more transparency. However, the media is not the solution to every problem. What we need most is a more tolerant social atmosphere as well as a more open and law-abiding system," comments Yu Guoming.

Looking at the prosperity of probing stories in Chinese press, an editorial of a Guangzhou-based newspaper writes, "This has been a natural consequence of a market economy. Newspapers must change their role of a government institution to the role of an enterprise. Otherwise, they will be eliminated by the market. People buy the newspaper because it prints what people love to read, it speaks the mind of the people and it attacks the persons and the things the people hate. And the newspaper gets a market. When the newspaper gets a market, it will become bolder."

Commenting on the Chinese press today, University of California, Berkeley, Graduate School of Journalism Dean Orville Schell said recently, "Megaphones for the party or free-standing independent watchdog? In China it's now a real mish-mash. And no one dares to even talk about it in public because such discussion can only get one in trouble. So China just sort of muddles along with a very murky, incomplete conception of what its ideals are." This statement is typical of many American researchers who are out of touch with Chinese reality today. This could be caused partially by language problems of reading Chinese publications or partially by their negligence of Chinese publications.

As a matter of fact, most Chinese journalists understand very well in what direction they are pushing the press reform. While many Chinese journalists agree that one of landmarks of modern civilization is pushing political democracy through supervising by public opinion and "supervising by public opinions has become the leading power of maintaining a benign political and economic cycle of society. A society is not a healthy society without supervising by public opinions. Supervising by news reporting and opinions has become a social checking power as important as government laws and morality." Some journalists look at the prosperity of probing stories of government officials as a consequence of the development of a news market. As Xinhua reporters Fu Xingyu and Ji Kaixing observe:

> "The marketization of news in China has turned the role of news reporting as a political propaganda tool to that of industrialization and popularization. With the increase of personal news consumption there will be a decline of news consumption using public money. It will become a life or death question for news media that does not serve the economy and the society, if it does not care about ordinary people's economic and spiritual life, if it does not meet the demands of the market and the audiences. Economists and journalists are of one view that any news organization will be washed out if its news reporting does not meet the taste of the audiences. The press era of relying on the financial support of political parties and government will be gone very soon."

CONCLUSION

THE FIRST DAY OF A NEW CENTURY

Beijing, 1 January 2000, 6:30 am: The air was cold and the streets empty as I rode my bicycle to Tiananmen. Barely awake from the previous night, I felt compelled to watch the dawn of a new century—China's century—from Tiananmen Square, the symbolic center of China.

Beijing's frosty early morning air clung to my fingers, piercing my gloves as I rode through the silent, seemingly abandoned streets. The early dawn was dark gray, the color of Beijing in stark winter. I rode through narrow wind-swept *hutong* alleys. As I pulled out onto Tiananmen Square, I could see that, to my surprise, the vast expanse was brimming with people after New Year's Eve of the millenium.

A party atmosphere, carried over from the previous night, had pushed through dawn, right into the center of China's most sacred political ground. Squeezed between each other, people strained their necks to get a glimpse, a mere glimpse of the green-clad soldiers carrying China's national flag. They marched out from the gates of Tiananmen under Mao's impassive gaze, to the flag pole standing solitary above swarms of onlookers below, also anxiously waiting from this historic vantage point, to see the first dawn of a new century.

As the early morning sun strained to push through the gray clouds heavy with the pollution that hung across the city, I thought back to when I first arrived in China nearly 20 years before. China and the United States had just established formal diplomatic relations a year and a half before. At that time, crowds lined up every evening with coupons to purchase rationed staples under a system of command economics. The most simple of free markets had just begun to spawn, however, private enterprise as such was all but unheard of. Everyone wore gray, blue or green—nothing else. One did not dare give so much as a gift of perfume to a girl for fear of her being labeled politically incorrect. Restaurants closed at 7:00 pm sharp. City lights went out shortly after that. Living standards were harsh, commodities rare, and lifestyles simple.

Twenty years later, standing in Tiananmen Square at the dawn of the new century it was clear in my mind that China had transformed. As the early winter sun scratched through the gray clouds, light touched on the modern chrome glass Oriental Plaza of Hong Kong tycoon Li Ka-shing, who had displaced the largest McDonald's restaurant in the world and destroyed countless ancient and historical buildings in order to construct a cement and glass monument groping to express modernity. Free markets had come of age and now virtually dominated China's trendy retail sector. Private enterprise on the back of an Internet revolution had become the fastest growing sector of the Chinese economy. Around me in the morning crowd I could smell the local brand Yue-Sai perfume amidst multi-colored purple, yellow, and green dyed hair of China's youth having partied the previous night away.

There was little in the way of ideology in their minds as China's big red flag unfurled in the frosty dawn. There was a sense of pride however, that China had come a long way, underscored by the numbers of people who came out that morning to watch the national flag rise over Tiananmen on the first morning of a new century. At moments such as this, where a point of transition is marked, one cannot help but wonder what the future will bring. This sense of anticipation could be felt among the throngs gathered in the early gray dawn, as they waited for the sun to rise.

THE IDEOLOGICAL ROAD FORWARD

China's road toward economic and moreover ideological transition began at the Third Plenum of the 11th Congress of the Communist Party of China in 1978 when Deng Xiaoping tipped the scales against Mao's appointed successor Hua Guofeng. Hua had adopted the line that the Party must adhere literally to Mao's dictums while Deng argued for a more pragmatic line. The "open door" policy was adopted together with reforms leading to the *chengbaozhi* or "self-responsibility" system, the first stage in the evolution toward private enterprise.

By 1982 when the 12th Party Congress convened, *chengbaozhi* had gained momentum nationwide. Free markets were sprouting and Deng's reform program was coming into its own. The 12th Party Congress dropped the word communism as a goal unto itself, replacing it with the more philosophical and less politically charged Marxism. Further reforms were put into play. By the time the Chinese Communist Party convened its 13th Congress in 1987, Deng's reforms were in full swing.

The year 1987 proved to be a high water mark. At the 13th Party Congress, Deng introduced yet another bold challenge to more conservative ideologues. Deng espoused that China was not a communist country per se, but rather a "socialist country" adding that China was "only at the first stage of socialism" which "would last for a relatively long period of time."

In short, while acknowledging the idealistic merits of socialism, Deng pushed the goalposts of achieving true socialism into the unforeseen future.

The side effects of Deng's bold initiative sparked inflation, corruption, and in turn, protests against both. The events that unfolded in 1989 were followed by a reactive freezing of credit by international lending institutions, which in turn caused foreign investment to dry-up, and growth to slow down. In order to energize stalled reforms, Deng Xiaoping once again took the initiative. In 1992, he took a "southern inspection" trip in the tradition of the great emperors Kang Xi and Qian Long, reviewing the Special Economic Zones of the south which had been pioneered at his behest nearly a decade before. Looking out upon these laboratories of market economics, Deng declared his experiment a success and a model for the rest of the country.

More conservative stalwarts in Beijing got the message. By the autumn of 1992 the 14th Party Congress had enshrined Deng's new principle of "constructing a socialist market economy with 'Chinese characteristics'" as the new mandate of the Communist Party of China. China entered a period of unprecedented 15% growth and in turn uncontrolled inflation of 24% by 1994. Zhu Rongji, then vice premier carrying the portfolios of economics and finance, personally took the reigns as central bank governor. He introduced a series of measures that brought inflation under control while maintaining high growth, leading in turn to the development of his "macro-control system," which combined market economics with a formula of state guidance and, at times, intervention.

Deng Xiaoping passed away in 1997, the year in which Hong Kong returned under the "one country two systems" principle, setting a precedent for Macao which returned under the same framework in 1999 and serving as a basis for solving the Taiwan issue. With Zhu having steered China's economy through a "soft landing period," confidence in the future was at a peak.

That year, State Chairman and Party General Secretary Jiang Zemin convened the 15th Party Congress which would in turn prove to be yet another watershed in China's reform process. While openly recognizing the importance of Marxism, Leninism and Mao Zedong thought in China's historic development, Jiang was emphatic that Deng Xiaoping thought, or pragmatism, would "lead China into the 21st century."

Jiang declared that the notion of "public ownership" no longer had to be restricted to State ownership was tabled together with open recognition of the importance the private sector has come to hold in China's now "mixed economy". A program of enterprise restructuring coined as "grasp the large and release the small" would witness the consolidation of large industrial groups while permitting smaller enterprises to liquidate or sell their assets to the market and even private investors. Jiang announced a comprehensive program of accompanying health care, retirement, banking, finance, and social welfare reforms, which would be necessary to accomplish the ambitious and far-reaching goals which he set out at the 15th Party Congress.

FOREIGN INVESTMENT AND WTO

In 1979, within a year of announcing the open door policy at the 11th Party Congress, the Chinese-Foreign Equity Joint Venture Law was adopted by the National People's Congress, becoming the first piece of legislation to sanction direct foreign investment. To present, this has represented the basis upon which China's entire legal framework for foreign investment has been constructed. Now, with countless laws, regulations, measures, rules and notices from the National People's Congress and State Council to virtually every ministry, bureau and local government department connected in any way with foreign investment, China has a well-rounded and to some extent, labrynthine legal system covering foreign investment and trade.

WTO entry is now causing this system to evolve further with a massive streamlining underway to clarify and rationalize often discordant departmental regulations. This process of streamlining foreign investment and trade legislation will require the amendment and re-promulgation of much existing legislation. While this process will in the short term lead to inevitable confusion and even frustration for many foreign investors seeking clarification for areas of investment, where multiple government departments' coordination and decision input is involved, the end result will be a system for making investments, that is clearer, simpler, and far more straightforward and user-friendly than the previous.

Of critical importance, the lifting of former restrictions on key sectors such as telecommunications, infrastructure, banking, insurance and services, regardless of the phase-in process required, will allow for more expansive direct foreign participation in sectors which previously were closed or tightly guarded. The significance of WTO entry cannot be underestimated in this regard, as it now sends a positive signal to institutional investors as well as multinationals investing or providing services in this market, thereby opening the gates to what could be unprecedented inflows of foreign investment in the coming years.

Such investment inflows will in turn stimulate yet even greater changes and propel forward not just China's economy, but social transition as well, forcing a competitive environment upon enterprises which have survived to date under the lethargic protection of State monopoly or support. Attitudinal, and in turn psychological, changes will follow. To a great extent, the legal, political, and institutional transitions which are now occurring in parallel, reflect this momentum which has already been put into play.

At the same time, investors cannot be unrealistic about the extent to which changes will take place. While enormous efforts have been undertaken to date in constructing a modern legal system, the enforcement of that system is still often restrained by traditional thinking, lack of education, local protectionism, and disparities in income and knowledge which are still endemic problems running through various levels of Chinese society.

These are especially significant obstacles in rural areas and interior provinces, where the impact of coastal urban growth, and information and technology has been limited by economic, social and geographic factors.

"ONE GUARANTEE"

On March 22, 1998 Premier Zhu Rongji announced his new cabinet at the close of the first session of the Ninth National People's Congress, introducing an administration which would be set in place and administer policies spanning the millenium. Zhu used this opportunity to introduce his ambitious program of comprehensive reforms, which he described as *Yige Quebao, Sange Daowei, Wuxiang Gaige*, or "One Guarantee, Three Achievements, Five Items of Reform."

The "One Guarantee" in fact consisted of three key elements: maintaining a high rate of economic growth, low inflation, and a stable renminbi currency. Although GDP growth was targeted at 8% in 1998, due to the effects of the Asian financial crisis it fell to 7.8% that year and 7.6% in 1999. However, due to careful policies of intervention known in the Zhu administration as the "macro-control system," China's growth recovered to 8.2% in the year 2000. Meanwhile, inflation was pushed to all-time lows of negative 2.8%.

Zhu resisted pressure from the World Bank and IMF—the so-called "Washington consensus"—which called for the devaluation of China's currency (a policy which had virtually trashed the economies of Indonesia, South Korea and Thailand making them all but colonies of the World Bank and IMF). Ignoring the arguments of Washington D.C.'s think-tank institutions, Zhu instead relied on his own policies of market guidance, continued demand for Chinese exports, and China's high level of foreign exchange reserves in maintaining a stable renminbi currency.

Throughout and after the Asian financial crisis, China's foreign exchange reserves continued to rise on the back of strong exports supported by pro-active policies to encourage exports and domestic economic structural adjustments. The result was that China emerged from the Asian financial crisis first, taking its position as the strongest and probably healthiest regional economy. As a result of Zhu's successful economic policies, the past economic development formulas touted by the Washington concensus have now been brought into serious question by economists and intellectuals in both developing and developed nations.

"THREE ACHIEVEMENTS"

Zhu's targeted "Three Achievements" represented the framework of an ambitious and far-reaching reform program to be undertaken within a three-year period (1998–2001) spanning the millenium.

The "first achievement" called for pulling the medium and large-scale state-owned enterprises out of the red. Without question, the reform of China's state-owned enterprises had been identified as one of the economy's major problems, as without undertaking dramatic structural reforms, these enterprises could not become efficient in China's increasingly competitive domestic market, much less compete internationally. Furthermore, much of the nonperforming assets being carried on the books of China's state-owned banks represented loans extended to state-owned enterprises unable to service their debts.

While many questioned Zhu's ambitious target for solving such a massive problem, requiring pervasive structural adjustments involving key pillars of China's old state-dominated economic system, Zhu put the problem into perspective explaining that, "The foreign media have exaggerated this problem ... There are more than 79,000 state-owned enterprises in China, some of which employ less than a dozen people. Many of these are losing money, so if you look at the total number of enterprises in China, it appears that many are losing money. But you must remember that China has some 500 large-scale enterprises, of which only 10% lose money. Taxation revenues and profits from these account for 85% of the revenues and profits of the whole nation. Of these large enterprises, only 50 are losing money. I am quite confident that we can get rid of the loss-making enterprises in three years."

Based on the principle of "grasp the large and release the small," major industrial enterprises in key sectors were merged, resulting in a rationalization of production functions while the smaller enterprises were often bankrupted or sold. The total number of large and medium-sized loss-making enterprises halved as guided mergers took their toll. The shock of enterprise restructuring sent tens of millions of workers to *xiagang* or "step down" from their positions in what amounted to effective unemployment. At the same time, private sector growth lurched forward as necessary retraining and re-employment programs came into play. Workers, both employed and laid off, were forced to look to society and commercial medicare and pension programs which were quickly displacing the iron rice bowl system that the state-owned enterprises once provided.

The "second achievement" would involve overhauling China's banking and financial system. It had become clear that the problems of state-owned enterprise reform were integrally entwined with the banking system. Wang Zhongyu, State Council Secretary General and former Minister of the State Economy and Trade Commission, explained the dilemmna as: "The state enterprises have been the biggest debtor for the state banks in the past and this situation will persist for a long time ... Most of the loans from state commercial banks were to be issued to the state-owned enterprises. But there are some problems, such as too many outstanding loans to the enterprises, which they fail to repay over long periods. The result is low efficiency of loan utilization and insufficient availability of capital to other enterprises."

Tackling the problems in China's banking system called for a comprehensive overhaul and redefinition of functions, beginning with the role of China's central bank, the People's Bank of China. Concentrating on banking matters alone, issues relating to securities and insurance were soon spun off into the newly-formed Securities Regulatory Commission and the Insurance Regulatory Commission.

In turn, the state-owned specialized banks—the Bank of China, Construction Bank, Agricultural Bank, and Industrial Commercial Bank—shed their policy loan portfolios to the newly established Agricultural Development Bank, State Development Bank, and Exim Bank, in turn concentrating on purely commercial banking matters. A number of shareholding banks came into the fore and urban credit cooperatives were converted into local city-level shareholding banks serving the needs of their communities. The boldest move aimed at trying to untangle the state-owned enterprise triangle debts has involved the four state-owned specialized banks which carry the burden of bad loans, each establishing their own asset management company to purchase their non-performing assets and eventually turn these around.

The "third achievement" called for streamlining China's bloated government bureaucracy. Since the commencement of economic reforms in 1978, China has evolved from a non-materialist to overly-materialist society. During this rapid transition, power associated with government position had become a tradable commodity. By the late 1990s, official corruption, an outcrop of economic reform, had itself become the greatest impediment to such reforms.

Zhu's logic was straightforward. Too many underpaid officials sitting around government offices approving projects for enterprises busy running businesses was simply a formula for using power to squeeze money. Zhu's objective was to cut the government bureaucracy in half while raising salaries for those remaining cadres. Such a program involved a process of weeding out incompetent cadres by instituting higher educational requirements, and a system of examinations for promotions, in an attempt to forge a real civil service.

The number of ministries was also slashed in half under Zhu's administration. The former industrial "line" or sector ministries (Coal, Metallurgy, Light Industry, Textiles, Power, etc.) which represented the old command economy system, were converted first to bureaus under the comprehensive administration of the State Economy and Trade Commission, and then reduced in status to mere departments of this macro-economy coordinating commission. Zhu divided the ministries under his administration into four categories: "macro-control departments" concerned with issues of economic coordination, finance and banking; "specialized economic administrative

departments" covering issues ranging from foreign trade to communications, construction, transportation and water supply; "social departments"
covering education, technology, natural resources, and social welfare; and
"State political affairs departments" covering foreign affairs, defense, health
and ethnic minorities. Zhu's program of restructuring represented probably
the largest single overhaul of China's government administrative structure
since the founding of the People's Republic in 1949.

FIVE ITEMS OF REFORM

Zhu's "Five Items for Reform" involved grain distribution, capital raising,
housing, medicare, and the overhaul of China's financial and taxation
system. These five items of reform basically covered: housing, grain supply,
capital circulation, fiscal and taxation, healthcare and pensions. In short,
Zhu undertook a complete overhaul of China's former iron rice bowl
system where people looked to their enterprise or government unit for
housing, medicare, pension and a host of basic "guarantees." In order to
make the "three achievements" a reality, the "five items of reform" would
need to be adopted simultaneously, addressing a host of interlocking issues
at one time in order to unlock the remaining barriers to deepening China's
economic reforms.

Zhu's intention was to replace this system of past guarantees with one
in which individuals would have to rely on their own savings, and look to
the financial sector for the appropriate tools with which to obtain their
once expected assurances. Essentially, housing, medicare and pensions were
being pushed to the market with a new system of taxation kicking in to
support government efforts in creating a social security system. In short,
for the first time in nearly 50 years, people were being told to take out
insurance to cover their medical expenses, create pension funds for their
retirement and obtain a mortgage loan from the bank to buy a home.

With increasing numbers of people being laid off, grain distribution
reform necessary to guarantee ample supplies of low cost staples became
more important than ever. Premier Zhu stated that, "Because of our bumper
harvests, we have successfully accumulated such grain reserves that even
if there are [natural] disasters for two years, nobody will go hungry."
However, to maintain such supply, subsidized payments to farmers had
to be guaranteed, requiring that embezzlement of staples by corrupt local
officials be stopped.

In parallel, the government's budgetary needs would shift from dependence on state-owned enterprise profits to taxation of enterprise and individual income. This major structural re-orientation in China's fiscal system
in itself represents one of the most far-reaching adjustments impacting
China's economy. Likewise, capital circulation reform has become a critical

piece in the package of measures given the importance of allowing both the private sector as well as those state-owned enterprises with legitimate fundamentals to have access to necessary capital to implode critical mass required in building strong businesses for the future.

NEW CIVILIZATION

The unleashing of a market economy has brought with it a radical shift in people's thinking. Within the mere span of 20 years, China has gone from a non-materialist society structured around principles of ideology to a now overly-materialist society driven by values of conspicuous consumption. While standards of living have improved alongside massive infrastructure development and growing productivity, there has been a rapid break down of social morality and an unfortunate loss of ideology and principles in general, leading to corruption and a new proliferation of social vices and rise in crime.

China's leadership, recognizing the dangers inherent in this ideological vacuum, is seeking to piece together a new framework of social values more appropriate for China's modern, and often trend-driven society, than the older more rigid moral structure espoused by the Communist Party in the past. This process began with the "spiritual civilization" campaign in which Jiang Zemin sought to balance spiritual civilization (covering a range of concerns from family values to environmental protection and appreciation of the arts) against "material civilization," which valued money and its buying power foremost.

Jiang later launched a program of "three talks education" which called for: "talking politics," which meant lashing out at corruption and improper abuse of political power; "talking study," which demanded that government officials have a clear understanding of the meaning of Deng Xiaoping's reforms and how they should be implemented; and "talking healthy atmosphere," which called for everyone in government to do something about the deteriorating social morality for which official corruption had unfortunately become a major contributing factor.

This was followed by Jiang's introduction of a new theory called the "three representations," which essentially brought into play past values of the Chinese Communist Party such as Mao's "representing the people's interests" and Deng's "representing modern productive forces," together with Jiang's "representing advanced civilization." In short, while representing the past values of the Party, cadres had better start representing the new concerns of society at large. In other words, if Party cadres cannot uphold idealism while keeping pace with the times, then the Party as an institution may itself be in danger of being dated. In short, Jiang has called upon Party members to not only keep up with the times but to try and keep their thinking one step ahead.

CHINA'S CENTURY

China's century has begun with the unfolding of the Tenth Five-Year Plan which calls for: continued steady GDP growth averaging 8% per annum over this period; a call for raising efficiency in enterprises both public and private; new pioneering efforts at technology research and development; and raising living standards from what is called *xiao kang*, or relative comfort, to *gengjia fuyu*, or affluence. There is no question that this task will be difficult to achieve; however, if successful, the country will witness an unprecedented transformation of living standards and in turn, values within Chinese society.

At the first stage of China's economic growth plan for the new century, an active fiscal policy will be applied, feeding into major infrastructure development programs focused on developing China's western and interior regions. China's immensity, in terms of both population and regions, and in the disparate levels of development, has created a unique situation in developmental economics unprecedented elsewhere. In short, China represents a microcosm of the traditional relationship between the developed and underdeveloped worlds, with coastal cities on par with the key capital cities of Asia, and rural regions which are all but untouched by this coastal development. Growth in China's vast underdeveloped interior will create an expanding domestic market which will fuel the expansion of China's coastal and industrialized regions, reducing reliance on exports, as a prime engine for growth.

A major infrastructure development program is underway involving the laying of vast networks of roads and rail lines, and the construction of new urban areas to concentrate disparate townships. The laying of electric lines and water supply systems are all feeding into the creation of healthier communities in the interior regions which in turn will anchor much of the floating population which has been drawn to the coastal regions by the massive construction spree of the 1990s. The first stage of this process will be driven through China's own version of Keynesian economics involving government support funded through a series of mega-bond issues.

In the next stage, however, a revamped banking system should offer new financial strength to fund China's emerging blue chip—often called "red chip"—enterprises, which will be encouraged to invest into these regions. Hopefully they will be drawn there by opportunities arising from new-found consumer demand on the back of enhanced lifestyles and income. Emerging markets are expected to form on the back of the growth initiative driven through State funding and guided infrastructure development.

The ongoing push in converting the old iron rice bowl system into a modern, commercialized social welfare system involving the insurance sector together with pension fund managers will have probably one of the most far-reaching and deepest impacts on the psychology and outlook of China's next generation workforce. The conversion of public housing into commercialized real estate and the introduction of housing loans and the realization of a credit system in general, will in turn rationalize the construction and property development sectors. Ownership of one's own home will in itself transform public outlook, values, and demands for a higher quality of life.

The explosion of China's retail consumer sector will be further stimulated by WTO entry and the opening of this once protected area to foreign participation. New concepts entering on the back of proven Western consumer business models will merge with the traditions and habits of Chinese consumers, in turn creating a unique and challenging domestic market energized by new trends and aspirations. This force, in itself, will be one of the major magnets drawing China's industrial sector to seek new management systems, techniques and approaches, merging Western experiences with the realities and limitations set by China's developing market and consumer behavior patterns.

The Internet revolution has come to China, but beneath the fast-money venture capital-driven excitement which permeated hotel conferences throughout the year 2000, a sharpened awareness of the enormous value that digital and information technology will have on China's system has become a driving priority of China's leadership. Both policy makers and the corps of highly-trained young intelligentsia emerging from education institutions throughout China, will be seeking to maximize such technology in the interest of both system reform, and research and development for commercial gain. The impact of this revolution will initially be seen in the enhancement of China's banking and financial system, where risk analysis and the development of a credit system will depend on the effective application of information technology. When applied to research in China's science and technology institutes, the results may be more surprising, even phenomenal.

Mobile telecommunications coming to China in the 1990s allowed the country to leap-frog out of an outdated telecommunications system into one as advanced as any other in the world, largely due to the fact that a fresh infrastructure platform could be developed on a what was previously a blank slate. China also demanded the latest in technology, and Chinese consumers the latest in mobile phone styles and high-tech fashion. These demands exceeded the expectations of many investors, who soon realized that only by grasping the rapidity of change in Chinese consumer psychology could one stay ahead in the China market.

Yes, there will soon be a fusion of high technology and Internet with China's media, television, and communications systems, which will bring China to the forefront of worldwide developments in the information industry. However, amidst the excitement of such changes, it is also important to keep in mind that Internet business models developed in Silicon Valley may not work the same way in China. As with most sectors, a different Chinese model will emerge with time and a natural fusion of practice. Because like all foreign ideas, philosophy, technology, science, business concepts and models that have come to China to stay, grow, and foster—it too will have to adopt "Chinese characteristics."

INDEX